A Commentary on
THE GOSPEL OF MATTHEW

UNLOCKING THE NEW TESTAMENT

A Commentary on

THE GOSPEL OF MATTHEW

David Pawson

ANCHOR

Copyright © 2023 David Pawson Ministry CIO

The right of David Pawson to be identified as author of this Work has been asserted by him in accordance with the Copyright, Designs and Patents Act 1988.

First published in Great Britain in 2020 by
This edition published in Great Britain in 2023 by
Anchor which is a trading name of David Pawson Publishing Ltd
Synegis House, 21 Crockhamwell Road,
Woodley, Reading RG5 3LE

No part of this publication may be reproduced or transmitted in any form or by any means, electronic or mechanical, including photocopy, recording or any information storage and retrieval system, without prior permission in writing from the publisher.

**For more of David Pawson's teaching,
including DVDs and CDs, go to
www.davidpawson.com**

**FOR FREE DOWNLOADS
www.davidpawson.org**

**For further information,
email: info@davidpawsonministry.org**

ISBN 978 1 913472 09 2

Printed by Ingram Spark

Contents

Chapter	Reading		Page
1.	*1:1–17*	Genealogy	9
2.	*1:18–25*	The Nativity	25
3.	*2*	Bethlehem	43
4.	*3*	Baptism	67
5.	*4:1–11*	Temptations	81
6.	*4:12–25*	Ministry	99
7.	*5:1–13*	The Sermon On The Mount	107
8.	*5:1–13*	Rewards	129
9.	*5:14–48*	Action	135
10.	*6*	The Christian Life	153
11.	*7*	Do Not Judge	173
12.	*8*	Healing	189
13.	*9*	Forgiveness	197
14.	*10–11*	Disciples Sent Out	201
15.	*12*	Supernatural	207
16.	*13*	The Problem Of Evil	231
17.	*14–15*	Death And More Miracles	245
18.	*16–17*	The Divinity Of Jesus	255
19.	*18–19*	Sayings And Responses	267
20.	*20*	Landowner And Labourers	275
21.	*21*	Jerusalem	289
22.	*22–23*	Challenges	301
23.	*24–25*	Destruction Of The Temple	313
24.	*24–25*	The Second Coming	325
25.	*26*	Passover And First Trial	363
26.	*27*	Roman Trial And Execution	375
27.	*28*	Resurrection	385

A COMMENTARY ON THE GOSPEL OF MATTHEW

Addenda

1. BETHLEHEM (2)	
(MATTHEW CHAPTER 2)	*397*
2. THE PROBLEM OF EVIL (2)	
(MATTHEW CHAPTER 13)	*413*
3. WORK: LANDOWNER AND LABOURERS	
(MATTHEW CHAPTER 20:1–16) (2)	*443*
4. DESTRUCTION OF THE TEMPLE (2)	
(MATTHEW CHAPTER 24)	*463*
5. EVIDENCE FOR THE RESURRECTION	
(MATTHEW CHAPTER 28)	*465*

This book is based on a series of talks. Originating as it does from the spoken word, its style will be found by many readers to be somewhat different from my usual written style. It is hoped that this will not detract from the substance of the biblical teaching found here. As always, I ask the reader to compare everything I say or write with what is written in the Bible and, if at any point a conflict is found, always to rely upon the clear teaching of scripture.

David Pawson

Foreword

The first edition of the New Testament Commentary on Matthew by David Pawson was published with many gaps. This NEW edition is an attempt to include much of the important content that was originally missed.

This book was not written as a commentary, but is more a collection of individual sermons relating to Matthew's Gospel, given by the late David Pawson over a period of time during the 1970s.

The reader is advised that the book does not flow as one might expect from a traditional commentary due to the fact that it is based on a series of talks.

There may also be various references to real events at that time and therefore the reader will need to take the time to understand the context in which many references are made.

Some of the chapters/talks may be standalone talks, e.g. Chapter 7: The Sermon on the Mount. As such, themes may be duplicated or repeated throughout this book. Each chapter should therefore be taken as a standalone 'teaching' unless there is a specific link to a series of talks.

In reviewing and including each chapter/talk in this book the editors felt that it was important to maintain the integrity of individual talks rather than edit to integrate multiple talks into one chapter.

Several talks have been included as Addenda. One of these is on Matthew 20:1–16. Whilst it references Matthew 20, this specific teaching is more a topical message about "work" than a commentary on Matthew Chapter 20. It is felt that the reader may appreciate the inclusion of this and the other messages and therefore we have included them as addenda.

We trust you will value the additional content included in this edition.

1
GENEALOGY

Read Matthew Chapter 1:1–17

When reading this genealogy, you may have thought: "Well, I wonder what on earth he will get out of that." I think I can honestly say that we get nothing out of it that God did not put into it. For the preacher's job is not to read his own thoughts into scripture, but to get God's thoughts out of it.

The genealogies of scripture are often despised or neglected, and there are plenty of them – all this "begetting" that went on through the centuries. People have often said to me, "Do you believe that all the Bible is inspired by God?" I have said yes. Then they have almost invariably responded, "What use are some of the passages?" When asked what kind of passage they mean, they refer to the genealogies, as if it really was a waste of time for God to give us all these unnecessary family trees. What spiritual good can they do to us two thousand years later? We shall see.

At Chalfont St Peter I once asked a lady missionary to give her testimony. She got up and said, "I was converted through reading the genealogy in Matthew chapter one." So we were all agog to learn how that passage had led her to the Lord. She said, "I had heard about Jesus, but for me he was a figure in a stained glass window – he wasn't real. One day I read Matthew chapter 1 and suddenly I realised he must have been a real person for there was his real family tree. I surrendered to Him."

So if the genealogy led just one person to the Lord it was worth it, but I believe it is going to lead us all nearer to the Lord.

Just imagine that you are in part of the world where there is only one Bible for every thousand believers.

Do you know what they do in those situations? They tear the Bible up and they give each person a page. You might have Matthew 1; that might be all you have got to feed your soul on, and to be your spiritual nourishment. On one occasion when I prepared to preach on this chapter, I said, "Lord, you give me out of it what we need today." Then I got so much in one week that I could understand someone feeding their soul for months on this passage.

Of course, it would be thoroughly bad journalism to begin a story in this way. The writer of a magazine article would not dare to begin the life of a man with a list of all his forbears – just a long list of names to wade through. It would not be good writing by modern standards, but many modern people do not want to study, they just want to read quickly – get something sensational; get a headline or two and put it away again – whereas reading the Bible is like panning for gold. Have you ever watched a film of a prospector panning for gold? With his sieve he digs into the mud and gravel and dirty water, and shakes it. What is he doing? Why is he wasting time shaking mud and pebbles? It is because every now and again something glints, something shines, and he picks it out and there is a gold nugget. This is what Bible study is like. As we shake this chapter with many names in it, and as we rake a little, we find this. Something will glint. We will seize it and look at it, and it will shine as God's truth into our souls. So I spent a week "panning", sieving this chapter of scripture. There is gold here for those who really are prepared to study, not just quickly read a few verses for the day.

We need to consider two things. First of all, we need to consider the author of this list, and then we need to consider the reader. That will begin to unlock it for us. The author was a man who collected taxes, and therefore he was handy with pen and paper. When he left his tax collecting he started collecting the teachings of Jesus. This man was called Matthew – the name means "gift of God", and what a gift of God he is to us – if

Matthew had not collected Jesus' teachings we would never have got the Sermon on the Mount, for example.

This is the first of the four Gospels in the New Testament, but it was not the first to be written. Why does it appear first in the New Testament? Would it not have been better to begin with Mark or Luke, which really get straight into the account? Mark particularly does not waste words. "Immediately" – is a favourite word in Mark, and it would have been good journalism to put Mark at the beginning. Why does Matthew start with this list? What is he after?

Of course, the Gospels are not photographs – they are portraits of Jesus from different angles in different roles. I have seen a few paintings, photographs and statues of Winston Churchill. Each of them presents a different characteristic: some his determination as a war leader, some his skill as a politician, some his recreation as a painter. You see the full-orbed character of Churchill through the different portraits.

In the same way, you see the full character of Christ through the four different portraits in Matthew, Mark, Luke and John. Each of them is painting a different picture – not a contradictory one, but filling it out with a new aspect. If Mark talks about the Son of Man who is the Suffering Servant of the Lord, and Luke talks about the Saviour of the world, and John paints the Son of God, Matthew paints the King of the Jews. That is his object. We now suddenly realise why Matthew is the first in the New Testament, even if it was not the first to be written. The answer is that it is the nearest Gospel to the Old Testament, the most Jewish one that picks up the threads of all that has gone before.

A New Testament is only half a book, only "part two". Therefore, Matthew chapter 1 is in a sense a recapitulation. It is a brilliant way to do it. By giving Jesus' family tree in just half a page, Matthew is saying: look at two thousand years of the story thus far, and see Jesus as the completion of the story. It is a brilliant recap of two thousand years of God's dealings.

Therefore, those who compiled the New Testament for us put it right next to the Old. It is right next to Malachi, and though there is a gap of four hundred years between the two books, those were lost years because during four whole centuries God never opened his mouth once.

No prophets came; not once did a man say "Thus says the Lord" in those four hundred years. They waited for God to speak again. Then God began to speak again. So Malachi and Matthew are squeezed together. The Word became flesh and dwelt among us.

What about the readers? Matthew is writing for Jews. This is one of the reasons why we Gentiles don't take to Matthew very well. We love Luke's Gospel, which is written for Gentiles. When I suggest that someone start reading the New Testament I always suggest they start with Luke unless they are a Jew. If you bear in mind that the author was a Jew, writing for Jews, writing about the King of the Jews, then you will understand why he starts with this list. Matthew is beginning the second half of God's book. So he is looking back and sees that there is a continuity of the story. History is "his story"; BC and AD belong together and he is writing the final chapter of it. Writing for Jews, he has to prove that Jesus was a Jew. Now frankly to us it hardly matters what Jesus was by nation or nationality, as long as he is our Saviour.

We Gentiles, I think, would not have been too worried if Jesus had been a Russian or a Chinese. We might even have liked him to be English. Some of our Sunday school pictures even seem to imply that he was fair-haired and blue eyed. That is not true. But to us as Gentiles, as long as God sent his Son into the world, that is the big thing; but to a Jew no, it has got to be a Jew. There is a profound reason why Jesus was a Jew, a Hebrew. So Matthew, in presenting Jesus to the Jews, has to begin by saying he was a Jew. Here is his family tree. Check it for yourself. He was a Jew and he could trace his history right back to Abraham. The first thing he said was that he is a Son of Abraham and Son of David. Those are two phrases to which we will return.

Right at the beginning we learn that this book is the *good news* of Matthew. Though Malachi and Matthew belong together, the last word in Malachi is "curse" and the beginning of Matthew is "good news". That is the difference between the Old Testament and the New Testament.

Pedigree is important, depending on what is in it. I do not know if you have ever checked your lineage. A lady in Devon by the name of Pawson got us back to about 1485. She dug out all sorts of things about us. I am not sure I was terribly happy about it all, but that is on my father's side. I was a little happier on my mother's side because we could claim at least one titled gentleman, Sir John Sinclair, as part of the family tree. Then we got a little further back and found that Sinclair was Spanish, "St. Clair's", so that was quite unexpected and we began to go a little quiet on it.

While we were living in Lancashire an American came, having saved up to come over and visit his birthplace. On his birth certificate it said, "Number 1, Southall Street, Manchester". When he got there he found it was the address of Strangeways Prison, and that he had been born in prison. His mother had been a prisoner when he had been born. It doesn't always do to dig up your background, or to trace back your family tree. We find out some strange things. There was a jobbing gardener in Buckinghamshire who discovered that he had in fact inherited a title and a fortune, and he had become a lord of this realm. He inherited that because he had the right pedigree; there was something in his family tree.

Now Jesus was not only the Son of Abraham, He was the Son of David. Jesus was not just any person. He was not just an ordinary man; he was already extraordinary. He was a real man, but he had royal blood flowing through his veins. Through these two thousand years of history that family tree had been recorded by someone to prove that Jesus was to be King. This is what we find when we study this.

This connection with David is stressed in two unusual ways – one simple, one subtle. The simple way is this. David's name is mentioned five times in this genealogy. It is the only name that appears that often, so that the emphasis in this family tree is on David. There is something more subtle though. The Hebrew language has no numbers and no vowels. So instead of using numbers they use letters. For numbers, "a" equals "1", "b" equals "2" and so on – like Roman numerals. Furthermore, when they wrote David, "D-w-d" would be the nearest way we could get to in English. They missed out the two vowels and they just had three letters. The "D" was the number "4", the "w" was the number "6" and the "d" was the number "4". Add that up – fourteen. At the end of this genealogy you can see that there were fourteen generations from Abraham to David, fourteen from David to the Exile, and fourteen from the Exile to Jesus. To a Hebrew, fourteen spelled in letters is spelled, "D-w-d" – David. You get the message that is coming through loud and clear.

Only a Jewish mind would get that message. It is written for the Jews. The whole thing fits and it cannot be a coincidence. There is some pattern emerging through this family tree that points to this name "David – Son of David". This phrase is terribly important. It is used more often in the Gospel of Matthew than the other three Gospels, but it is there all through the Gospels. It is so obvious that a blind man can see it: "Son of David, have mercy on me." On Palm Sunday the crowd shouted, "Hosanna to the Son of David!" Read the Epistles and you find that a favourite phrase of Paul is the "seed of David". Read the last page in the New Testament and you find Christ saying, "I am the Root and the Offspring of David...." From the first page to the last page of the New Testament: "David" – this name runs right through. It is vitally important; Jesus was the Man born to be King.

To us it is commonplace to say "Jesus Christ". Do you realise

Matthew Chapter 1:1–17

that is something that most Jews in the world cannot bring themselves to say? One word (Jesus) is a name and the other (Christ) is a title, but we have used the title so much now that we think it is the name. When we turn the word "Christ" back into Hebrew, and get the word "Christ" back from the Greek into the Hebrew, we get "Mashiach"; "Messiah" – the Christ. Who do they mean? That word for the Jews sums up a hope that has burned in hearts for centuries – a hope that one day there would come a Son of David, who would sit on David's throne, and bring Israel through to peace and prosperity again. They never had it as good as they did in the days of King David. All down through the centuries the hope was passed on that the Christ would come. When Jesus came, Matthew says he was the Christ, and they did not see it. They panned the pebbles in the mud and they never saw the gold. It is the greatest tragedy of history.

It is an intriguing fact that the Gospel of Matthew is the fortieth book in the Bible. The number forty in the Bible is invariably connected with a period of testing, whether forty years in the wilderness or forty days in the wilderness. Forty days is a period in which people are tested; either they come through, having passed the examination, or they fail, but forty is God's examination. Matthew's Gospel is the fortieth book in the Bible; there are thirty-nine in the Old Testament and the fortieth describes the testing of the people of Israel. It was so obvious that he was the King of the Jews that even a Roman governor, who did not know the Old Testament, wrote down on a piece of board: "This is the King of the Jews," and it was stuck on his cross.

Even Pontius Pilate could see it was true, and he didn't have any of the knowledge that the Jews had. The fortieth book symbolises for me the testing of the people of Israel. Would they recognise their own King? They did not. They even went to Pilate and said, "Write, 'He said, I am the King of the Jews,' but don't write 'This is the King of the Jews'." Pilate, with the only burst of courage he ever showed, said, "What I have written, I have written." It remains written in God's Word above the cross, "This is the King of the Jews." It is Matthew's genealogy that proves his right to the throne of David.

We have not looked at any details as yet. Let me make a very obvious point. Someone kept this genealogy. The genealogies of Jewish families were kept in various ways. They could be remembered by the individual. Since they did not have many books in those days they had to train their memories. We have to write things down on note pads, the back of envelopes, on all kinds of things. They used to write it in the family Bible cover in the old days. Have you ever seen a family Bible with a family tree in it? But they had to remember it and the whole thing is arranged for memory. That was one way: remembered by the individual and recorded by the family. A family, if they could afford it, would write down the family tree on a scroll, on a piece of parchment, and keep it.

It would also be registered by the government for purposes of taxation. Now the government keeps my national insurance number and all my other numbers in some computer, but in those days they kept the family tree in the tax office. That is why Jesus was born in Bethlehem – because his family tree was in some tax office. He had to be born in Bethlehem because he was of the house and lineage of David. Matthew was a tax collector and I believe he went along to the tax office, pulled open a filing cabinet and said, "Let's see that record of Jesus." I have the feeling he went along to the tax office to get it. I am reading between the lines, but it is exciting, isn't it?

First of all, I am going to look at the men in this story and then I am going to look at the women. That is in itself a story. I could preach a sermon on every one of these names. Notice first that the legal descent is through the father. Today there is a great debate going on in Israel: who is a Jew? They are tending to talk about having a Jewish mother's blood in you or a Jewish grandmother. But in those days the biblical principle was clear: the legal descent was through your dad, your abba, and it came down through the male side. Therefore it is the male line that is vital to a genealogy.

We have here a list, for the most part, of men. Some of them are extremely well known to us – Abraham, Isaac, Jacob, David. You know about these people. It would take a long time to look at each of them. Some of them are little-known farmers. We know a little about the governor Zerubbabel. Some of them are quite unknown. Who on earth was Azor? We will meet him in glory and ask him then. Do you know anything about Salmon? This is a mixture of known and unknown. Take a little lesson from that straight away. God uses a whole company of people to accomplish his purpose – some are famous and some hardly known, but God has the names, and that is the important thing. You may not be in the public eye in serving the Lord, but you could be a vital link in God's chain for someone, a vital person in what God is doing in the world. Do not worry if you are not known. You almost need to read the whole Old Testament to understand these men. They are real people, heroes of history, flesh and blood. Try to get the feel of this. You are going to meet them; you are going to live with them; you will shake hands with some of them. They are real people, not just names in a dry old book.

There is more than physical heredity here, there is spiritual heredity. There is sin going down the line. These were not all good men. The only thing mentioned here of David is the bad thing he did. These are bad men as well as good men. Most of them are a mixture of the two, saints and sinners. Not only does sin go down this line, but faith goes down the line. It is not only a line of flesh, it is a line of faith. Abraham was the father not only of fleshly descendants but of all those who shared his faith. These were men of faith.

I am going to pick out two names because there is something quite unusual about them. The first is the name Jeconiah. He is the last just before they went into exile and the first when they got back. Why do I want to think about Jeconiah? Well let me tell you the strangest thing. It is an illustration of the fact that you will never understand the New Testament unless you read the Old. In the Old Testament in the book of Jeremiah, Jeconiah is one of those who has helped to bring the nation so low in sin that God says: Off to Babylon with you; get out, I am not having you in my Holy Land. Jeconiah was one of the leaders in that breakdown of that nation, and God put a curse on Jeconiah.

The curse was this: "No offspring of yours will ever sit on the throne of David." Here he is in Jesus' family tree. Now there is a puzzle for you. "No offspring of yours, I curse you with this." It is a curse that lasted all the way down the family; no offspring of Jeconiah would sit on the throne of David. No offspring ever has done because Jesus was not physically descended from Jeconiah. Do you see that? If Jesus had been the physical son of Joseph, then the curse of God from the Old Testament would have been undone. But the fact that Jeconiah has his name in that family tree means that Jesus could not be born of Joseph, and yet He needed the family tree. He needed the legal descent.

So that makes us turn to Joseph. You notice he is not described as the father of Jesus. All the others are "father of..., father of..., father of...," then it says "Joseph, husband of Mary, of whom Jesus was born." Now note that legal inheritance is always by legal descent not by physical descent. This is absolutely vital to understanding the excitement of the end of this genealogy. Jesus was, of course, conceived out of wedlock; He would therefore have had no family tree. He would have come under the law of God in Deuteronomy 23 which states that, "A bastard should not be allowed in the temple of God to the tenth generation." It was Joseph who gave Jesus not only his legality, but his title to David's throne. How the purposes of God can hang on the decision of one man; that he should entrust us with so much. But Joseph was engaged to Mary.

Now engagement was, as we will see in the rest of Matthew 1, a very serious relationship. It was more than engagement here in our modern society; betrothal was a binding thing. Therefore, if your fiancé died while you were betrothed you were a widow. More than that, if you broke that engagement it was a divorce. The marriage had not taken place, and had not been consummated, but during the engagement period you were as good as married legally.

When Joseph found out that his wife had already conceived, being a fair man, he decided to divorce her privately. Had he gone ahead with that, Jesus would have had no claim whatever to the throne of David. Now does that grab your attention? Joseph had the whole line of God in his hands at this point. God sent an angel to him and the angel said: "Don't be afraid to take her as your wife, she has not been unfaithful to you, it is the Holy Ghost operating. She has conceived, but by him, not by any man, so take her." Therefore, they got married before the baby was born, and therefore, they had to go to Bethlehem to be taxed. For this reason, Jesus was born "once in Royal David's city". The whole of God's plan came true.

So Jesus' right to the throne of David did not depend on his physical birth, but on his legal descent, and the willingness of Joseph to be involved in the situation, for Joseph passed on the legal inheritance that made possible the King of the Jews and the Saviour of the world. Did you realise that? There it is at the end of this thing: an ordinary carpenter, knowing that he had the right to the throne of David passed it on to this boy he had not fathered. Had he not done that he could have kept it for one of his own boys. He could have told one of his own sons: "You are in the line, and you may get the throne." The throne of David had been vacant for six hundred years, but everybody in that line hoped that a son of theirs would get on the throne, but Joseph gave it away. Jesus had the title.

Now let us look at the women. It is astonishing to find women at all. In the genealogies of the Old Testament, women do not figure, but in the New Testament, women have a new place and a new honour. Here they are in the genealogy, but what a mixture of women. There is Rahab, a Canaanite, a prostitute in the worst city of those days, Jericho; yet, because she stepped out in faith and accepted the invading army of Israel as the true followers of God, she became an ancestress of our Lord Jesus Christ. Faith brought her into the line in more ways than one. Then we look at Ruth, a Moabitess. The same law in Deuteronomy 23 that forbids bastards to enter the temple, links with Moabites and forbids them to enter. Here she is in the ancestry of our Lord. Then we see Tamar, a deliberate seducer and adulteress (and see also Genesis 38) is here too. Then we find Bathsheba, not named because she was more sinned against than sinning, and her name was not to be dragged down. She is simply described as Uriah's wife, but it is not a very edifying part of the story.

One commentator pointed out that if Matthew had ransacked the pages of the Old Testament for improbable candidates he could not have discovered four more incredible ancestors for Jesus Christ. What does it say to you? I'll tell you what it says to me. It doesn't matter what you have been, it is what you become; it doesn't matter how low you have sunk, it is what God does with you. How like God to choose women like that. Then, of course, the general impression this might give of women is redeemed by that lovely name "Mary" at the end. That teenage girl unspoiled who said, "I'm willing. Do to me your handmaid whatever you want. I'm willing." She never even defended herself against the gossip; she never even tried to explain to her own fiancé, she just submitted to the will of God.

Verse 17 completes this part of our study. We have just touched on some of the fascination that lies behind this genealogy. If you have time, take this genealogy, use a concordance, and look up each name and study what experience went into this family tree – it would take you days to do that, and you could feed your soul on it. Is v.17 just pointing out an unusual coincidence that there were fourteen generations in the three stages? No, I think it is telling us three vital things about God. Number one: the *patience* of God. Forty-two generations – two thousand years – God took, and we might say, "Hurry up, Lord! We've been waiting centuries!" But through all those generations God knew exactly what he was doing. They came and they went, but God went on working out his purpose as year succeeded year. He is still wonderfully patient. Fourteen generations to complete one stage, another fourteen to complete another; and another fourteen.

Secondly, it tells me about the *purpose* of God. These three fourteens mark three stages of Israel's history. Stage number one was from Abraham up to David – the build up of the nation. They reached their peak under David; they never had so much territory, so much peace, so much happiness. David was a man after God's own heart and a man loved by the people. The next fourteen generations went all the way down again until God kicked them out of the land. You can read the sad story in 2 Kings of how they sinned against the Lord – even those kings, increasingly, of whom it states: "He did what was evil in the sight of the Lord." Down and down they went. A nation follows its leaders up and down.

Stage number three: there were six hundred years in which no one sat on the throne of David at all. There was just one brief period under the Maccabees where they gained independence and they put some people on the throne to reign as kings, and they crowned them, but they were not of the line of David. Jews celebrate Hanukkah, the Maccabean independence, and there was restoration of a kingly line, but it was not the line of God. No, for that third period, another fourteen generations, there was no king on the throne of David and they waited – until a little baby in a manger at Bethlehem cried his first cry. There came wise men from the east: "Where is he that is born King of the Jews?" At that time the man that claimed the title "King of the Jews" was Herod and he did not have the pedigree. Half his blood was Edomite and he had no right to be there. Do you see the purpose unfolding? It is, of course, the same pattern that other empires have had. The British Empire rose and fell, and will never be the same again. The same could be said of Rome, Greece and Egypt. The difference is this: to the Jews, God sent the Christ – not to any others.

This also tells me about the *power* of God. David Wilkerson gave a remarkable prophecy on 8 August, 1973. It came in a vision he saw in his sleep. He woke up shouting these five words, which God had put on his lips: "God has everything under control!" That is the message for today. Two thousand years of history may look chaotic to some people – they may think of it as a kaleidoscope of events getting nowhere fast – but when you read a genealogy you see that God has everything under control. It is all moving to his planned destiny. That is what this genealogy tells me.

This is the last genealogy in the Bible except for Luke chapter 3, which is simply another version of Christ's genealogy. Why do we not have any more? Why do we not have Paul's genealogy, or Peter's or John's? Why is Jesus the last person to have a family tree in the Bible? The Old Testament is full of them. I recall when our church read the Bible right through from cover to cover, non-stop, and some people got the first ten chapters of Chronicles. The Old Testament is full of genealogies and begetting and family tables. Why do they stop? The answer is they stop because they have all reached the end. When Jesus, who is called "the Christ" was born, they did not go any further. It does not matter now who your ancestors were, what family tree you have. What matters now is whether you are *in Christ*. Jesus, the Word, became flesh. Those who are God's children are born of God, born from above, born of the Spirit. You only have one family tree when you are born of the Spirit.

When God made a promise to Abraham and a covenant with

him, he said: "Abraham, I'm going to make a great nation of you; I'm going to give you this land. Everything is for you and your seed." The word "seed" there is masculine and singular. In other words: to you, Abraham, and one male descendant of yours. The promise came to Jesus; the promise of Abraham was inherited, and once it has been inherited that is it. The promise has been received.

It does not matter where my name or yours is written on earth or what our family tree is – but it is vital that your name be written in one of God's books. The original is in heaven and there are no copies on earth. It is the Lamb's Book of Life, and right there in that book is my name written in God's book. Here is an exciting thought that came to me: Matthew 1 is my family tree! Why? Because I am mentioned there at the end of verse 16: "Christ", and I am *in Christ*. "If anyone is in Christ" is the New Testament definition of a Christian. You may go to church, but that does not make you a Christian. You can "put on" Christian behaviour. You can imitate other Christians, you can sing hymns, you can read your Bible – but that does not do it. What makes you a Christian? To be *in* Christ makes you a Christian, and that puts you into Matthew 1. It puts you into the final stage and this becomes *your* family tree. You inherit the promise by being in Christ, and then Abraham is your father. So I was excited to read this genealogy. What a joy to be one of the family, and Jesus is not ashamed to call us brethren.

2
THE NATIVITY

Read Matthew Chapter 1:18–25

I would guess the nativity is the best-known narrative in the whole Bible to the world of unbelievers. Most people in the Western world know at least the basic details. They have seen nativity plays; they may have heard it at school or Sunday school, and the nativity still exercises fascination even amongst those who will never darken the door of the church all year. Some will turn up for midnight mass or a Christmas Eve communion, and for carol singing. People who do not seem to know God personally will sing about the coming of his Son.

Yet Christmas has the least Christian impact of any period in the year. The number of conversions to Christ goes down over Christmas as the number of suicides goes up. The ultimate, deep questions about Christmas are very disturbing. Why is it that Christmas has so little impact on people? They hear the story of the gift of God's Son year after year after year, and never seem to receive that gift. What is it? I have come to one or two conclusions about this. One is that a baby is less threatening than a man, and the world prefers Jesus as a baby. A baby cannot tell you what to do. A baby cannot order your life or challenge you about your sins. You can pick up a baby and put it in a manger, and you can keep it there. The baby Jesus is preferred by the world of unbelievers because they dare not face the man Christ Jesus. I believe that to be one reason.

A second reason why Christmas fails to make its impact is again that the idea that God has become like us is much more congenial to our nature than the idea that we are to become like him. Therefore Christmas, rather than the Ascension, is what the world likes to hear about. The thought that he has come and he has mixed with us and he is one of us – that is great, and it is a thrilling part of the story. But the thought that I have got to get myself fit for heaven? That is not so congenial to the world.

Another reason is quite simply that we surround fact with so much fantasy that the impact of the whole is lost. I wish I could do what the Scots have done and put all the rest of the trivia of this time into Hogmanay, get rid of all the Christmas tinsel and fairy lights and get back to fact. What strikes me in the story of the birth of Christ in the Bible is how factual, simple and straightforward it is. It is simply an account of what actually happened. It is not dressed up. It is not disguised in things that do not appear at other times of the year. There is no description really anywhere of the feelings of the people involved. The scene that we dress up on Christmas cards was such an ordinary scene.

So let us get back to the facts in this passage. Each year, every minister in a sense has the horrible feeling, "I've said it all before for so many years. Can it be fresh? Can I find anything new here?" There is the subtle temptation to try to introduce novelty and to read into it what God did not put there first.

One year I had a little card on my mantlepiece which read: "A happy Jesus Christmas!" What one wants to do is indeed put the name "Jesus" back into it – not the "Christ-Child" or the "Holy Babe" but "Jesus". "You will call him 'Jesus'"– Why? Because he will save people from their sins. That is what it is all about, and it is the one thing people do not want to hear at Christmas. "Jesus" is the one name you do not hear the world using much at Christmas. This is the important aspect of Christmas that they are missing: Jesus. This is the Saviour, and this is the fact.

First, I want to deal simply with the narrative of his birth. There are two sides inextricably woven together. On the one hand there is the natural aspect – things that occur at every birth. On the other side is the supernatural part of the story, things that we

Matthew Chapter 1:18–25

are not accustomed to. These two sides intermingle beautifully to make the whole. What is happening is this: two worlds are meeting – the natural and the supernatural. Heaven and earth are kissing and therefore you cannot separate out the human part from the supernatural part. That is why the nativity play has to be done as a whole. You have got to have the angels as well as the shepherds or you spoil the narrative.

Let us look at the natural side first. Jesus was conceived out of wedlock – that is the first complication. That is happening every day hundreds of times, so there seems to us to be nothing very extraordinary in it. But what we need to understand is that the marriage customs in the Middle East were rather different from ours. Officially and by mutual social consent, we still have a two-stage marriage though it is rapidly disappearing. I mean that first you get engaged and announce publicly that you are engaged to be married. That is an understanding; it is something that can be broken and indeed often is, but it is announced to society. Stage two: there is the legal marriage and the consummation of the marriage. Those two things happen together, usually on the same day, some months or even years after the engagement but it is a two-stage process.

In Jewish society and biblical days, it was a three-stage process. First you were *engaged*, and you did not choose that. Your parents probably arranged it when you were a child. Stage number two: you were *betrothed* and that was the legal ceremony. From that point on you were legally married, and if your betrothed died you were a widow or a widower. It was a legal contract, but, and this is the complication: you did not consummate the marriage physically for another twelve months, and the consummation was stage number three. So you were engaged, maybe for some years; then betrothed (legally binding) for twelve months, and finally the marriage was consummated when the bridegroom came to the bride's house to take her to his home and consummate the marriage there. Until then, he would just visit her.

In our society the stages have pretty well become one now, and in many cases have become none. Now it was while they were in the second stage, not the first, that someone – we do not know who – discovered that Mary was pregnant. Legally, the only way to deal with that was by divorce because it was the next step back from engagement. Joseph resolved to divorce her quietly – privately. In fact, you could divorce in such circumstances by simply having two members of the public witness you giving your fiancée her divorce and breaking the legal contract. Two witnesses would need to be present to show that it was on adequate grounds, and of course in this case it was. Had Joseph divorced Mary, of course, Jesus never could have been the Son of David. He would never have received the title to the throne of David. The whole story of the Gospel would have collapsed. So that gives you the background, and therefore we find in an ancient Hebrew writing this strange phrase: "a virgin who is a widow". You can only understand that phrase if you have got the message.

Now she was discovered by *someone* to be pregnant. Was it Joseph? Was it her mother? She did not tell anyone. She was used to keeping things in her heart and pondering them. One of the things that moves my heart very deeply was that in v. 10 it says that Joseph was in an agony of mind. The Greek verse means to be in an absolute agony of mind; torn between two. Imagine the feelings of Joseph – falling in love with this lovely, devout, beautiful girl; she had got everything and he could hardly believe that she had said "yes" and would marry him. He really must have had her up there on a pedestal, to have such a girl legally betrothed to him and looking forward to the end of twelve months when it would be possible to consummate the marriage. He really had everything, and suddenly he discovers that this good, beautiful girl who was coming to give herself to him and who he assumed had not been with any other before him is, in fact, in this condition. It says he was in an absolute torment. What could he do? Should he go through with it?

On the other hand, it says he was a righteous man, which means he was a man who stuck strictly to God's will and God's law. God's law was divorce in these circumstances and the man was torn in two. You know, we do not have one word from Joseph's lips in the whole of the Bible. Have you ever noticed that? Strong, silent man that he was, you get a sense of his feelings, character and personality. He could have really put Mary in the middle of the village square and said, "Look at her! She's let me down. I was engaged to her and betrothed to her, and look what she's done to me!" Human nature can be very vindictive when it is disappointed and frustrated – but Joseph was a righteous man. He did not do what he felt like doing; he did what he felt God said should be done. After an agony of mind, he was coming to the following conclusion: I will divorce her privately with just two witnesses, and we will try to keep the whole thing quiet.

But before he did so, the supernatural side of the story entered. It ceased to be an ordinary human situation; the kind of situation that people are constantly meeting, and which requires great wisdom, understanding and righteousness to deal with properly. Joseph received supernatural help – he got a visit from an angel. It is intriguing that he had that visit in his sleep. In the Bible, why do many messages come to people in dreams? I think it is because in your dreams you have no choice but to accept anything. Is that not so? In your dreams, the most incredible thing you just simply accept as normal. A pink elephant may come flying in and say, "Hello," and you just say, "Hello," in your dream; it is acceptable in the dream world. Very often, therefore, God can get through to us while we sleep because our minds are not defended against things. Our minds are open to the most unusual thoughts. This is the simple reason why sometimes if you have a problem, and you go to bed and sleep on it, you will wake up in the morning with the solution. The Bible says, "He gives to his beloved in sleep." He gave Solomon a dream and gave him an answered prayer in a dream and gave him the gift of wisdom while he slept.

An angel came and spoke to Joseph in the dream because he would have been thrown off balance if the angel had come in broad daylight. He was a carpenter; a practical man, thoroughly down-to-earth. The important thing is that when he woke up, the dream stayed vividly with him and stood the test of Joseph looking at it in daylight. You have got to test dreams because a dream can come from your subconscious as well as from God, and it can come from demonic influence as well. It does not mean that because you have had a vivid dream God has spoken to you. But, tested, you can know whether it is of God, and sometimes God has spoken clearly in dreams.

Joseph woke up. He was told that the pregnancy was not due to infidelity on Mary's part. That is an extraordinary fact. A waking man in his senses in broad daylight could not have coped with that fact. It was the first time it had ever happened, and yet the angel just reels it off as a kind of matter-of-fact statement: "It's all right; she's with child by the Holy Ghost" – as if this is a normal occurrence, something perfectly straightforward. To God, it is.

To the God who created the stars and the planets, to produce a baby in a girl who has never known sex, is nothing. It is so ordinary, so everyday to heaven because heaven is a place where miracles are happening constantly, and God's creative activity is producing something new all the time. So the angel just speaks in a matter-of-fact way. It is all right; it is the Holy Ghost who has given her this child. Of course, this virginal conception of a male baby had never occurred before in the history of the human race. To a down-to-earth carpenter this was said. No wonder it came in a dream.

Can we find a parallel anywhere in scripture? Some women like Hannah and Sarah were barren right up to the time they had a child, and clearly the Holy Spirit enabled them to be fertile after knowing men. Elizabeth was another. So, the Holy Spirit had acted already on women who seemed not to be capable of being fertilised, enabling that to be done by their husbands. Now that is a totally different thing. This was the first time it had happened without a man being involved at all. The only parallel is in Genesis 6 where one possible meaning of the first six verses is that evil spirits had impregnated human women, and the result was a kind of horrible beings called Nephilim, whatever that means. It is sometimes translated as "giants", sometimes as "monsters" but in Genesis 6 there is the possible interpretation – I believe it could well be the right one – that evil spirits, fallen angels impregnated human women and produced monsters as a result of this terrible cross-breeding between species which God had clearly forbidden.

If that is so, there had been virgin births by evil spirits before this, but there had never been a virgin birth by Holy Spirit. The next time Holy Spirit (without the definite article) came on Mary was on the day of Pentecost when she was filled with Holy Spirit and spoke with tongues along with the other 119 believers. Twice did the Holy Spirit come on Mary in power – the first time to produce a baby within her.

I have a scientific cast of mind. It is part of my background and training, and I find myself asking: how did the Holy Spirit do it? I hope it does not sound irreverent, and I can only speculate, and yet I want to try to help you to realise that it really was a physical thing. There are two ways in which God might have done it physically. One way is that Mary's egg was fertilised by God, and therefore that she contributed the human characteristics physically, and that Jesus would be physically like his mother and have a physical resemblance to her. There would be only need for one very tiny addition of a chromosome which is an absolutely microscopic thing – only the strongest microscopes can see them. Otherwise the birth would have been of a little girl. Other claimed virgin births which have been investigated by scientists, and a few accepted as possible virgin births, have all been of girls because a woman can only produce a female egg. The woman does not have the capacity to produce a boy. It is the man who puts that vital little chromosome right in the egg and makes it a boy. So either God took one of Mary's eggs in which case Jesus would have resembled this lovely girl and added in the chromosome, which would change the egg to a boy, and people would have recognised him as Mary's son.

The other possibility is that in fact, God simply used Mary's womb to carry a fertilised egg which he created in totality. In that case, Jesus would not have resembled Mary or any of his physical forebears but would have been programmed or patterned according to the genes which God created – in which case he would simply have implanted in the womb this egg; it would not have come from the ovaries. Now, I think like this because I want to get into the miracle of the Incarnation.

The birth of Jesus was a natural event. He came into the world the same way you and I did. It was an ordinary birth. It was a virgin conception. That is what had happened that lifts it out of the ordinary. I just want to feel that God got right into the world which science looks at.

I saw a photograph of a little baby being formed in a womb. What a photograph! The things which we have at last been able to photograph and at last been able to watch with sophisticated equipment are things which God watched thousands of years ago (see Psalm 139). He formed my inward parts; he watched me when he knitted me together in my mother's womb. God was watching the wonderful process all the time.

I want the world of science – the material world in which people live – and the supernatural world, to get together. That is why I talk like this – so that we can see God working in the world that scientists discover; God doing things and watching them long before we see them. God in this world, God right down here, God in the material – God handling that fifteen-year-old girl's body in such a miraculous way. The whole thing makes you want to bow down in wonder, love and praise that ever God did it. It is so ordinary to angels but extraordinary to us.

The second thing I want to address is the nature of this birth. Why a virgin birth? We have looked at the how, and we must leave to God the exact how. I have given you the two possible ways he could have done it; I don't know which one it was. I just have the feeling that he did allow Mary to contribute to the physical body of our Lord Jesus, but that is only my feeling. When I get to heaven I will ask – but why a virgin birth? That is more important – not how, but why.

Let me just rule out one answer to that: the idea that sex is sin. I am afraid that deep down this has been a tradition in the church for too long. That is why the belief arose, mainly in the Roman Catholic Church but not exclusively, in the perpetual virginity of Mary, as if somehow she had to be pure from having physical relations with a man. If that is true, then celibacy is holier than marriage – which the Bible does not teach. I think we have got to kill this one because it says very simply that Joseph did not know Mary until after Jesus was born, which is as plain a statement as you can have that, in fact, Mary was not a perpetual virgin. She lost her virginity soon after Jesus was born, and there were other brothers and sisters.

Those who try and twist the Bible and say it says "cousins" instead of "brothers and sisters" are not being true to God's Word. No, it is not because the relationships between a man and a woman are somehow dirty or sinful. Sin can make it that way, but God made male and female for each other. He made sex first for partnership rather than parenthood; not just to have children but that one might be a helpmate to the other. This has implications for many practical questions of behaviour. But when God made them for each other like that, he said, "Now that is very good." They can now have companionship.

In that sense, this is not the reason why there was a virgin birth. Then why was it a virgin birth? One possible reason (not given in the Bible) is this: where a man and a woman produce a joint, fertilised egg to become a baby, they have created a new person who never existed before. Each of them has contributed something to the other, and each of them has contributed certain characteristics to the new, unique personality. They have created a new person, who did not exist before. The Son of God was not new – he had existed from all eternity. This was no new person arriving on the scene; this was a very old Person, the Ancient of Days. This baby was not a new personality, a new character; this baby was the embodiment of a personality who had existed from all eternity. Therefore, a normal conception, a normal fertilisation would not have been possible. It would not have been the right one because what was needed was not a new personality but the embodiment of someone already existing. Therefore, you would have expected there to be a new way to be born. That is why Sarah had a miraculous child by Abraham. Hannah had a miraculous child – Samuel. Elizabeth had a miraculous child, but by her husband. Mary had a child, but not by Joseph.

Now let us look at the prophecy in Isaiah 7:14, which gives us the real answer as to why it had to be a virgin birth. You find that in the Revised Standard Version it says, "Behold, a young woman will conceive and bear a child, and they will call his name Immanuel" – a young woman. I want to tell you that I take my hat off to the translators of the Revised Standard Version for an accurate translation. The word used there means, "A young woman of marriageable age"; it does not necessarily mean a virgin. It usually meant that, because one would expect a young woman of marriageable age to be a virgin, but the word itself does not specifically mean that. It means a normal, young, teenage girl to be married, and in God's sight normality means virginity. Therefore, it has the implication of being a virgin but not the stated meaning. When the RSV came out, there was an outcry from some people who thought they were decrying the virgin birth. They were not; they were trying to be accurate translators.

Matthew Chapter 1:18–25

When it comes to the New Testament, then Matthew gives the interpretation to that word – "a virgin", and he is right to do so. There is the clue to the tension between the two, and it is a little complex. In the Old Testament, many of the predictions have a double fulfilment. In other words, they are fulfilled in one event and then also fulfilled a second time. Many of the prophecies of the Day of the Lord and the coming of the Lord split into two fulfilments, and we know that Jesus came to this planet Earth once and will come again. Sometimes both events are included in the one prediction "the Lord will come".

In exactly the same way, if you read Isaiah's prophecy carefully, he is predicting that a boy will be born within the lifetime of the people to whom he is speaking, if you read on. He is speaking of someone to be born long before Jesus was born in Bethlehem, and he is speaking of a girl of marriageable age producing a little boy who will be called Immanuel. The first fulfilment of the prediction was in the days of the Old Testament, before certain historical events were to happen. If you read on through the next two or three verses of Isaiah, you will see that. But when Isaiah predicted this, God was giving him a double fulfilment.

The first time it would be a young woman of marriageable age by her husband; the second time it would be a young woman of marriageable age without her husband, and therefore a virgin. It is Matthew who says that this fulfilment (a virgin) has now come true. Isaiah was looking forward to two events and seeing them both together, and God could see them separately. Matthew brings us the second fulfilment, in which case we can use the word "virgin" and realise that God included that originally.

Here is the big answer why it had to be a virgin birth: because it had to be Immanuel. It had to be "God with us", and if it had not been a human birth it would not have been *with us*, and if it had not been a divine birth it would not have been *God* with us. Do you see that? It just had to be a human mother and a divine

Father; there was no other way it could be done. For, if he was to be our Saviour he had to be one of us. He had to know what it was to be tempted. He had to know what a battle we face. He had to get inside and lift the load. He had to get into our very humanity and take our sins upon him and lift them off us. He had to get right into the battle. He had to come right down and, therefore, it had to be of a human being.

If Jesus was *only* a human being and then people had seen him as the great reformer, the great teacher, the great example, then he could not lift us now; he could not get us any higher than a human being can lift us. One thing he would not be able to do is forgive all our sins because only God can forgive all sins. He had to be human and divine. There is only one way for those two things to get together. God in his infinite wisdom chose this teenage girl. The Holy Spirit came on her, and the divine and the human met in her womb. God the Father sent his Son and the miracle of the Incarnation took place.

"Immanuel" – the last bit of that word, "el", means "God" and you find it in so many words: Isra-el, Nathana-el. In the name "Elijah", "El" means "God", and "immanu" means "near". Imminent means "near in time", "immanent" means near in space, or "within", and we keep using these words: imminent, immanent. Immanuel – God near; God touchable; God with a face; God in the here and now; God within reach of ordinary human beings like ourselves. God is near. "Call upon him while he is near. Let the wicked forsake his way and the unrighteous man his thoughts. Let him return to our God for he will abundantly pardon." That is the cry of Isaiah, and hundreds of years after Isaiah said it, God came so near that Isaiah's words come home with more force. Call upon him while he is near – he is here and he is here now. "Son of David, have mercy on me," said the blind man, and had he not cried out that, he might have missed the chance of seeing because Jesus was just passing by. God was near. Call upon the Lord while he is near; present help in time of trouble.

Matthew Chapter 1:18–25

We have looked at the narrative of the birth, we have looked at his nature – now let us look at the name. Names are very important. I think we want to give our children unique names. My wife and I got a book full of names. We went into separate rooms in turn, and we wrote a short list of names that we liked, came together, and found that about (I think) eighteen or fewer were in common. Then we went separately again and put them in order of merit and saw it was a real operation. We finally boiled it all down. They were unique names to us. If you said their names, they would bring an immediate picture of one person.

"Jesus" was a common name in those days. You met it everywhere. It is almost the same as the word "Joshua". In fact, the way the Israelis say the name Jesus today, "Yeshua", is very like "Joshua". The pronunciation of "Jesus", of course, is very different in different languages, but what does "Yeshua" or "Joshua" mean? It means: "God saves." That is a lovely name.

God the Father chose the perfect name for Jesus – the name that fitted everything he would do. Legally, in Hebrew life, only the father could name the child. God the Father didn't say "Joseph, name the child." Through an angel he said: "You shall call him Jesus". It was the first time his Son had had that name, because he did not have it while he was in heaven. He had it when he came to Earth because what he would do on earth would precisely fit that name. God had the unique advantage of knowing exactly how it would turn out. There were, as I have pointed out, many other people called "Jesus". There are at least five in the rest of the New Testament. One had the surname "Barabbas". Jesus the Christ and Jesus Barabbas were presented to the crowd as alternatives. Barabbas means "son of the father" – Jesus, son of the father. "Which shall I release?" asked Pontius Pilate, "Jesus of Nazareth or Jesus, son of the father?" It is a remarkable irony of history.

But what does the name mean? Jesus did not come primarily to save you from your loneliness, frustration, boredom, discomfort, ignorance, fears or anxieties. Every one of these things is a by-product. *He came to save us from our sins*. The tragedy is that we want to be saved from everything else but this, and the world is looking for anyone who will counsel them about any problem but this. Anybody who is willing to lend a listening ear can find a ready stream of people to come and talk about this, that, and the other problem. Of course, it is a part of human life and these problems are valid in themselves, but Jesus came to deal with one thing primarily, and all the others are related. He came to save us from our sins. This was not an almighty experiment; this was not a trial. It was something that was bound to succeed – he shall save his people from their sins. This is not something he may do, not something he is hoping to achieve, but he is going to do it. He shall – and it is the first promise in the New Testament. Let us claim it. He shall.

I want you to notice one letter in that sentence. It is the most crucial letter "s" at the end. I have been guilty of this myself and I think you may have been too. We want to be saved from the penalty of sin but do we want to be saved from our sins – plural? If you take that seriously, you have got to take a pencil and paper and write down what sins they are from which you wish to be saved. As the Puritan preachers constantly used to say: "Descend to the particular; come down to the detailed." Come down to writing out what sins you want saving from. What are they? Lust? Pride? Greed? Gluttony? Envy? Whatever they are, write them down and say, "Lord, will you save me from that and that and that?" To save us from them is what Jesus came to do.

This sentence, "He shall save his people from their sins," does not mean *primarily* that he shall save you from hell. It means primarily that he wants to save you from your besetting sins (plural). The world says you cannot change human nature; you cannot break these things. You cannot be free of the chains of your character and habit, but Jesus Christ came to save his people from their sins. If he has not saved you from any particular sin yet, he is not your Saviour. Now that seems a strong statement

Matthew Chapter 1:18–25

but I make it; I believe it to be thoroughly scriptural, for his name is Jesus, He shall save his people from their sins. He breaks the power of cancelled sin and sets the prisoner free. It is no use our going around saying, "He has saved me from hell, I am saved for heaven, it is all done," if I have not been saved from a single sin. As a well-known evangelist put it when he made an appeal: "Don't come out to the front unless you are willing to leave your sins behind on the seat you leave." That is the gospel. That name "Jesus" becomes precious not to those who just say "I've been saved from hell and the penalty," but to those who say, "He has set me free from this and this, and I am free." That is the freedom that he came to bring. That is what the word "save" means primarily.

"Jesus" is the highest, most powerful name because that is what he came to do. He was followed by men and women who had been set free from their sins. What sins has Jesus saved you from?

Jesus does not save people by his birth. His having been born only made it possible. His life only made it demonstrable. It is his death, resurrection and ascension to intercede for us that makes salvation possible for us. The world can celebrate Christmas and go back to their sins so quickly, and even carry their sins into their Christmas celebration. That is why thinking of the Christ-child makes no difference to people. They are not saved from their sins at all because they do not go on from Christmas to Easter and to Pentecost.

Notice these words: "For he will save his people..." His people, not the world. Whether Christmas has any final influence on my life depends on just one thing: am I one of his people? How do I become one of his people? The same way Joseph and Mary became his people. How did they become his people? Mary became one of "his people" when she said, "Be it unto me according to your Word. I am your handmaiden." Joseph became one of "his people" when he awoke from the dream and did as he had been commanded; so both of them became part of "his people". The people who will be saved from their sins are those who do what God tells them, and who become part of the story themselves, and who are willing to be used by God. He shall save his people.

One final illustration: back to World War I. You have heard this recounted so often but in that war the first Christmas morning (1914) dawned. It was a lovely, fresh, crisp, frosty morning. No guns were firing between the trenches. There were no trees; they had all been blasted away, and there was just that bare, pock-marked mud of the front lines. Then, at about ten o'clock, someone threw a snowball over to the other lines. Shortly afterwards, the sound of carol singing was heard in the trenches. No one knows whether it was first heard on the British or the German side. But somehow it very soon was taken up until snowballs and carols were being exchanged over the ranks – over the lines. Then by midday the soldiers had come out. The senior officers were very worried because both sides were mixing freely and were singing carols about the Christ-child. "Still the night, still the night," and it was floating backwards and forwards over the lines. Then, at the end of the day, they turned around and went back to their trenches. December the 26th dawned, and with the first ray of dawn a hand grenade went over, and a shell, and another shell, and soon men's lives were being blasted to bits again. Why? It is a mad world. Why? It is because people do not notice the name of the baby. It is because they like a bit of celebration, especially in the middle of winter when it is cold and dark. It lights up the streets; it cheers us all up and keeps us going. That is how it started – as a mid-winter festival. We like it, and by Boxing Day we have forgotten that the baby was called "Jesus". We want to be saved from war and hunger and disease and all the other things that afflict us, but Jesus came to save you from your sins. Do you want saving from those? If so, then Christmas will mean an entirely different thing to you.

We look at the wonderful narrative of Jesus' birth. We look at the nature of this baby – divine nature and human nature meeting, so that he was very God of very God and also true man. If you stop there, then there will be no effect. But we go on and we look at the name of this baby – Jesus. That is the name you have got to use. Next time you are being tempted, next time your besetting sin is getting on top of you, just say aloud the name "Jesus". Call on the name of the Lord.

3
BETHLEHEM

Read Matthew Chapter 2

The more I study the Christmas story, the more convinced I am that conditions today are very much nearer to the conditions two thousand years ago, especially in the Middle East but also throughout the whole world. One of the notable things about the time in which Jesus was born was the vast improvement in communications. There were Latin words and the Greek language was everywhere and we too are in a world where communication has vastly improved in recent decades. But the most striking similarity, which makes me wonder again how near we are to the second visit of our Lord Jesus to this planet, is in the fullness of time of the first visit and the second where conditions adjust right. The second similarity is this: when Jesus was born, the Western world, dissatisfied with its own religion, was looking to the East for new spiritual information and the so-called mystery religions of the East were creeping through to the West.

Today, Zen Buddhism and yoga, and I don't know how many other Eastern meditational practices, are creeping over into the West. The West is becoming more Easternised. When Jesus was born, the Eastern part of the world was becoming increasingly Westernised and looking to the West for salvation and hope, and right in the middle of that situation, the Christ came. The parallel is almost too extraordinary but there it is. So, in our Lord's day, two thousand years ago, the Roman world was increasingly looking to the East for a new religion, and widespread through the Orient was the idea that there would be born in the West a King of the whole world, and it is the result of that two-way looking that you get the Christmas story and the wise men coming all the way from the East to find this new King.

Now, Matthew chapter 2 has been grossly romanticised. I am sure that if you study your Christmas cards you will see by how much. Everything has been done to these wise men. They have been limited to the number three. They have been made into kings. They have been given different coloured skins. They have even been given names, and all of it is pure legend. We have also romanticised chapter 2 by cutting out the side of it we don't like to hear. We don't like bad news at Christmas time, it spoils the story. We don't like bad news at Christmas because it is the one time that we want to shelter ourselves from the horrible things that happen. So, the story of Herod and the Slaughter of the Innocents is cut out of the Christmas celebrations. It hardly appears in a Nativity play but we are going to see that it is a vital part of the story.

Now let us look at chapter two. It begins with the word "after". One of the things we have done to the Christmas story is telescope it into the compass of our half-hour Nativity play and therefore we get the shepherds and the wise men together at the manger. That, of course, never happened. In fact, it was after – long after Jesus was born. He was not in a manger when the wise men came. The census was over and Mary and Joseph had got rooms now; more than that, they had actually got a house. They had decided the right place to bring up the Son of David was in the city of David. No doubt Joseph's carpentry trade was already getting orders and so he had taken a house and it was probably months, maybe even over a year after our Lord was born that these wise men arrived in the little town of Bethlehem. That is just to clear up the picture for you so you can get the animals and this manger and the shepherds out of your mind now. We are looking at something that happened much later; a separate event altogether. Now, Christians usually celebrate this event the Sunday after Christmas, which again gives us the impression that it happened almost immediately. But, of course, the Bible condenses history enormously and condenses the story of Jesus. By the third chapter of Matthew, we have jumped to almost thirty years later. That is the kind of express train account we have got. So, this is something quite separate from the Christmas story. The wise men are not part of the Christmas story, they come much later. Let us see it as a separate event and look at it in itself.

There are four things I want to say. First, we will discuss the magi. You can call them magi or wise men or what you like but I am not happy with the New English Bible calling them astrologers because they were not. I am going to talk about the magi and their star, then Herod and his priests, and finally Joseph and the angels.

First of all, these magi – who were they and what were they? As far as we can tell, they came from Persia, what is now Iran. They were the ancestors of those we now call Farsi, which similarly means Persians. They were men who studied as far as they could within their limits with serious scientific observation the universe around them, and among the things they studied were the stars.

Now, in calling them astrologers, we do them far less than justice. They were men who observed this incredible kaleidoscope of lights above us and tried to find some order or pattern in the sky and then relate that pattern to the existence of men. That is a scientific approach. So, at first, they noticed that some of the stars were in groups that stayed roughly the same shape and they began to give names to these constellations, these groups, and those names have come all the way down to us even today. In fact, this preoccupation with the governing of human life by the stars out there comes out in our very names of the week – Sunday, "the day of the sun", Saturday, "the day of Saturn". These names have come right through in our daily life without our realising it, but they noticed there were certain clumps of stars that had patterns. Any psychologist would have a great time working out what motives led them to see an animal in this and a man's face in that and a sword in the other.

You and I have stood on a starlit night, we have tried to pick out the Great Bear and the Little Bear and Orion's Belt and all the rest of it. They first noticed these patterns, then they began to notice that they moved in circles, all except one star in the middle – the North Star. But the rest were on the move and there was a cycle. So, they began to count the number of cycles and they began to divide the cycle, the heavens, into sections – the houses of each constellation. The signs of the zodiac grew out of this. Now, so far there is nothing wrong with this kind of study of the stars; nothing wrong at all. They were identifying what was happening, labelling it and getting to know the pattern of the stars.

The crucial question came when they asked this: are the cycles of human life related to the cycles of bodies in the heavens? Is there any connection between what happens up there and what happens down here? And it is that question that is the critical one. Of course, we are now realising scientifically that this is so. We know that there is some relation between sun spots and my irritability. We certainly know that the tides ebb and flow because the moon is travelling around the Earth and that the waves that you watch and the sea coming in and going out is due to a heavenly body. We know, for example, that every particle of my body came from the stars. I am made of stardust. That does not make me a star or a superstar but it is a thought, isn't it? Every atom in my body was once part of a star whirling through space and here I am, the result of the stars, sitting here on Earth. Yes, you can say that is up there and we are down here, there is some kind of connection – but there are three possible answers to the kind of connection.

One is that the stars affect human life. The second is human life affects the stars and the third is that God controls them both.

In some areas of life, the first answer is right; in other areas of life the second answer is right. A child throwing a teddy out of a pram moves the most distant star – so I am told by a scientist. This idea was popularized in chaos theory as 'The butterfly effect' where a butterfly flapping its wings in Tokyo causes a tornado to occur in Texas. I find it incredible, but he says that any movement in the universe affects the whole universe. In many areas the third answer is the right one. Now, it is when you tie everything to the first answer that you become an astrologer. That is to make your decisions by the stars and to fall for the belief that the day you were born and the place where you were born puts you under a certain arrangement of the stars, decides everything that happens to you.

Now, that is astrology and it is a most dangerous device of the devil. As soon as you explain everything that happens in terms of the stars, you are right under the power of evil forces. Shakespeare gave the answer in one of his plays. He said, "The fault, dear Brutus, is not in our stars but in ourselves". You cannot blame the stars for the way you got out of bed this morning. It may explain certain events on earth but not others. As soon as you treat the stars as governing us fatefully like that then, frankly, you are finished as far as belief in God goes. That is why the Bible condemns astrology so severely and if these wise men were astrologers, pure and simple as we know them today, they would not have found Jesus Christ through their understanding of the stars. They are rather different.

You see, our knowledge of the stars can lead us in many different directions. It can lead us to say, "There is no God." Or it can lead us to say, "When I consider your heavens, the work of your fingers, the moon and the stars, which you have ordained". It can lead you to God. Science can lead us either to science fiction, as it has done in many cases, or to reality – it is what we do with our knowledge. These magi did the right thing with their knowledge of the stars and they found Jesus, but there were other magi that didn't. There are two other magi mentioned in the New Testament. Did you know that? One is called Elymas, one is called Simon, and in both cases, they were men with occult powers, men in the grip of Satan, men who did not find Christ but were against Christian things. The reason is they turned their knowledge of the stars in the wrong direction and made the wrong deductions from it.

The wise men studied the stars and they particularly looked for a King to be born in the west and they kept looking west. What kind of a star did they see? We know because Kepler told us that in 7 BC Saturn and Jupiter, two of our planets in our solar system, met, or appeared to meet, in the sky and became a vivid, bright conjunction of stars. Kepler worked back from modern records to establish that. Was that what they saw? Halley's Comet flew across the sky, the western sky, to these men in 11 BC. Was that what they saw? Or even more extraordinary, we know from contemporary records that between 5 BC and 2 BC a dark star called Sirius, rose very brightly at the same time as the sun rose in the morning but at the opposite end of the sky, and the dark star rose brightly in the morning. Now the interesting thing is that the name of that dark star means "Birth of a prince". That may well have been the star they saw, but with their knowledge they did not say, "The stars are affecting something on earth." They rightly said, "Something on earth is affecting the stars."

Now do you see the difference from astrology? An astrologer says that when you are born it is the stars that affect you and you have to move according to the stars, but these astrologers said the opposite. They said, "What is fixed is what's happened on earth. It is the stars that are having to move according to what is happening on earth," and throughout the Bible because God is in charge of the stars, as well as affairs on the earth, he is able to rearrange both, and they were reading off the heavens what was happening on earth. Most modern astrologers do the opposite and read off the heavens what is meant to happen on earth, what is fixed. Anyway, they saw the star.

The important thing is this: here were men without the Bible, without any Jewish background – though they must have heard of the Jews and indeed Jews were living over in Persia at this time after the exile – they had none of the things we have but they had sufficient knowledge of God and his ways to be able to follow that knowledge until it led to fuller knowledge and led them to Christ. If a man is prepared to follow what little light he has got and go all the way with it and really follow it through he will come to Christ. I believe that God has given light to people who have never seen pages of the Bible. If they follow through with what they have got, they will come to Jesus Christ. We are only judged by the light we have received, and these men would not have been judged because they had not met Christ; they would have been judged because they had not followed a star had they not done so.

Now look at the three stages of their pilgrimage: a star, the scripture, and the Saviour. There is a progression here. It is as if having followed one thing, God gave them something more, and having followed that he gave them something more still. Any man can find God if he seeks him with all his heart. But the secret of these wise men is that they dropped everything else and they made this the one big thing in life. There are many people I meet who would like to find God; who would just like to know him and like to add him to their many acquaintances, who drop into church from time to time and pretend to be interested but it has not become the primary quest of their life. They play at it from time to time; they are not prepared to drop everything else and make this the one goal. This is not the most important thing to them and therefore no wonder they don't get through to the Saviour. But you show me a man who is prepared to make any sacrifice, who is prepared to drop anything to find the truth and I will show you a man who will get through to Christ – a man who is this serious.

These wise men, having got the one little glimpse of

knowledge, did not follow a star, incidentally. Don't get this idea that as they rode on their camels across the desert this sort of star went ahead of them. They did not follow the star like that. They saw it appear in the East – that means "in the rising". Actually, the Greek there "in the rising" means they saw it appear in its rising. When they saw that they said, "The Prince is born, we must set off," and they followed the whole way without another glimpse of that star. Not until they got near Bethlehem did God vouchsafe them another glimpse of what had guided them. So, walking blindly in a sense, just one little glimpse, those wise men had decided to drop everything and whatever it cost, find out the truth that they had glimpsed through the star, and so they set off following the star. It therefore was not long before God introduced them to someone who knew the Bible, and that is what happens again and again. A man may just have a glimpse of God in the middle of a battle and maybe years later God directs him to someone who knows the Bible and can take him a step further.

So, they set off blindly into the west, not really knowing where they were going, but determined to get all the way and find what they were looking for. It probably took them many months to get there. God does not always reveal himself quickly and, in fact, I find great insight into God's character in the fact that the shepherds, simple ordinary working people, just had to walk a few hundred yards but the clever ones, the intellectuals, had to go hundreds of miles and many months. It is often the case that simple people with little education seem to get straight through to Jesus. The intellectuals take such a long time to come. They have so many questions to answer, so many signposts to pass and they eventually get to the same place, but much later.

God in his mercy reveals himself to the poor before the rich, to the simple before the clever. He wants all of them but he has his own way of bringing the right ones first; they had a long way to go and so he brought them to somebody who knew the Bible. They used their natural sense; they used their nous – that is Greek for common sense. They went all across the desert and they said, "Where do we find him now? We'll make for the capital; we'll make for the palace." That was human logic but it shows again how human logic can result in a search for entirely the wrong place. It was logical that if a king were born, he would be in the palace. We look for him at the centre of things but they were looking wrongly. There comes a point where intellect has to give way to revelation; where scripture has to take over; where your brain cannot take you any nearer to Christ. So, they got up to the point where their brain had taken them as far as they could and then through an incredible series of circumstances, men who did not really want to follow the Bible themselves opened the scriptures to the wise men.

One of the most challenging things I got for my own heart from this chapter 2 was just this: the men who opened the scriptures to them did not bother to go with them. You can know the Bible, you can be able to quote it, you can have it all off and you cannot join in the quest to find the Saviour. That is a challenge I throw out to you if you know your Bible. Do you join in the quest of those who without that knowledge utterly sincerely are looking for Christ? That is the important thing. Scripture is only a means to the end; it is not an end in itself. The tragedy is that the scribes and the priests, who knew their Bibles, said, "It's got to be Bethlehem; it says so in the Bible." At least they were fundamentalists. They believed literally the scriptures in which it says, "Bethlehem and Judea". They knew that must be the place, but they didn't take one step towards Bethlehem.

These men, who were Gentiles right outside the religious tradition, just went shooting past the religious leaders because they wanted to get to Christ. The religious leaders only wanted to be teachers. It is a challenging thought, and I share it with you. So, having studied the scripture, they made off for Bethlehem and now they reached their goal. They had followed a star, they had followed the scripture, they had now found the Saviour – that was it; suddenly it was all worthwhile. I just want you to pause and think about the tremendous faith they must have had to look at a baby and say, "That's what we're looking for." There was not a single sign of royalty, no carpets on the floor, no gold crown, and all these halos and things you see on your Christmas cards, not one of them was there. All that they found was a working man and a baby boy a few months old, yet immediately they knew who he was. Of course, they had been given a little help in this. God had given them a special last touch of guidance.

How varied is God's guidance. We try to put God's guidance in a straitjacket and say it has got to be this method of guidance or I don't know what his will is, but here is God guiding through creation, through revelation, through experience, through so many different ways and God is infinitely varied in his guidance. He guides us according to our needs at the time and he knew that just before they got to Bethlehem they needed one more bit of guidance, a last homing in, and suddenly for the first time in months they saw the star again. This time they saw it because it was down near the horizon. That is because Bethlehem is 4,600 feet above sea level, nestling in a saddle in the hills and it is right against the skyline, six miles south of Jerusalem, slightly higher than Jerusalem; they saw that star sitting right on top of the roof of one house.

The last bit of guidance they needed took them right to the house. Now there is sheer faith; they just walked in and they did not say, "This can't be, it must be some mistake, let's just nip back up to the hill and have another look at that star." They did not say anything like that; they fell down and they gave. I read a little devotional comment on this. I don't remember the exact words, but I found the gist of it very moving. They not only gave but they came and they saw and they worshipped. It is one thing to give, it is another thing to come and see before you give. It is still another thing to worship as well as give.

You see, the Christ does not just want our gifts – otherwise we could just stay at home and send a cheque instead of going to church. He wants us to come and worship and give. It is all part of the total picture and these men came to give themselves before they came to give their gifts. Before they opened their treasures, they fell down. They came to offer themselves as subjects to this new King. They came to say that whatever happens in your own country, whether your own people receive you or not, remember there is a little bunch of loyal men way out in Persia. You will always find them ready to follow you. It is a most lovely moment when they fall down and worship. Many things have been read into the gifts they gave. The usual interpretation, which is appropriate, is that gold is for royalty – for a king; incense is for a priest or a god and myrrh is for a corpse to embalm. You can hardly have had three more appropriate gifts for the Christ child – for his kingship, for his deity, and for his mortality and suffering. They were terribly appropriate but I want to read one or two other things into the gifts.

First of all, the sheer value of them: these men opened their treasures. Not for them a little bit of money that was left over after they had spent everything else on themselves, for them their most precious possessions. They knew that if you come to Christ, he may take from you your most precious thing, but even that is hardly worthy of the person you have come to. They opened their treasures, their most valuable possessions. In other words, a gift is of value to Christ only in terms of what it cost the giver; not in terms of what it will buy but in terms of what it cost. They opened their treasures. Furthermore, those treasures are interesting. Gold would be the profit they made on their work; incense and myrrh were used in incantations to the stars away in the East. It is as if they are surrendering the very things that might have been used for the wrongful application of their knowledge. The very things that would have been used in astrology they surrendered to the Christ. It is as if they were saying, "We want nothing more to do with the occupation that has led us away from you or could have led us away from you." It is very exciting to see that happen – it still does happen on the mission field and it still does happen here. I once preached knowing that there was somebody in the congregation listening to me in whose back garden there were ashes from a bonfire of black magic books, a surrender of things that could lead astray, lead away from Christ. Well, they brought their gifts. We must leave the wise men; we could say many things about them but I won't.

I shall move on to Herod and the priests. Some years ago, I read up on Herod in order to preach on him and was reminded of what an incredible character he was. But it is a very different picture now in verses 13 to 18, from light to darkness. I know you only see a star when it is dark or when it is just sunrise or sunset but through the first part of the chapter there is a tremendous impression of light, isn't there? Light everywhere, gold shining, star shining; but when you get to the middle section suddenly the storm clouds gather and the shadows come and there is darkness and horror. There is Herod with a black face and a black heart devising black deeds and then there is the slaughter of maybe twenty or thirty innocent babes – it is a horrible scene. Now, Herod had a very mixed character. Not for nothing was he called "The Great". One contemporary historian called him "a very fine beast". That just about sums him up – half Jew-half Edomite, half descended from Jacob, half from Esau, both lines from Abraham, of course.

Jacob and Esau were in the mixture and I am afraid the worst part of Jacob as well, and yet he was good as well as bad. Mind you, he was larger than life, everything was on the grand scale; everything was a gesture. Herod the Great – but here are some of the good things he did. First of all, he was a very efficient governor. He managed for thirty-three years to keep the Middle East at peace and that was an incredible achievement. That is why Jerusalem was disturbed when there was news of another king. They feared civil war. He was also a tremendously constructive

Matthew Chapter 2

man: a palace on the western wall of Jerusalem, a fortress northwest of the temple, an artificial harbour in Caesarea whose remains you can still see, a new town of Samaria, new buildings everywhere, and today they are excavating the gigantic stones that Herod put in place.

Oh, you have got to see the stones to believe them – never had there been such stones. What a builder! More than that, he was a generous man. In times of difficulty, he would remit the taxes and when famine struck the land, he melted down his gold plate in order to feed the poor. This was Herod the Great, a man who kept peace and order, a man who was generous; a man who looked after the poor. What went wrong? Why was he so insanely jealous?

The answer is he had no right to be there; he called himself the King of the Jews but the Romans gave him that title. Herod was a brilliant politician; he managed to keep in with Augustus and Antony, which was an incredible feat. He was the only man who ever kept in with both of them and Cleopatra wanted Judea. She desperately wanted it and Cleopatra said to Antony, "Can't I have Judea?" But Herod got it and kept it. What a man to defy even Cleopatra and Antony. You can read the whole story if you are interested in history. But what went wrong? Well, first of all, he was very unpopular. He did build great buildings but not because he was popular. He was chosen by the Romans, not the Jews; a man of mixed blood was not acceptable.

Then, second, he was multi-religious and to the Jews this was horrible. He put up a new temple to Jehovah. It was still being built all through Jesus' life – Herod's magnificent temple to Jehovah. It was destroyed just forty years after Jesus died. If he built a temple to Jehovah here, he built another temple to a Roman goddess there and another temple to Augustus, the Roman emperor, in a third place. He was multi-religious and to the Jew that was not on. The third thing was that he was so desperately insecure that he could not stand a rival and there was one family in Judea which could claim the throne from him – the Hasmonean family. So, what did he do? He married the daughter of the family, Mariamne. Then he proceeded to murder the rest of the family, and one by one he had them assassinated until Mariamne was the only one left. Then he killed her, his own wife. Then he killed his own two sons – one by one. Then he killed others until finally that man must have assassinated thousands. He killed off all the Jewish Sanhedrin, the council, when he came to power lest anyone come against him.

I suppose the final touch of Herod was that when he died, he ordered all the noble men in Jerusalem to be killed at the same moment he died in order that there might be weeping in Jerusalem at his passing. He knew no one would weep for him. Now, why this insane insecurity? Well, as I have said, deep down he knew he had no right to be in the position he was. So, any rival was a threat and he dealt with them fiercely by force, shedding blood. Therefore, when the wise men came you can understand his reaction. He was an old man of seventy, and when I say old, seventy in those days was old. An old man of seventy had one foot in the grave when Jesus was born. Jesus was no threat. By the time Jesus grew up, Herod would be long since in his grave. But still there was the threat, and so Herod tried to destroy Jesus. To him, human life was cheap and the Slaughter of the Innocents reminded Matthew of something in Jeremiah. The saddest writer in scripture is Jeremiah – read the book of Lamentations: "Is it nothing to you, all you who pass by?" It is all there, the agony, and in Jeremiah's day he imagined a corpse weeping.

It is a most moving passage from Jeremiah 31: Rachel's tomb lies outside Bethlehem on the roadside where she died giving birth and Jacob buried her there by the roadside. Everything that happens in Palestine along the main road that runs like the Pennine Way along the rigid Judean hills passes Rachel's tomb. That tomb has witnessed sadness after sadness after sadness. If you read the story of the 1948 War of Liberation, you will read

Matthew Chapter 2

what happened outside Rachel's tomb. That tomb, which I have seen, wept with tears. I have seen the stones running as if with dew or rain and they have been tears of Jews. That tomb has seen sadness after sadness pass up and down that road outside Bethlehem. Jeremiah, in the days when the children of Israel were taken off in exile, said, "Even Rachel in her tomb is weeping as she sees them carried away in chains past her tomb." It is a most moving, poetic passage and you can almost hear the sobs of the woman inside her tomb mourning the sight of the prisoners going away. Now, says Matthew, it is all happening again. Rachel's tomb – you can hear her crying inside it for the families in the little town next to the tomb that had been broken. It is a pretty horrible thing but it shows the lengths to which men will go to keep Christ out of their life. It only happened because Herod had no room for another king.

Whatever your star has been, you are following it and you are determined to go all the way until you find the Christ. You will find him if you go through with it. As you read this chapter, God looks into your heart. He either sees a wise person who is determined to get through to Christ having come to this teaching because you are following a star, or he looks in your heart and sees a Herod. Herod was not so very different from any of us. Herod was a king on a throne who did not want anybody else ruling his country and your country may not cover a big geographical area. Your "country" may be just six feet high but that is your "country" and you are king on the throne. Christ comes and he has been born King of John David Pawson and I do not want another king. If I say I am on the throne, I am in charge of my life, I will decide what I do, I don't want another king in my life, one thing that is certain is this: if I turn Christ away from the throne of my life like that, I will hurt other people in doing so. I cannot avoid hurting others and causing them pain and suffering that they would otherwise not have experienced. So, there is a Herod in each of us that says, "I know I don't have the right to be king of my life but I want to be. I am the king of myself and I won't have another."

Let me move on to the third character I want to speak about: Joseph. Maybe the third kind of person reading this book now is a Joseph. Hallelujah for this. I dare say readers can be divided up into one of these three: you are either seeking the Christ Child and sincerely going on seeking him until you find him, or you have realised that he has come as a rival to yourself and he wants the throne of your heart and you don't want that. Or like Joseph, however God speaks to you, you are going to trust and obey. Hallelujah for Joseph. The more one thinks about him, the finer the character appears. Mary was willing to carry God's Son; Joseph was willing to carry Mary and God's Son, to take the full responsibility. Strong, silent man that he was, there is not one word recorded of him in the Gospels. This was a man who when God told him to do something, he got up and did it. God asks for no more – lovely man, Joseph.

Now, he was guided in dreams. You cannot take every dream as from the Lord; it can come from your subconscious; it can come from God, it can come from the devil. I think Joseph was quite clear that God had spoken because I do not think he was the sort of person who had dreams, or if he did, he didn't remember them. He was a good, hardworking man who went to bed and slept like a log. Probably Mary had a job waking him up in the morning. I think that was the kind of man he was. For him to have a dream was an event – and to have such a clear dream and remember it in the broad light of day, practical man that he was, I am sure that meant a lot to him and God spoke to him through dreams. Look, we have had God speaking through a star, through the scripture, through dreams. How many more ways are there in which God can guide through creation, revelation, and experience? But the important thing is he got up; he got up every time. If God said, "Go there," he got up and went. If God said, "Come back," he got up and came back. If he had not done so, we could say (humanly speaking) that Jesus would never have survived his first year. Or divinely speaking, we would have had to say that God had to make other arrangements.

The glory of this is that God never had to make other arrangements because Joseph did what he was told. He went to Egypt. It was a strange country to go to but it was the nearest out of Herod's jurisdiction. There were already a million Jews living in Alexandria so there were relatives and friends there. It was the obvious place to go but in going to Egypt, Joseph was unconsciously repeating history. Fifteen hundred years before, the same thing had happened. Jacob and his children had gone down to Egypt for refuge and out of Egypt God had called Israel. That is why Matthew points to the prophecy of Hosea, "Out of Egypt I've called my Son." It is as if the baby Jesus had to go through all the history of his race.

Jesus as a baby relived the whole of Israel's history. He went down into Egypt, he fled there, he was rescued from there, he was brought back to the Promised Land – "Out of Egypt I've called my Son." History is repeating itself. What Israel went through he went through. That is why when he was tempted in the wilderness as Israel was tempted in the wilderness, he replied to the devil by quoting from the book of Deuteronomy the very words with which God protected his people as they came back. You find if you study it carefully that the whole history of Israel is right there in Jesus' life. History was repeating itself in embryo in Jesus.

So, Joseph came back to Israel and found that Archelaus, the son of Herod, was on the throne. That was rather sad because Archelaus inherited all his father's bad points and none of his good points. When he came to the throne, he murdered three thousand rulers, leaders in the land, to make sure that he could have power. So, Joseph was afraid to go back to the city of David, Bethlehem, and another dream came. Why didn't the angel tell him in Egypt it would not be safe in Bethlehem? Because the angel only revealed step by step and had he not done so, Joseph might have stayed in Egypt.

Very often in my life and yours, the Lord only reveals one step and then he reveals that step was not leading straight ahead to another but leading off on a tangent, a new direction. You thought it was going that way and he took you one step that way, then he shot you off this way. That is the way he leads often – leading us one step at a time. So, he leads us one step this way and another step that way and on until we are in the place of his choosing, and the place where the Lord wanted Jesus as a boy was Nazareth. To be born in Bethlehem, to spend his babyhood in Egypt, and his boyhood in Nazareth. If you and I had been put in charge of the committee arranging the coming of the Son of God, we would have never thought of any of those things. It would have been incredible – God's ways and our ways are so different.

So back to Nazareth: a little village, totally unknown, nestling in a hollow on the edge of the Galilean hills looking down onto the plain which had the crossroads of the world in it. A most Gentile, cosmopolitan place with no religious tradition about it, well away from the religious leaders – notice that. There the boy Jesus grew up surrounded by the hills so he got a love of nature, able to lie down on the very edge of the precipice overlooking the plain of Esdraelon. There you can see the boy with his head in his hands, watching the armies of nations march to and fro and the travellers and the caravans and the traders. Seeing the whole world before him, just down there on the plain and catching a glimpse of a whole world that needed him. Only God would have thought of it. It was a relatively unknown place and yet Nazareth today is one of the most famous names in the whole world. Jesus of Nazareth, people did not know he had been born in Bethlehem – not until much later. So, he was always called "of Nazareth" – the very name has a ring about it that is precious to us.

Matthew says it was prophesied but you can search your Old Testament from cover to cover and you will never find the

Matthew Chapter 2

prophecy. It is a problem. One day I will ask the Lord about it. I cannot give you the answer. Some have said, "Well, maybe it's a prophecy that wasn't written down." That is a possibility. Some have said, "Well, the word 'Branch'," which was one of the titles given to Jesus by Isaiah, is in Hebrew nezer and very like "Nazarene". "Maybe that's what it means. It's a play on words." Well, we don't know and I cannot solve that one for you. Scholars have spent centuries discussing it and I am not likely to solve the problem when they haven't for so long.

Let me conclude by telling you five things about the real hero of this chapter whom I have hardly mentioned because the chapter hardly mentions him. The real hero of chapter two of Matthew is not the wise men, certainly not Herod, nor is it Joseph, though you can put yourself in one of those three categories as you read. The real hero of the chapter is the Lord himself.

There are five things I want to say in just a few lines, each about the Lord. Number one, the Lord conforms to his own ideas but never to man's. He had said it would be Bethlehem, so Bethlehem it would be. He kept his word. When the Lord says, "I will do this," he keeps his word and he always conforms to himself. Whatever he has revealed in the Old Testament he sticks to. But our ideas are just so way out to God that the way he does things are not the way we do them. We would have had the wise men on the welcoming committee. The shepherds could have come along a year later, but not God.

Second, God will fulfil his plan. He is the stage manager. Somebody has said that the Lord is like a master chess player. No matter what move you make he will always be able to make moves to achieve his objective. In a sense, that is what we see happening in Matthew chapter two. All the Herods in the world cannot stop God's plan being fulfilled. Yes, God may have to tell Joseph to get up in the middle of the night and flee in the darkness so nobody sees which direction they have taken but Jesus will be safe. And the glory of it to me is that all the world's dictators and rulers cannot stop Jesus coming again to this planet and bringing his Kingdom. God fulfils his plan.

No matter what men may do, God just makes a move and what they attempt to do is undone. Herod no doubt went to bed that night thinking he had finished with the Christ and that he was safe. He had done nothing of the kind. His epitaph was written by an angel: "Those that sought the child's life are dead," and that is still true of every world dictator. Stalin said he would wipe out Christianity from Russia and it is in this way that dictators today try to kill the Christ child. They try to kill him in Christians, which is the only way they can get at him. So, they try to kill the Christians and those who sought the Child's life are dead. Stalin is dead and every other dictator who has tried to stamp out the Christ by stamping out Christianity is dead or will be – but God's plan will be done.

The third thing about God is that he is willing to give light to those who are willing to seek with all their heart. He is willing to lead them if they are willing to be led. If I seriously mean business and I am not playing at it, if I really say that I am prepared to go all the way, whatever it may cost of my treasure, my job, whatever happens I am willing to go all the way because I must find the truth and I must find this King, then God is willing to lead me and all those who are willing to be led and he will take us the next step and the next step and give us more light.

The fourth thing is this: God is a God who hides himself. You know, you can read the whole of this story and you can put it into a Nativity play without thinking about God once. You can think more of the angels whom he sent than about the Lord. "How silently, how silently / The wondrous gift is given! / So God imparts to human hearts / The blessings of his heaven." But you get the impression here that God is not on stage; that he is controlling from behind, that the strings are being pulled from up above.

You cannot see God, not directly, and that is why Herod could go to bed to sleep after he had done all that he had done because

God had not forced himself on Herod, or anyone else for that matter. God does not force himself on people, not now. He will one day when he appears in his glory but for the moment a man can come to church for a couple of months and he can go away for the next twenty years and God will not force him to come back. A man can catch a glimpse of the Christ at a distance and he can go and forget all that he has seen and God will not force him to remember it. God is a God who hides himself. He does it so silently, so gently, so quietly that you can ignore him.

The fifth thing I want to say about the Lord, who is the hero of this chapter, is perhaps the deepest thing I want to say and the most difficult for us to accept: the Lord is a Lord who allows the innocent to suffer. You see, God caused the slaughter of the babies in Bethlehem, didn't he? By sending Jesus he caused that to happen. He must have known it would happen and he did not step in and save those babies, did he? And he could have done and this is the whole big problem of suffering. Why does God allow the innocent to suffer? Why did he allow those twenty or thirty families to lose their baby? They might never have had another one. Why did he allow it to happen? He is a God who is prepared to let the innocent suffer and yet here the conflict posed, the question posed, by suffering is at its fiercest because he told Joseph to save his baby.

Here is a God who protects his own baby and lets other innocent babies be killed. That is how the world cries out against God: "God, why did you let this kind of thing happen?" And you can put that question in many other forms but it is there in this chapter. Why should God protect his own baby Son and none of the others, when in a sense his Son was the cause of it and these others were innocent? It is called the Slaughter of the Innocents. This is called Innocents' Day. Well, we have got to face something very honestly here.

First, we have got to say that God is a God who will allow pain and suffering if out of it good will come; that God is a God who will let the innocents suffer and who will allow us to hurt each other. That God is a God who will give Herod a great deal of rope. Ultimately, he may hang himself but God is that kind of a God and he has given you that freedom too; the freedom to hurt your children, the freedom to hurt your friends – God has given you that freedom. He does not protect people against each other. He allows us freedom both to help and hurt each other. We have got to face that fact, but I want you to go a little further than this story. True, he saved his own baby out of this and let others die without lifting a finger to help them. But why did he save his own baby? Was it because he was going to protect him all through his life and bring him to a peaceful old age in bed? No. Someday the greatest innocent was going to face the greatest suffering by God's will and God would allow it to happen and bring good out of it. The cross was to happen thirty-three years later.

If God had never sent Jesus to Mary, Mary would never have had a sword piercing her own heart. God is prepared to cause pain if his purposes need that. The evil in the world is to be allowed some freedom, but as I see it, if God had allowed Jesus to be slaughtered by Herod, the death of Jesus could never have been a sacrifice for sin. Has that thought ever struck you? It could not have been. Why not? Because it would not have been a voluntary sacrifice – a baby's blood could not have cleansed your heart. A baby's blood could not have cleansed any of us from sin. For the baby would not have chosen it, the baby would have known nothing about it. One flash of a blade in the sun and the baby's head would have rolled and the baby would not have even suffered for a minute. But it was God's will – he knew that evil can never be dealt with unless an innocent does suffer and he was waiting for someone who would voluntarily accept this suffering and go through that suffering, even though it might last hours and he would bear it all for the sins of the world. So, God had to save his baby from that. Why then did he not step in and save the rest of the babies?

Do you realise that had he done so, Herod would have known he had failed and Herod would have never let up? He died in 4 BC and he was probably alive for another two years after Jesus was born. Jesus was born about 6 BC, as you probably know – the calendar was mistakenly arranged and Herod was alive probably two years after Jesus was born – and had those babies in Bethlehem been protected, Herod would have stopped at nothing to get after the one baby who had escaped. As it was, he thought he had succeeded. The baby Jesus in Egypt was safe, but thirty-three years later, he, the only innocent man who has ever lived, the only man without sin, voluntarily choose to suffer death on the cross. If he had not done so, then you would not be reading this. If he had not done that neither you nor I would be able to rejoice that we can bring gifts and offer them to him, that we can fall down in worship, that we can come and see; that we can know the Christ child, that we can have these privileges. It is not because of his death; it is because of the cross and his death that these things are possible.

Well, there is the meditation for this chapter. It is just the fruit of thinking about the story in between many other things. Who are you? Are you a wise person who really wants to find the Christ and is prepared to go all the way whatever it may cost you to find the truth and to find him who was born to be King? Praise God, you will find him. Are you a Herod and have discovered that he is the biggest rival you have ever had? He is a rival to your very partner's affections. He is a rival to your ambitions. He is a rival to what you want to do with your life. He is a rival to certain relationships you have got which you want to keep. He is a rival to certain things which you enjoy doing and which you do not want to give up. He is a rival and he comes to take the throne and you have realised this and you are plotting even now. Though you may go to worship him, you may also think at times, "How can I get rid of him? How can I get all this out of my life?" When you do that, you are Herod.

Are you Joseph? If God speaks to you through a sermon, through a dream, through a flower or a tree, do you get up and go? Do you want to just get up and be where he wants you to be, whether that is Egypt or Israel or Bethlehem or Nazareth or India or Africa or Greenland? Someone told me of a friend or a relative of theirs who said, "Lord, I'll go anywhere in the world but don't send me to a hot climate; I can't stand a hot climate." Where did the Lord send him instead? He was up in Greenland as a missionary. The Lord just took him at his word and said, "Off you go there. I'll send you up there," and he got up and went. From what I know, if God had sent him to a hot climate, he would have gone. There are young people and old people to whom God says, "I want you somewhere else, I want you to go there." Are you a Joseph? If so, maybe God says, "I want you to just stay here in your town. I want you to be a shining light here. I want you to have the Christ child in your home." Are you a get-up-and-go Joseph?

Finally, do you really know the Lord? We want to see stars; they are pretty spectacular. We love reading the scriptures but the whole point of it all is to get through to the Lord. He is the Lord who hides himself, but also the Lord who leads those willing to be led. He is the Lord who makes his plan come true always but does it through human beings who respond to him. Above all, he is the Lord who is willing to let you suffer here in order that his will may be done, willing to cause you pain and sorrow in order that one day you may rejoice with him in glory – that is the Lord.

4

BAPTISM

Read Matthew Chapter 3

Baptism – have you wondered what it is and why we do it, what it is for and what its point is? Is it just a piece of religious ritual for church membership? Is it a telling testimony to the people who are present that you know and love the Lord Jesus? Well, it is the latter, but that is not all. Is it some kind of therapeutic experience for each individual, to give them a cleansing experience in the Lord? Yes, it is that, but it is something much bigger.

I want to try to paint the broadest canvas I can to show you the place of baptism in the eternal purposes of God and to try to help you to see what God is doing in the lives of the tens of thousands of people who are baptised into Jesus Christ each day. It is something very big that is happening. Most things can be explained by going back to their origins and seeing how they started. I go back to the very first baptist, a man called John.

John's mother was decades beyond bearing children. She was not fertile and that boy should never have been born though there was something different about him even from his conception. He is the only man that I have ever heard of who was baptised in the Holy Spirit in his mother's womb. What age do you need to be to be baptised in the Holy Spirit? You have got your answer.

After he was born his parents realised there was something very different about this man and as soon as he was old enough, he opted out of society. He cut himself off from social life. He was not only a total abstainer from alcohol, but he also cut himself off from social contact and went to live in one of the most barren, desolate spots. He had only one set of clothes: one garment and one belt, both of them from the animal world, and everything he ate came from the insect world. He lived the life of a hermit, yet he was never alone. Because he opted out of society and because he went to live in that place where there was absolutely nothing to distract him, nothing to look at, nothing to do; no sports to play, no books to read, he had absolutely nothing but God.

So he spent his time with God and for about twenty years God shared secrets with this man. You know, I think I can understand why he went into the wilderness, why God wanted him there. It was because those secrets were so exciting, so tremendous. I know that if God had told me those secrets and I was living in a town, I would have been straight round to the next door neighbour to tell him; but John had to hold those secrets for twenty years and God went on showing him his mind and heart, and God told him something he was going to do. John must have been bursting to get out and tell people that, and God said, "No, stay here. Stay here and wait for my time."

His thirtieth birthday came and went and then God whispered in his ear one day something like this:

"It's time to tell: go."

"Where?"

"I want you to go to the River Jordan."

"Why there, Lord?"

"It is the lowest part on my Earth."

That was a good enough reason. If you start at the bottom you can only go up and that is where people are – at the bottom.

"Any other reason, Lord?"

"John, that's where my people came into this land many years ago and I want them to come in again. Only this time I want them to come in wet, not dry."

"Why? You're not going to part it for them this time?"

"No. This time they will go into the water and enter my promised land washed and cleaned, and now John, I want you to tell them the good news."

Matthew Chapter 3

"The good news? What is it?"

"The good news is this..." and God told him the secret.

You know, if you were the people in those days and I told it to you, you would be out of your seat. Here is the secret: the Kingdom of heaven is near. Does that get you excited? Let me put it into paraphrased English and I think you might get a little more warmed up: God is about to take over the government! Now do you realise what a secret that was? To be able to say to the nation: God is going to look after the government! He is about to take it over. Let me briefly give you a little history lesson because then you will understand what that meant to people in those days.

Over the previous five hundred years they had been downtrodden by one invading enemy after another. The Assyrians had come and gone, so had the Babylonians, the Persians, the Egyptians and the Syrians; the Greeks had come and gone, and the Romans had come and they had not gone. During that entire period spanning five centuries, only for one brief interlude did they get their independence (under Judas the Maccabean) and they soon lost it again. When the Romans came, they put the hated Edomites, the descendants of Esau, on the throne, and the sons of Herod split the country up into separate parts and each one of them got one.

When John announced this news, it was against this chaotic background. Not only was it occupied by enemies but it had been divided up and other enemies had been put in charge of each part. Imagine how you might feel if this happened to your country. Can you sense what a tremendous thing it was to say, "God is about to take over the government." Their hearts must have leapt within them.

Now, of course, we cannot get quite as excited because we have not known a successful invasion of this country since the year 1066 when one King Harold had to defend the South and another King Harold invaded from the East into Lincolnshire.

We do not know what it is to be under a dictatorship. We talk of throwing one government out and having another lot in. We talk as if we are the government and in fact we are in a sense. We do know constant change of government and I predicted years ago that we are going to see increasingly frequent elections. Why? Because it is one of God's laws of history. He has written certain laws into nature and other laws into history and you cannot break those laws, you can only illustrate them. The law of gravity is written into nature, and if you fall off the cliffs of Dover you will not break the law of gravity, you will only illustrate it. In the same way, there are laws of history and I came upon one in the book of Proverbs: "When a nation sins, it will have one government after another."

I want to show you the connection between baptism and the Kingdom of God; baptism and the government that he is about to introduce. We still baptise for the same reason as then: be baptised for the Kingdom of heaven is near. Now let me spell it out. Let us just try to imagine that God has taken over Number 10 Downing Street. Some of the things that will then happen in our land will thrill us. Some of the things will kill some of our newspapers. They will not know what to report. Let us start with some of the good news. First of all, unemployment would slump. In God's Kingdom, under his government, no one will be out of a job. If you become a citizen of God's Kingdom, he will have a job for you to do which only you can do – a unique function for you to fulfil. There will be no inflation. You will be able to walk the streets safely at night. You will not need to lock your home. Have you ever counted up the number of keys you have to handle and use daily? That is because you cannot trust people. There will be other benefits too. There will be no vandalism, no violence, a disarmament programme will be implemented and we will beat our swords into ploughshares, our spears into pruning hooks, and we could direct our efforts into many profitable ways of helping mankind. There will be no boredom, no frustration;

Matthew Chapter 3

no "permissive society". Are you beginning to get excited by this? Do you still want the Kingdom of God to come? Do you still want God to take over the government?

What kind of government will it be? It will not be democracy. It will be a single party system and there will only be three party members: Father, Son and Holy Spirit. There will be no elections for the government. The government will elect the citizens; the citizens will not elect the government. Do you still want this government to come? There will be no debate, no discussion, no opposition allowed to the laws. Do you still want the government to come? Let me spell it out even further. One of the immediate effects, I believe, if God took over the government of our land, will be a reduction in the standard of living for every one of us because the Bible makes it absolutely clear that when God governs, he redistributes wealth and status. One of the most revolutionary statements in the world, is not to be found in the *Communist Manifesto;* it is to be found in the song of a fifteen-year-old peasant girl from Israel when she knew she was going to have a baby. This was the song she sang, which we call the *Magnificat,* the "Magnificent Song", the song that magnifies the Lord, and she said she knew what was going to happen. She said he will bring the rulers down from their places and exalt the lowly. He will fill the hungry with good things and send the rich away with empty hands. That is the most socialist programme you have ever heard. That is what God would do if he took over the government, and since we are one of the best-fed nations in the world there would be an immediate redistribution. Half our food that we eat today has come from other nations, and most of it from poorer nations. God has a heart for the poor and the needy. Do you *still* want God to take over the government? Or are you beginning to think a little more seriously about this?

I have mentioned the material side, now let us move on to the moral side. What would God do to our laws if he took over the government? It would be easy enough to pick up some of the legislation of past decades and say, "What would God do about that?" It is a preacher's fodder. He would immediately alter our divorce laws for example – there is no question about that. They have become so lax and easy that many marriages now finish on the rocks.

I believe he would alter the abortion laws. I believe he would bring in laws that would strengthen our welfare of the homeless and the helpless, but there are other laws. Would you be happy for a six-day week to return? That is shaking you a bit but according to my Bible, one of God's laws is "Six days shalt thou labour." That is God's law. Are you still happy about him taking over the government? Let us go a little deeper: God's law not only covers crime (and crime is what a person does to other people), his law covers vice – which is what a person does to himself, and vice is not punishable under present laws, but it is punishable under God's laws. God's laws cover not only what I do but what I think and what I feel and what I say.

You see, if God took over the government, the one thing that would be certain to happen is that he would eradicate the root cause of all our troubles. The root cause is not the economic system, the root cause is not the way our industry is managed, the root cause is not the value of currencies. The Bible tells you what the root cause is. How do wars start? James says in his letter, they start when people want something they have not got and they fight for it. God's laws would come right down to the matter of pride, greed, lust, anger, envy and sloth, and his laws are against all those things – the sins which wreck society. If God is given the government, he will eradicate those things.

In other words, John the Baptist was the first to realise that if God is about to take over the government, then that takeover will be followed by a purge. Every time a government is toppled, every time there is a *coup d'état,* every time there is a revolution, it is followed by a purge. It is no comfort to me to know that I was in the thirteenth category of the list of those who would be eradicated if Communism took over Britain. There were twelve other groups above clergy but we came in the thirteenth category. John the Baptist realised that if God is going to take over the governance, he is going to eradicate every greedy person, every proud person, every lustful person, every lazy person, every envious person. John cried in the wilderness: Listen! The Kingdom of heaven is near – God is about to take over the government. Purge yourselves before he purges you.

That was his message and written right into his whole message there is this element of threat and I must be true to it if I am to preach the Word of God. He says: the axe is at the foot of the tree and if there is not good fruit that tree will come down and get burnt; God will come as King, his winnowing shovel will be in his hand and he will toss people away and the chaff will be burned. There is a threat there. Did you see it? And John had to pass that message on. There he was, one man alone in this rather strange, unkempt garb and he was just shouting to the people: God is about to take over the government! They came in their thousands from every quarter of the land. Why did they come? Why was his mission such a success? You could say, "God was with him, and whatever God is in will succeed." I would agree with you, but there are human reasons also.

The basic reason why John the Baptist was so successful that revival came to that land is this: they believed what he said. Of course they did – they had been praying for it, longing for it, expecting it for a thousand years. Not only were they praying and longing for it, they had a promise in black and white from God that he was going to do it. They had the promise that one day a child would be born and a Son would be given and the government would be on his shoulders. They had that promise and they knew it must happen. John the Baptist studied the same prophet, Isaiah, who said that one day there would be a voice in the wilderness crying: Get ready; make the roads straight.

You really see this vividly when you go from Jerusalem to

Jericho. You can go in twenty minutes now. The coach goes straight down that fifteen miles along a wide road that hardly bends. It was a road built by the Americans for King Hussein when that part was in Jordan. As you go down you can look at the side and I could look at the road I used to go down from Jerusalem to Jericho when I first went out there – and you can see a road that is narrower and more twisting. If you look more carefully still, you can see the old Roman road of the New Testament days and that really does wind in and out of the ravines. King Hussein wanted a road that would take him straight to the capital, so they filled up the valleys and they brought the mountains low and they made the rough places smooth and the highway was there, leading right into Jerusalem for the king. John the Baptist saw that he was actually the fulfilment of Isaiah's prophecy. There will be a voice (you do not even need to know the name) and he will say: I'm getting the road ready. I am filling up the valleys, bringing down the mountains; I want a straight road so that when the king comes he can come in and take over the government. You can understand that if people believed that, they would say: Tell me, how can I get rid of this pride; I'm a greedy person, what do I need to do? John the Baptist was absolutely specific. He was not one of these preachers who roamed around and said vague things. He told soldiers they must stop threatening and stop bullying. There were people who came to him who were crooked accountants, who were involved in the kind of business deal that has been unveiled time and time again in modern times. He said to them: "You get your books straight; get your accounts right." There were people who came in nice clothes and John the Baptist said, "Have you got more clothes at home in the wardrobe? Then go and give them to somebody who hasn't got anything to wear."

Who says the Word of God is not relevant? John told them to be content with their wages. He was hardest on the rich and religious but do you see what he was doing? He was saying: Start

Matthew Chapter 3

living now as you would expect to live under the government when God takes over. Get ready for it by anticipating it. Don't be purged after the government has come. Purge yourselves now. Get into this water and wash, and I have an amnesty for you from God himself. Get into this water and as far as he is concerned the past is wiped clean. All your greed, all your pride, all your lust, all your anger, all your sloth – gone! When he comes he will find a people ready to be citizens of his Kingdom. That is John the Baptist.

John the Baptist was calling on people to turn away from their sins and come and get washed and step back into their own land which God had promised them, with a clean record so that when the King came there would be no purge. No wonder they got into that water – and fast. So fast that he had to stop them coming in, so fast that he had to turn some down who were not ready. They were so eager to get into that water but John the Baptist realised his limitations. It is one thing to persuade a person to turn away from their sins; it is another thing to keep them away. Even if you did manage to keep them away, what would you put in their place? For a life that has simply been emptied of sin is a dull, boring life. Make no mistake about it. The Bible is utterly honest and says that sin is a pleasure for a season and if you take all those pleasures away from people and put nothing in their place, what are you left with? A bunch of miserable, religious people. You are left with a bunch of Pharisees and it will not be long before another law that God has revealed to us will apply. That is that human nature abhors a vacuum and that worse will come into a life that has been cleaned out and emptied.

John realised he could get people to turn away from their sin but that was all he could do. He could get ready for the Kingdom but could not bring it, and even when the Kingdom came he would not be a part of it. In fact, Jesus once said among those born of women there had been none greater than John the Baptist – but even he is less than the least in the Kingdom.

So, John's message was: God's man is coming after me. I am not even fit to undo his shoelaces, but he will do for you two things that I cannot do for you: I can get you to turn away from sin and get your past right but how can I guarantee you will stay that way? What you need is someone who will take away your sins. Not just get you to turn away from them but to take them away from you. One day, John pointed to the One who is God's man to take away the sins of the world. But he didn't say "God's man", he said: "That is the Lamb". To every Jew that means one thing: It means a lamb with its throat slit – a lamb that has been killed and whose blood has been splashed around. This was the Lamb of God who by having his life taken and his blood spilt would take away the sins.

But that is not enough – to take right away, what have you got left? People would say, "You've taken away everything I've enjoyed doing."

John also said that Jesus would baptise people in the Holy Spirit. He would fill them up. Empty, sinless, religious lives are the most boring people you will ever meet. It is precisely one of the difficulties of the church today – that there are so many of us who have got ourselves emptied of some sins, just enough to be miserable. That is why you will find public houses where some patrons look much happier than in church. If you just got a few sins cleaned out and got no further than that, you would be miserable and you would say every Sunday, "O God, have mercy upon us miserable offenders...." Jesus would not only take away the sins, he would baptise in Holy Spirit and fill in the blanks and give pleasures for evermore.

So John knew his limitations but he still baptised. However, baptism is much richer in meaning than John's baptism. So much richer has it become since Jesus came that, in fact, if you had only been baptised by John, we would baptise you again in Jesus. It happens in Acts 19 because now we can fill it out and we can say two things that John could not say. First, we can say

"Repent", which he did say, and "Believe." Not just turn from your sins but turn to the Saviour; be filled with the Spirit. We can now offer the positive and I tell candidates who are being baptised in water: Until you are sure that you have been baptised in the Holy Spirit (as sure as you are that you are going to be baptised in water), there is going to be an emptiness in your life that is dangerous.

The Lord wants to fill and we can say another thing that John could not say. He said, "The Kingdom of heaven is near." But now we can say the Kingdom of heaven is here because the truth is that God is governing now, and the government of God has arrived. It comes out so clearly in the Lord's ministry when he casts out demons. He said, "If I by the finger of God cast out demons then the Kingdom of God has come upon you." On another occasion he said, "The Kingdom of God is among you." It is in your midst and wherever Jesus moved, the government of God was established and in life after life after life, so now we can see that living in the Kingdom is living in the Spirit. Do you see the connection?

Listen to just one text: The Kingdom of God is not eating and drinking but it is righteousness, peace and joy in the Holy Spirit. That is what the Kingdom is and we are heirs of the Kingdom. That is why our call to baptism is a call to become a citizen. The nearest secular equivalents that I think of are naturalisation or seeking political asylum. A candidate for baptism is saying: God, I seek political asylum under your government; I want to come right in now.

How patient Jesus is. Thank you, Lord Jesus, for your patience. When Jesus went back to his Father, all authority in heaven and Earth was given to him – all, not some; the whole lot.

We are under the government of Jesus now – and let it be known – and not only as individuals. As an individual I am under the government of Jesus. I obeyed the first law of that government. I did it a bit late but I did it and I went into water and I was baptised. That is his way of naturalising you. But what is the church? It is a community of individuals who are seeking in their life together to demonstrate the government of God. That is why we don't need a church police force. That is why Paul says it is disgraceful if a Christian takes another Christian to court. That is not how God's government works. You settle that under God.

We are the people of God and we believe that one day the government of England will be in the hands of Jesus. It is only in the hands of others by his permission right now but one day it will no longer be in their hands by his permission, it will be under his direct control. He will take it over and the kingdoms of the world will become the Kingdom of our Lord Jesus Christ and then he will hand it all back to the Father for whom it was all made.

If baptism is coming under God's government, if it is accepting citizenship in the Kingdom, then it involves all that I said earlier for the individual. His laws begin to apply immediately and there are some people who would say after all that, "I'm afraid I'm not very sure that I want to be in the Kingdom." It sounds repressive.

Ever since the Garden of Eden, Satan has been able to plant this lie deeply in our thoughts and there are millions who honestly think this: that God's restrictions on us prevent our freedom, and it is a lie. God's laws were given to us so that we might be free. In the book Deuteronomy, the phrase I underline again and again (concerning restrictions covering every aspect of life – domestic, agricultural, sexual, the lot) is at the end of a chapter when it says "that it may go well with you." God's government is a wealthy estate and he wants things to go well for you.

I received a letter from a girl thousands of miles away whom I have never met, who thinks she may not have long to live. She had been a drug addict for years. She did her own thing – she was free, she thought, and then she came under God's government and now she is free. She collected flowers and leaves, pressed them and put a beautiful thing together and posted it to me as an encouragement. She did not know me personally but the recorded talks that reached her had brought her to the Lord. She is free; she is under God's government – there is beauty in her life. If you asked her if she had one regret, she would say that she did not come under his reign earlier.

God is going to take over the government – every knee shall bow and every tongue shall confess that Jesus Christ is Lord. I beg you, purge yourself before his government purges. It will have to come, but praise God that he has lengthened the day before the purge comes, so that you might wash yourself. Praise the Lord for his patience. Thank him that he did not take over our government yesterday and decide to purge every sinner from this land, but he is going to do so, and so I plead with you: wash. It is Paul who says: murderers, adulterers, fornicators, thieves, drunkards, homosexuals, greedy persons, idolaters – none of these will have a share in the government of God; such were some of you but you were washed.

5
TEMPTATIONS

Read Matthew Chapter 4:1–11

On one particular day John had seen his cousin Jesus coming along the riverbank and, to John's astonishment, Jesus asked to be baptised. We know from the other Gospels why John thought he should not be, and why Jesus knew he should be. I am not going to dwell on that. The simple fact is that Jesus was baptised, and if Jesus was, and calls me to be, can I refuse? There were, however, unique features of Jesus' baptism.

First, Jesus saw heaven being torn open, which means that the clouds parted, and suddenly, they saw right up through the heavens to the deepest blue of the sky, and way down through the gap in the clouds there came a white dove – not the symbol of peace as we often think it is, but the symbol of God's power: the dove that brooded over the chaos in Genesis 1:3 and brought the order of the universe out of the chaos; the dove that brings order and power; the Holy Spirit was coming. Jesus did not preach a single sermon or perform a single miracle before this moment. Why not? Because, being a real human being as well as the Son of God, he could not do it without the Spirit's power. Jesus needed an anointing of the Holy Spirit with power to do what he did. As the great American evangelist D. L. Moody once said: "If the Holy Spirit, who came down on Jesus and enabled him to do what he did, is available to a man today, what could that man not do with that same Spirit?" Then he wrote in his diary that night, "I intend to be that man", and that day Moody began his great work.

If the power of the same Holy Spirit who came down on Jesus at the Jordan River is available to us, then the truth of what Jesus later said can be seen clearly: "...anyone who has faith in me will do what I have been doing." [I wonder if any Christian has ever had faith to believe that Jesus meant what he said.] He continued: "He will do even greater things than these" (see John 14:12). Lord, we believe, remove our unbelief! That was the vision, and it should encourage every Christian today to seek the Holy Spirit's anointing with power.

Second, there was a voice, which was obviously God speaking. Notice that God quotes the Old Testament twice – but then he is only quoting himself, because it was his Word originally.

What God said is interesting. It comes from Psalm 2:7 and Isaiah 42:1, and it refers to two things that he had said hundreds of years earlier. One was "You are my Son", which in the context of Psalm 2 is part of a coronation service for a sovereign. But in Isaiah 42:1 the words "in whom I delight" refer not to a sovereign but to a servant. Here is the amazing thing. Psalm 2:7 concerns the highest position that a person can have, a sovereign ("You are my Son"), but Isaiah 42 ("in whom I delight") concerns the lowest. In the account of Jesus being baptised, we see that the Father wanted him to combine the highest and the lowest – greatest sovereign and humblest servant – in his ministry. That is what his baptism meant to Jesus. It meant taking the responsibility of being King of kings and Servant of servants. How do you combine the two? I only know that when I look at the life of Jesus Christ I see the highest and the lowest perfectly combined. I see someone who can wash feet and wear a crown with equal dignity. I see someone who fits anywhere in the social scale. I see someone who is equally at home with the highest and the lowest in the land – with the religious and political leaders, and with women of the streets.

A vigil followed. I have read elsewhere that Jesus was alone for forty days after his baptism, yet he was anything but alone.

Matthew Chapter 4:1–11

I know there were no human beings, but it was a pretty crowded scene in the wilderness. The Spirit led him into the wilderness, so the Spirit was with him; Satan met him there, so Satan was with him; he was with the wild beasts – they prowled around him – and the angels came and ministered to Jesus. If you have no other human beings near you, that does not mean you are alone. Sometimes when you are sitting by yourself, with nobody in sight, the room seems crowded. We need to remember that the angels worship with us when we are in church. Jesus was not alone in the wilderness. The battle had begun. On the one side the Spirit and Jesus and the angels; on the other, the wild beasts and the devil. Natural and supernatural forces were engaged. It is significant that it was *after* the high moment of Jesus' baptism that this battle took place. There is a spiritual battle that is going on, and we are fools if we think we can just have nice times in church without engaging in this warfare. But Jesus went into it, and he came out in the power of the Holy Spirit, and the first round was won. Following that victory, he began to preach and liberate the victims of Satan in Galilee – the first public episode in his ministry.

Humanly speaking, the temptations happened when he was all alone, which means that he must have told people later what happened. He must have shared this very deep experience with his disciples for their encouragement. The first thing I want to say about the passage is this: *temptation is not sin*. Our Lord, in telling us that he was tempted, is making it quite clear that you can be tempted and still live a perfect, holy life. It is one of the things that will happen to you however far you progress in the Christian life. Until you are in your grave, you can expect to be tempted by the devil.

What can we learn from our Lord's bitter experience here, right at the beginning of his ministry? Before he preached to the crowds and before he performed a miracle, he had to fight and win a private battle. He was now baptised, he was now full of the

Holy Spirit, and I want you to notice that it was the Holy Spirit who led him into the place of testing, of temptation. When you say the Lord's Prayer, you ask, "Lead us not into temptation," and people have said to me, "But surely God the Father wouldn't lead us into temptation." Yes he would, and he did with the Lord Jesus. The Holy Spirit led him right into that place where he was going to be exposed to all the attacks of evil. He was led into that barren strip of territory about thirty miles long and some ten to fifteen miles wide, that is on the eastern slope of the Judean hills as they go down to that deep rift valley in which lies the river Jordan and the Dead Sea. It is a rain shadow – there are no showers here, so there are no trees, there is no grass, and there are deep rocky ravines and in those days there were wild beasts. The hyenas would laugh at night, and there, in the middle of that dreadful place, Jesus stood – alone and yet not alone.

Notice three things about this temptation: first, *the moment when it occurred* because that will tell you when to expect the devil to attack. The devil does not stay with you. Indeed, one of the things I want to make clear is that the devil, not being God, cannot be in more than one place at once. Some Christians talk to me as if the devil lives with them. If so, they are jolly important people because while he is with them he cannot be with anyone else. We must get this quite clear: the devil is not God, and like any other angel, whether good or bad, he can only be in one place at a time – but he was in this place.

When are you likely to encounter the devil, or what is probably a much more common experience, one of his agents? In his book *The Screwtape Letters,* C. S. Lewis has this fundamental insight: that the devil stays in his office, and sends his agents to do his work, and they report back to him, and what we often call "the devil" may be no more than one of his minor agents sent to us. But here it was the devil himself. When did he attack Jesus? Because this is a clue to the moments when he will attack you. He attacked Jesus after a high moment of spiritual experience.

Matthew Chapter 4:1–11

Jesus had been baptised and it had been a great baptism. The Holy Spirit had come down, the heavens had been opened, there was a voice like thunder, and very shortly afterwards the devil came.

If you have a blessing today, I can tell you this: the devil will try in some way to arrange that you lose the blessing soon. If you have had a great time, expect trouble. If you have had a high moment of assurance so that you know you are a child of God, then expect the devil to say, "If you are a son of God..." and to cast doubts almost immediately on what you have been assured of in the Lord. Another thing is that this temptation came to our Lord after an exhausting period, after six weeks without food and in the extreme heat of the daytime and cold of the night. It is often when you are exhausted that temptation can come with greater force. The devil loves to hit someone when they are down. When you are tired, even just physically tired, when your body is crying out for refreshment, it is then that you need to be on your guard.

Consider the *method* that Jesus used to deal with temptation. Have you noticed that Jesus used certain weapons? He used the scriptures, and in fact, if you want to deal with the devil, do throw the book at him – literally. Martin Luther used to throw his inkpot at him, but the Bible is heavier, spiritually and in other ways. Jesus, the Son of God, who knew the Father so intimately, used the weapon of quoting the Word of God – taking a piece of truth and throwing it at the liar, for the devil is a liar, and this is one of the best ways you can use. It was, of course, the Old Testament that Jesus threw, and it was the book of Deuteronomy. If you want to be able to deal with Satan, do get to know Deuteronomy. What a book to go to when you are trying to deal with temptation! You try it. Read it through in the next week or two.

Another secret of Jesus, as part of the method he used to combat the tempter, was to use the *power* of the Holy Spirit. He was full of scripture and full of the Holy Spirit. The two together enabled him to be invincible, even though the attacks of Satan were very deep and cutting. There are Christians who know the scriptures well, who can quote the text well, and who have got the Word stored up in their heart, but who lack the fullness of the Spirit, and they lack the power that is needed to draw from that Word the right weapon – for the belt of truth is the Bible, but the sword of the Spirit is that which the Spirit draws from it for the particular occasion of your battle. Therefore, we need the Spirit.

So there are those who are full of the Spirit, but who are not feeding on solid teaching from God's scripture, and they too will lack a vital dimension when the devil comes. But those who are full of scripture and full of the Spirit are more than a match for Satan.

The third thing that we want to look at is the *meaning* of these temptations. Here I want to correct, if I may, a lot of misunderstanding. There are those who approach the three temptations of Jesus as though Jesus were sorting out his motives; as if he was primarily concerned with why he was going to do things in his ministry. If we approach the temptations with these spectacles on, we will say that he was being tempted to get food without work, power without responsibility, and excitement without risk. Certainly, those are three temptations that *we* are all prone to, but I do not believe that is the basic meaning of the temptations.

The second approach, which is more common and taught quite widely, is that Jesus was not thinking through his motives concerned with himself, so much as his methods concerned with others, and how he was going to do his ministry – that he was there in the desert, thinking out possible ways of doing it, and that his temptations came through this. According to this approach, the temptations are interpreted like this: that he was being tempted to use the material rather than the spiritual approach – bread rather than preaching; that he was being tempted to use evil means for a good end, or that he was being tempted to offer sensational proof to make people believe.

Matthew Chapter 4:1–11

I still do not think that is the meaning of the temptations, for both these approaches make one fundamental mistake, which is that they are approaching the temptations through the mind of Jesus, but you will never understand a temptation until you approach it through understanding the mind of Satan. The question is not, "What was Jesus hoping to achieve?" but, "What was Satan hoping to achieve?" Then you will understand the temptations. We have got to see what the enemy was trying to do when he tempted our Lord. It is not so much Jesus thinking the thing through, it is Satan trying to think it through, and trying to gain an advantage.

We need to remember that we are dealing here with real things, not imaginary ones. We are dealing with real places. I used to have the idea when I read this story as a child that it all happened in the mind, that it was a kind of series of pictures in Jesus' imagination, but when I went to the Holy Land I stopped thinking like that. I saw the places and they are real. That wilderness is so real, and in one part of it there is a special stone which the Arabs call bread stone, which just looks like crumbled pieces of bread lying on the desert floor. A hungry man would see that almost as a mirage.

It is all real, and that pinnacle of the temple was real too. It towered ninety feet up, and from there you surveyed the whole area of the temple, with people like little ants running around in the courtyard. That mountain is real – way above Jericho they still point to the traditional mountain (I daresay it is the real one) and in Jesus' day from the peak of that mountain you could see ten different kingdoms. I for one have no doubt that was the mountain that Jesus climbed up, then looked out over those kingdoms and saw in them a microcosm of the kingdoms of all time and space.

We know we are dealing with reality because Jesus was a real person, but let me tell you that the devil is real, not a figment of the imagination. If you do not believe in a personal devil I honestly wonder how much experience you have of a personal God. The devil is not a little imp but a very intelligent being, far more intelligent and powerful than any of us. He knows how to twist you around his little finger. You will never beat him on your own. The angels are real too. I have said that Jesus was not alone when he was tempted: there were wild beasts, there were angels, there was the devil, and there was the Holy Spirit.

So that is the first key to unlocking what happened: this is not imagination and not picture language, it is reality. The second important key is this: to realise that this is only a tiny bit of the Bible, and whenever you want to understand one part of the Bible, the best thing to do is to look at all the other parts of the Bible. The Bible is a self-interpreting book: one passage unlocks another. What other passages in the Bible would help us to understand the temptations of Jesus in the wilderness? I will give you three. Firstly, John the Baptist went to school in the wilderness, that is where he learned. Now for six whole weeks the wilderness is to be the school in which Jesus learns something absolutely vital to fulfilling his mission: he learns obedience by what he suffers. The wilderness is a school. When you are going through the wilderness, God has sent you to school. When you are going through a dry patch, when you are going through an area that seems to have nothing attractive about it, remember that God has sent you to school. He wants you to learn something, and that is the first clue.

Let us look further back into the Old Testament. God sent the people of Israel to the wilderness for forty years. Why? To send them to school and to teach them things that would prepare them for the promised land. The wilderness was their school: the Sinai Desert. The book of Deuteronomy contains the lessons they learned in an account of their schooldays. This is why Jesus, to beat the devil in the wilderness school in which he was now learning, went back to the old school textbook of Deuteronomy. He quoted the very lessons that Israel had to learn when they were hungry in the wilderness, and they lacked bread, and had to be told that there were more important things than bread – one of the hardest lessons we have to learn.

The third passage of the Bible that helps me to understand this one is Genesis 3 – Adam and Eve in the garden. There is a clear link here. The devil sought to rob them of paradise, and by disobedience he achieved it – but you notice that the devil did it by offering food. When the second Adam came to the fight and to the rescue, the devil tried exactly the same tactic. He is not terribly original you know, and we are not ignorant of his devices: he started with food again, and tried to rob our Lord Jesus of his paradise and his obedience. So we are to use the rest of the Bible to understand this passage.

Another key is that we must understand that these are the temptations that came to the Son of God. Have you been tempted to turn stones into bread? Why not? Because you are not the Son of God.

We need to remember that Jesus' sayings are simply replies to what the devil thought up. These thoughts did not come from Jesus because Jesus was good, and therefore these evil thoughts had to have come from someone else. Alas, I can be tempted from my own imagination, because it is not developed perfectly as Jesus' was. Therefore, these wrong thoughts had to come from outside and come inside, whereas for me they can often come from inside, and I must not blame the devil for what has come from me. We sometimes do blame him for things for which he had no responsibility. Consider a man who forgets to set his alarm, he gets up late, he's in a bad temper, he argues with his wife about the way the breakfast is done, and he goes out to town in a foul mood, and he gets to the station and misses the train, and when he does get to the office he is in such a bad mood that he tells off a junior colleague, and he goes on like this all day. He attends a fellowship meeting at night and says to a fellow Christian, "Oh, the devil had a good go at me today." The devil probably had nothing to do with it. He forgot to set his alarm and everything else followed from that. The irritability and all the rest came out of his own flesh. But that could not happen with Jesus – the evil thoughts had to come from outside him.

So if we are going to understand the temptations let us start with the mind of the devil and approach it through his evil imaginations. Think first of the first temptation. The devil is taunting him as well as tempting him. I don't know how long you have ever been without food. Do you fast? The Bible assumes you do from time to time, but I daresay you have never fasted for six weeks. We do not have to. We have plenty of food. Jesus was without food for six weeks not by his choice, but by the Father's choice because he had told him to go somewhere where there were no food markets, and where there was not even grass to eat. Jesus had been without anything to eat for a month and a half. There are a few streams running through that wilderness and so they obviously slaked his thirst – but there was no bread.

His body was crying out for something to eat, and the devil said: If you are the Son of God, you can do anything; you can take stones and turn them into bread. Of course God can. The amazing thing is that a few weeks later, at a wedding reception, Jesus was going to turn water into wine. Why was it wrong to do such a miracle at this moment? The reason is very simple. The Father was going to teach his Son Jesus a most important lesson: no matter what need your body is crying out for, his will must be done first.

Now, you see, it is not much of a temptation to me to steal. I do not know why it is that wealthy people are caught so often shoplifting – people who don't need to walk out of the shop with something they have not paid for. I am not tempted to do that in this affluent society, but supposing my three children had not had anything to eat for months, and I went round a supermarket and noticed there was nobody looking, what would come first – God's commandment "You shall not steal?" or my family's empty stomachs? That is the kind of situation that is terribly poignant, and we do not know what this pull is. We have not been in situations where we are as desperate as that, but Christ was desperately hungry, and the Father was testing him: Will you remain obedient to me even though your body is crying out for a little bit of bread? Will you put your principles before your appetite? Jesus was right up against this. If he had not fought and won the battle, then, three years later, when his body was crying out in agony to be free from the nails, do you realise he would have stepped off the cross? Because he could have done that easily. If Jesus had once allowed physical desire to have priority over the Word of God then he could not have stood the cross. It was only possible three years later because he had already fought and won this battle, but when the body is crying out for some relief – if God has told you to do something – you remain obedient.

So, we know what the devil was trying to do. He was trying to break this, and therefore Jesus went right back to the experience of Israel in the wilderness when they were hungry and without food. God had said, "You leave Egypt and go to the Promised Land," and they were hungry and without food, and God had allowed the hunger to see if Israel would put obedience first and keep right on. But no, they talked about the onions, the garlic and all the tasty stew that they used to have in Egypt, and their bodily desires were pulling them back from God's will. We are physical creatures, our physical needs are sometimes so overpowering, but God says, "Will you remain obedient to me when your body is crying out for some relief? Will you still do my will?" You have to learn that, and there is only one way to learn it, and that is to be put into a situation where your body is needing something and God has said "Do that." Jesus had been led into the wilderness deliberately to take him away from food, to teach him through hunger that man does not live by bread alone.

However much bread you give anyone, he is going to die.

Even though we have enough food to eat, we are all going to die. You cannot live by bread alone. You can keep your metabolic rate going by bread alone, but you can't live – for that is not life, it is just existence. I pity and feel deeply for some poor people who are living for just one thing: to keep body and soul together, just scraping to keep going.

Jesus knew that God the Father was testing him, and that obedience was more important than a square meal. What a battle! He won it.

Let us look at the second temptation mentioned here. From the pull on the flesh, on the body, Satan now turns to a more subtle one: the pull of the world, or of power. Here is the pull of wealth, the subtle pull that comes to us when the devil offers us this world and he says, "It's mine to give you." I am afraid that is true. The devil is claiming that he could give Jesus power and wealth, and he could, and he can give you power and wealth. If you want power and wealth, do not come to Jesus – he never offered it. If you go to the devil, he will give it to you on his own terms, and they are terrible terms. So in the second temptation Jesus is being shown all that he wanted, and this was why it was such an awful temptation. Jesus had come from heaven to have all the kingdoms of the world. The Bible says that this is what he had come to do. The devil said, "I can give them to you if you will just bow down and let me boss you."

It was a bargain; it was Christ being offered the post of Antichrist, and one day the devil will offer to a human being all the kingdoms of this world. The Bible predicts such a world dictator before the end of human history, and the devil will offer it to that man, and that man will get it by devilish means. He will be in the grip of Satan and that is the way Satan is increasingly going to control this world. At the moment, Satan controls so much of it, but not on a world scale because there is no world government. Satan's ambition is to have one-world government ruled by a one-world dictator who is himself ruled by Satan, and in this way he will have totalitarian control over every member of the human race. Satan said, "Look, I'll give you everything on earth." What a temptation!

The tragedy is that on a much lesser scale the devil has said to some of his agents: "Go to that businessman and tell him, 'You can have the biggest business in this line in England if you will do it my way. You can have that rise if you will compromise my way. You can have this promotion if you will not let on that you belong to me, and if you do not let on that you have principles, you can have it!'" The devil can offer it to anyone, and we are led along – the power and the wealth that this world offers are things that our flesh desires. Jesus wanted all the kingdoms of the world, but he only wanted them to give them back to the Father. There is only one person that you are to bow down to.

I do not know if the day will come in this country when it will be as it was in Ancient Greece, where business was so tied up with pagan religion that you could not open a shop without bowing down to pagan idols; you could not join the equivalent of the Chamber of Commerce unless you did this. To be quite specific, here is an illustration: freemasonry, with some of the rites and religious implications of that. I was once asked by a senior man in freemasonry, "Why don't you join us? I could get you in, there are many ministers in, and it will help you on. You'll get the best churches, you'll get promotion, you'll get help, and you'll always have friends wherever you go. It's a great thing to be." He pressed me as a young minister to become a freemason, but I knew enough about the religious rites to say, "I can't bow down to that." You see, the tragedy is that if you are willing to compromise, if you are willing to go along a bit with things that are not Christian, you will get on. You will be helped. You will go up the ladder, but who wants to go up it without Jesus Christ? Who wants to go up it without God? Because if Jesus had got all the kingdoms of the world and the devil had given him this power and wealth, do you know that he would have lost it when he died? No matter what power or wealth you get in this world, if you get it Satan's way you will lose it very quickly. Two people were discussing a wealthy man who died and one said, "How much did he leave?" The other said, "Everything." All the human power you can gain just goes like that. It can end with a bullet or a germ, or just being born too soon – it has all gone. Jesus would not bow down to Satan and he would not dabble in anything of Satan's – and he came through victorious. The result was that later, when the devil came back, Jesus was able to deal with him. When the devil came through Simon Peter and offered Jesus victory without a cross, Jesus said, "Get behind me, Satan."

The next temptation is to appeal through popularity. The temple was not far from the wilderness – twenty minutes' walk would have got him there. The temple is now gone but you can still see the stone platform on which it stood, and if you stand on that platform, you look forty-five feet down to the Kidron Valley. On top of that platform there were the towering porches of Solomon's gateway and pinnacle on top, and every morning a priest used to climb up the tower to the very top of the pinnacle so that he was the first to see the sun rising over the Moab Hills to the east. He would then call down to the courtyard and they would offer the morning sacrifice.

Jesus climbed that pinnacle, and he stood at the top and the devil stood there too: Jesus, you know if you jumped off there when the crowds are looking up, and you just floated down, you would have them all in the hollow of your hand. Give them the proof they are looking for, give them sensationalism; give them something that will get them talking for months – the greatest publicity gimmick there has ever been. The devil was offering to be our Lord's PR man. Can you see this? Even more, do you notice that he used the scriptures? Oh, how subtle he is. Do you know the devil has studied them? He knows them very well and he can always quote out of context. If you study the text he quoted at this point, he missed out the most vital phrase that told us that in fact the promise of God – to protect his children and bear them up lest they dash their foot against a stone – would only apply if they were in line with God's will at the time. How important that is. In fact, if I took this text, I could just go to Beachy Head and walk straight off the cliff and say, "See you down at the bottom, we'll sing a chorus" – but I tell you it would not work. That is not because of any scientific law that states that gravity must always operate. It does not always operate – man can walk on water – but because I would not be in line with God's will to do it. The devil was using this text to say to Jesus: Give them what they want. Get the popularity; start with a great crowd that are hanging on every word; do an almighty conjuring trick.

There are still people who want to see miracles for this reason and this only. They say, "Go on, you perform a miracle and I'll believe." Don't you believe it – if a miracle was performed in front of their eyes they would say, "He had something up his sleeve." They would look for an alternative explanation and they would not be convinced. Do you know what would have happened if Jesus had thrown himself down? They would have scraped his body off the paving stones of that courtyard. The promise would not have held because it was not in the Lord's will and Jesus would have been buried that day.

Now we are getting very near to answering the question "What was the devil trying to achieve?" Two things: our Lord's disobedience and therefore our Lord's destruction. King Herod, at Jesus' birth thought: I'm the king of the Jews; there's no room for two of us in this nation. When Jesus arrived and was baptised and began his ministry the devil realised: there is no room for both of us. And there wasn't – there isn't room for both in your heart. You cannot follow the devil and Jesus at the same time, and the devil knew that here at last was the one who would open the prison doors; the one who would set his victims free; the one who would open the Kingdom of heaven to all believers. The devil knew that his days were numbered; that he was going to lose his power, that he was going to lose his kingdoms, and his reaction was the same as Herod's: How can I get rid of this man?

Herod had tried it by killing every baby boy under two years old; the devil was more subtle. The devil knew that if Jesus disobeyed his Father, he would destroy himself. For that is what you do – that is what I do if I disobey my God in heaven – I kill myself, either quickly or slowly. "Whatever a man sows that shall he also reap. If he sows to the flesh, he will reap death," and it is written right through the scripture. Do you know that the devil was trying to kill Jesus before he got to the cross and died on it? That is what he was after – he was trying to destroy him one way or another and bring him under the curse of God. Jesus was the very first person ever to be able to say no to the devil. Whether it was the power of the devil, the pleasure of the flesh, or the popularity of the world, Jesus said no.

The devil is so subtle, so powerful. His main aim is to destroy you, and he will do it by your disobedience. He does not bother with those who are not Christians. Why should he? They are no threat to him, they do not bother him, but the day you become a Christian, that day you are on his lists. You have got your name into two books. One is the Lamb's Book of Life, and the other is Satan's register. He will seek to do everything he can to drive a wedge between you and your heavenly Father. He will appeal through the needs of your body, he will appeal through the opinions of society around you, he will appeal to you through those incentives of power and wealth and all the glitter of a world that is fast passing away, and you will not be able to say no yourself, but if you call on the name of Jesus you can be sure that the devil will run. "Resist the devil and he will flee from you," and that is why we read, at the end of this temptation period, "The devil departed." As we noted earlier, the devil cannot be in more than one place at a time. We sometimes talk of the devil as if he were divine, but he is not. He is only a fallen angel, a spirit being, but an angel cannot be in more than one place at once. He is not omnipresent and he is not omnipotent. He is not all-powerful, even if he is stronger than we are. This means that the devil literally left Jesus at this point. He did not hang around. He came back some months later and I find that that is how his agents behave too. Temptation is not a constant in my life, and the devil is so subtle, he sends his agents to tempt me and then they go away again. They do not trouble me for quite some time until I have forgotten them, and then suddenly they are there again. Have you had that experience? You have had a big battle, and have really been going through it, and the Lord brought you through it and you were victorious. Did the powers of evil go on trying? No, they just left you and you went on in victory, and you forgot all about it. Then, bang! That is why, for example, it says in the book of Job that God said to Satan one day in heaven, "Where have you been?" Satan said, "I've been going to and fro in the earth." You see? "I've been moving around." I wonder where Satan is right now. I wonder where he is concentrating his own personal interest. Like the evil supervisor that he is, he leaves it to his angels. He has one agent whose charge is Britain, another whose charge is America, another whose charge is Russia, another China, and he uses these princes of nations to go and do his evil will with the leaders of nations.

So he sends his agents, but where is he? If you ever have a personal encounter with the devil, it is a terrible encounter. I pray you never will. Jesus did on just four recorded occasions. The devil himself gave Jesus personal attention and Jesus said no.

I know that the enemy's forces are everywhere in our world. I do know that you will meet them. I do know that they have a personal programme to destroy you by getting you to disobey God, and I know that Jesus, who won that victory after the devil departed from him, came into Galilee full of the Holy Spirit. It is that personal, private victory which you have against the forces of evil when you are alone that enables you to go into the public eye and there to have the victory for Jesus.

6
MINISTRY

Read Matthew Chapter 4:12–25

Jesus began his ministry when John was put in prison. John and Jesus were not rivals. Some people tried to set them off one against the other, and they came to John the Baptist one day and pointed out that Jesus was getting a bigger congregation. The devil loves to set the people of God against each other like this. But John's reply to such talk was along the lines of: that does not matter, I came to get ready for him and if I get smaller and he gets bigger that is as it should be; if I become less and he becomes greater, that is right and proper. What a big man it takes to say that. John was thrown into prison. He had done all he could to get people ready, so now Jesus must start.

It is interesting to notice not only the time when Jesus began but the place, Galilee. I can see a lot of interesting things in that, but I shall give you only two. One is this: it was where he *lived*. It is comparatively easy to go and preach somewhere else, but in front of people who know you, that is not always the case. I remember the first time I had to preach in front of all my family and relatives. I would much rather have gone and preached in front of a million in America than preach in front of those few. Jesus began to preach in Galilee, where he had been a carpenter and everybody knew he was the man down the street if you wanted a table mended.

The other interesting thing is this: Judea is on the road to nowhere; Galilee is on the road to everywhere. I have no doubt that he chose to start his ministry there because it was at the centre of the world. Imagine a map of the region. There is a road that goes from Europe down through to Arabia and ultimately to the East. There is another road that comes from Asia through Mesopotamia, through Damascus, down through the middle to Egypt and to Africa, so that those three continents were linked by a gigantic crossroads, and the junction was about three miles from Nazareth in Galilee, at a place called Megiddo. It always has been the crossroads of the world, with Nazareth just above the crossroads – so it was called Galilee of the nations, Galilee of the Gentiles – and everybody came through Galilee one way or another. One of the places on that main road was a fishing town called Capernaum. Jesus was choosing to begin his ministry at the very point where news of it could go to every part of the world, and perhaps that is why he began in Galilee.

There are three features of his wonderful ministry that come out in these verses. The first is the remarkable *pattern* of his ministry. What did he actually do? The answer is very simple: in his grace and power he met the threefold needs of people: physical, mental and spiritual. The ministry of our Lord was to the *whole* of the person, and it was for the *whole* world. We find this balance: he preached to meet all three kinds of needs.

Take first the *preaching*. Jesus believed in preaching. This was the fundamental priority of his ministry. He did not begin with healing, he began with preaching. And the church, in the days when it spread so rapidly in its first three hundred years, always had this priority: there was healing and there was teaching, but they *began* with preaching. They did not begin by opening a school or a hospital, they began with preaching and the other things followed. This is the emphasis of our Lord's ministry because this is the way in which God meets the deepest needs of people. As we saw earlier concerning the ministry of John, the deepest need of every man and woman on earth is the need of forgiveness. Why did Jesus begin with preaching? Because the world is in the grip of Satan, and Jesus came to set people free from that grip. The world was full of vice, crime, disease

Matthew Chapter 4:12–25

and death, pain and suffering; but all these things were caused by one thing only, and that was the grip of evil.

The Kingdom was now *at hand*. Jesus said, "My Kingdom is not of this world". What does it mean? It means this: wherever God's power reaches out and controls, that is the Kingdom of God. Jesus said, "...if I drive out demons by the Spirit of God, then the Kingdom of God has come upon you" (see 12:28). Wherever a life is being touched by the power of God, there is the Kingdom. If we would like to live in the Kingdom of God, we do not need to move house or change jobs, we do not need to get on a boat or a plane. You can live in the Kingdom of God at this very moment if you allow God's power to take hold of and control your life. This is tremendous because it means that God has power over disease, over death, over fear. He has power over all the things to which we are prey.

Therefore, if I allow the power of God to enter my life then I am in the Kingdom. I shall see these things under his control, and he will control these things within my own life because I shall be within the reach of his power. This world is *not* the Kingdom of God – according to Jesus it is the kingdom of Satan. That is why our newspapers are full of lust, cruelty, bloodshed, suspicion and hatred – because this world is not the Kingdom of God. But wherever someone comes under the power of God, and the evil things are removed from their life by God's power, that person has entered the Kingdom and is living within the reign of God. God is reigning over their life. The good news that Jesus preached was that the Kingdom of God is breaking into this world *now*; it is very near *now;* you enter it *now;* you can live under God's power *now;* you can have God's power conquering the enemies in your life *now*. That is good news, tremendous news – it is a gospel. So, Jesus came preaching the *gospel* of the Kingdom of God which was at *hand*.

The next key is to *repent*. How can we hope to be in the Kingdom of God and ask God to deal with our enemies if we do not want him to deal with our sins? How can I ask God to get disease out of my life if I am unwilling for him to get envy out of my life? How can I expect God to give me the victory over death if I do not want the victory over bad temper? In other words, you cannot have God in bits and pieces, you cannot have God help you with one enemy if you want to hang on to another enemy. All the enemies of God and all the enemies of men must be dealt with at the same time. While I may feel that my sickness is an enemy that God should help me to conquer and should banish from my life, I must also realise that gossip and worry are just as much enemies of God as illness and disease.

How then do I get ready for the power of God to break into my life and give me the victory? The answer is: I repent. In calling people to repent, Jesus was saying just what John said before him. In other words, when God comes, he comes to put everything right, not just what we want put right. So the need is to repent, which is to change our minds and to hate the things we have done that were wrong. Let me underline this. Most of us are sorry when we have done wrong if the wrong catches up with us and we suffer for it. The real test of whether we have repented is whether we feel sorry about the things we did that were wrong that nobody knows about and that have not cost us anything. If we do, we are repentant. A man who was asked by a magistrate, "Are you sorry about this?" replied, "Yes." The magistrate continued, "What are you sorry about?" and he answered, "I'm sorry I was caught." The criminal was being absolutely honest, and he had plenty of remorse, which he expressed in that court, but he was not repenting. Cain never repented of the murder of Abel; he may have been terribly sorry he did it because it cost him so much, but he was never sorry about the thing he did. The repentant person will say, "Lord, I have asked you to get me out of this trouble, I have asked you to banish this enemy, but I am sorry about all the other things now and I am asking you to put all of it right," and then believe the good news.

Jesus' teaching was for the *spirit*. It was also to the *mind*. One of our greatest needs is to get the truth, to know the difference between true and false, right and wrong. The third area of Jesus' ministry was healing for the body. All of us face sickness sooner or later. We find that whatever sickness Jesus encountered – sometimes acute conditions such as fevers; sometimes chronic sickness; sometimes illnesses which in those days were incurable – Jesus was able to deal with it. Usually he did something physical – he might touch the sufferer. There was no situation beyond his control. Just imagine what would happen if a man arrived in your town who could cure every known disease. Supposing you heard that he was at the bus station and he was curing every known disease without a failure yet. What queues there would be! People say that health is everything, but it is not and the Bible does not say it is. Those who think health is everything would do all within their power to get near a man like this, and people flocked to him. So, the pattern of our Lord's ministry is wonderfully balanced. All the needs of mankind – physical, mental and spiritual – come within his reach. Therefore, our ministry, following his, must be balanced and must seek to meet all the needs of people – in his name.

To extend his ministry, we now see that Jesus called other people to share it. This would mean extending it in space while he was still on earth, and extending it also in time after he left earth. So he called men to be his disciples and apostles. I do not know whether you realise the excitement of this, but when you read the story of how he walked along the shores of Galilee and called four fishermen, it was the beginning of the church. That was the beginning of a human society which would last two thousand years and more. Every group of believers calling themselves a church began on the morning Jesus walked along that shore and said to four fishermen, "Come, follow me." So simple a beginning, so utterly sublime. It is remarkable that the church should have started in that way, not with a committee, not with a great assembly, not with a procession, not with a lot of hullabaloo, not with a lot of different vestments, not with a lot of paraphernalia; just four fishermen and Jesus walking along the seashore. Maybe the church would be more effective today if it had managed to retain that simplicity.

They had met Jesus before, when they had been with John the Baptist down by the Jordan River. Now we notice two things: first of all, what they were (or, rather, what they were not); and, secondly, what Jesus said to them. First, what they were. They were young, so they were not very experienced or mature. Most of them were probably in their teen years or early twenties. They had not had much education such as we have in this country. They were ordinary people who worked with their hands. From the world's point of view they were nobodies. And God chooses nobodies. He does not choose people for what they are but for what they are not. This is the story of the Bible; this has been the story for two thousand years. He takes a cobbler in Northamptonshire and turns him into a William Carey. He takes a parlourmaid from London and makes a Gladys Aylward of her. Thank God he chooses nobodies! If God had said that he needed a church of rich people, clever people and good people then there would be no hope for most or all of us. But he did not start that way, he started with a group of ordinary, young working men and said, "Follow me". In other words, everything that they would be was because of him. They would therefore give glory to God and not to themselves. They were nothing. Of course, as fishermen they would be tough, they would be brave, they would be patient, but they were just fishermen and they were certainly not very religious people.

Jesus chose them for what they were not, rather than for what they were – ordinary, practical, down-to-earth, uneducated men; he told them to follow him, and he would make them fishers of men. Notice he made a demand and an offer simultaneously. He never makes a demand without making an offer, or an offer

Matthew Chapter 4:12–25

without making a demand – the two go together. The demand was "follow me" – unconditional. He did not lay down any terms. He did not say, "Is there a shop steward of the fishermen's union that I'll have to negotiate with? What wages will you require? How many hours will you work for me?" He said, "Come, follow me." Only the Son of God has the right to tell a man to do that. Unconditional! It was going to be a kind of slavery and yet perfect freedom. So Jesus made the demand with no conditions, no terms – and they did follow him, leaving immediately. It meant giving up a good job; and, in some cases, leaving their relatives. Simon had to leave a wife, presumably. Zebedee the father was left by James and John. It meant, ultimately, leaving their life, because only one of those original disciples died of old age in bed; the others were martyred, yet they had followed him immediately. When Jesus calls you to follow him, you cannot make conditions or terms, you cannot say, "Well, Lord, I will follow you if...", or, "I will follow you but...." There are cases in the Gospels of people who have tried to do this, but there can be no "buts", we are simply to follow.

The offer was a wonderful one. If they followed him, he would make them fishers of men. They were pretty good at handling those nets, but he was going to help them handle people. Notice he did not call them to an easy life. This fishing would be more demanding. He does not call us to a life of ease, but if they followed him, they could do a job that they had not been doing before. So, these were the human partners in his ministry.

Turning to the divine partner, we recall that prayer was more important to Jesus than sleep, so he would get up very early in the morning, and he would get alone with the Father, who was his other partner. He was down-to-earth with the men he chose, and he was up to heaven with the Father he loved. Jesus was not a mystic shut away, he was right in the middle of human society, and he would get up before daybreak and pray. This is the secret of ministry: to get right in among ordinary folk and love them as he loved them, and to get right away from them and love God. It is this combination of getting into society and out of it again that marks the life of Jesus. Once again, I am impressed with the balance of our Lord's ministry. As far as the pattern goes, he balanced their physical, mental and spiritual needs; and he balanced the divine and the human; the earthly and the heavenly – what a balance there was in his life.

7
THE SERMON ON THE MOUNT

Read Matthew Chapter 5:1–13

By some standards the Sermon on the Mount is one of the shortest sermons preached; by any standard it is the greatest. We are going to spend three chapters looking at this sermon. We shall have to travel quickly and may miss some of your favourite points in the sermon; you can put them in yourself.

By way of introduction, look at the place, the people, and the purpose for which this sermon was preached. The place: why did Jesus go up into a mountain? To get away from the crowds, to have room for a multitude, to separate from the merely curious or perhaps to use one of God's pulpits, one of those hills to which we lift up our eyes for help. The hills of Olivet, of Carmel, of Sinai all come to mind as being God's natural pulpits. One cannot help drawing the contrast and making a comparison with Sinai and the revelation through Moses. Now a man greater than Moses is here whom Moses himself predicted and about whom he said, "Whoever does not listen to that prophet will be destroyed from among the people." So much then for the place, one of God's pulpits.

Who were the people to whom this sermon was addressed? A lot of scholars' ink has been spilled over the question, "Is this for disciples or for everyone?" The answer is that he began with his disciples and he finished with a multitude and I am presuming, therefore, that this sermon is primarily for those committed to Christ but that he did not mind those who were not committed overhearing the conditions of discipleship. I have found that this sermon has a double value in preaching. It not only helps disciples to realise what they ought to be, it also warns would-be disciples about the conditions under which they are called to follow the Lord Jesus Christ – it is for both. The purpose of the sermon is a very serious one. This is obvious from the fact that Jesus sat down and the fact that he opened his mouth. God does not waste words and if God tells us these things, they are important. Our Lord is speaking ex cathedra and he sat down and when a rabbi sat down, he was going to speak the Word of God. So here is our Lord speaking ex cathedra from his seat.

It is also serious because he opened his mouth. Now, obviously you have got to do that to speak. But whenever that phrase is used it seems to underline that we should listen very carefully to what is going to be said. There is a kind of deliberate approach to the sermon. He sat down, he opened his mouth and he taught them. Now, there are those who feel that in the Sermon on the Mount our Lord was telling us how to work for our salvation and that this sermon belongs to a very limited period of history in which salvation by works was being offered to the Jewish people. I cannot stop now to argue that one except to say that I think there is a misunderstanding. This is not how to work for your salvation but how to work out your salvation. It is working, yes – but not working for, it is working out – working out what God has worked in.

For Christianity is concerned with behaviour as well as belief; with conduct as well as creed; with consecration as well as conversion; with how you go on as well as with how you start. I think it was Matthew Henry who said that this sermon is not so much concerned with the credenda (the things to be believed) of the Christian faith as with the agenda – what needs to be done. Here we have the working out of salvation, now let it work; this is how it should work. Now we approach the first section of the sermon and we notice that the sermon begins with character before it deals with conduct and that is quite deliberate and of far-seeing importance.

The Christian life is first of all what you are before ever it becomes what you do, and that is precisely the opposite notion to the one most widely held among unbelievers. Ask an unbeliever what a Christian is and he will answer in terms of what you do. Being kind to grandmother and the cat, trying not to do anybody any harm, leaving the world a little better than you found it – all in terms of doing. Christ teaches us that Christianity is first of all what we are and what we do will be the fruit of what we are. Conduct will spring from character. It is much more important to be a Christian than to do things Christians do. The one follows from the other and so our Lord begins with being a Christian. And therefore, this is the opposite of the world's notion as to how you begin.

Now, there have been arguments as to whether the beatitudes are in chronological order. You begin by being poor in spirit and you finish up by being persecuted. It is true that there are certain progressive ideas in the beatitudes but when I preach on this, I put a little phrase on the outline in the handout: "Beginning and Continuing". I have the feeling that these attitudes, these attributes of Christian character, these ingredients of the recipe for a Christian disciple are in fact attributes which are needed all the way along and we are not to regard any of them as belonging to the earlier stages, or any of them as belonging to the later stages. They are continuing as well as beginning. So, we turn to what Billy Graham has called "The Beautiful Attitudes", which is quite a useful definition.

We begin by looking at the meaning of the word "blessed". By the way, when you read it do read "blessed". "Bless-ed" is a very old fashioned way of saying the word; it is blessed. Oh, how blessed are the poor in spirit. Now what does Jesus mean? It is obvious that the word means, basically, happy. Still to this day, a popular name for Greek boys is Makarios, as you might call a little girl "Joy", so little boys are still called Macarios. However, I think it is the triumph of hope over experience to call any child a name of character. We called our third child Angela, or angel. I am afraid it has not worked! Now, the word Macarios or blessed means more than happy, it means to be in a happy place or position. It means to have within oneself all the conditions needed for true happiness. The very name Cyprus means "Happy Isle" because of its fertility. The earliest settlers believed it contained all that was necessary within itself for its inhabitants to be truly happy.

The word "blessed" means a person who has within himself all that is necessary to have true happiness, but the word "blessed" means even more than that. It is a congratulatory term and, if I may, I'll just draw your attention to the Greek and point out that the verb "are" is not included in the original. It is not blessed are the poor in spirit – it is blessed the poor in spirit. It is a congratulatory term. It is a statement. We could translate it as "Oh, the happy position of the poor in spirit." We have got right into our subject. Now here is the interesting thing – here is our Lord's answer to the question, "Who is best off in life?" Or "What is the life that is most worth living?" His answer is quite different than the answers of many of the great philosophers of history.

There are three basic answers to this question. Some say the answer is to be found in what you have. You are in a really happy position according to what you have, whether it is wealth or health or friends or faculties, whatever it may be. A second category of answer to this question is that the real life worth living is to be found in terms of what you do. If you have many hobbies or interests, if you have travelled widely, if you participate in cultural activities, then you will be in a happy position. But our Lord's answer to the question of what it is that makes life most worth living is that it is not in terms of what I have, not in terms of what I do, but in terms of what I am. Here is the real secret for the real world in which I live: it is not the world outside but the world inside.

Matthew Chapter 5:1–13

I went to a conference in Swanwick many years ago and I suffered from violent toothaches the whole conference. I finally had it pulled out rather roughly in a little back room down the road in Ripley after two days of sheer misery. The weather was excellent, the speakers were great, the fellowship was wonderful, but the real world I lived in was the world inside and I was not in a happy position even though I was among Christians and in Swanwick and enjoying perfect weather. Just multiply that by the spiritual dimension and you have got the meaning of the beatitudes. The real world in which you live is the world inside and the happiest position is the position of the life that is right inside and that has the ingredients of Christian character. It is to these that we now turn.

The first is the key to the rest and in a sense is the fundamental first step of the Christian life, although it is a continuing as well as a beginning attribute. It does not say, "Blessed are the poor spirited." Christians are not called to be sissies and namby-pambies who wouldn't hurt a fly with neither backbone nor staffing – that is not the beatitude. Nor does it say, "Blessed are the spiritually poor." There is no blessedness in a poverty-stricken prayer life or in a poor understanding of the Bible. There is nothing blessed in half-hearted worship. There is nothing blessed about being spiritually poor. What, then, does it mean?

The word "poor" is a relative term. We use it in Britain but we do not use it in the same sense as they use it in China. In Britain it means someone who has not got everything that we think is necessary for life. It means someone who is deficient in the things that they need, but that is not the meaning on our Lord's lips. Taking it a stage lower down it means not only someone who is deficient, who has not gotten everything they need, but someone who is destitute – someone who has nothing. That is one step further down – that is to be really poor. There is a step lower still and that is someone who has got worse than nothing, who is up to their eyes in debt. Charles Dickens and his portrait of debtors' prisons in The Pickwick Papers reminds us that the word "poor" in Britain, not many years ago, meant someone who had less than nothing and who was up to their eyes in debt with no hope of ever getting out of it. That is the meaning of poor in scripture.

A study of the Prophet Amos reveals this straight away. It is the situation of being so utterly poor that you not only have nothing yourself – you have less than nothing. You are so much in debt that you will never get out of debt. Apply that to the spirit and you have got the meaning. It is someone whose pride has been progressively destroyed by poverty. If you have less than everything you need, your pride will lead you to struggle to maintain your existence. Did you ever try to help an old-age pensioner? If you had absolutely nothing, your pride might lead you to starve rather than beg; but if you are a debtor your pride is completely swallowed and you are ready to accept charity from anyone who will help you out of your impossible situation. You have got to swallow every bit of pride you have got and throw yourself on the mercy of someone who is charitable toward you. To be poor in spirit before God is to realise not only that I haven't everything I need – not only that I have nothing that I need, but that I am up to my eyes in debt and there is no way out of this situation except by throwing myself on the charity of God. Martin Luther said, "We are all beggars," and that is the beatitude. George Bernard Shaw said, "Forgiveness is a beggar's refuge. We must pay our debts like men." I fear that he is now paying his debt.

You either come to God as a beggar or you come not at all. "Blessed are the poor in spirit." Now, a friend of mine is a minister in London and a man came to him one day and said, "Do you mean to tell me I must come before God with open hands and outstretched arms and confess my life is a failure and that I can't do anything without him. I'm damned if I will." The minister rightly replied, "You're damned if you won't."

It is this pride in us that will not allow us to come poor in spirit. When I read the words from the lives of the saints, they were people who were beggars. They were people who were utterly humbled. Listen to Charles Wesley: "If so poor a worm as I". Listen to Isaac Watts: "A wretched, poor, and helpless worm". On William Carey's tombstone is written: "A wretched, poor, and helpless worm, On Thy kind arms I fall." It is those who have found that the kingdom of heaven flings its gates wide open to beggars and to no one else. Theirs is the kingdom of heaven.

Now I come to number two: those who mourn over sin. Now, there is a paradox in this beatitude. "Blessed are those who mourn, for they shall be comforted." Isn't that an extraordinary thing to say? "Never man spake like this man." Jesus said, "Blessed are those who mourn, for they shall be comforted." The word "mourn" means to be overcome with grief, to agonise, to ache in heart, to have tears coasting down one's cheek. "Blessed are those who mourn". Now, there are two mistaken views about the Christian life that I come across. Number one: Christians must never be happy. Some years ago, I heard about a Scotsman who was brought before the elders of his church for smiling on the Sabbath. Those days are fortunately gone but there are still some who think that every time we have a service, we ought to have a funeral and that we ought to dress as if we are going to a funeral. This is the idea that Christians must never be happy.

This beatitude does not say, "Blessed are the moody" or "Blessed are the morose," or "Blessed are the miserable." It says, "Blessed are those who mourn". The opposite idea, which is equally mistaken, is that Christians must always be happy, and we all know the cheerleader who goes around saying, "Now come on, it's raining outside but we're great inside, clap your hands and let's get going." That is the kind of cheerleader approach to the Christian faith. But I do not think a Christian must always be happy. We follow a man of sorrows, acquainted with grief and there are times when a Christian will mourn and blessed are those times. Now let us say straight away that it does not mean bereavement. I am afraid I do not feel that this verse ought to be read at funerals. I do not think it refers to that kind of mourning. Nor does it refer to that weeping that comes from sympathising with sufferers – mourning for others.

This is essentially the godly grief that produces repentance towards God and carries no regret. The world tries to make a joke about sin and to laugh it off but that will bring regret. Godly grief does not try to laugh it off but instead it faces seriously the sin of our own heart and it mourns over that sin. I do not make this a generalised rule but I have noticed that where there have been tears at a conversion, there is a lasting conversion. Where there has been a genuine weeping over sin, there is cleansing and healing in those tears. That is not to say we must work up weeping or must expect it or stimulate it. I am just making an observation. If you have never wept for yourself, I wonder if you would know the blessedness about which our Lord speaks here. When you consider the opportunities you have wasted, the Spirit you have grieved, the people you have hurt, is that not enough to make you weep? It ought to be. The glorious promise is that those who weep like that will be comforted.

Now, this word is so misunderstood. "Our minister never preaches comforting sermons." Have you heard that? Or said it? What they mean is that he never preaches coddling sermons or cotton-wool sermons, but the word "comfort" has in the middle of it the word "FORT". I put it in capital letters for you. It means to put strength in you, it means to garrison you, it means to make you strong. In the Bayeux Tapestry, that embroidered comic strip of William the Conqueror, there is a picture – one of the scenes – and it shows a battle in progress and it says, "Bishop Oden comforts his troops." Do you know what he is doing to them? They are there in a line facing the enemy and he is standing behind them with a sword and he is prodding them in the behind. He is tarring them into battle. He is pushing them on. He is strengthening them to fight the enemy. Now that is not many people's idea of comfort but frankly, when people in a congregation look as if they are sitting on drawing pins, and sometimes they do, they are being comforted. They are being strengthened, they are being helped to face the facts and come out a stronger person, and those who have learned to mourn will come out strong. Funnily enough, in Britain tears are regarded as a sign of weakness but according to our Lord's thinking, this kind of tear is a sign of strength, of comforting from the Lord.

Now we turn to number three: meekness. Said an Indian Hindu to C. F. Andrews in the days of British imperialism, "Sir, the Englishman may inherit the earth but if you call him 'meek' he will be insulted," and that is the general reaction to the word meek. Let us say straight away it does not mean blessed are the weak, nor does it mean blessed are the mild. I do not like that word "mild" one bit. One of the things about which I am not too happy with Charles Wesley despite loving him in every other respect is the fact that he it was who put meek and mild together. Our Lord was not mild; the one who could whip moneychangers out of the temple was not mild but he was meek. The word does not mean a feeble, frail person who is easily pushed around, easily knocked down. I do not think we should give that impression. It is a strong word – it is used of our forces held in check. It is used by the Greeks of breaking in a horse. I used to do that when I worked on a farm and breaking in a horse is not trying to make it soft. It is seeking to control the energy there is there and when it is broken and all that energy is still there, it is still strong but the energy is now channelled into useful purposes. It is now meek; it is not weak; it is meek and it is still strong.

That is why the meekest man in the Bible was Moses. Now, if the Bible did not say that in Numbers 12:3 would you have ever thought it? If I asked you who was the strongest man in the Bible you would say Samson. You would be wrong, of course

– he was the weakest. If I asked you who was the wisest man in the Bible you would say Solomon but he was not, he was one of the most foolish. A man who could have as many wives and concubines as that was not very wise. If I asked you who was the meekest man on earth, well, you would have to say Moses because the Bible says so but he was not. All of these people had to be supernaturally trained and moulded before they were wise or strong or meek. When I read the story of Moses, I don't think of him as meek. Do you? But he was. All the forces of his character were moulded and held in check by God and used for good purposes. That is meekness. It is a man who has got himself completely in control and therefore does not react by instinct to what happens to him.

We shall see much more of this later where our Lord draws certain pictures of meekness: a man who is injured but never thinks of revenge, a man who has suffered injustice but never thinks of his rights, a man who has been insulted but never thinks of his reputation. It requires strength of character to be meek and not to hit back. There was a newspaper that held a competition for the most striking headline and one of the entries was "The Meek Shall Inherit the Earth Next Wednesday." Isn't that interesting? For the ordinary Englishman's reaction to this is it is not true – but if you hold yourself in check and do not assert your rights and stamp your reputation and take your revenge, you will be pushed out.

Life is a jungle and it does not work this way – but, in fact, Jesus is saying, "It will work this way." It is a quotation from Psalm 37:11 where it refers not to the earth but to the land of Canaan, where the people of God are assured that if they hold themselves in check, if they are meek, then they will be given the land of Canaan – but if they try to grasp it by asserting themselves, they will lose it. Said a wealthy landowner to an artist painting in one of his fields, "All this land is mine." The artist replied, "But the landscape is mine." Blessed are the meek for they shall inherit the earth, and it is literally true that God will one day give the whole earth to those who did not try to grasp it but to those who are fit to have it. Paul was able to say, "as having nothing, and yet possessing all things". All things are yours because you are Christ's. That is literally true and will one day be seen to be true.

Hungry and thirsty are two words that we do not understand. I have never been hungry in my life. I have had a good appetite; I have been without a meal or two but I have never been hungry in the way that many people in the world are hungry with that gnawing pain which dominates all else. I was once thirsty. I was once stuck in the Arabian Desert with a broken-down Land Rover and no water and I began to realise what thirst is after a bit. You begin to think of lots of water in your mind; you begin to roll your tongue around your lips and begin to wonder what it feels like to drink water again. Now, in the Middle East, the words "hungry" and "thirsty" mean things that you and I do not understand. They mean to be so desperate for something that all else is excluded from your desire.

Blessed are those who are desperate for righteousness. It is our next beatitude: consuming passion, a grand desire, an overall ambition. Now, the world has a hunger for happiness. Happiness here and holiness hereafter, if there is a hereafter. That is the world's priority, but the Christian's approach is precisely the opposite. He knows that holiness here and happiness hereafter is God's plan. Happiness is a by-product of holiness – holiness being defined in both the negative and positive way. Negative to be free from self, free from sin, free from temper, free from envy, free from malice, free from jealousy, free from impatience – but not just free of those things because a life that is empty is filled with far worse spirits – but full of love, joy, and peace toward God as well as patience, kindness, and goodness towards others, and also faithfulness, meekness, and self-control towards self – this is holiness.

The word "holiness" is nasty to some people, it is monastic to others – but to us who know Jesus Christ it is a lovely word; it means to be like him. Now, I ask you, in the centre of these beatitudes, is that your grand passion? May I put it like this: everyone in a chapel on a Sunday morning is exactly as holy as they really want to be because the promise here is that this is one thing you may have because it is the one thing God wants to give you. How hungry are you for it? If you are hungry, he will satisfy you and that means that I am just as holy as I really want to be – no more, no less. Is not the prayer upon most of our lips in fact, "Lord, make me holy but not just yet?" We would love to be a saint, but we would not necessarily like to have to do all that is required of the saints. I had a man say his ambition was to be an ex-missionary. Do you understand that? Well, wouldn't it be nice to be an ex-saint? But there is an appetite for holy things that we have got to have. Do you covet it in others? Do you seek it in yourself? Do you take time to be holy? Then you will be because you are satisfied. God will fill those who are desperate to be like Christ.

The next beatitude is to be merciful. At this point we run into people who say this is not a beatitude, it is a bargain and therefore it belongs to salvation by works. Now, it is not a bargain with men and it is not a bargain with God. There is no guarantee that if I show mercy to men they will show mercy to me; the world is not like that. Nor is it a bargain with God as if there is a pact of mutual lenience between us. You do this and I'll do that. This is not the meaning of the beatitude. That would contradict the whole of the gospel, which is not a bargain nor a contract; it is a covenant freely entered into by God through his grace. Well, what does it mean? We know what showing mercy does mean from Luke 10 where the parable of the Good Samaritan defines it for us – he that showed mercy.

It is first of all a thing of the heart – it is to feel compassion for another in need. It is, secondly, a thing of the will. It is to do something about that need and to express the compassion by binding up his wounds, setting him on an ass, and paying the innkeeper tokens for his keep; but it is primarily a thing of the mind. The whole point of the Good Samaritan was it was a Samaritan and there was this gulf between the Jews and the Samaritans. There was a racial gulf between them and they were not even on speaking terms. Do you know why the Jew was going down the road from Jerusalem to Jericho? To avoid going to Samaria. It was the long way around to Galilee and he was deliberately going down that road to avoid meeting a Samaritan. That is the setting, that is the point of the story, and those two Jews, the priest and the Levite, went past; it was the Samaritan traveller who stopped.

Now let me bring this up to living memory. In a gold mine in Johannesburg one of the overseers, a white man, was trapped underground, and so dangerous was the condition of the gallery in which he was trapped that no one went in to fetch him out until an African at risk of his life crawled in and pulled that man out to safety. The man was unconscious, taken into a hospital but he recovered. Now, when he recovered, they told him that but for this man's courage, he would not be alive. The man said, "I'd love to meet him; bring him in, please," and they brought in this man and when the man in the bed saw the colour of his skin, he turned over and would not shake hands with him and would not speak to him. Now, supposing that European was again trapped in the mine, and supposing again someone was needed to go in. Would that African go in a second time to save him do you think? If he did then that would be showing mercy.

For the very word "mercy" means that it is to do something that is not deserved – it is not just doing good deeds. The parable of the Good Samaritan was not told us simply to do good deeds; it was to do good deeds particularly to the enemy, particularly to the undeserving. The Samaritan showed mercy to the one who fell among the thieves because the Samaritan knew that the Jew would probably not even bother to thank him and would still despise him. Blessed is he that showeth mercy. Why? Because he shall obtain mercy. What does that mean? I think it means first that this quality of mercy, which is not strained, which follows the gentle dew of heaven, is a quality that especially appeals to God's heart and the reward, in a sense, is two-fold. I do believe that our fellowship with God and our forgiveness, which we need daily for the daily sins we commit, is conditioned by our passing on that forgiveness that we are taught in the Lord's Prayer, "Forgive us our trespasses, as we forgive those who trespass against us."

This is not for purposes of salvation but for that daily communion with the Lord. As much of a need as our daily bread, our daily food is our daily forgiveness and it is conditioned in so far as we pass on to others the mercy that we have received. If we are not forgiving, then in that daily sense, we cannot be forgiven – the two go together. If my heart is refusing mercy to another, how can I come for that daily forgiveness which I need for communion? The Parable of the Debtors tells the same story but in the future. It seems to me to suggest that just as there is a reward in heaven for all a Christian's service, there is a place in Christian life for reward. We shall be judged not for purposes of punishment but for purposes of reward. There is, as it were, an undeserved reward, a reward out of proportion for those who have shown mercy because this quality is particularly precious in God's sight and the reward for showing mercy in Christian service will be even more than is deserved. It will be a particular example of God's mercy itself; it seems that this quality is nearer to God's heart than many others. I shall leave those thoughts with you.

We could therefore reverse the beatitudes because this will give us the secret of being merciful. Blessed are those who obtain mercy for they shall be merciful – that is where it starts. It is only when you have got a living sense of the sheer, undeserved favour of God that you can show this to someone else. Look at the hymns; look at the texts that spring to mind. It is of the Lord's mercy that we are not consumed. We sing of how his mercies are new every morning. It is a mercy that we can sit in church on a Sunday morning, it is a mercy when the sun is shining, it is a mercy that we have got enough to eat and enough to wear. It is a sheer mercy. Do you deserve all this? It is a mercy – as new every morning as the paper. His mercy made me free. God be merciful to me, a sinner. When you think like that you can show mercy to others and as you show mercies to others more mercy flows into you.

Number six: blessed are the pure in heart. Sin blinds and it is a mercy that it does. For if a sinner looked at God and could see God he would shrivel up. This reminds me of a wonderful hymn:

> *Eternal Light! Eternal Light!*
> *How pure the soul must be*
> *When, placed within Thy searching sight,*
> *It shrinks not, but with calm delight*
> *Can live and look on Thee.*

A sinner could not look at God. There is a holiness without which no man could see the Lord. Blessed are the pure. Now, there are two things in this beatitude regarding our religion. First of all, it is a religion of the heart. Let us get that quite clear. It is not something that we put on outside – that is the whited sepulchre – it is something that begins within. After all, sin is of the heart. "As a man thinketh in his heart, so is he." The heart is the source of dirt. What makes a man dirty? It is not what he puts into his mouth but what proceeds from his heart – all evil thoughts, fornications, and adulteries come out of a man's heart.

After all, the heart is the part of us which God will judge – for men look at the outward appearance. The Lord does not see as man sees; the Lord looks on the heart. It is a heart that first responds to the gospel. If you believe in your heart and confess with your mouth you will be saved. It is in the heart that true worship takes place. "These people draw near to me with their mouth, and honour me with their lips, but their heart is far from me." Now we have changed the meaning of the word "heart". It does not mean, of course, the physical organ which pumps blood. It does not mean the seat of the emotions in the Bible – it has come to mean that with us.

The word "heart" in the Bible means quite simply the inside of a man. It would cover what we call heart, mind, and will. Our emotions, our thoughts, and our motives. It means the inside and we use the word sometimes like this when we say, "Now the heart of the problem." We mean the real inside of it – that is the true meaning of heart in the scripture. Not your emotions but the real inside of you.

The second thing that this tells us about religion is that it is not only a religion of the heart, it is a religion of purity. Clean heart. I discern a kind of progression in scripture here – the law in Leviticus seems to place tremendous emphasis on clean hands. Then in the Psalms we read: "Who shall ascend the hill of the Lord? He that has clean hands and a pure heart." Then we come through to the gospel and Jesus says, "Blessed are the pure in heart," and he was criticised because he let his disciples eat with unclean hands. There is a kind of progression here and the heart of it is a clean heart. Now, what does a clean heart mean?

First, it means a heart that is free from mixed motives, a heart that is single, that is not double-minded, that is not half-hearted but has a pure motive, that desires God for his own sake. The second thing is it means a heart that is free from dirty desires that spoil even the holiest thing we do. Both people will see God. I remember a man who was as rough a man as I have ever met before he knew Christ. He never looked at nature; he always saw nature through the steamy window of a pub parlour. Yet I went to walk with him in County Durham after his conversion and you know, every blade of grass, every cloud in the sky, every leaf on the tree spoke to him of God. He could see God everywhere. A man who had never bothered to look at nature before, he was now pure in heart.

There was a little boy who said to his daddy, "Daddy, have you ever seen God?" His daddy said, "Now don't trouble me with questions like that, off you go away and play." So, he went out into the streets and he saw a man coming down the road with a dog collar on. He went up to him and he said, "Have you ever seen God?" "Well now, that's a big question from a little boy. I'll tell you when you're a bit older." So, he went on down and found a dear saint sitting by a river and he said to this dear old man, "Have you ever seen God?" The old man lifted his eyes and he looked around and then he looked down into the little boy's face and he said, "Sometimes lad, I think I see nothing else." Blessed are the pure in heart, for they shall see God and one day they will have a vision of God direct, face to face, no longer through a mirror obscurely but then face to face; no longer through the mirror of the Bible, the mirror of nature, the mirror of saints, but face to face. This beatitude seems to suggest what we see then will be determined by how holy we have been here. There seems to be some suggestion that we will see more of God if we have been pure in heart.

So, we move on to number seven: blessed are the peacemakers. There is a tremendous need for peace in the world, which I do not need to underline – international peace. Do you know that a historian has worked out that we have only had three hundred years of peace in the last four thousand years? Isn't that an amazing figure? Britain has been engaged in numerous wars through history – minor and major, cold and hot. Racial peace, industrial peace, ecclesiastical peace, domestic peace – well over a hundred thousand divorces a year – personal peace. What H. G. Wells said of Mr Polly is true of most of us: "he was not so much a human being as a civil war". Peace. It does not say blessed are the placid. I find some people are always at peace because they have got a lovely placid temperament. How I envy them. They seem to just sail through life so delightfully.

It is not blessed are the placid, nor is it blessed are the popular where everybody is your friend. Nor is it blessed is the pacifist – I do not think that is going deep enough into this beatitude. Nor is it blessed are the politicians, though they desperately try to make peace. Nor is it blessed are the peace-lovers who like peace at any price. It is "blessed are the peacemakers" and that may mean that you are regarded as precisely the opposite. Jeremiah was when the false prophets cried, "Peace, peace." Jeremiah said, "There is no peace." Isaiah said, "There's no peace for the wicked." Jesus said, "I came not to bring peace but a sword." The peacemakers will often be thought of as just the opposite. These that have turned the world upside down have come hither also. Of course, they were quite wrong – they were telling the world right way up. If you are living upside down and somebody comes along who is the right way up, Einstein's theory of relativity means that you regard them as turning you upside down and this is how peacemakers are often regarded.

Who then are the peacemakers? They are not those who keep fighters apart and enable them to live in peaceful coexistence. They are those who come with a ministry of reconciliation and base it upon atonement. Therefore, the first peacemakers are the evangelists. Wherever a man pleads with men on behalf of God to be reconciled to him through Christ there is a peacemaker. He may not be regarded as that but he is a peacemaker. Blessed are the evangelists, the peacemakers of the world. This is not only those who announce the peace that the blood of his cross has bought. The pastors are peacemakers, for not only is peace needed for there to be reconciliation between God and man but there needs to be reconciliation between man and man, and between Christian and fellow Christian, and some Christians have a unique ministry of peacemaking in this regard. After all, such people will be recognised as sons of the God of peace.

And now the final one. One of the rarely praised virtues of Jesus is his honesty. He is absolutely honest. He did not tell people it was a bed of roses, he said it would be a crown of thorns. He did not offer people a cushion by the cross. He did not call them to a picnic but to a battle. I am very disturbed both by preachers and testimonies that imply the opposite.

I have had more trouble since I became a Christian than I ever had before and so have you. Christ said, "In the world you will have tribulation." The word "tribulation" comes from tribulum, which was the threshing sledge. You will go under; you will be refreshed in life and Jesus was honest. He did not promise an easy life, so never preach that if you come to Christ your troubles will be over. That is a lie anyway. I heard a testimony at a youth rally from a girl who had been converted one month. She said, "I've been wonderfully happy for a month, all my problems have been solved, all my troubles are over." I felt like saying, "Just you wait sister; just you wait," but she had been led to believe by the one who led her to Christ that that is what she ought to expect, but Jesus never said that. He said, "If you follow me, you'll be hated because I am. If you follow me, you'll have to carry a cross every day. If you follow me, you'll be persecuted. If you follow me, you'll have a tough time." He promised them a cross before he promised them a crown.

Jesus was absolutely honest with would-be disciples that if they followed him they might have nowhere to lay their head. "If you follow me, you'll have to give up everything, you'll have to get rid of your money, you rich young man." He was honest and here he says, "You'll be persecuted." Now, some of us are persecuted because we are offensive. We have got to be honest here because we have got the wrong way of doing and saying things. There is no blessedness in that. Even if you are a saint, you will be persecuted for two reasons. Firstly, because you are a peacemaker and people do not like peacemakers. Secondly, because of beatitudes one to seven: whoever would live a godly life in Christ Jesus will be persecuted because they are different. As a follower of Jesus, you are the conscience of mankind; you are the different person who disturbs.

Your standards are so much higher, and because they are in a state of enmity against God, they will have the same enmity against God's people. This explains other than this, the anti-Semitism which has been the characteristic of every race, including the British, where Jews have settled. It is because men are in rebellion against God, and the nearer you are to God, the nearer you share in that antagonism. But Jesus says, "Isn't it wonderful to be persecuted?" On the title page of John Bunyan's autobiography this text is written: "all who desire to live godly in Christ Jesus will suffer persecution". Did that man understand that? But it is a blessed state. Oh, how happy when you are persecuted, when people gossip about you, when they speak against you. Now, is that true? Yes, it is. First of all, it is because it is reassuring you that you belong to God. There are two things that prove to you that you are one of God's people. First, that you love the brethren and second, that the world hates you – it is reassuring.

Secondly, it is refining. The church is never so strong as when it is persecuted – and a Christian is never so near the Lord. A pastor in either Tibet or Nepal was imprisoned along with seven of his baptised converts. There was a prayer meeting in an Indian church for them in prison. One after another prayed, "Lord, keep them safe. Lord, set them free from prison. Lord, bring them back to us." As they prayed around the circle, they came to a dear Indian woman who said, "Lord, why did you give them the privilege of going to prison for you and not us? Why can't we suffer for you?" The whole prayer meeting changed. She was the first person in that prayer meeting who regarded persecution as a blessed experience and the others felt a little embarrassed at their prayers. So, this beatitude is not only reassuring, it is refining – it is rewarding. There is a special crown for the martyrs.

You spend your future with those who suffered before you – the prophets – and this beatitude came true in both parts from the very beginning of Acts, in which the disciples suffered and rejoiced that they were worthy to suffer for his name.

Finally, we come to verse thirteen – the influence of this kind of character is described as salt. The last beatitude said what the world will do to us. Now, Jesus tells us what we will do to the world: we shall be salt. Now, I have heard many sermons on this. I have preached a few but I have usually got the meaning a little wrong. I used to think it was a nice flavour that salt gives to anything else but that is not what Jesus meant. Then I would talk about salt being a preservative, but that is not what Jesus meant. Elsewhere Jesus described the two things he had in mind. He said, "If the salt loses its flavour it is thenceforth good neither for the dunghill nor the field." The dunghill was of course the ordinary backyard primitive sanitation of those days. It was the earth closet, and salt was used as the disinfectant on the dunghill to stop infections spreading. The other use, because the salt contained part ash and other helpful elements, scraped as it was from the shores of the Dead Sea, was of a fertiliser in the field to make things grow in the barren soil.

These are the two functions of salt in our Lord's mind. To discourage the growth of evil and dangerous things and to encourage the growth of good things; to act as a disinfectant and a fertiliser, that is what this kind of character outlined in the beatitudes will do. That is a lovely thought but the Christian is the disinfectant and the fertiliser is this dirty and barren world – discouraging evil things from spreading and encouraging good things to grow and it does not take a lot of salt to have an influence. Salt influences out of all proportion to its quantity but in proportion to its quality and therefore it must not lose its flavour. A little bit of a scientist, I used to wonder how can salt (NaCl) lose its flavour? It is chemically impossible. Now I know that Jesus was right after all. It loses its flavour not by changing its substance but by being adulterated by other substances. A man who wanted to make money on the market would mix a bit of sand in with his salt and sell it at the same price. The more he mixed in of other things, the more worthless it became. A housewife would buy some, she would taste it, she would realise it was adulterated and since she would throw it out the front door it would be trodden under the feet of men. Adulterated salt is of no use.

The worldly Christian is of no use to the world. He neither acts as a disinfectant nor a fertiliser and even men despise and reject a worldly Christian whose character is not different. I have noticed this: a Christian who is really different will be persecuted by others and respected by them and when they are in trouble, it is to the Christian who is different that they will go. They despise the Christian who tries to be worldly. So, salt is out of proportion to its quantity but in proportion to its quality in its influence on the world.

8
REWARDS

Matthew Chapter 5:1–13 continued

At 5:12 in this passage we have a key phrase: "A great reward is kept for you in heaven". Reward is a moral incentive. It is a totally naïve, idealistic view of human nature to think that we will ever arrive at this stage on earth where we do good simply in order to do good. It is naïve to expect people to serve simply in order to serve. Fallen human nature demands incentive and some kind of push, but redeemed human nature also needs the same incentive. All talk of serving God without any thought of reward is being more pious than Jesus himself, who for the joy that was set before him, endured the cross and despised the shame.

When I realised that reward for Christian service is something God is offering us, and looked at that in the Bible, I was astonished. The New Testament is packed with the concept of incentive in the form of reward. So, I make no apology for this. God does not expect us to be "good for nothing". Therefore, in his grace and mercy he has given us some profound teaching about reward. This world is based on the fact of recompense; on the fact of punishment for wrongdoing and reward for doing right. Every parent knows that this is how you will train your children – by punishing wrongdoing and by rewarding right doing. God is a Father training us as his children. Let us tackle a few questions around this thing called "reward".

First: who gives it? There is a simple, stark choice with which Jesus presents us as Christians: you must choose in life who you expect to be rewarded by. You can choose between people and God; you cannot choose both. You either live for the rewards that people will give you or you live for the rewards that God will give you, and which you choose will determine your behaviour.

People praise those who seek human reward – that is what they are after. They may get that, but there is no reward in heaven for them. But you, when you pray, get by yourself; shut the door, pray in secret and the Father, who sees in secret what no man sees, rewards openly. When you give, don't let your right hand know what your left hand is doing. Look for your rewards from God. That does not mean you will get no recognition from men; it is lovely when somebody who has been working for God gets recognised by people. Sometimes the reward and recognition may come at a human level; sometimes it may not. It does not matter whether it does or not.

In some churches, there is a service for the Lord which is not seen by the rest of the fellowship and may never get a vote of thanks at a church meeting. They are in a stronger position for the rewards of heaven than those of us who do things in the public eye, where the pressure is on to seek human recognition. Give thanks to God if he has called you to a secret task. Someone used to fill up six or seven hundred glasses with wine every time we had communion in one church where I ministered. I have thought about that and the washing up of all those little glasses, and the fact that God sees what is done in secret. Here is the first question: Who are you expecting to get a reward from? If you are looking to people then sooner or later in church work you will be insulted, you will be offended, you will be upset, you will be overlooked, and then you will stomp out in disgust if you are looking for human reward. But if you are looking for your reward from God, you will rejoice that nobody knows about what you have done. You will rejoice that the Father's eye is upon you: he is the God who rewards us. I want to go further than that and say that God is a God of such grace that unlike rewards from people, his rewards go way beyond anything we deserve.

I think of the parable of the labourers in the vineyard, which in modern terms we might call the parable of the wage differentials. The man who had worked all day and the man who had only worked the last hour in the vineyard were rewarded. Most got far more than what was a just reward for their work. Jesus showed us that this is how God operates; that is the Kingdom of heaven. If you are working for a reward in heaven, you will get far more than you deserve.

The next question is: Why does God need to offer me rewards? Why do I need an incentive? There are at least four reasons given in the scriptures why I need an incentive. First, I need an incentive *to look for God in the first place*. The Bible promises a reward to those who do. Whoever would come to God, says the author of Hebrews, must first believe that he exists. That is the first basic step if you are going to find God. The second is that you must believe that he rewards those who seek him. Ask, and you will have it given to you. Knock, and you will have it opened. Seek, and you will find.

The second reason I need an incentive is *to be sanctified by God*. It is the easiest thing once you become a Christian to settle down and be satisfied with where you have got to, but I need an incentive. I am in the running; I am in a race. There is a prize offered to me – to forget the things that are behind and press on toward the goal, for the prize is the high calling of God in Christ Jesus; to press on and seek that holiness without which no one can see the Lord. Do you realise that the Beatitudes are just one statement of prize after prize that is waiting for those who are poor in spirit, for those who hunger and thirst, for those who are pure in heart, for those who are reviled? Every single beatitude is simply a statement of a reward waiting for holiness. Great is your reward in heaven. It awaits those who reach the winning post – they even knew this in the days of the Old Testament. David said, "In keeping of your commands, there is great reward" – "great reward" is the same phrase.

The third reason I need the incentive of a reward is to *serve the Lord with diligence,* to keep at it, not to retire. In the Christian life there is no retirement. Paul, at the end of his life, says: "I've run the full course. I've kept at it and there's a prize waiting for me." You get a sense that he is just reaching the finishing line: "I have finished the course and now I am just waiting for the crown that is laid up for me." What an incentive to holiness and to serving the Lord. In Colossians 3:23 we are told: "Whatever you do, work at it with all your heart, as though you are working for the Lord and not for men. Remember that the Lord will give you as a reward what he has kept for his people; for Christ is the real master you serve."

It is not just your Christian service that God is interested in rewarding; it is your daily work. So, you can be going for that reward tomorrow morning in the office, or the shop, or the factory, or the kitchen. Is that not exciting?

The fourth thing I need the incentive of a reward for is to *suffer for the Lord's sake*. There are increasing indications that we are going to suffer as a church in this country. God is beginning to bless us; he is beginning to build up his Body in a new way. He is pouring out his Spirit. We are now not bothered about trying to get the denominations together but about getting Christians together. If God is doing this, and he is doing it in other countries too, why is he doing it? He is getting us ready for tougher times, mobilising his people for battle so they will stand shoulder to shoulder. If you are going to suffer you will need a reward for your suffering. Even Jesus needed that reward and for the joy set before him, as I have said, he went through the cross, but the joy was set before him. You can put up with a lot if you can look forward. A mother going through the pains of child labour is looking forward to the joy of holding the baby in her hands and the pain is lost in the joy.

Paul uses an accounting term: "I reckon up that the sufferings of this present time are not worth comparing with the glory that is going to be revealed." The eternal perspective enables people to go for the martyr's crown, for the joy set before them. In the letters to the seven churches of Asia in the book of Revelation, every one of them finishes with the offer of a reward to him who overcomes: I will give them a new name; I will put them on the throne beside me. The Lord is offering rewards.

The next question is: When? Do we get our rewards in this world or the next? I am thrilled to be able to tell you: both. One reward is rest. That does not mean sitting in an armchair for all eternity. It means the kind of retirement in which you can just do what you enjoy doing. That is real rest.

How many people in a humdrum job are just waiting for the day when they can build a little bungalow somewhere and do what they enjoy doing? But the New Testament teaches that part of your reward is a house eternal in the heavens, a city with foundations. Abraham looked for that reward; that was what he was looking for – a city. That is why he was content to live in a tent from eighty years of age until his death. His reward was a mansion up above.

Another part of your reward is *rejoicing*. "Well done, good and faithful servant. Enter into the joy of your Lord." I tell you, heaven is going to bring you real, deep happiness. Lasting happiness is part of the reward that only Jesus can give.

Next: *radiance*. You are going to shine like stars in heaven. When you look at the sky, notice that the stars are different in brightness – and the saints in glory are going to vary in their brightness. How bright do you want to be? Just a tiny little flickering light or would you like to shine like one of the strong stars that pierce the gloom? In the book of Daniel, you come to the following phrase: "You shall shine like stars in heaven". The word "glory" is used more than any other in connection with the reward.

There it is: *renown; prestige,* crowns. Paul again and again takes the world of athletics and says: "they do it for a fading crown". In those days, they did not get a metal shield, they got a wreath of laurel leaves, which was placed by the emperor on their head. A man who could walk down the street with the laurel crown on his head was considered the greatest. But laurel leaves do not last very long and that faded so quickly.

Paul sees all these people striving – and when they get that, where do they go from there? It goes, but we are working for an unfading crown. I know that many persecuted brethren are going to be wearing crowns in glory. There are crowns for martyrs, crowns for faithful servants; crowns for those who are faithful unto death. I cringe when I hear that word used at a funeral of someone who has died naturally. It is not those who are faithful until death; it is those who are faithful to the point of dying for Christ – there is a special crown for them.

Finally, there is royalty: "You shall reign with me"; "You will sit on thrones with me". Royalty, this reward, is variously described in scripture as satisfying, enduring and incorruptible. To serve God faithfully now is to enjoy part of that reward now. You could wear on your tee-shirt, "By Royal appointment" or "OHMS: On His Majesty's Service". Hold your head up high.

Royal service is reward enough – by appointment to the King of kings and the Lord of lords. I tell you, when the Lord calls you into service for the church, he is not asking you to do him a favour; he is doing you a favour. He is putting you in the race; he is putting the reward in front of you. He does not want you ever to say, "Well, I'm getting on, so I'll leave it to the young folk now." There is no discharge in this war. He wants you to get to the end of your days and be able to say, "I have run the race. I have finished the course. Henceforth, there is laid up for me a crown, and not for me only, but for all those who love his appearing."

9
ACTION

Read Matthew Chapter 5:14–48

We now move from the attributes of a disciple to the actions of a disciple – from what we are to what we do. We consider two areas of Christian behaviour or Christian conduct: the social area and the spiritual area. The difference between these two areas is this: our social behaviour should be made as public as possible, but our spiritual behaviour should be made as private as possible. Our purity should be shown to all people; our piety should never be shown to any. Any reversal of these two is an offensive kind of witness. If we parade our piety and keep our purity hidden, then that kind of testimony is far from helpful to the cause of the Kingdom.

We deal first then with our social behaviour – our purity, our standards of morality. Jesus said of us here the same thing which he said of himself: "I am the light of the world"; "You are the light of the world." In the New Testament, light and darkness are moral qualities. God is light and in him is no darkness at all. People do not like the light because they live in darkness and prefer to keep their deeds dark. Essentially then, light is to be placed in as public a place as possible where it can have the maximum influence on others, where it can both expose what is hidden in the darkness and guide those who desire to be guided by the light. This is what we are to do and, in my view, the hardest teaching to follow in the Sermon on the Mount is to first let your light shine before men – by nature we do not want to do that – and, second, to do it in such a way that they give the credit for your standards to your heavenly Father. The light of Christian morality must be held up to the public gaze if it is to be of any help at all to others.

From speaking of the light, Jesus goes on to speak of the law. He has not mentioned the Old Testament, except by indirect quotation and implication, and there may have been those who thought that he was propounding a new religion. So, for the next few verses he describes his attitude to the law of God. There are two heresies which have appeared all the way through church history. One is to set the New Testament over against the Old, and that heresy is as old as Marcion. The other is to say that Christianity has no prohibitions – that we have changed from the negative, "Thou shalt not" to the positive "Thou shalt". Both these positions are over-simplifications and Jesus corrects them in these verses.

First of all, he says the purpose of the law is for it to be fulfilled and not abolished. Now what does the word "fulfil" mean? Some people assume that it means to be "filled full". In other words, to expand and explain. But taking it in its normal usage in Matthew's Gospel it means to be done; to be executed. Something that was spoken about by the Prophet is now translated into an event; the law of God is to be fulfilled; it is to be done. Jesus came, among other things, to get it done – both in himself and in other people. He did not come to abolish it, but to get it done. It is true that he got it done by planting his Spirit within people so that their very love fulfilled the law. He did not do it in the old way by imposing external prohibitions, but he was fulfilling it in getting it done.

Verse 18 includes a double negative and a "truly", which emphasises the verse tremendously, he talks about the permanence of the law and this would earn Jesus the title of "Fundamentalist" today. After all, the "jot" was the smallest vowel and the "tittle" was the point of a consonant. If a preacher says "I believe the Word of God to the smallest vowel and the point of a consonant" he is a fundamentalist, but Jesus made it absolutely clear that he did not come to alter, add to, or subtract from the Word of God – it was there and he came to get it fulfilled. Any interpretation of the next part of the Sermon on the Mount, which suggests that he was correcting and altering the law of God (for example, on divorce) is a sheer contradiction of this verse. Our Lord would have been inconsistent if that had been what he was doing.

Notice that there will be no Bibles in heaven. You see, the Word of God will not pass away until heaven and earth pass away, but we won't need Bibles in heaven when we see God face-to-face and know even as we are known, and understand as fully as he understands us. We are not going to need a Bible then; we have God himself in direct communication – but until the end of the world we do need the Word of God and Jesus was not going to alter that in any way.

There is a perversion which is an interpretation of the Word of God that relaxes the standards of God. One of the most disturbing things about a spate of publications back in the 1960s, particularly in the realm of morality, was a change from the absolute to the relative – saying that a thing is "almost always right" instead of saying it is always right. To drop from a hundred to ninety-nine as your standard is a radical change and we need to be very much aware of this. Jesus tackles in six examples the kind of scriptural interpretation which relaxes the commandments and teaches others so to do. You cannot understand the Sermon on the Mount except against the background of the teaching and practice of the Scribes and the Pharisees – the interpreters of scripture in those days. They were fundamentalists themselves, but their interpretation had the effect of altering the scripture. I have noticed that in most cults and sects a fundamentalist attitude is combined with an interpretation of the Word of God, which alters it in subtle ways. This we are going to see in these six examples.

In v. 20 he says that in the practice of the law we have got to do better than the Scribes and the Pharisees. They have failed to make the grade. Now this is an extraordinary statement, for the Pharisees were outstanding in doing good deeds: they were outstanding in attending worship, they were outstanding in studying scripture, they were outstanding in practising prayer, they were outstanding in self-discipline, they were outstanding in evangelism. They would come from sea and land to make one proselyte. Yet Jesus says: Unless you can do better than that in keeping the law of God you will not reach the Kingdom. Now before you can exceed, you must equal, and that must have been a shattering statement. What he is hinting at, as he will show, is this: all of this that they achieved was outward rather than inward – the letter rather than the spirit – and therefore it resulted in a self-centred righteousness instead of a divine righteousness. He is going to illustrate that in six different ways, to which we now turn.

Before we look at these six ways, may I underline for you that Jesus said, "You have heard that it was said...." The two key words are "heard" and "said". He is not referring to the Old Testament but to the oral interpretation and tradition of the Scribes and the Pharisees. If Jesus quoted the Bible he said, "Have you never read what was written?" But here it is talking about what was heard and what was said. In other words, he is dealing with the fallacies of second-hand Bible study. Who has not ascribed to their own interpretation the infallibility that belongs only to the inspired Word? Now, may I say that all of us are guilty of this kind of confusion. The easiest form in which this happens is if you get a Bible, which includes between the lines of the Word of God the comments of men. It is so easy then to take that person's or that committee's interpretation as the infallible Word of God and to fail to distinguish between what God said and what man said about what God said. The use of Bible reading notes can be a similar delusion or snare. I was interested to learn that in the early days of the Scripture Union there were no notes – you had to read the Bible by itself. Do not get me wrong, Bible study notes can be a tremendous help, but I advise people: as soon as you can do without them, do without them. When you can walk, throw the crutch away and see how you manage.

Now, that may sound like extraordinary advice, but it is because the subtle temptation when you are using notes is to spend far more time on the notes than on the Bible. The best sort of notes are those that do not spoon-feed and do not give it all, but encourage the person to go back to the Word and get it for themselves. This is why I have stood on the principle of the right and duty of private interpretation of the Word. My purpose in expounding the scriptures is to encourage people to go and read them for themselves – not to accept my interpretation. No interpretation is infallible, but if it encourages you either in hearing the Word expounded or in reading Bible study notes to go back to your Bible and regard that as the main source of your convictions, then that is the whole object of the exercise. Our whole aim is to get people into the Word, where there they may find the Word of God as it actually is. All of us, I am afraid, read back into scripture what is not there.

Our Lord's interpretation of scripture is set over against the scribal interpretation of scripture. This is not the New Testament correcting the Old. This is not Christ correcting his Father's laws. This is his interpretation as against the Scribes', and the difference was that his carried the authority of God and theirs did not. So, we address the examples. He gives two examples of where their interpretation was far too narrow and limited – it was the letter and not the spirit. There is a danger in being a "Letteralist". The first example is murder and their addition of the words "liable to judgment", which do not occur in the Old Testament, reduced the "sin" to "a crime", and "the court before which you were responsible for it" to "a human court". In other words, it limited that commandment in its scope to the crime of murder, and the possibility of execution by a human judge, whereas the obvious intention of the commandment was very much broader than that – it was to cover many other things.

You can kill in thought and in word. You do not have to stick a knife in someone's back to be a murderer in God's sight. God hates all forms of murder, whether in thought or word or deed. The commandment is intended to say just that to us, and the "Letteralist" approach limits it to crime.

One of the things that I find most difficult today is to get across to people the difference between sin, crime and vice. Vice is what you do against yourself. Crime is what you do against others. Sin is what you do against God. That is a very broad distinction but I think it holds. I may have no vices and no crimes in my life, but that does not mean I am not a sinner. Hollywood has got these three terms dreadfully confused. The commandment "Thou shalt not kill" was dealing with sin, not with crime. It was meant to convey to us the thought of God about our relationships with other people, and anger breaks that command. Wishing somebody dead (which is the heart of temper) is murder. It is the wrong, sinful attitude. Our Lord says that makes you just as liable.

Arrogance is another. "Raca" is onomatopoeic, a spitting word. It is a word of abuse or contempt, like "nitwit" or "rabble" directed at people, and that is murder. It might not be a knife, it might just be spit. They spat on Jesus before they crucified him. They were murdering him then. It was an act of contempt to spit at him. Even if you are using a rather ineffective weapon, in practice it is murder. Abuse is yet a third way of breaking this. The word literally is "moron". To call somebody a moron is to put them beyond redemption, beyond appeal; to condemn them. Now, our Lord used the word "moron", but frankly only God has a right to use it, because only God knows who really is one. Jesus once said, "A man who lives entirely for money, who pulls down his barns and builds greater, and thinks of nothing else is a moron." Jesus did say that, and he called two other people morons. But he taught that when you do that, without the knowledge which God has, when you take it upon yourself to dismiss someone as an utter moron, you are virtually killing them in thought. Now this, of course, is a very high standard. It goes to the spirit of the law rather than just the letter and it means quite frankly, that there are many more murderers around than we usually realise.

There is within many of our hearts the seed of this sin. Therefore, on the positive side: settle out of church and out of court. Go out of your way to be in a right relationship with people and not a wrong one. I heard of a Methodist missionary in the South Sea Islands of the Pacific who was holding a communion service and they were coming forward to the front to kneel down to receive the bread and the wine. Then as one man knelt down he began to shake. His face was filled with rage and he jumped up and ran out of the church. A minute later he came back in, calm, and knelt down and took the bread and the wine. The missionary asked him after the service, "What on earth went wrong?"

He replied, "Well, I'm just visiting this church but when I knelt down, I found myself kneeling next to the man who ate my father. I was so angry with him that I realised I just couldn't stay for communion and I ran out, but as I ran out of the door I saw a picture in the sky of Christ on his cross, and Christ was saying, 'But you did this to me.'"

He said, "So I dealt with it outside the church and came back in and knelt down next to him."

That is very practical. Before a man eats of that bread or drinks of that cup let him examine himself. Settle out of court too, for once the sentence has been passed it is too late to try to put a situation right. Put the thing right. Our Lord always matched a negative injunction with a positive one. The negative: "Don't be angry, arrogant or abusive"; the positive: "Settle out of church and out of court."

The second example is the matter of adultery. Now sex is prominent in our society, in our nature, and in our Bible. It is the most realistic book and it says a great deal about this. And so it needs to, for this is a vital part of life. God has two simple standards regarding this matter. From these two standards, every other injunction may be deduced: absolute chastity outside marriage; absolute fidelity inside marriage. That is the simple teaching of the Word of God which our Lord endorsed and which Moses taught. "Thou shalt not commit adultery" being concerned with the second of those standards. Both were being relaxed by the Pharisees, by being quoted out of context, and the devil loves to quote the Bible out of context.

I notice, first of all, that in both these two examples Jesus speaks to the men. Ancient society blamed the women, as modern society tends to do. We say far more about loose women on the streets than the men who are their clients, but if there were no clients there would be no women there. Our Lord put the responsibility for sexual standards of behaviour on the men and he spoke to the men. Now this was radical and revolutionary, and see what he says – the context of the seventh commandment – "Thou shalt not commit adultery" is the tenth Commandment, namely "Thou shalt not covet thy neighbour's wife." The interesting thing is the Pharisees never talked about the tenth one. Why not? Because they could not keep it. Paul of Tarsus said this: "As touching the law, blameless." Now that was external, but the one Commandment that he could never keep was the tenth: "Thou shalt not covet". He tells us that in Romans 7. It is not just what we do, it is what we covet and what we desire. Our Lord seeks to distinguish lust from love. He is teaching that you need not climb into someone else's bed to break this commandment, you can do it in look and in thought as well as in deed.

Do you remember the account of the time when they brought to him the woman taken in adultery? I may be wrong here, but I think when he said "He that is without sin", he did not mean sin generally, because that would be a foregone conclusion. He meant "whoever is clean in this matter", and you notice it was the eldest men who went first. The youngest are more brash and more willing to justify themselves, but those who know – the eldest – went out, even to the youngest. What a searching and challenging experience. That this is needed is of course obvious from the Bible itself – the lust of the eyes goes with the lust of the flesh. The case of David and Bathsheba is enough warning to us about this very matter. It was Job who said to the Lord, "I've set a watch on my eyes, lest I look at a maiden." Now that doesn't mean you are never to look at a girl. Bishop Taylor Smith is our outstanding example here. He said he enjoyed looking at a pretty girl but he turned his enjoyment into a prayer. He thanked God for making someone so beautiful and he prayed that she would be given extra strength for the extra temptations that she would have to face. To the pure all things are pure, and he could look at a pretty girl like that. Jesus knew the dangers and he taught that you break this commandment by doing it in look and thought.

Now from two commandments which were interpreted in too limited a way by the scribes, he turns to two things that were interpreted in too broad a way by their additions, alterations, and interpretation. You can either make the scripture too narrow or you can make it too broad. We can get so legalistic that we miss the spirit and intention of a particular injunction – I am not free of it, and neither are you.

One area that was being handled by some in too broad a way was divorce. Moses did say that if you divorce your wife, give her a Bill of Divorcement. In other words, do it legally; do it properly. But this was said in a particular context. It did not say you can divorce your wife for anything provided you do it properly, but that was what the Jews had begun to think. By the time of our Lord's earthly ministry, one more liberal school of Jews was arguing that you could divorce your wife for burning the breakfast, or for talking to a man in the street, or for having too loud a voice, or for putting too much salt in the soup, or for being quarrelsome. It may sound incredible, but that is why they asked Jesus whether a man can divorce his wife for every cause. They were already broadening it out. How had they done this? Let us go back to Moses. Our Lord agrees with Moses. Deuteronomy 24 states that if a man marries someone and finds right at the beginning that there is an unseemly thing in her then he must write out a Bill of Divorcement. This nearly happened to our Lord's own mother. Joseph was betrothed to Mary and he found her with child and being a just man he resolved to divorce her privately. Now, that was in accordance with the Mosaic law. The unseemly thing was obviously something which prevented that woman from coming as a pure virgin to begin a one-flesh relationship with her man. You notice it referred to something that happened before the marriage, not something that happened afterwards, but which was only discovered at the beginning of the marriage. He had to produce proofs to the relatives of this unseemly thing.

Now, our Lord makes only one exception to his divorce position and it is the exception which Moses made. It is the exception of something that happened before marriage. The biblical evidence is very clear. There is not a single case of fornication and adultery ever being mixed, confused, or interchanged. As many Bible Dictionaries now admit, the word used refers to premarital intercourse and to nothing else. Therefore, there is no ground of divorce in Christian thinking for anything that happens after marriage.

Jesus taught that the original intention is that the man and the woman leave their families and become one flesh and cleave to one another. That is the intention. The only exception is where one of them is not really in a fit condition to do this, for they have already had a one-flesh relation with someone else. Where that is discovered then the marriage does not get off to a right start, and this was a concession to the hardness of the human heart, which finds that sort of thing difficult to forgive and forget. Jesus made the concession as Moses made the concession, but the point is this: he is teaching that in arguing about the exception, you have made the exception the rule.

If I focused on the exception I would fall into the same trap as the Pharisees. The rule is the thing, not the exception, and the rule is absolute fidelity inside marriage. It is a permanent state of one man with one woman – monogamy. That is the principle, and therefore remarriage is adultery and seventy-five per cent of the divorcees of this country remarry. It is possible, of course, to get a separation without going the whole way in a divorce, but most divorces are for remarriage and our Lord did set a standard. It is a difficult standard, a hard standard, just as is the standard of absolute chastity outside marriage. The question is: Are we to lower God's standards to human nature? Or are we, by God's grace, to raise human nature to God's standards? That is the final issue before us.

The next example is much the same thing – an exception became a rule by faulty interpretation. These days, this is less relevant to our society because swearing in this sense is not too common. I know the ordinary kind of swearing. I have worked among working men. I worked with a man who had the dubious reputation of being able to swear longer than anyone else without repeating himself, and I know the atmosphere with which many have to work, but that is not the kind of swearing mentioned here. Here is the thought: here Jesus is thinking of the swearing which is the use of an oath to make a man speak the truth.

It is a recognition of the fact that it is not easy for us always to be truthful and to speak the truth, the whole truth, and nothing but the truth. In certain circumstances it is absolutely vital that a person speaks the truth, and one way of doing that is to bring the fear of God into his heart by making him swear by God to tell the truth, the whole truth and nothing but the truth, and overcome certain other motives by making the fear of God the main motive. Mind you, where the fear of God is absent there is absolutely no point in making someone swear such an oath and I cannot help feeling that handing a Bible to a man in the witness box in a court in this country has become an absolute formality because there is not the general fear of God, which an oath exploits to get the truth. But where you have got people who believe in God, as in the Jewish nation, then they could use oaths, and did. One of the Ten Commandments forbade them ever to take the name of God in vain.

Now from that very limited used of oaths the scribal interpretation had made swearing a very common everyday thing because they had developed a casuistry that said: "As long as you don't use the name of God, it's alright. You can swear by heaven, you can swear by earth, you can swear by your head – all sorts of things." You know, common or garden swearing started that way. The word "bloody" is a shortened form of "By our Lady" as you may have realised. It is simply an oath which got into everyday speech and something sacred became something profane, and most profanity deals with the two sacred areas of life – sex and religion – and profanes the sacred.

That is what happens when oath taking becomes frivolous and common. Jesus is teaching that whatever oath you use, God is in the situation; if you swear by your hair, you cannot alter that; if you swear by the earth, it is God's footstool. If you swear by heaven, that is true, you are swearing by God's dwelling place. In other words, you cannot speak without God being involved in what you say, and the real intention is that all your speech should be in the presence of God, and therefore you should be a person of integrity. When you say yes, it should be the sort of yes that knows God is listening. When you say no, it should be that integrity of speech that knows that for every idle word men

Matthew Chapter 5:14-48

will be judged on the Day of Judgment. Our speech betrays us.

Now, there are many ways, of course, of being dishonest. Exaggeration is a very common one in Christian circles, about the results of a Crusade; about blessing on a particular occasion. It is very easy to try to magnify the Lord by exaggerating the extent of our experience of his glory. There is also the dishonesty of remaining silent and not saying what should be said. There are many ways of doing this, but the intention of the scripture is that your speech should be such as to reflect your awareness of the presence of God at every point.

It is said of George Fox (who I am afraid carried this to illogical conclusions by refusing to take an oath even in court) that when he said "Verily" it meant, "verily", and there was no changing George Fox. That should be our integrity of speech. You do not need to be saying all the time, "Honestly, honestly...." Some people who are always saying that make you wonder very much whether you can take seriously anything that they say, and if they have to keep saying "honestly", you wonder what they mean when they leave it out.

There are occasions when an oath is right. Jesus himself, on occasion, was put on oath and put himself on oaths. So did Paul. Paul would swear by God or say, "Before God I lie not." There are times when something of such crucial importance needs to be said that you can say your, "Verily, verily" – you can say more than "Yes" and "No". But that is the exception and the general rule is this: I see nothing in this verse as the Essenes and the Quakers did, to forbid oath taking in a court or on certain occasions. This is dealing with everyday conversation.

Now we come to two further examples, which were interpreted in too harsh a manner. Harshness again is a besetting sin of Christians. It was said of one great expositor of the Word that he had so much love for the Lord that he hadn't much left for people. Do you know what I mean? We can be hard in our rigid interpretation, in our logical deductions – so hard that we escape the real import of the Word of God. The first is the matter of vengeance, which must be properly applied.

The one thing we need to remember is this: "Vengeance belongs to me," says the Lord, "I will repay." To take from God the responsibility of vengeance and exercise it personally is too harsh an interpretation. Moses three times said, "An eye for an eye and a tooth for a tooth." But look at the context. First, it was said once when there was an injury to an unborn child because of an assault on the pregnant mother – a very serious crime indeed. The second time, it was for the deliberate disfigurement of a neighbour, and the third time it was for perjury in a court that caused an injustice to another. Those are three very serious crimes. This was not a general principle; it was only in those three cases.

Furthermore, it ensured that there was a strong deterrent for the serious crime of injuring an unborn child, deliberately disfiguring your neighbour, and causing an injustice to someone else by perverting the legal process. Moreover, this *lex talionis* (the oldest human law in existence) limits the amount of retribution in strict proportion and is there for an expression of justice, not a barbaric thing. The most important thing is that in the Old Testament "an eye for an eye and a tooth for a tooth" was a responsibility that had to be placed in the hands of the judges – the legal authorities, and never in the hands of the individual. But when the scribes interpreted this verse, they said it gave anyone full permission to give him a black eye when he gave you one, and this was an utter perversion. It justified private revenge, and it led to the conception of the Jew which appears in Shylock with his pound of flesh in *The Merchant of Venice*.

I have some wonderful Christian friends who would disagree, but I don't think our Lord was dealing with the question of public and political pacifism. He was dealing with personal revenge. The question of pacifism must be settled on other scriptures, Romans 13 among them, but it is not dealt with here. He is not saying we

Matthew Chapter 5:14–48

must not apply justice, as Tolstoy thought he was saying and as Gandhi thought he was saying.

Nor is he cultivating indifference to social injustice. Some have thought that "Resist not evil" meant that you must not tackle social injustice. That again is a perversion. What was his meaning? He gives four examples to show it: If you are injured – no revenge; if you suffer injustice – no rights; if you personally are insulted and suffer indignity – no reputation, and if you are the victim of importunity – no return. These are four examples of personal dealings.

The second is injustice – if somebody takes something from you that is a luxury, give them something that is your necessity. You can do without a coat but you cannot do without a cloak in the Middle East. The coat is a luxury, it is the underwear. The cloak is what you sleep in. You have got to have a cloak, which is why Amos and the Old Testament criticised those who took cloaks from the poor. Have you ever heard the cynical proverb "Where there's a Will there's relatives"? More families break up over that than perhaps anything else, but Jesus is teaching that when that happens – when they take something from you by law – let them have something more. "If anyone compels you to go one mile...." Now remember that this was an occupied territory and a Roman soldier had the right to lay the flat blade of his spear on anyone's shoulder and compel them to carry his baggage a statutory thousand paces. In an occupied territory it was with great reluctance that Jews submitted to this indignity of having to collaborate with the enemy. Jesus said, "Go a second mile." As somebody has delightfully commented: "The first mile is rendering to Caesar the things that are Caesar's, and the second mile is rendering to God the things that are God's." Going the second mile – you notice the positive again. If somebody hits you on the cheek, turn. If somebody takes your coat, let him have your cloak. If somebody compels you to go one mile, go two miles. Every time it is a positive injunction.

The next is: "If a beggar comes to you, give him what he asks." Don't expect it back again. I remember having supper once with Toyohiko Kagawa, that great Japanese Christian. I remember him saying, "Why should the devil have all the world's spendthrifts?" He said this to justify his own reckless generosity with his fortune in the slums of Tokyo.

Jesus is the perfect example of these four injunctions. They struck him on the cheek at his trial, but he did not strike back, he let them do it again. They took his clothes off him, and he was stripped naked. They compelled him – exactly the same word as here – to carry his cross, and one of his last acts was to be generous to a dying thief who begged something from him. He was the perfect example of all of these things. Jesus always practised what he preached.

The final example is that of malice. Here we come to the heart of the Sermon on the Mount, and the most blatant misinterpretation of scripture the Pharisees ever made. Moses had said, "Love your neighbour", and the logical expositors got to work on this phrase. They said that means that if you have got to love some people you have got to have a different attitude to others, and the opposite of "love" is "hate" so there are others you have got to hate, and the opposite of "neighbour" is "enemy" – "neighbour" being regarded as a fellow Jew and a friend, therefore "enemy" is regarded as a Gentile, therefore this really teaches you to hate. It all sounded logical to them.

May I give a modern example? I do so with hesitation, but I think it illustrates what I mean. The fact that the Bible states that God predestines us to our salvation does not logically mean that he predestines others to damnation. Now to our logic it seems to follow, but I wonder if it doesn't lead to too harsh an interpretation. Most theological systems are logical. I find the Bible is not always logical. I cannot reconcile human responsibility and divine predestination, except that I must believe that God has free will as well as that I have a choice to make.

I find that both the Arminian and the Calvinist would love to rewrite the New Testament in certain parts. I am content to leave it at: whoever will may come, and only those whom the Father draws will come. I must beware in my interpretation of being too logical and drawing what, to me are valid deductions that become too harsh.

So, they say: "Love your neighbour" – right; logically that must have a corollary: "Hate your enemy." Jesus taught us that it is not a logical deduction. You should argue from love rather than logic when you interpret a passage like this, and so in the heart of the Sermon on the Mount he tells us to love our enemies.

The Old Testament said that. Proverbs had said: "If your enemy hungers, feed him; if he thirsts, give him water to drink, for you will heap coals of fire on his head." A young Christian in India reading that said, "Oh that's terrific! I'd like to see him scorch." Well, that is not the spirit of the injunction. Actually, it goes back to a practice in Egypt where a penitent sinner would walk to the temple carrying a metal tray of burning charcoal on his head as a sign of penitence. It really means to be penitent, and if you return good for evil that is likely to lead to penitence. A young man went into the barrack rooms. He knelt down to say his prayers by his bunk because there was nowhere else to do so, and two heavy army boots were thrown very hard at his head and caused him much pain. A sergeant sleeping opposite had thrown them. The following morning when the sergeant got out of bed there were his boots back again by his bed, polished. The sergeant said, "I've got to find out what makes a man do that," and he became a Christian as a result.

To return evil for evil is animalistic. To return evil for good is satanic. To return good for good is human, but to return good for evil is divine. Jesus taught that even the worst men, tax collectors, even the people outside God's people, the Gentiles, have a reciprocal decency. That is innate to our humanity, to return good for good. You are arguing from the scriptures if you are human, but you are to be like God – perfect, as he is perfect. Just as he loves all, you are to love all. That is what the word "perfect" there means. It does not mean the absolute perfection. The word means to be complete in your love, and he sends his sun on the good and the evil. God's providential care is over all his creatures. His sun and his rain come to all. We are to love all as he loves all – that is the spirit of "Thou shalt love thy neighbour". Who is my neighbour? Read the story of the Good Samaritan again – anyone in need, whether he is your neighbour or not; whether he lives next door to you or not; whether he is of your race or not.

10
THE CHRISTIAN LIFE

Read Matthew Chapter 6

We now come to the spiritual behaviour of the Christian, and there is a complete change that is required which we have not always found easy to learn. Our purity, our moral standards must be put on a lampstand for everybody to see. We must nail our colours to the mast here. We must let everybody know where we stand on these issues. Chastity, fidelity, charity, the lot – we must let them see, but we must not let them see our religious side; we must keep it quiet. In a word, the secret of true religion is religion in secret. In the background again are the scribes and the Pharisees, I am afraid, and the three examples are the three pillars of Jewish piety: giving, praying and fasting. Our Lord assumed his followers would follow these three pillars and that believers would fast, as well as pray and give. It is strange that fasting has become an optional extra for those ascetic saints who care to do it, but it is as much part of the Christian life as praying and as giving. Christ did not say: *if* you pray; *if* you give, *if* you fast. He said *when* you do.

The first thing is the need for secrecy. The Pharisees took steps to make it public; when they gave, they literally blew a trumpet before them. They rationalised it by saying, "This will encourage others to give." Now, I share this with you not because I want to be critical of a brother, but one of my earliest memories as a small boy was going to a missionary meeting where the chairman at the time of the offering took out his cheque book, told us the amount he was writing on it, put it in the plate and said, "There, I want that to encourage you to do your best." That left an abiding impression on my little mind, but not of the right sort. We can publish subscription lists; we can do it openly. They did it in their way; we can do it in ours. It is still done by us in different, more refined ways.

Fasting – they disfigured their faces. They used plenty of eye shadow and they went out and looked dreadful. People said, "Are you ill?" So, it was paraded. Jesus taught us to take positive steps to keep it quiet, not positive steps to make it public. When you give, don't even let yourself know what you are giving. If you do not think of your gift, you are not likely to display it to others. Can you forget the gifts you give? That is a happy kind of forgetfulness. It was said of one great saint that he always forgot a good turn he did, but he never forgot a good turn he received. That is a lovely memory to have. When you pray, deliberately get away from others if it is at all possible. Edward Wilson used to climb into the crow's nest of the Terra Nova in the Antarctic Expedition, and got right away from them. When fasting, you put your best clothes on and look fit and healthy.

Dare we apply this to ourselves? I'm going to be very direct here and phrase questions that could cause furious discussion. I do not believe it is good advice to tell a Christian who is going into the Forces to kneel down by their bunk on the first night. I do not think that is what our Lord meant when he told us to shine in public. Frankly, if a man is a real Christian the men in the barrack room will find out quickly enough from his moral standards. They do not need to see anything else. The problem of mixed motives when you pray before others is a real problem. I spoke at the opening of a church building, and the end wall, which was on the main street with many people passing by, was a sheer sheet of plain glass. I noticed that for the whole service people were looking in curiously, and I wondered if that was really in the spirit of this. I have worn a dog collar (I did for ten years when I was a Methodist minister) and I began to wonder: Am I in their minds parading my piety? I began to wonder whether that was one of the reasons men changed their conversations when they saw a dog collar.

Should we really wear a badge that tells others we read the Bible? I am throwing out questions to try to show we have got to look at ourselves and not just laugh at those people who blew their trumpets. The one part of our life that ought to be kept strictly secret is our devotional behaviour; our quiet time should be kept quiet. Now that is being very direct but Jesus taught us about the mixed motives that come in when anybody else knows about this, and you know they know – they are a real hindrance. He says, "You will get your reward," and the wording he uses means that is all you will get. They have their earthly reward and that is all they do have. They have a reputation for being spiritual, but that is all they get.

He said that your Father is the only one who needs to see your piety. It is only possible to be free from hypocrisy and full of sincerity if we take positive steps toward secrecy. The need for secrecy is really the need for sincerity. With the best will in the world, if we do a thing in front of other people, we are tempted to be aware of their reaction to what we do. Now let your light shine, let your moral standard shine, put your purity on a pedestal for all to see so that they may glorify your Father – but your religion, your piety, is between yourself and God alone. The implications of this for the Christian witness are far-reaching, and we need to remember them. We need to ask at every point whether we ever parade our piety, in even the most subtle form.

We come at last to the Lord's Prayer. Our Lord interrupted here to give us a prayer, which is to be the model of our prayer when we pray in private. Again, I think we are literalists when we use the Lord's Prayer on so many occasions, and we repeat it. I always thought that "chart" was the next word in the second phrase of the Lord's Prayer. We said it so often as children: "Our Father chart in Heaven." I know somebody else who thought God's name was "Harold". For years they said "Harold be thy name", just because we repeat the words *ad infinitum*. How often do we really understand or think of what we say when we say the Lord's Prayer? It is not to be rote, it is to be a model.

How should we pray? When we have got right alone by ourselves, when we are quiet, when we are not in front of others – just to God – how should we pray? Jesus practised and preached prayer, but he never used the Lord's Prayer himself – it would not have been appropriate.

"Forgive us our trespasses" is a prayer he did not need to pray himself, but it is a prayer we need to pray. He makes the point that what we pray matters. To put it differently, it is not the quantity but the quality of prayer – not the length but the depth.

We do need *form* in prayer. Can I put it in a cliché? Without fervour, form becomes formality – but without form, fervour becomes fever. Therefore, it is a balance between form and fervour which is to be the way in which we engage in prayer.

For one, I am certainly not against liturgical prayers. I notice in Acts 2 that, "They continued steadfastly in the apostles' doctrine, fellowship, the breaking of bread, and the prayers" – badly translated as "prayer". "The prayers" means the set prayers, the forms of prayer, but they filled them with fervour. Now here is a form which can be filled with formality – or fervour, and it becomes real prayer. Notice that it is brief. It is also simple; a child can begin to use this prayer. But notice that it is profound – you will still not understand it at the end of your Christian life. Notice that it is comprehensive – it covers everything. Notice that it is universal, since it can be translated into any language and be used. Notice that it is a challenging prayer. Robert Louis Stevenson jumped up from the breakfast table once and ran out in the middle of family devotions. His wife went out after him and said, "What's the matter?" He said, "I can't pray the Lord's Prayer today, I'm not ready." I wish we could be like that when we repeat the Lord's Prayer.

Now let us look at it. The person to whom we pray is "Father".

Matthew Chapter 6

It is a family prayer. Occasionally in scripture he is said to be the Father of every creature, as the begetter of every creature. More often he is called the Father of the Jews. Still more often, he is the Father of Jesus Christ, and, by adoption, our Father. When a little baby in a Jewish family is taught to speak, they are taught to say "Abba", which is the equivalent of "Dada". "When we shout out," says Paul – not when we think but when we cry out involuntarily – "Abba, Dad!" – it is the Spirit himself bearing witness with our spirit that we are his children.

I was once in a prayer meeting in the Shetland Islands where I began my ministry. A dear old fisherman got up during the church prayer meeting and he just said, "Abba, Abba," and that was all he said. What a prayer: "Father". To think that the eternal God who set the stars on their courses and made everything that is, is my Dad. They said to Jesus once, "Would you teach us to pray?" They didn't say, "Would you teach us how to pray?" They had been taught how to pray by their parents; they were good Jews. Their question signified: would you teach us to pray like that? He said: When you pray, say, "Dad, Abba". But lest that intimacy be abused it is "Our Father in heaven...." That will introduce respect into the intimacy.

It is also "Our Father" that balances the individual and the corporate. Do you notice that even when you are alone you should say "Our"? That will alter your petitions pretty quickly; that will affect your prayer – if you regard yourself as one of a group when you are alone in your room and you say, "Our Father, we need this...." When you went into your room privately yesterday, did you pray "my" or "our"? What a wonderful thing to go into our room for private devotions. Even when you are alone, that is the way to pray – "Our...." It corrects those selfish prayers that focus on "my" and "me".

Notice the six petitions: a beautiful balance of three each – three for the needs of God, three for the needs of ourselves. "Your, your, your..."; "Our, our, our...." A believer's first concern in prayer is what God wants from us, not what we want from God. In this first set of three we have Father, Son, and Holy Spirit. Your name, your Kingdom – you cannot think of that without the King, and the Kingdom will come when the King comes – and his will.

In an early manuscript version of the Lord's Prayer, instead of saying "Your will be done" the phrase is, "Your Spirit be given" – because who can act in accordance with God's Word without the Spirit being given? So, you have Father, Son and Spirit. Daily bread is the Father's responsibility and gift. Forgiveness is that which is obtained from the Son through his blood. "Lead us not into temptation" – it was the Spirit who led the Lord into temptation in the wilderness and it is the Spirit who we look to when it is time for us to be led out of it.

Let me just look at each of these phrases a little more deeply. The name of God is the revelation of his nature – what God is. If you are going to reverence God's name, if you are ever going to hold it in awe, then you have got to know what he is like. The name "God", the name "Father", the name "Lord" – you will not take it in vain if you know who it refers to. A man who works in a factory said to me once that somebody was taking the name of Jesus in a blasphemous way. This Christian turned around and said, "Would you mind not talking like that? You're talking about someone I love." It was a lovely way to deal with it. It was not so much a reprimand as it was a request. That is reverencing the name: "May thy name be hallowed" – may people whenever they hear the name "God" pause, stand and think. Perjury, profanity, flippancy, incredulity, hypocrisy, familiarity, blasphemy – there are dozens of ways in which God's name is not hallowed by so many people.

The second thing: his Kingdom may come now. Scholars have argued as to what this means, but frankly it means two things to me. You can tell a person's theology by what they think "Kingdom" means. The word "Kingdom" is crucial to your theology, and as far as I can see it, humbly, in scripture, it means two things. It means a present slow process, and a future sudden crisis. The parables include both. The Kingdom comes as an individual enters into the reign of God by faith and repentance, and the Kingdom comes when the King suddenly returns in his glory to establish peace and righteousness. When I pray "Your Kingdom come" I think of both a present process and a future crisis.

When I pray, "Your will be done" it is not resentment, it is not resignation, it is resolution. There are two words for the word "will" in scripture. They shade into each other in meaning, but they are distinct in their central meaning. One means *decree* and the other means *desire*. The word used here is "desire", not "decree". His will that all should be saved means he desires that all should be saved, not he decrees. Here it is not "By decree be done" – that is fatalism, resignation. It is "Your desire be done"; it is resolution. The emphasis is on the word "done"; "Your will be done". Let us go out and do it. That is the prayer.

"Give us this day our daily bread." The Roman Catholics interpret that as the sacraments. The Douay Version translates this phrase as: "Give us this day our super substantial bread." Spot the deliberate mistake – it sticks out like a sore thumb; but neither is the daily bread the scriptures. Evangelicals go to the other end of the scale. It means daily bread. The word translated "daily" really means this, as we now know. William Barclay revealed this in his research. It means: for the next twenty-four hours. So it is really: Give us this day our bread for tomorrow. We are to live just a day at a time like that, and acknowledge that our physical sustenance is a gift.

"Forgive us our debts." It is not really the things we have done; it is the things we have left undone that we need to pray about here. Forgive us what we owe to you. Even when we have done our best we are unprofitable servants. We are still poor in spirit; we are still in debt. Lord, forgive us our debts. The condition –

not the basis of that forgiveness but the condition – is that we are prepared to pass on God's mercy towards what has not been done.

Finally, "Lead us not into temptation". I would disagree here with the New English Bible. It does not mean "test", it does mean "tempt". God does lead people into temptation. He does not tempt them, but he does lead them into temptation. The Spirit led Jesus into the wilderness to be tempted. God is in control of how much we are exposed to the devil, and if we trust God he will not let us be tempted above what we can bear. He will control our exposure to the devil, but sometimes as a discipline he exposes us to the devil so that we might learn the hard way that we are not trusting God. This is a request to God not to expose us too much to the devil – that we might learn the easier, not the harder way, to let the Holy Spirit garrison our hearts. But "Deliver us from the evil one". I wish we could get back to what Jesus said. He said, "the evil" which means "the evil one". You start the Lord's Prayer with God, and you finish with Satan – that is the right order of prayer. You come into God; you go out to Satan. You need to ask God to deliver you from Satan when you go out into the world again.

To say "Yours is the Kingdom," is an act of faith. To say "Yours is the power" is an act of hope; to say, "Yours is the glory" is an expression of love. To say "Mine is the Kingdom, the power, and the glory" would be to fall into the very error of pride into which Nebuchadnezzar fell when he said, "Is not this great Babylon, which I have built by my mighty power, for my majesty and glory?" To say "mine" is to be proud, but to say "yours" is to be humble.

"Forever and ever." Then the ringing certainty of your prayer: "Amen" – so shall it be. It is the same word as "verily" – truly. That is how we are to pray. To pray for what God wants from us first, then to pray for what we need from him.

We move to Jesus' teaching on not laying up treasure on earth but, rather, laying up treasure in heaven – which leads on to not worrying. Worry is a terrible hindrance. It leads to a nervous state which saps one's energy and it denies God. What is the antidote? Is there a cure? Yes, there is. Just as the cure for the wrong fear is the right fear, the cure for the wrong worry is the right worry. Get worried about God's Kingdom; seek his concerns, then you will not be worried about food and clothing. Cure one concern with another. Seek first his Kingdom, his righteousness, and all these things shall be added. In other words, when you are in Christ's service, you can run an expense account on heaven. There is a condition here. He is not saying every one of my children need not worry. What his teaching means is this: you need not worry because I know you have needs and I will provide. So we can now afford to be generous. It is your Father's good pleasure to give you the Kingdom. Therefore, you can afford to give. You can afford to be generous because you are very rich. Look what is coming to you. The amazing thing is that whatever the Christian gives does not go on the debit side in their heavenly account, but on the other side. That is how you lay up treasure in heaven – by giving. God's mathematics are exactly the opposite of ours: whatever you give makes you richer; whatever you get for yourself makes you poorer. That is God's heavenly bank account and you have got an account right now with God as a child of his. So he says, "Lay up treasure in heaven". That is the best of all bargains, isn't it?

The reason is that where your money goes and where your material things go, there your heart will follow. I heard a lovely story of a little boy in a church and one day a missionary came to that church called Mr Burt. At the end of the missionary meeting, there was an offering to help Mr Burt and his work overseas. This little boy put a penny in the offering. A year later, Mr Burt came back to the church and the little boy said to his parents, "I want to go to that meeting."

He was so keen that they asked him, "Why are you so keen to go?"

He replied, "When he was here last time, I gave him a penny and I want to hear what he's done with it!"

Now, he was absolutely true to real life in this. Where you have put your money, there your heart will follow. That is one of the reasons for giving to missionary work: giving yourself to it, your heart will go after that gift.

Fear arises because a Christian is thinking too much about the *people* in this world and not enough about God. Greed and worry come because one is thinking too much about the *things* of this world. Dangers come because the Christian is thinking too much about either the people or the things in this world and too little about God and the next world.

Discipleship

There are two main subjects that we now deal with towards the end of this great sermon – The Attitudes of a Disciple and what I have called The Aberrations – the mistakes, the misleading of a disciple from his course. Take first the attitudes of a disciple; now, our attitudes are revealed in relationship to things and in relationship to people. And our attitudes to possessions and people are going to affect our character very deeply and are going to reveal our discipleship.

Christ said more about money than about any other subject. He said more about money than about prayer, more about money than about heaven, more about money directly than about God directly. Now, if you question this, get a red-letter New Testament in which the words of our Lord are printed in red and go through and mark every verse that has some relationship with money or possessions and I think you will be quite astonished. He knew perfectly well that this is a major part of ordinary life and therefore the attitudes of a disciple to this are important.

Over half the verses of chapter 6 are about material things. The chapter begins with giving money and the rest of the chapter – or most of it – is about our attitude to the things of the flesh, the things of the material side of life. Money was invented as a help, but in fact, though it is a great help to physical life – it saves barter and tithe barns and all sorts of other things – it is not so much of a help to the spiritual life, and it facilitates the physical but it hinders the spiritual. There are two wrong attitudes to money–not just one, but two. One is when you have too much of it and the other is the attitude when you have too little of it. One is avarice, one is anxiety, and both are silly and sinful and our Lord approaches it both from the point of view of common sense and from the point of view of spiritual principle. The tenth Commandment is concerned with greed or coveting. Francis Xavier said that in all the years in which he had sat in the confessional box and listened to confession, he never once had a single person who came and confessed the sin of covetousness. And I think if you asked any priest today the same question, he would probably underline this. All sorts of other sins are confessed but this one is not. It was the one that Saul of Tarsus found that he could not keep even though as far as external life went, he was, as touching the Law, blameless.

We know that the Pharisees combined a deep piety with love of money. The statement is made in Luke chapter 16. We know that the children of God had a hankering after the "flesh pots of Egypt" from time to time, and this acquisitive instinct to collect, to hoard, to amass for oneself is deeply rooted in human nature. Therefore, our Lord says a negative and a positive thing about wealth – a negative thing based on the temporal approach and a positive thing based on the eternal approach to these things. The negative, temporal approach says first, don't be silly and second, don't be sinful. And the silliness of it is this: even if you lay it up for yourself, you can't keep it. First of all, we live in a dangerous present and no matter what form of investment you adopt, it is not secure. Said a dear lady to me as she showed me a teapot on the mantlepiece full of dirty pound notes rolled up, "When I put those by, I thought they would really look after me in my old age, I thought they would really see me through and now they're hardly worth a quarter of what they were."

There is no form of security. I know that property seems to go on increasing in leaps and bounds. They did not put their money in pictures or property then, they put it in clothes, fine clothes – but the moths got at them; they put it in grain – but then, of course, you had the rats in; and they put it in coins and in precious metals – but these can be tarnished and rust. We live in a dangerous present as far as amassing or hoarding goes. Even more important, our Lord taught us that if that is our aim in life, then it is a desolate future.

Two people sitting on a bus were discussing the death of a wealthy man announced in the press and one said to the other, "How much did he leave?" And the other said, "Everything." A shroud has no pocket. And the Lord called that man a moron who thought that he could go on building up his personal fortune – "For tonight thy soul shall be required of thee." It is a silly thing to do, to live for your investment of material things. It is not only silly; it is sinful because of its effect on your personality. The Ebenezer Scrooge complex is composed of a distracted heart, a darkened mind and a divided will.

A distracted heart because, if I can make a rather poor pun – where your investment is, there will be your interest. And the heart will be where its money is. And one of the great by-products of increased giving to missionary work is that you are more interested in missionary work because that is where your money is and you want to know what it is doing. And from a purely business aspect, it is a good commercial policy to get people to give more to missions because they will want to know where that money is going and what it is doing and will begin to ask questions about the missionary society.

The darkened mind is this. Our eye – what we see – as to whether we are looking for things that we can grasp or things that we can give will have an immediate effect on the mind, on our thinking. The eye is a window and through it either comes the darkness of grasping and greed or the light of generosity. And if *I* use my eyes to look at the things that I want all the time then my mind will live in darkness. But if I look out on things that I can *do* and *give*, then my whole body will be full of light. And our Lord often used the word *evil* as a synonym for a grudging attitude and the word *good* as a synonym for generosity. There are only two men who are called good in the New Testament apart from Jesus and our Lord said, "Why do you call me good?" But there are two men called good, and they both had the same first name (they had different second names). Both were called Joseph. There was Joseph of Arimathea and Joseph called Barnabas, and both of them were those who gave property to others – one a tomb and the other a field. In the parable of the labourers in the vineyard, the master of the vineyard said, "Is your eye evil because I am good? Are you grudging because I am generous?" This is how it translates in one New Testament in modern English. And there is this darkened mind.

Thirdly, there is a divided will. Now, it cost thirty pieces of silver to buy a slave in those days, that was the price. And that put you one up; the status symbol was not a swimming pool or two cars or a radiation-proof shelter in the garden. The status symbol in those days was to own a slave – that put you up into the next bracket of society. Now, if you just could not get there by yourself, you got a friend and you said, "Look, I can raise 15 pieces of silver if you could raise another 15. Let's have a slave between us, and that will move us up the social bracket." But you know, it never worked out. Even in voluntary employment, it is very difficult indeed to work for two bosses. I was once in that position in secular employment where I was responsible to two people, and it just did not work. Now, this is not employment, this is slavery being considered and a slave has no rights even to his leisure. Can you imagine being a slave of two owners, both of whom in a sense had a right to everything that you were? It just cannot be done; it does not work out. Sooner or later, you begin to veer to one or the other. You cannot be a slave of God and mammon. You cannot be bought body, mind and soul by both. It just does not work out.

And this divided will is one of the most eroding factors in Christian discipleship. That does *not* mean that money in itself is evil. It does mean that the *love of money* is the root of all kinds of evil. Matthew 25, Luke 16 and 1 Timothy 6 tell you what to do with your money. Lay it up for yourself – that is a good injunction; lay it up for yourself, but not on earth – have a good account in heaven. Our lord frequently mentions the motive of reward and he does not say, don't lay up for yourself treasure at all but give it all away, he says, lay up for yourselves in the right place. Now, this is just sensible. It is not being too spiritual. It is saying, you want to lay up treasure for yourself? Fine, do so; but just make a good investment. And Matthew 25, Luke 16 and 1 Timothy 6 tell you how to do just that.

Take Luke 16, a parable that Christians find embarrassing – use your money to make friends for yourself. *There* is a text for you to preach on! And you know, when I first read that, I thought, but that is exactly what my unbelieving neighbours do – making a financial contribution for a cocktail party. What are they doing but using their money to make friends? But surely our Lord would not say that kind of thing. If we just look at it, we see that he qualified that statement by the whole context of the parable of the unjust steward, which I haven't space to expound fully. He simply said that the unjust steward was wise because of two things: first, he realised that he would be better off spending his money on people than on things, and second, he would be better off spending it for the future than the present. And the children of this world are often wiser in their generation than the children of light. But the people we are to spend it on and the friends we are to make are those people who will welcome us *in heaven*. That alters the whole perspective, and the people on whom to spend your money if you want to be welcomed in heaven and if you want a nice bank balance there are, first, the unsaved who will bless you for giving that money so that a missionary might go and tell them the Good News of Christ, and secondly, the saved who are in need and who will thank you in heaven for helping them in that need. This is the way to invest in the future and it is very practical and very down-to-earth advice.

In the days of Vespasian's persecution in Rome, the Roman prefect burst into a Christian church meeting for worship and said, "Show me your treasures." They had come to take away everything of value. So, a deacon of the church took him to a door at the back, threw it open, and said, "There are the treasures of our church." And inside was a group of widows and orphans being fed. This was the treasure the church had laid up in the city of Rome. They were investing in the future.

John Wesley went through sixty thousand pounds in his lifetime and 300 years ago that was a not inconsiderable sum of money. But when the capital gains tax came in, in those days – or not quite the capital gains tax, it was a straight capital tax and they have been thinking up new taxes from the year dot – they wrote to him and asked him to declare his property and he wrote down "Seven silver teaspoons – some of which are in Bristol and some of which are here in London." And they immediately sent an inspector of taxes to deal with him. But in fact, they found that he had returned an accurate tax form.

Now, the other wrong attitude to possessions is that of anxiety when you have too little. Avarice is when you have too much and want to lay it up for yourself on earth; anxiety is when you have too little. We need to remember that our Lord was speaking to people who worked for a wage a day at a time and a Roman denarius was a modest amount by today's standards. Furthermore, we need to remember that he was speaking to people who had no pension, no dole, no national assistance, nothing – so that, if they didn't find a job that day for that day, they would go without. That is the background of the parable of the labourers in the vineyard, and the background of the shop steward on that day who had some comments on the wage differential.

Now, this is the background to the whole teaching. Our Lord is telling us not to be anxious. Those people who had far less than I imagine any reader of this book has. Thirty pounds a week is wealth by biblical standards, which is why *poor* is a relative term. When our Lord speaks about the dangers that come to rich people, he refers to thirty pounds a week and over. That is rich, that is wealth according to his standards. So, it was to people who had far, far less than we have, and if he told them that it was sinful to be anxious, how much more do we sin when, with much greater resources, we are anxious about material things?

Again, there is a negative and a positive and our Lord balanced these two aspects of teaching. May I say that in our existential age in which tolerance is exalted to be a virtue and in which truth is regarded as relative, if we are ever going to preach the truth, we have got to preach it negatively as well as positively. You have got to tell people what it does not mean as well as what it does in an age in which relativism is the approach to truth. Only in this way can you define absolute truth in a relative age. And our Lord was always doing this – what it is *not* and what it *is*. The negative, the positive. And the negative is this: don't be anxious. Now, of course, the Authorised Version is one of those translations that is most unfortunate. It was understood 350 years ago but it is misleading today. For instance, we read: "Take no thought for tomorrow". But our Lord never encouraged idleness; he never encouraged lack of thought. Nor did he ever discourage forethought. He encouraged us to think ahead.

Tyndale, Cranmer and the Geneva Bible have the word "Don't be careful for tomorrow." And that originally meant to be full of care, like Martha "troubled about many things". And *don't be anxious* is perhaps the best translation – don't *worry*. Now, worry is obviously silly for four reasons. Under my heading

Matthew Chapter 6

The Foolishness of Anxiety, it is first of all Unreasonable; it confuses a living with a life. And that is a great confusion. I have noticed, even in talking to church people, when they talk about their grown-up sons and daughters and say, "They've done very well," I say, "What do you mean by that?" In nearly every case, it is answered in terms of making a living. This is a disturbing feature of our thinking. "He's done very well. He's getting sixty thousand pounds a year and I didn't get half that at his age; he has done very well." To confuse a living with a life is an unreasonable approach to a rational human existence.

Secondly, it is unavailing. You cannot lengthen your life by worry. I think "add one cubit to his stature" refers not so much to the *height* as to the *length*. Our span of life is not likely to lengthen with worry; it is much more likely to do the opposite.

Thirdly, it is unnecessary. It is using up energy with no result because you cannot turn the colour of your hair by worry. Now, I always wondered about this. You certainly cannot turn white hair black but I think you can do the opposite by worry. But you cannot alter life radically by worry; you cannot achieve your purpose.

And fourthly, I would want to say it is unnatural. Man is the only part of nature that worries – the birds do not. Oh, they can feverishly search for food but they are only concerned with getting food now; they are not worried about three weeks' time, not to my knowledge. My dog gets worried when there isn't food there, but he is not worried about next Thursday, I am quite sure. The flowers do not worry. Now, it is really a libel on God if you worry. It is saying that God is the sort of Father who is more interested in his pets and his garden than in his own children. That is how our Lord is putting it. Is God the sort of Father who would look after the sparrows and the daisies and not his own children? Is he more interested in his pets and his garden than his own children? That is a libel on God. "Your heavenly Father," said Jesus, talking, of course, to believers – this is not a general principle, it is to those who are his children.

He says, not only is it silly, it is sinful because it is a libel on God. It is an ungodly thing to do. Gentiles can worry, let them worry, that is their privilege to worry because they haven't a heavenly Father. It is an ungodly thing to do because it is practical atheism. "O ye of little faith." He says you have got just enough faith to get saved and none to live by. You have got a little faith because you are his child but you haven't enough to be his child day by day. You have got faith to *become* a child of God but not faith to *continue to be* a child of God. "O ye of little faith." If you worry, you do not trust. If you trust, you do not worry – easier said than done, I know, but it is a simple fact.

Now the positive side is this. The secret of tranquillity is twofold. The first is to get your priorities right and the second is to get your programme right. The two secrets of a serene life. Now, we have had a lot about priorities and goals and balancing our roles in life. Our priorities are our first concern in dealing with worry. What is your first concern? That will determine how concerned you are about food and clothes and the things by which to live. Well, our priority is to seek first the kingdom – that means to set your priorities in heaven rather than on earth – and to seek first the kingdom of righteousness, which is the priority of the inward over the outward. Notice that it does not say to seek *only* the kingdom of righteousness but rather "seek *first*". Of course, we must give thought to food and clothing, especially if we have a family. "He that provideth not for his own household is worse than an unbeliever" – a quote from the New Testament that is very practical and part of Paul's advice to people with families. But it does say that is not the priority in life. Seek that first; seek these things second, but seek that first, and your priority will keep your thinking in perspective.

And the second thing is: your programme is by nature divided into units of 24 hours. Our spiritual trust should be divided into the same units. To live a day at a time. It does not mean that I don't think about next week, but it does mean that as far as the problems and burdens of life go, I do not try to carry them before I meet them. I do not cross my bridges before I come to them. Sufficient to that unit of 24 hours is all that you have to carry – "as thy days, so shall thy strength be". Or as someone put it the other way round to me about a conference: "As thy strength, so shall thy days be."

Paul said that he had learned in all things to be content, with much or with little, with all things or with nothing. Now, which do you think is the most difficult for human nature – to be content with much or content with little? I don't think there is much to choose between them, do you? I meet some Christians who are very well off indeed. I meet other Christians who are very poor, but I find that God can produce contentment in both situations, and when he has *that* he can use a rich man's wealth and a poor man's poverty for his glory. And both are wonderful lessons, to be content whether you are rich or poor. I find generally among unbelievers that it is the rich who are less content and who get more anxious, but here we have two wrong attitudes: avarice and anxiety.

11
DO NOT JUDGE

Read Matthew 7

Now our attitudes to people, a most vital part of daily life. And we are dealing first with the charity of our mind, the discrimination we must exercise, and second, with the charity of our hand in our distribution of gifts. Regarding the charity of mind, let me say straight away that this first phrase, "judge not", in chapter 6 has been widely abused to mean that you must never examine another life, that you must never discriminate, that you must never venture an opinion, that you must never come to a conclusion about another because anything like that is judging. Now, let us try and get rid of that. First of all, there must be judgement in society; that is God's will. Romans 13 is the classic passage on this. There must be judges in society so this does not cover that. Second, there must be judgement within the church. 1 Corinthians 5:12ff states something like this: You are not to judge outsiders but you are to judge insiders. Now put him out from your fellowship until he repents, this man whose life is a contradiction of the gospel. There is a place for judgement within the church. I would say that one of the difficulties of having a separate church for young people is that that church will lack one of the marks which the Reformers said was vital to a true church: the mark of discipline and the power of the keys. And I would add to the definition of the church "organised with a common discipline", and this is where the older need the younger and the younger need the older if we can possibly get them together.

If we are going to have a separate church for young people, we must appoint elders from among those young people to exercise the discipline – as happened to a church of young people in Stockport who met in a youth club. Local churches would not have them in though there were 200 young people in the Coach House as it is known, and so they finally became a church, a young people's church – the Coach House Church. But they immediately had elders and sacraments and everything that made them a proper church. But it was the discipline that they lacked until they were properly formed into a church.

There is a place for judgement in the church. There is a place for judgement in the family. If a man cannot rule his own household, he is not fit for the household of God. There is a place for judgement – to spank or not to spank, that is the question. But what does this mean? It means that again, there can be too much discrimination and too little in our relationships with people and "judge not that ye be not judged" refers to *too much*. It means to make yourself the judge rather than the jury. It means to sentence or condemn rather than to examine. The word *judge* does not mean to *try*, but to condemn, to write off, to sentence. And it obviously refers to that hypercritical, censorious attitude which is always writing people off and this kind of thing, of course, is wrong in the Christian. If it meant that we are never to examine and assess another person, then our Lord contradicts this just a few verses later when he talks about swine and when he says, "Beware of false prophets". How are we to do either of those two things if we are never to examine and assess another life? But it does refer to this attitude of condemning everyone and everything too easily.

Criticism works this way: you will always criticise those who are nearest to you. Did you realise that? You think through who, if anyone, you have criticised in the past week. Were they people in China? Or were they people who were close to you? The reason why we do it to people near to us is because that takes them down a peg or two and therefore lifts us up a bit. So, you don't criticise someone down the road in another church nearly as much as someone in your own – if you are doing things

Matthew Chapter 7

naturally. Alas, if you are not careful you become critical of fellow members of your church without even realising it, because it is not your enemies you criticise, it is your friends. That is why Jesus, speaking of our concern for our enemy, now goes on to speak about criticising one's brother. This is the opposite of the world. The world has deep concern for friends and criticism for enemies. But Christians need to go much deeper.

At this point, our Lord uses humour. You know, I think we often miss humour in our Lord's teaching because we are Western and not Eastern. I have read some of the passages from our Lord's teaching to Arabs and found that they saw the funny point. They saw the humour. When Western literal-minded commentators come to our Lord's words about the camel going through the needle's eye, they have got to say there is a little gate in Jerusalem that is too small for the camel – rubbish! There isn't a little gate in Jerusalem like that. The guide will show you that because he is paid to show you what you want to see but there isn't any such thing. It is hyperbole, it is humour. If you read to a Middle Eastern congregation today the idea of a chap carefully getting the teaspoon and getting that little gnat out of his coffee and then swallowing the camel hump and all, he would be rolling in the aisle. And here is humour again. Here is a chap walking about carrying a roof joist stuck in his eye and he says, "Excuse me just a minute, would you mind holding this; there's a little splinter in your eye." Of course, it is ludicrous. This is Eastern humour and it depends on quite a different sense of proportion to our Western literalism. But time and time again, commentators miss the humour of this, as when Isaiah asks whether the clay says to the potter "You've given me no handles." It is a humorous thing. And when you read the Bible through the eyes of the Middle East, the humour of it comes out.

Now, notice that our Lord is not saying you must not point out the splinter. He does say, get rid of the roof joist and *then*... then you can see properly. It might not even be a splinter at all, or it might be another roof joist but at least you will see what it is. And with humour he gets across the point. The Oxford Group used to say that if you point at someone else, you have got three fingers pointing back at yourself – same point. The next thing he says is that you not only contradict yourself because you suffer from worse, but you condemn yourself. Every judgement you make of someone else shows the light that you have and therefore that is the standard by which you will be judged. And if I condemn a man for that splinter, it shows that I understand that that is wrong. Therefore, if there is any trace of that in my life, it will be judged in my life because my criticism of him shows that I knew perfectly well that it was wrong. "For with what judgment you judge, you will be judged". "Therefore," said Phillips Brooks the great preacher, "if you see a fault in any other man or any other church, look to see if that fault is in yourself or your own church" – wise advice. The other extreme, of course, is too little discrimination, assuming everybody is perfectly all right; that kind of facile and naïve interpretation of human nature, the original goodness of man.

Now, our Lord says that we are not to be the judge who condemns everyone but we do need to be the jury and examine; we do need to try. And there are certain people who are neither fit nor able to receive sacred things. There *are* people who are dogs. Here is a text for you: "Beware of the dogs" – straight from Philippians 3, which is a grand text. There are all sorts of dogs in the world but when you go to the Middle East and see the wild dogs inhabiting the ruins in the Arabian Desert, you know what our Lord meant when he said dogs. And swine too. There are certain people, if you gave them holy things, they would despise the gift and attack the giver. Our Lord did not say a word to Herod. He said, "He's a fox that man," and he would not say a word or do a thing in his presence because that man was just out to exploit our Lord for a bit of entertainment in the court. And our Lord was not going to play with such dogs and with such a fox. We need discrimination. Our Lord did not use the word *Father* much in public, if at all. It was too sacred a thing to bandy about freely. I think this applies to our witnessing and to our worship. We need to be very wise as to what we give to people too quickly, too easily, before they are ready to receive it.

Now, when he says, "Judge not, that you be not judged," he does not mean that you must renounce all critical faculties. If he meant that, if we were never to examine each other positively, then I would never write a reference for anyone, nor should anybody ever sit on a magistrate's bench, nor should there be any school or university examinations. What Jesus is now talking about is *condemning*. It means writing someone off, saying he is beyond redemption. It means saying he is hopeless – we can't do anything with him. Only God has the right to be such a judge.

One of the most frightening things that Jesus ever said is right here: that with what measure you judge, you shall be judged. In other words, on the Day of Judgment, when one stands before one's Creator, all he has to do is to play back a recording of the faults I have found in other people and said so, then to examine my life with what I have criticised in others. Can any of us stand before God if that is how he is going to judge? For we know we have condemned in others what there is in our own heart. This, then, is the secret of harmony with other people.

There is the secret of holiness before God. This is practical. Jesus spoke in pictures so that his hearers could see the truth. As his hearers listened to him, they could say, "Oh, now I see." The pictures he paints are of a tree and of a house. It is a law of nature that a tree can only produce after its kind; what the tree is, that it will produce. It is also a law of human nature that what you are in yourself, that is what you produce. You cannot produce anything else. What is stored up in your heart will come out of your mouth, which is why Jesus said on another occasion, "Every man will be judged by the idle words that proceeded from his mouth." What is so important about the mouth? Simply, when you open it, what is in your heart comes out unless you keep a very tight grip of yourself and you are one of those who speaks in a very reserved way and is careful and considerate in what you say. If you are really free and if you are really relaxed and if you let your mouth take over, it will reveal what is in your heart.

Jesus teaches that every man and woman, over the years, has built up a treasury in their heart. Thoughts are stored in your heart; all the experiences of life are there. Your heart has become more and more full of treasures, either of good things or of bad things. When you open your mouth, the treasures will come out – the things that you have stored up. You might have someone to tea and just talk casually. The things that you have stored in your heart are what will come out. As someone thinks in his heart, so is he. Jesus is saying that a bad tree cannot produce good fruit and a good tree cannot produce bad fruit.

The things that come out of the mouth can be unreal. In casual conversation, the things that come out will be from your heart; in formal and official circles, what you say may not be from your heart at all. This is the big danger in religion – that you say things that are not from the heart. "Why do you call me 'Lord'?" So do watch your language. When you are not consciously controlling your mouth, your heart is revealed. When you are consciously controlling your mouth, it is all too easy to lapse into hypocrisy.

You will never get fruit without roots. Going deep down to the invisible, Jesus changes the picture from fruit to foundation. He tells us the secret of holiness before God, and makes it absolutely clear that the secret of holiness is not the number of sermons you have listened to – everything rests on what you *do* with the teaching.

Now we turn to charity of hand. This is not a misplaced section on prayer as some have thought, though verse 7 is a classic law of prayer. We are dealing with charity of hand and the obvious approach to it is to look at the generosity of God – every good and perfect gift comes down from him. Hidden in the English, but apparent in the Greek, is the law of the need for persistence in prayer. The literal translation, using the continuous present tense is this: "*Go on* asking and you will receive. *Go on* seeking and you will find. *Go on* knocking and it will be opened to you." And the humorous picture of our Lord springs readily to mind of that poor chap in bed with all his family and listening to the continuous banging on his front door – "I need bread; I've got a visitor. Come on, wake up." He has got to get up sooner or later. If a reluctant *man* will respond to persistence, how much more will a generous God respond to those who *go on* asking. And it is the nature of parenthood to give good things. Notice our Lord's view of human nature – "If you then, *being evil*" – which is our Lord's doctrine of man in a nutshell. Nevertheless, he admits that evil men can do good things and he says, "If you then, being evil, know how to give good gifts to your children, *how much more* will your Father who is in heaven give good things to those who ask him!" It is the argument from the lesser to the greater; it is a contrast rather than a comparison. Now he comes to the revolutionary Golden Rule, the simple precept – *do as you would be done by*. Is it original? William Barclay culled a list of parallel quotes from various sources. Jewish sources – Tobit: "What thou hatest do to no man." The Rabbi Hillel: "What is hateful to thee do not to anyone else." Then there is Confucius: "Do not to others what you would not wish done to yourself." The Stoics taught this: "Do not to another what you do not wish to happen to yourself." Epictetus said: "What you avoid suffering yourself seek not to inflict on others." Buddhist philosophy says the same.

Do you notice anything? Every one of these quotations is negative! *Don't do* what you *don't* wish to be done to you. And our Lord's *revolutionary* reinterpretation of this principle, which human wisdom everywhere had discovered, was *Do unto others!* By nature, we think negatively about our responsibility to our fellow men and by nature, the unbeliever will say, "I've never done anyone any harm" – as the ground for his acceptance. But our Lord is interested in what we have done that is good, whether we have positively loved the Lord our God and our neighbour as ourself. It is not only a simple precept; it is a scriptural principle. This *is* the Law and the Prophets. Love thy neighbour as *thyself*.

Now I come to my final section, which is The Aberrations of a Disciple, the mistakes he can make. The sermon finishes with three serious warnings. It also finishes – and if you are a preacher please note – with an appeal for decision and a verdict, which it does by presenting the alternative courses ahead of the hearers. That is brilliant homiletics. And our Lord was a matchless teacher and preacher. He speaks of two roads, two trees, and two houses.

First, what is your goal? A Christian is one who lives like Abraham with his eyes fixed on the future, seeing the Invisible, looking for a city whose builder and maker is God. He has got a perspective that is in the future. He does not make comparisons in the present but in the future. If you once begin to make comparisons in the present, you are finished; you will get on the wrong road. You have got to keep the comparison of the goal ahead. Now, Psalm 73 is the classic example of this. The poor old psalmist is saying, I just don't understand it, Lord. These wicked people, they die peacefully and prosperously in their old age; they have no pangs, they are so comfortable. And here I am; I've cleansed my heart in vain; I'm troubled all the day long. Have you ever felt like that? Then he says, "Until I went into the sanctuary of God; then I understood their end... Surely you set them in slippery places; you cast them down to destruction." And with the new perspective, he gets quite a different slant on life. "You will guide me with your counsel, and afterward receive me *to* glory. Whom have I in heaven *but you?* And *there is* none upon earth *that* I desire besides you." Suddenly, the whole perspective is changed because the comparison is with his goal. When he compared the roads, he came to a wrong conclusion and decided he had wasted his time trying to be a godly man. But when he got his eyes on the goal again, the comparison fell

Matthew Chapter 7

away and he was through the danger.

Now Jesus said that if you compare the roads, you will make the wrong decision. Look at the road to hell. He warns that it is wide. Oh, you can take a lot of luggage with you on the road to hell. You can take a lot of broadminded ideas – it is a wide way. It is not only wide, it is easy, it is congenial to your nature. You can saunter, you can stroll, there are no steep hills, no sharp bends. It is an easy road. And it is a full road; if you want company, then as somebody said, "It's heaven for climate but hell for company!" And the road is the same way. If you want to walk with rich people, nice people, clever people, rational people, eloquent people, happy people, even good people, then the road to hell is the road to walk – most of them are on it. That's company. What a cavalcade marching for a cliff.

The other road that leads to heaven is not a very attractive road. It is narrow. Let us tell young people it is narrow. Let us warn them before they put a hand to the plough. It is narrow. It is so narrow – the gate is so narrow to it that you have got to leave behind your sins; you may have to leave behind your friends and family, though you would want to try and bring them with you. You will have to leave behind a lot of your ideas. It is a narrow road and the world *considers* it narrow, and they will tell you that you are narrow. But it leads to life.

And secondly, it is hard. Let us tell young people it is hard to be a Christian. I am quoting Browning there. It is hard to be a Christian. It is. The entrance fee is nothing but the annual subscription is everything – it is hard. And it is empty. Believe not those who say the upward path is smooth, and that is probably why it is empty. There are not many. You may be the only Christian in the place of your work. You may be the only person in your class at school. It is a lonely road and we must face that. You have Christ but you don't have many others. We are in a minority and many Christians are very lonely. It is the only religion in the world you cannot be born into. Is that why there are so few? Bunyan's *Pilgrim's Progress* is a matchless embodiment of this section of the Sermon on the Mount. He did not have many companions through his journey; it was a narrow, hard and empty road and that is why he so often lost sight of the Celestial City and his goal; he saw an easier road through By-path meadow. He saw congenial company this way and he got off the road because he lost his goal. And of course, the real difference is in the destination – one leads to destruction and the other to life. Christianity is the way *to* life as well as a way *of* life.

Now we come to the second danger, which is that you get the wrong guide. You need guides but there is an awful danger that you get the wrong one. From the very beginning of God's revelation of his Word to men there have been those who *claimed* to reveal his Word but who were false prophets, and our Lord warns Christians about this. There are wolves and John Wesley's comment on that term *wolves* is this: "These are far above the rank of ordinary cut-throats; for they murder the souls of men." False prophets – they are ravenous. That means they are desirous of their own power, prestige, and popularity. They are greedy for themselves. Now, to identify them is very difficult, first of all because of their teaching. They say nice things; they cry peace, peace, when there is no peace. They talk of heaven – but not of hell. They talk of God's pardon, not of his punishment. They talk of his mercy but not of his justice. And I find the false prophet does not tell a lie, he tells a half-truth. Oh, it is very difficult to spot that. And it requires very careful analysis.

Secondly, you cannot tell him from his appearance. Do you know that the shepherds in the Middle East wear a fleece? And the sheep see him as one of them. He wears a coat just like them; he wears a fleece when it is cold. But here is a *wolf* who wears a fleece. His appearance is that of one of the flock. I find that one of the most difficult things in these days is to remind myself that the people who are the most dangerous guides to the flock are those who look like sheep; that the devil will come as an angel of light, that Antichrist will have the appearance of a lamb. Have you ever noticed that in Revelation? And how very easy it is to be misled by someone who apparently is a caring shepherd, a nice man, a Christian in appearance but who, nevertheless, by his perversion of the truth is going to lead people astray.

You cannot tell by his fervour. He might cry, "Lord, Lord," but that does not mean that the Lord knows him or has that intimate relationship with him that makes a true prophet. And you cannot even tell him by his miracles. Jesus said he will perform miracles in my Name. He will do wonders and signs but the power is in the Name, not in the prophet, and we need to remember that.

Now, in these days it is vital for us to discern and test all things, not to quench the spirit but to test everything and prove what is good. There are good things happening, there are counterfeit things happening and we need the discernment of the Spirit lest we be led astray by false guides. The only real test of a prophet is the fruit that he bears; in his own character the fruit of the Spirit and in other people's lives in attaching people to the Lord and to his church, rather than to the prophet. This is a very good test. Does that man when he has ministered leave people nearer to the Lord and more dependent on the Lord, or does he simply draw after him his own followers and fans? What is a man's lasting work?

Emil Brunner, the great theologian, was walking along Oxford Street and he saw a man with a sandwich board, which had written on it something along the lines of "Eat at Joe's"; I forget what it was exactly, it may have been something a little more respectful than Joe's but it was eat somewhere. And Emil Brunner looked at the man's face and it was pinched and hungry and Emil Brunner said, "That is my life as a theologian; I'm advertising God and I'm hungry." And it was then that he left his lecture room and threw himself into the evangelism and social service which characterised his life for a number of years. But in the case of the false prophet, it is all on the hoarding, it is all on the advertisement. In himself, there isn't the fruit that comes from abiding in Christ.

Jesus finishes this sermon with an illustration from his carpentry days. He would have recalled seeing some houses built well and others built badly. I remember going to visit a family home many years ago. It was a beautiful house in the woods on a lovely residential estate. But when I got there, I couldn't believe my eyes. The whole place had been dug around – it looked as if they were going to put a moat in with great heaps of sandy clay in trenches around the walls. What was it? It was the foundations which needed taking down. The builder had not made them deep enough. Jesus is teaching us that when you listen to preaching you are building something as you listen. If you enjoy a sermon, are moved by it, but then go away and do nothing about it, you will have built a structure (life) that looks all right superficially, a life that looks Christian. You may live in that life for quite some time, but when the crisis comes, when the crunch hits you, your Christian life will collapse – it will have no foundation on the rock. But if you listen to the sermon and listen to the Word of God, and go away and do something about it, then it will be hard work; it will require effort – you will have to dig deep and get down to the bedrock of what you are really like and get down to the bedrock of what life is really like, and get down to the bedrock of what God is really like. Then, when a crisis comes, your Christian life will stand firm.

That is the secret of holiness before God: to listen to his Word and then do something about it. In your relationships with others, have a concern for your enemies and refrain from criticism of your friends. The secret of holiness with God is to bear the fruit that comes from having roots and having a foundation on the rock.

It has been said that the Sermon is a mirror to show the dirt, for it leaves you with a dilemma. When I read through the life and the teaching of Christ, I know that is right. I know it is the truth. I know that is the way; I know that is the life – but I just cannot do it. That is why I need a Saviour and Lord. That is why people do not live the Sermon on the Mount – not until they find

Jesus Christ. That is why it is silly to say, "If everybody lived like this, our troubles would be over." Of course, they would be, but nobody does live like this until Christ forgives their sin, begins his work in their heart and begins to live his life in them. For all the good things we have read in these passages so far are perfectly true of Jesus. As they spat on him, whipped him, mocked him and laughed at him and nailed him to a block of wood, he said, "Father, forgive them, for they know not what they do." Not long afterwards, one of the early Christians who was stoned to death showed that he now could live the Sermon on the Mount. As the first Christian martyr breathed his last, he said, "Lord, lay not this sin to their charge." It is possible to live like this, but not by yourself. You will only do it with Jesus.

Finally, the ground. As a carpenter, Jesus would have delivered doors and window frames to the building estate where the builder was busy and he knew perfectly well about jerry building and this is his subject now – jerry building. For the benefit of any overseas readers, that means building in a poor and shoddy manner, it means building a bad house that will not last and which is not a good building. Jesus knew all about this. I will never forget, up in the Shetland Islands when I was shown a house that was built on sand, that had been standing for seventy years without a crack. The real secret for this was that it was built on wet sand, on a spit of sand that joined one of the islands to another and the man had built it on the wet sand and the wet sand did hold. Mind you, the waves went over his roof – he never had to wash his windows when the wind blew in Shetland. And there it was, the dampest house I have ever seen, but it stood. It rather shook my understanding of this verse.

I always used to think that in fact these two houses were built in different localities. I now know that this is not so. Jesus had been a carpenter in Nazareth. Now, the geography of Nazareth is this: it nestles in a kind of deep saucer among the Galilean hills. You may have had the privilege of seeing this. The erosion of the hills has filled up the bottom with silt and sand and if you are going to build a house in Nazareth, you must go down through the sand until you hit the rock. A jerry builder will only build on the top and then the wadis fill up with water in the rainy season and the water just scoops out the sand and the loose silt from under the corner of a house and a crack appears in the corner and bit by bit it becomes an unstable house until finally, one day there is a big storm and the rains fall – notice the rains are part of the storm, not just the wind – and the rains pull the rest of the foundation away and down it goes. Jesus had seen this happen. And it was not the locality of the building; it was *how deep* the builder went. That is the difference – not location but depth is the point here.

A man who builds on sand is shallow; a man who builds on rock is deep. That is the real picture he is painting. And he simply says that if you listen to me preach and go away saying, "What a wonderful sermon, very interesting preacher this morning" and do nothing about it, you are shallow, you did not go deep enough into my Word. But if you go away and say, "Lord, what will you have me do?" If, having seen ourselves in a mirror we do not forget what we have seen but go away and put it into action and become a doer of the Word and not just a hearer, then we have gone deep enough to build.

> *Isn't it strange that princes and kings,*
> *And clowns that caper in sawdust rings,*
> *And ordinary folk like you and me,*
> *Are builders for eternity?*
> *Each is given a bag of tools,*
> *An hourglass and a book of rules,*
> *And each must build, ere his time is flown,*
> *A stumbling block or a stepping stone.*

Matthew Chapter 7

You are building. When you sit and listen to a preacher, you are building – either on sand by just listening, or on rock, by going deep enough to change what God has revealed in your life. Do you realise that Jesus, in this whole sermon, has been talking about himself? That is the subject of all preaching. Whether you are preaching doctrine or ethics or apologetics, Christ is the subject of preaching. And he was the subject of his own preaching. He has been speaking of judgment, of the road that leads to destruction, of the tree that will fall and be put in the fire and of the house that will collapse. But who is the Judge? "And then I will declare to them, 'I never knew you; depart from Me, you who practise lawlessness!'" *I*. But he has also been describing himself as the Saviour. Which is the way that leads to life? Listen to what Jesus said: "Abide in me, and I in you. As the branch cannot bear fruit of itself, unless it abides in the vine, neither can you, unless you abide in me. I am the vine, you are the branches. He who abides in me, and I in him, bears much fruit". How do I bear fruit in the Lord's service? And who is the Rock of Ages? Jesus. And if I go deep enough into the scripture to find Jesus, I have found the Rock on which I can build, and it is on his words that the church must be built. So, he finished the sermon, and there was great astonishment. I am not surprised, are you? They had never heard a sermon like that in all their lives. I can imagine them letting out their breath at the end of it. They were astonished. Why? Because he knew what he was talking about.

The scribes preached second-hand stuff but when Jesus preached, he preached as one who had *authority*. It was the Word of God that he spoke because he *was* the Word of God. And as Moses had said – with this I began and with this I end – "every soul who will not hear that Prophet shall be utterly destroyed from among the people." Amen.

12
HEALING

Read Matthew Chapter 8

Right in the middle of a country lane Jesus was met and worshipped by a leper. Why was the leper not in the town? Because he was not allowed there, he had to live outside it. He had heard what was going on in the town, wondered how he could reach Jesus – and there he was, coming along the road! No wonder he ran up.

This man who was condemned to a living death said with astounding faith, "Lord, if you are willing, you can make me clean." That was great faith being shown by one who had an incurable disease. Jesus had compassion on him and touched him and said, "I am willing. Be cleansed!" and he was.

This man's need was obvious, his faith is obvious, he was healed, and the next thing that is obvious is his disobedience. Jesus told the healed leper not to tell anyone. Jesus told him to go to Jerusalem, where he would be inspected, get a medical certificate and go back into society. But the man went rushing down the road, and to everybody he met he said that he had been healed by Jesus. Jesus could not even get into the towns, he had to keep away from them, so that he might preach where only the fit could reach him. We see the problem and, again, the wonderful balance in his ministry. While he had deep compassion for people in physical pain and suffering, he had a deeper compassion for people in sin – people who were facing a suffering in the next world that those living in this world never dreamed of – so he went on preaching.

Now we come to the case of the surprising soldier. It was a remarkable background. The centurion was equivalent in rank to a regimental sergeant major. You would not generally think of such a man as a deep, mystical, religious person, would you? If you have had any experience of RSMs, you will know that they are often the backbone of the army – utterly reliable, men of strength and character.

This man was a most unusual soldier. As well as being a strong character, a leader, a well-trained military man, he had tremendous sensitivity. First, he was sensitive to his slave. Do you know what they used to do with worn-out slaves in those days? They would put them in a room and shut them in with no food, or put them out in the yard to die. A slave was no more than a tool, and when a slave was worn out he was discarded – not worth feeding. But here was a man who said, "My slave is sick" – and his concern was not only for the soldiers beneath him but for the slaves. That was almost unheard of in the ancient world.

More than that, here was a man who was in the position of trying to keep the peace and who out of his own pocket built a needed place of worship for people in an occupied territory. That was unusual – yet he had built a synagogue. You may have seen the ruins of a synagogue in Capernaum that stand there to this day. That is not the actual synagogue referred to here, but it is built on top of the one that the centurion built, and to this day the ruins that you can see are Roman architecture with Hebrew symbols worked into the stone, and bear testimony to this man who paid for an architect to put up a lovely synagogue right there in Capernaum – for the Jews, who were normally despised by the Romans. Their religion was thought odd. What a remarkable soldier!

I want you to notice one little thing. Nowhere in the New Testament is a soldier told that to be a soldier is a dishonourable profession for a believer in Jesus. On the contrary, centurions seem to stand out as fine men. There is one at the cross saying, "Surely he was the Son of God." There is another called Cornelius in Acts 10. These were men who stayed in the army and who were never told to stop being soldiers, even by John the Baptist, when they said, "What do we do to repent?" They were told to be just, honourable soldiers. So it has been ever since. Some of the finest Christians in our times have been soldiers who have understood Christ well. This man was going to understand Jesus Christ very well because of his military training and background.

Notice his humility, again remarkable in such a character. The Jews said he really was worthy for Jesus to do this thing for him. But the soldier's message was: I am not worthy either to come and speak face-to-face with you, a Jewish rabbi, nor to have you come into my Gentile home. What a man! He stands out as having the right scale of values. But let us ask what he thought about Jesus. Let us get inside his mind and heart. Here is the most incredible fact of all: he believed that Jesus could do anything by word of mouth alone, whether he was present or not. That is astonishing faith.

You see, Jesus had already been healing people by laying his hands on them and touching them. This man affirms that he didn't even need to come and touch the slave. Wherever you are, just say the word. Most people needed the touch of Jesus or needed to feel the hem of his garment or to have some tangible sign of Jesus' presence so they might believe in his power – but not this man. He was in the same position that a believer is in today. We cannot see Jesus. We cannot touch the hem of his garment. He is at the right hand of the Father in heaven, and the faith that is required of us is the faith this centurion had, which is to believe that he only has to say the word and it is done. Of course, we have far more reasons for having that faith than this soldier did. He had not met Jesus, he had only heard about him. Jesus had not yet died and risen again as we know he has. This centurion was outstanding, and he had the utmost confidence in Jesus.

The reason he did was this: the key word is "under". He recognised Jesus as a man under authority. That is the opposite of what you would have thought. He said, "I also am under authority, and because I am under authority I can tell people what to do." Now, if that centurion had not had the rank he had, if he had not been in Caesar's army, if he had just been an individual, he could not have told another man "Go!" and had the man go. But he had taken a commission.

I remember the time I took a commission, and still have the certificate. The Queen, bless her, gave it to me. I don't think she did it personally but there is her name on it anyway. The commission put me straight in at the rank of Flight Lieutenant. This was quite unusual for me. I had been used to a voluntary society of a church where you ask somebody to do something, hoping that they will feel that the Lord is leading them to do it. But now, suddenly, as an officer I could say to someone, "Go!" and, lo and behold he did. It took quite a lot of getting used to at first! That was no power in myself, no power of personality. I was under authority because the Squadron Leader above me could say to me, "Go". I was now in a chain of command, so with the Queen's commission, I could give an order to anybody below my rank. Because I was under authority, it was as if the Queen was telling that person to do something.

This soldier, when he heard about Jesus, saw this: That man is under the authority of the King, under the authority of God. Therefore, he can order this disease to leave my house. He can say to it: "Disease, quick march!" and the disease will have to go right out of the house, right out of the slave. That is how he came to his faith. That is how many soldiers have come to their faith – they have recognised authority. Since conscription ended, several generations of young people have grown up that find it very difficult to recognise authority, and that makes it hard to accept the authority of Jesus. But in a society where you recognise the chain of command and accept it, then you recognise the power of the Lord in people. This centurion was declaring: I also am a man under authority, and I tell slaves what to do and soldiers what to do, and they do it. So, when you are under the authority of God, all you have got to say is, "Disease, quick march!" and it is done. What faith!

So, what did Jesus think of the soldier? He was surprised, and that shows the true humanity of Jesus – he could be surprised by something. He was delighted, and he said, "I haven't found such great faith, not even in Israel." The word "marvelled" which is used here is only used twice in the ministry of Jesus. The other occasion was when he had preached in Nazareth, and it says, "He marvelled because of their unbelief." Do you remember that? He could do nothing in Nazareth; he was helpless to help people. You can imagine the thrill in his heart: he had never expected a Roman soldier to have the kind of faith he had expected in his own people and had not found there. That is what Jesus thought of this soldier.

So, I challenge you in this way: the trouble with Nazareth was familiarity, and the great blessing that came to the centurion was due to faith. These are opposites. Jesus marvelled at Nazareth because through their very familiarity with him, they could not believe in him – "Isn't this the carpenter's son?" But a total outsider with no such background said, "Jesus, just say the word and it's done." For those of us who have been brought up in Christian churches, in Sunday school, in Christian family homes – one of the perils of that is the familiarity that makes it hard to believe things can happen. You will be shamed and embarrassed from time to time when someone with no Christian background, no church upbringing, comes to Jesus and says, "Jesus, say the word," and things happen that you have never seen before. Do you expect Christ to do something? Do you expect him to touch lives? Do you say to him, "Jesus, just give the word..."?

The ministry in Capernaum continues, and Jesus is a guest of Simon the fisherman. Maybe that is one reason why he made Capernaum such a base. It was in fact the fishing base for the Sea of Galilee, which is thirteen miles long and eight miles wide and full of fish, unlike the Dead Sea where there is not a single fish. I have accompanied fishermen in Galilee at night on their fishing expeditions, and they hang a lantern over the stern of the ship. The fish are attracted to it as they would be to the light of the moon. Then the net is thrown down and pulled back, and in a reasonable catch there might be eight or ten fish. Something very different from that is going to happen shortly. There was a problem. Simon's mother-in-law was sick (and I am afraid I am rather naughty, saying that means the first Pope was married). When Jesus came into a house, sickness had to leave. It happened frequently. So he healed her, and she immediately began to wait on him and serve a meal. It is interesting to note that the healing led straight to service.

Now let us leave the home and go out into the street where there are dozens of people sick and needing healing, and that requires explaining. Capernaum today is in ruins. There is nothing there except an empty shell of a synagogue and the remains of a few homes. Why was Capernaum so packed with sick people? The answer is that two miles south, along the west coast of Galilee, is a place called Tiberius, which to this day is packed with sick people, because in Tiberius there are hot springs springing from the depths of the earth and, like Harrogate or Bath, it has become a spa for sick people. There I met Jews from all over the world who had come specifically all the way to Israel and to Tiberius to "take the waters", either by drinking or bathing in them. They are foul waters, full of sulphur – they smell, but they believe it heals, and here at the spa in Tiberius were hundreds of sick people, and they heard that up the coast in Capernaum there was someone who was healing and was successful every time. You can imagine the crowd rushing to Capernaum in the hope of being healed. That was why the street on any given morning was packed with sick people. I like this: Jesus touched each one. There was a big crowd, the street was crammed, but Jesus did not do any mass healing, he went to each one, touched them, and there was no failure, Jesus healed everyone. And once again, demons are on the scene. Jesus did not go looking for demons; they came looking for him. That is important because I am afraid there are some people who are looking for demons everywhere, even today. On this occasion they were shouting to get attention. "This is the Son of God," they shouted, and once again, Jesus wanted people to know that, but he did not want the demons to be the ones to tell them. He was waiting until Simon Peter the fisherman would say: I know who you are. So, with this demoniac man shouting at the top of his voice, Jesus silenced him because the demon knew he was the Christ, the coming King, the anointed one. Because he knew – and it was right, it was true – Jesus did not want him advertising him.

Soon, the disciples were left in complete bewilderment by the calming of the storm. Who is this man that even winds and the sea obey him? They were so near the truth there. He was God! That was how he could control the weather, and they could have guessed even then who he was. The demons had already told people who he was but Jesus had told them to keep quiet. Now the disciples were seeing for themselves.

The Sea of Galilee is surrounded by steep hills on all sides, so it is in a hollow and 600 feet below sea level. During the day what happens is this: the sun heats up the water of the Sea of Galilee and in the afternoon the hot air over the water rises and sucks in cold air, down all the valleys around, from every direction. So if you are in a little boat in the middle of that, you are stranded in the wind and you cannot move anywhere. I have been in a larger boat in the middle of an afternoon squall on the Sea of Galilee and it is frightening. In fact, they forbid anybody to go out in open rowing boats in the afternoon in Galilee because there is real danger. Suddenly, this beautiful still lake is in turmoil and the wind is blowing at you in the middle from every direction and you cannot escape. Furthermore, the boat was a bit overloaded – all the twelve disciples were in it, water was coming over the edge, and they looked to be in real danger of drowning. For fishermen to be afraid of drowning means they were in real danger. It must have been very frustrating that Jesus slept through the whole thing. He was fast asleep, and not troubled, so they woke him up and said, "Lord, save us! We are perishing!" He rebuked the winds and the sea and there was a great calm. Then he rebuked the disciples and said, "Why are you fearful, O you of little faith?"

He could sleep through it because he trusted his Father, but they obviously did not trust him yet. It was a very sharp rebuke to the wind, the waves and the disciples. It was then that they asked who on earth this was.

13
FORGIVENESS

Read Matthew Chapter 9

A paralysed man was brought to Jesus and we notice what faith is from this – it is not just accepting a creed, it is being absolutely determined to find Jesus, and it is being utterly confident that he is the one to help us. Now, why did Jesus deal with the sins of the paralytic rather than only his sickness? Was it just a case of seeing another need that the man was not aware of and simply doing the whole job at once? Was he just saying that as well as this paralysis you have got something else so we will just clear this up first, then tackle the main thing? No, there is something much deeper. This is not true in every case, but I believe in this man's case his suffering and his sin were directly related, and that is why Jesus dealt with it. He did not deal with others in the same way. Psychologists will now tell us there is nothing difficult in imagining that paralysis can be brought on by wrongdoing and by guilt. Jesus could always diagnose perfectly – he was the best doctor of people. He saw straight through to the cause of this difficulty in this man's case, and he dealt with the cause, not the symptoms. He dealt with it straight away and said to this man, "Son, your sins are forgiven". Then to prove that this was the real trouble and to show them that he had dealt with the problem, Jesus released him from the consequences of the cause, saying, "I tell you, get up, take up your bed and go home", and he did. The key factor here that caused the opposition was not the fact that he healed a paralysed man but the fact that he dealt with sins. In other words, if only Jesus had stayed with physical diseases he would have been perfectly all right. If he had gone round the world just helping sick people to be better, the cross would never have happened. Why then did he not just remain on earth as a physician as he could heal people? Surely that is a wonderful mission in life; surely to heal sick people is one of the noblest things you could do. Why did he prejudice, indeed jeopardise, the ministry of healing by doing other things as well? Could he not just have left the religious side alone? No, because Jesus came not to save people from sickness primarily but to save them from sin. That is why he had the name he had, and he had to deal with this at whatever cost to himself. He was claiming a divine prerogative – to forgive sins! Then we meet the tax collectors, who were collaborators. Can you understand what it was like to make a friend of one of them? Imagine what it was like to be such a person – to be a social outcast, and for the sake of money to have cut yourself off from your people. Jesus straightened out a man like that, and became unpopular as soon as he did so. But he called this man, who from collecting taxes became a man who collected stories about Jesus, and ultimately, we got the Gospel of Matthew.

Apart from the tax collectors and his friends within the trade there was another group of people who tended to mix with them for the same reason – and they were social outcasts. The word "sinner" is a peculiar word in the Gospel. Are we not all sinners? Yes. But the word as they used it meant people who were in a state of excommunication from their local synagogue. They were people who were not allowed to go into the congregation – they had broken the laws of God, whether knowingly or otherwise. They could not or would not live up to the religious standards imposed by the preachers of the day, so were simply untouchable. Here were two groups of people who had difficulty in mixing in ordinary society and were out on the fringe. Because they were outcasts they tended to mix together. Matthew (Levi) threw a party for them; he invited them along, and Jesus was right in the middle of the party. The thing that upset others was that Jesus would mix with religious outcasts. The first problem, as we saw with the paralytic, was that Jesus would bother about sins. If only he had stuck to healing he would have been all right. There would never have been a cross. The other problem was that he would bother with sinners. But Jesus came to deal with sinners and he came to deal with sins.

14
DISCIPLES SENT OUT

Read Matthew 10–11

This last bit of Jesus' ministry in the north was a real turning point, where disciples became apostles, which means "sent ones", and those who had been called to be with him, having studied him, were now called to deputise for him. They were sent out to do what Jesus had already been doing, so they were first commissioned and then he commanded them to do certain things. In commissioning, he gave them power and authority, and they needed both. He told them that they were to preach and to heal, as they had seen him do, but without him. That was the crucial changeover. The commissioning must have been done with something like the laying on of hands. That is how it was usually done in those days. He gave them certain commands which they were to follow. They were to take nothing for themselves – no money, no spare clothes, no bread. Why were they sent out with nothing? The answer must be that they were to depend on the people they went to for food, for a change of clothing, for any money. They were to go with nothing at all and I can imagine that was quite a test for them.

They were to stay in a house that was "worthy", where their peace would come upon it. But if the people did not receive the disciples, they were to shake the dust off their feet as they left, as a testimony against them. That, of course, was a well-known sign of disapproval. So off the disciples went. They were to preach, saying: "The Kingdom of heaven is at hand." They were to heal the sick, cleanse the lepers, raise the dead and cast out demons.

Persecution would follow. Yet they should not fear people but fear God. The theme of what the right fear of God is like is developed in this section. It is vital to look at the situation not from the point of view of what men will say or think but from the point of view of God. Here is an illustration. Somebody says to you, "Are you a Christian?" You are in a situation where you know you ought to declare yourself and say that you are a Christian. People in the office are discussing what religions there are in the world and what religion each one favours and you are present. You are saying to yourself, "I'm awfully afraid to confess I am a Christian because maybe I don't live up to it very much, and I am a bit embarrassed to acknowledge it." That is thinking of men, but if you think of God, this is what he would say in that situation: If you don't admit you belong to me, I cannot admit you belong to me; if you are ashamed to admit it, I am ashamed to admit it. When you are the coward and you do not say "I'm a Christian" when you should, if Christ is asked at that moment by the angels, "Is he one of yours?" he will say, "I can't acknowledge him, not at this moment. One of mine would acknowledge me." On the other hand, the moment you acknowledge publicly to others, "Yes, I do belong to Jesus Christ; I know him and I love him" – then at that moment Christ can say to the angels, "That person is mine and I acknowledge them openly. They belong to me." Now that is the direct consequence of what we do on earth. It is of the greatest importance what the Lord says about us and thinks and feels, not what other people do, and that will alter you tremendously.

So, next time you get a chance to nail your colours to the mast, remember that Christ can acknowledge you in heaven too, and say: Look at that person, one of mine – openly acknowledging them. But if we deny him, he has to deny us because we were not being true to him at that moment. Another thing that he looks at is rather puzzling at first. He says that you can say anything you like against the Son of Man and it could be forgiven, but if you speak against the Holy Spirit, it cannot be forgiven. Many have been puzzled by this: that the worst blasphemy that a man can make against our Lord Jesus can be forgiven, but the same thing against the Holy Spirit cannot be forgiven. People have asked why. The answer is very simple. It is true to history too – many of the Jews said horrible things against Christ. Some called him a blasphemer and wanted him put to death as a criminal. But seven weeks later, three thousand of them repented of that and were converted by Peter: "You crucified this man who is the Son of God. God has made him both Lord and Christ, this Jesus whom you crucified." They repented, and they said, "We are sorry we said it." They found forgiveness. The reason is that the Holy Spirit convicted them of sin. So, the Holy Spirit can convict us – if we listen to him – of the wrong we have done to Jesus, and, when we see that, we can repent and be forgiven. If you sin against the Holy Spirit in this way, who is going to convict you of that? Who will tell you that you have done wrong then? The answer is no one, because there is no one else to help you.

You see, Jesus came to those who had spoken against God the Father, and then the Holy Spirit came to those who had spoken against Jesus, but there is going to be no one more. If I will not let the Holy Spirit speak to me and if I deny his voice, and if I speak against the Holy Spirit, then frankly I have come to the end of the road because there is no one else to help me. Can you see that? Therefore, we must be careful when we speak. We must have a great fear of speaking against the Holy Spirit. Jesus' teaching means that the blasphemy against the Holy Spirit is to look at what the Holy Spirit is doing and say: "That is of the devil." When you say that, there is no hope for you, and then you have reached the end of the line. If the only person who can convict you of sin is the one you are calling the devil, then who will now do so?

Jesus teaches that when you are in a tight corner, when you have been arrested, when you are being tried for being a

Christian, that same Holy Spirit whom the world is blaspheming is going to be your greatest help. Do not be afraid, you may find yourself in a court of law. You may find yourself in the dark because you belong to Jesus. This does not cover being in the dark because you have committed a sin which is also a crime, but if you are there in the name of Jesus, don't worry! You may not be a preacher, they may have taken your Bible from you, and you may not know what to say, but do not be afraid of man, because the Holy Spirit will put words in your mouth. There are such amazing examples of this. Read the life of Stephen; read the life of Paul, Peter, James and John; when they appeared in court they always had the right words from God. It has been shown to be true through the ages. You find that whenever people of God have stood on trial, the Holy Spirit delivered them from fear of man and put words in their mouths. Let the fear of the Lord take away fear of people. In every situation you will find the Holy Spirit will help you.

Jesus did not expect everyone to accept the ministry of those he sent out. They were to tell hearers that the Kingdom of God is near – but he expected many people to reject it, and now he said some of the most terrible things, which almost make you shudder to read. Do you realise that if you send a missionary anywhere you will make some people worse off than they were before that missionary arrived? Some will be better off, but many will be worse off. The tragedy is this: if you have brought a person to a church service you could have pushed them nearer to hell. We have to face this unpleasant truth, that when you preach the gospel to someone you have not left them as they are. You have either brought them nearer to God or you have pushed them nearer to hell. Every missionary we send out makes some people more guilty than they were before. You cannot remain neutral with the gospel. When you hear Christ preached you either come or you go. You either take a step nearer or you pull back – you cannot remain the same. The tragedy is that there are some things that are even worse than moral degradation. Jesus is teaching here that to reject the gospel is a far worse sin than anything that happened in Sodom and Gomorrah. We tend to think those are the worst sins in the book, but no, Jesus is teaching that the worst sin in the book is on the part of somebody who rejects you when he has sent you to witness, because in rejecting you they have rejected him; in rejecting Jesus they have rejected God. This makes us representatives and ambassadors when we witness, and that is a frightening thing. To be a disciple of Jesus and to meet other people is to put them in the position where they must either come nearer to God, or draw further from him.

15

SUPERNATURAL

Read Matthew Chapter 12

There was a remarkable revolution in people's thinking about the supernatural around the middle of the twentieth century. I was born into and brought up within the scientific era in which the natural was regarded as the real and the supernatural as unreal. It was widely thought that the only problems that mankind had to solve were the problems of the material world, and that final satisfaction and meaning came through material things. This was the whole atmosphere of my upbringing and it has had its effect on my thinking. This outlook, which confined reality to that which could be seen and touched, invaded and infected even the church, so that the supernatural receded from Christian thinking, all through the twenties, thirties, forties, and into the fifties.

I picked up a well-known twentieth century commentary which would have been on most preachers' bookshelves. I looked up this passage and the commentator said that the man who was suffering was under the delusion that he had a demon – and the commentator said that it was a delusion. That was written as a guide to preachers. It was published by the thousands and it is simply an example of how even preachers explained away the supernatural – the miracles became no more than coincidences. It was thought that God, if there was a God, was locked up in heaven and things that happened down here happened within the cast iron system of cause and effect so that there was no point in praying about the weather. God could do no more about it than you could – it was part of the physical universe that simply went on its way. This was the thinking of my background.

I will tell you quite frankly that I went to church for years and I never thought about demons as a possible reality. I read the stories; I accepted the scholars' word for it that it was a superstitious way of talking about mental illness. I honestly thought there was no difference between schizophrenia and demonic possession except that we changed our labels over the centuries. But that has all changed now. From one point of view, thank God it has. We are getting in touch with reality a little better. It happened shortly after the Second World War. Two world wars shattered the idea that science could solve our problems, that material things could bring final meaning and satisfaction. So there began to be a search for more reality, a search that looked beyond the visible world.

When we got to the moon and found it empty and came back, that was the end of it all. So people said: there is nothing to be found in this universe through the material, through the physical senses; we are going to explore elsewhere and try to find reality. So, having exhausted speed and noise and drugs and a number of other things, people began to say, "Let's see if there is a supernatural world." They began to look for it. If only they had believed God's Word first. For the revelation of God has been there all down the centuries. There is a supernatural world and it is more real than this natural one. It is in the supernatural world that you will find meaning, satisfaction and fulfilment, but – and here is the huge but – the Bible makes it absolutely clear that if you explore the supernatural world, you are playing with fire. For this reason: that there is evil as well as good in the supernatural sphere. This is a warning that goes unheeded today.

People are having to learn the hard way that when they step into the supernatural realm they discover evil, the like of which they never dreamed existed. They discover malice and destructive powers far worse than anything they have ever heard of in human nature. That is a warning the Bible has uttered all through the centuries and it has been ignored, and so people have been exploring the supernatural with no discernment, with no sense of danger. Often, they do it originally for kicks, for a bit of excitement in their boring life, for a new thrill. Once you believe in demons you do not rush to meet them. Pray for those who are in the frontline of this battle.

So, the word "demon" came back into our vocabulary. The word "exorcism" came back – a word we had hardly heard used for many years. The churches most of us were brought up in were not in touch with this kind of thing. It is new to many; it can be scary but it is part of the Word of God. So people are getting involved. I find two groups of Christians I am worried about. The first are older Christians who still do not believe that demons are real or that you find them anywhere. They lack experience and knowledge and have never come to grips with God's Word on the subject and that group worries me because they are out of touch.

Another group worries me even more, and that is a group of Christians who find a demon under every bush and go around trying to exorcise the common cold. This is not an exaggeration – I have come across that. To put every trouble that anybody has, or every minor depression, or every physical ailment, down to this is just plain silly and shows as much lack of discernment as the other group I have mentioned. It is very important in a day when reality has crept up on us again, to have true discernment; to keep a cool head as well as a warm heart in this situation of dealing with people.

Jesus was an exorcist. I believe he was the only person who had a right to the title "The Exorcist". I believe he is the only one who has been able every time to deal totally and adequately and permanently with every case of possession that he came across, not that this was his sole occupation and ministry. He did not go looking for this but his advent on earth provoked an almost unprecedented activity of evil spirits, for they recognised in his coming the beginning of their end. They recognised the greatest challenge they had ever had. So they said, "You Holy One of Israel, Holy One of God, what have you to do with us?" There are some nine recorded cases in which Jesus encountered them and there would have been many others, for the Gospels are only a tiny selection of all Jesus did, and if all he ever did was written in books, the whole world could not be a big enough library to contain them.

Jesus met people possessed by demons and this was such a man. We are not told of the cause of his possession. Did he dabble in the occult? Did he go into it for a thrill? How did he get involved? Certainly, he had no intention of becoming as involved as he became and I am quite sure that when he went into it he had no idea that this would rob him of two of his most useful faculties and break down his communicating abilities. He had no idea, but he lost his sight and his speech, and that was only the beginning of his troubles. It is only the beginning of the end, for evil spirits' intention is to destroy a human being until he no longer has any capacity to bear the image of God upon him. I think of the Episcopal bishop, Bishop Pike who explored the supernatural, got in touch with his own son, he claimed – his son had committed suicide. So, the bishop went to a medium and began to contact his son, he claimed to have had messages from the other side from his son and said it was all right for Christians to engage in this. How did Bishop Pike finish up? Those evil spirits he contacted (and he was not contacting his son, he was contacting the spirits who knew more about his son than he did) led him into the wilderness of Judea until he was lost and died out there in the rocky valleys all alone. That was the bishop's end. They destroyed him in the very place where Satan tried to destroy Jesus and they succeeded with that bishop.

That is the end of it all – the destruction of a human being so that he can no longer bear the image of God, however simply it begins – and one of the shames of our days is that Ouija boards are sold as toys.

Matthew Chapter 12

Jesus met the man who could not talk and could not see. Not everybody who is deaf or dumb has come to it this way, but this man had. This was not a dressed-up version of mental illness or emotional disturbance. This was a straight case of a man who was already in the grip of evil powers and people brought him to Jesus – the best person to whom they could have brought him.

Demons are more intelligent and more powerful than we are, and no human being can tackle them. Jesus could tackle them for two reasons: first, he is the Son of God and therefore he was above them to begin with; secondly, though, in coming to Earth he was putting himself within their sphere of activity, but he lived an utterly holy life here and they said: what have you to do with us, you holy one? It takes a divine person and a holy human to deal with this situation, and Jesus was both. So, Jesus set the man free and he could see and he could speak. The exorcist had triumphed.

Now, I don't want you to think it was easy for Jesus. It was a battle and it was to cost him his blood and his life. For the principalities and powers he challenged threw everything in the book at him, but ultimately there was the cross. It was not easy – he had to struggle with and bind the strong man before he could steal his goods. So, it was a spiritual battle – a heavy, hard one, and he sweated blood over it at one stage. But having triumphed over the principalities and powers, he made a show of them openly. In the cross he showed them up to be infinitely weaker than himself.

Consider the reaction of people to what Jesus did. It is a very strong message here. When the people saw it, they were amazed: Could this be the Son of David? Could this be the Christ? Could this be the One God has sent? Could this be the One we have waited for, for a thousand years? They were asking the right question and were on the track of truth but I want you to notice that also another group of people came to exactly the opposite conclusion and said: This is not God, this is the devil.

Here we have the same incident, the same evidence, the same person and two groups of people coming to totally opposite conclusions.

People believe what they want to believe. There is no such thing as objective belief in this sense. Firstly, every single one of us (including myself) has *chosen* to believe what we want to believe. I wanted to believe in Jesus, so I believed in Jesus. Secondly, the fact that all of us chose what we believe does not entitle us to that belief. The common view today is that since people choose what they want to believe and believe what they want to believe, that entitles all of us to believe what we want – but it does not. You may believe what you want to believe but the real question is: Does it correspond to the truth?

I believed in Jesus because I wanted to believe in Jesus and, hallelujah, it corresponded to the truth – it fitted. The facts are there, and what I wanted to believe proved true. Is it not great when you wanted to believe something you find is actually true? We are not entitled to any other beliefs than the truth, even though we believe what we want to believe. The people wanted to believe in the Christ, they wanted him to come, they wanted God to send the Saviour, and they were open to it. So they wondered about Jesus: Could this, the exorcist, be the Christ?

The Pharisees did not want to believe that Jesus was the Christ so they believed it was of Satan. Who was right? The Pharisees were not entitled to what they believed, nor is anybody else, however sincerely they believe what they believe. If they believe something that is not true, they are not entitled to that belief. We are not being intolerant of each other if we question someone's beliefs when we regard them as being in error. We ask: "Is what you want to believe right? Is what I want to believe right?" That is the important question. Jesus rebuked and argued with those who were not entitled to their opinion.

One of the things that some of us have been brought up to accept is that arguing is not a Christian practice. That is not true.

Mind you, the *way* we sometimes argue may not be Christian, but argument itself can be a very Christian thing and Christ was a great arguer. John Stott wrote a book studying the arguments of Jesus, and he called it *Christ the Controversialist*. It did not sell as well as his other books because it was such a controversial title. People do not like to think of Christ as a controversialist, but he was. He was an arguer. There is a difference between his arguments and ours: he won every time. Furthermore, it was always a one-sided argument. They only needed to say one thing and he said something back, and that was the end of the argument. Then they would switch to something else and he would say something else and that was the end of that argument. You study the teaching of Jesus – he did argue people into silence when he came across those who held their own opinion and knew it to be a wrong opinion. He argued them into silence and he argued them out of it.

Let us see how he argued them out of this one. They looked at Jesus exorcising a demon and they said, "He is in league with Beelzebub"– that is another name for Satan. Literally it means "Lord of the Flies". What a vivid description of Satan. If you lived in the tropics, you would understand that description so well. Flies get in everywhere – they get on your food, they irritate, they bring disease, they are always there. You cannot sleep without putting a net around you. What a vivid description: Lord of the Flies; the agents of the devil getting in anywhere, always buzzing around your head; always there; the prince of the power of the air, with his flies, right through the air. They said he is in league with him; this is one of the devil's flies. That is what they said about Jesus, that is what they are saying. He is one of the devil's flies buzzing around; a nuisance to be swatted. See how they were thinking?

Jesus shows that the Pharisees' thinking is inconsistent and illogical. He was pointing out that their argument was inconsistent with what we know of the devil. Have you ever known the devil gladly give up one of his victims? Here, then, was a very strange thing: a man who was in the grip of the devil was set free and they were saying the devil was doing it. This is strange, is it not? If you have struggled to set someone free from the devil, you will know that the devil will not let them go. Only the power of Jesus can loosen his grip. A house divided against itself will fall and if Satan is fighting himself he is finished – we do not need to worry about him anymore. But it is utterly inconsistent with fact, with our knowledge of the devil.

Next, Jesus was observing that it was inconsistent with their own religious practice. They believed in demons, practising exorcism themselves, so they wanted it both ways. When they did it, it was supposedly of God. Such is the perversion of our minds that in most of our arguments against the Word of God we are utterly inconsistent. We want it both ways. The next argument Jesus used against them was this: it is inconsistent with the very ordinary experience of life. If you want to burgle someone, the first thing you have got to do is deal with that person. They have to be out of the way before you can steal their property. In those days the owner was invariably in his one-room house, and if you wanted to burgle it, you would have to get in first, bind him and then you could spoil his goods. It does not make sense. You cannot release someone captive unless you first capture the captor. It is logical, isn't it?

When did Jesus bind Satan? It was during the six weeks in the wilderness when Satan tried to destroy Jesus – literally, by getting him to throw himself off the pinnacle of the temple on one occasion. If Jesus had done this, he would have dashed his brains out on the stone courtyard below because the promise that the devil quoted from Psalms was quoted out of context and not applicable to someone who deliberately threw himself off a tower. If Jesus had done it, he would have killed himself. The devil tried to destroy Jesus at the beginning of his ministry before ever Jesus healed a single person, before he preached a single sermon, before he did a single miracle. He had been led of the Spirit into the wilderness. Why? Because he had first to bind the strong man, then he could spoil his goods. So, some months after that wilderness temptation experience, when Jesus met a woman who had been haemorrhaging for years, he said, "You see this woman? She has been bound by Satan but now I am going to set her free." He could only do that because he had bound the strong man first. So, Satan was bound and Jesus spoiled his goods.

Now, those are logical arguments. There is no answer to them and they did not give one, but he now added solemn warnings. Warning number one: you cannot remain neutral once you have seen what Jesus can do for people. Once you have seen the power of Jesus to set people free, from that moment you are either for or against him; you either join him – and you join him in doing what he is doing in gathering people in – or remain aloof; becoming one of those who scatter. But once you have seen Jesus operate on people, once you have seen the power of Jesus and what he can do for others, then from that moment you cannot be neutral.

You are either going to come and help Jesus with his work and gather people for him, or you are going to be against him from now on. It is dangerous to come into a church and meet people who have been changed by Christ. You have then put yourself in a frightful position. You either come and join Christ in his work to set others free, or you are going to be among those who will make his work more difficult.

Solemn warning number two: when you see Christ at work and you do not accept it as God's work, you could put yourself in danger of committing a sin that could never be forgiven. I have heard sermons on the unforgivable sin and I have heard preachers play it down. I have heard preachers soften it. I have heard people say: "It is so rare you hardly come across it." I do not believe that. I believe it is a very common danger. Mind you, I have met all sorts of people who have all kinds of ideas.

It has nothing to do with sex, for example. As we discussed in the last chapter, out of thousands of sins that can be committed, there is only one that can never be forgiven. What is it? It is called blasphemy against the Holy Spirit. It is to say that what the Spirit of God is doing is not from God.

Now, that is all too common in our day, for the Holy Spirit is moving on a scale that some of us have never known in our lifetime and yet some Christians are saying, "This is not of God, this is of the devil." People are leaving churches because of what the Spirit is doing because it is new and because it does not fit in with their traditions and ideas. They are in mortal danger of doing this very thing. Now, let us look at it. If I say black is white and white is black, I am brainwashing myself and I am putting myself in a position where one day I will not know the difference. If I say good is evil and evil is good, there will come a day when I cannot tell the difference any more. You will have read George Orwell's *1984*. That book is based on the premise that for so long people have been calling black white and white black, and lies truth and truth lies, that there comes a point where people cannot discern the difference. A man can bring himself to that point by brainwashing. If he does so, what hope is there of repentance? How will he ever see what is wrong? How will he ever hate it? How will he ever turn away from it? Well, he will be unable to do so, because for repentance it is vital that we know that good is good and evil is evil.

If I see the Holy Spirit of God doing a work, setting people free – free from their sins, free from their inhibitions, free from their traditions, and I say that is bad, not good, I am in danger of brainwashing myself until I do not recognise what God is doing. There is a further important reason why it cannot be forgiven and will not be forgiven, and it is this: if I blaspheme against God the Father, if I call him all the names under the sun, if I use his name as a swear word, I can be forgiven because there is someone to persuade me that I have sinned – and that someone is Jesus Christ, the Son of God. When Jesus Christ came, he was able to persuade many that they were sinning against God. If I blaspheme Jesus and use his name as a swear word and if I say all these terrible things about Jesus and if I join a Jesus-hate club – even if I do all that – it will still be possible for me to be forgiven for there is someone who will be able to convince me that I have sinned – and that someone is the Holy Spirit. If I say these things about the Holy Spirit, there is no one left to convince me I have sinned. No human being can convince another that they are a sinner – only God can do that.

If I blaspheme the Son of God, there is God the Holy Spirit to convict me of that sin, and I know that is true because on the very day of Pentecost the Holy Spirit, through Peter's preaching, had convinced those who crucified Jesus that they had sinned; blasphemed against him. They were forgiven and baptised and became Christians. If I say these things about what the Holy Spirit is doing, God has no one else to convict me. There are only three persons of the Godhead and I have now reached the third and refused his enlightenment. Do you see now why it cannot be forgiven? It just can't, in the nature of things, and we need to be very careful.

I utter this solemn warning because I believe some are in danger of this: that when the Holy Spirit sets them free, they say it is not of God. I beg such people not to persist in an attitude that could lead to this, for Jesus gave these Pharisees a simple warning. He was not saying that they had committed this already or had got this far already. He gave them a solemn warning that they have put themselves on the road to it. He says there is a sin, beware, that will not be forgiven. In these days demons and angels are being thought about more, and the Holy Spirit is doing things that he did in ancient days that he did in the New Testament, things that we may not have been used to. In a situation that has not been our normal lot, many of us brought up in sheltered homes, with a Christian upbringing, have not come up against many things that now are confronting us face to face. In that situation, let us say, "O God, I want the truth. I want to know what is of the Spirit and what is of the devil. I do not want to make any mistake in this." So, Jesus was the exorcist.

The greatest freedom of all that we need is to be free from sin and from Satan. I know of no one in the whole world who can do that for you but Jesus.

Here is another solemn warning: words are enough to damn a man to hell eternally. (See 12:36f.)

Jesus was often using pictures from nature to describe human nature, because we are part of nature. Therefore, some of the principles on which nature operates, operate in us. Henry Drummond, in *Natural Law in the Spiritual World*, applied the laws of nature to the spiritual sphere, and showed there is a remarkable correspondence. Jesus was often doing this. There is one very important thing about a tree: it can only produce the fruit that belongs to that variety of tree. It does not matter what tree you plant. You cannot gather grapes off thistles or figs off thorns. Nature is always true to itself, and one of the laws of nature is that everything produces after its kind. That makes all animal husbandry possible, and all crop husbandry. If pigs had puppies we could not breed them and we could not have any agriculture. It is a law that runs right through nature that like produces like, and each species produces after its own kind. It is a law of human nature that you can only produce the fruit that belongs to your tree. If your character is represented as the tree, what is the fruit that you produce? The answer is: the words that come out of your mouth. What the fruit is to the tree, words are to you.

This is not about carefully prepared statements but when you speak in an unguarded moment, when something is blurted out, then you reveal what the tree is that has been growing in your heart for a long time. It is the odd moments of conversation, the things you say under pressure. Now most of us like to think that the real self is when we speak in a prepared way, and I am very careful with what I say – but not a bit of it. The real you comes out when your words come out spontaneously. That is why Jesus taught that it is for every idle word that people will be judged. That means every word that slipped out when they were not on duty – the words that come out on Monday morning, not Sunday night; the words that just slip through the guard – that is when you give yourself away.

I have the feeling that in the case of Richard Nixon what shocked America was not so much that they discovered that he had in fact been an accomplice in the cover-up of Watergate, but the coarse language that came out all the way through. It had never come out in his prepared speeches. It had never come out in the utterances in public, but when they heard the tapes and heard this man talk about those near to him within the privacy of the Oval Office at the White House, they were shocked. They felt they had not understood the real man, and now that his idle words were recorded and out they knew what he was. However, before we point a finger at President Nixon, let me ask you if you would be happy if your private conversations had all been bugged and were now being made public. I would not. Jesus said it is these words that God's tape recorder catches, for if I can put it in a simple way, God bugs every conversation. He is present, he is the silent listener at every conversation. Jesus said that there's nothing hidden that will not be revealed. What you have said in the bedchamber will be shouted from the housetops. That is shattering.

You do not need to talk to someone in a relaxed setting for very long before you get an impression of what they really are like. On the other hand, if someone is holding back and not responding immediately to your questions, you know they are being jolly careful. Ministers in the House of Commons get asked a tricky question and then they come back later with a very carefully prepared answer. You know there is something up; they have to be careful what they say. If we realise that our idle speech will give us away, we can try to be very reserved and careful, but that gives us away too. People say, "Why is he holding out on us?" and our speech is what reveals us. Jesus therefore said that your speech is enough to damn you. If nothing else were ever said on Judgment Day but a recording played back of all those bugged conversations in your life, then that would be enough because the Bible says: if you have never said the wrong thing, then you are a perfect person. You are holy, because the tree must then be good if you never say the wrong thing. So, Jesus is teaching us that it is not changing your speech that matters, it is changing the tree.

During my time as a chaplain in the RAF, I saw many young men come to the Lord, especially among the national servicemen, and we always knew when one had been converted and had become a Christian. He stopped swearing. We never told him to, and we never said it is wrong, but suddenly his speech was different. This was the proof to us there was a new tree growing inside. There had been a total change – a new nature had been given. He just stopped and his speech gave it away, and our speech does give us away.

How urgent it is that we seek the forgiveness of God before those recordings are made available.

Jesus came to show us what real religion is. Real religion is not what you say when you have prepared it, not what you say when you are reading it out of a hymn book or a prayer book, not what you say when you are being careful with your speech. Real religion wants to deal with you at such depth that your speech all the time reveals a new tree growing in you.

The next thing is the nature of proof and at first sight it seems to have little connection. People came to Jesus and wanted him to prove – visibly, to their eyes – that he was who he said he was. But they would not take Jesus' words from his mouth as revealing him. They would not accept the revelation that came

Matthew Chapter 12

in what he said, and so they said, "Teacher, we want to see a sign from you." They would not believe the words of Jesus and Jesus spoke of an evil and adulterous generation. What did he mean by that? It is a bit of an insult. He meant: you love your own ideas better; you do not want to believe. You can say of somebody who keeps demanding visible proof that they do not want to believe the words that they have heard. Jesus mentions two narratives from the Old Testament days and refers them both to the Day of Judgment again.

We move then to the story of Jonah, which is often misunderstood because it is thought that Jonah was alive inside the whale or the great fish, whatever it was. So many people have argued, "How could Jonah live inside the whale? Where did he get his oxygen?" It is true that in 1927 it was claimed that on a whaling ship in the Antarctic someone fell overboard and was later found inside the belly of a whale as it was cut up, and was just alive, though his body was terribly eaten away with the digestive juices of the whale's stomach. So, it has happened, but I do not believe that helps us any with Jonah.

I believe that Jonah was dead, that when he was thrown into the sea the whale wasn't on the surface with its mouth wide open to catch him. It says that Jonah sank down from the surface right to the bottom of the ocean, to the very roots of the mountains with the seaweed entangled around his head, right down to the bottom of the Mediterranean. It only takes about a minute and a half to drown. It takes fully that to get to the bottom of the Mediterranean Sea and the fish picked up a dead body and carried it around. I have seen a film of a whale do this. A member of our former church went out to California and became a trainer of whales, dolphins and porpoises. In one huge tank he had a big whale and a little dolphin and he trained them to do tricks. These two creatures had a very warm relationship. They were both mammals, both air breathing and they understood each other. The dolphin died, and for three whole days that great huge whale carried the dolphin around in its mouth and kept popping it above the surface to try and get it to breathe again, instinctively knowing that it was not getting oxygen. The whale picked up a dead body. For three days and three nights Jonah was dead inside that whale, and if you read chapter 2 of Jonah carefully, all the prayers that he prayed were prayers from Sheol, the world of the departed – prayers from the dead. God brought him back to life after three days and three nights dead in the belly of the whale.

Jonah was resurrected, one of the three resurrections in the Old Testament. He was brought back to life after that experience and Jesus reminded his hearers of the sign of Jonah as he was three days and three nights in the belly of the whale, the Son of Man was going to be three days and three nights in the heart of the Earth. There would be a miracle, like the sign that Nineveh had. But notice one important thing: the people of Nineveh never saw that miracle, they only heard about it. It was in the Mesopotamian Basin. They got the sign of Jonah, only in word, and they heard that he had been dead for three days and three nights and had been brought back to life. Nineveh heard it and believed and repented, and that is all the sign these people got.

Do you want proof that Christianity is true? I will give it to you. Jesus was three days and three nights in the tomb, but you might say, "I didn't see it." Nor did Nineveh, but they believed it. If you say, "Well, I can't believe it unless I see it. You are just telling me that happened, I can't believe it on your word," then one day, on the Day of Judgment, you will stand there and God will say to you, "These Ninevites believed it when they heard about it, why didn't you? Do you doubt my Word?" The signs that have come to us so often are things that we hear. Are we prepared to take God's Word for them?

Now Jesus gives the example of a woman – to include everybody. He talks about that fabulous figure, the Queen of Sheba – that romantic figure who haunted Hollywood film producers for decades. She was a real person and you may meet her one day. I do not know quite where she lived – it may have been what is now Yemen or it may even have been what is now Ethiopia, but somewhere in that southern part of Arabia or the north-eastern part of Africa – there lived this queen. She heard that there was a king a long way to the north who had riches and wisdom. She only heard it and she set off, and in those days such a journey was a long, hard one. She had nothing to go on but somebody's word, but she believed it. When she came and saw Solomon's glory and heard his wisdom from his lips she realised that she had not been told half of the truth. The important thing is that she believed what she was told.

When we speak to each other, we do not trust each other's words. We know that we are not people who can be trusted, and so we do not take people's word for it. We read things in the papers and they prove later not to be true. We hear things through gossip and they are later proved to be false, and we have got into this habit of not believing words at their face value, and not believing that words could reveal the truth about a person. Jesus' words revealed his true self. He was speaking the truth – about who he is – and his hearers did not believe it. One day they would be thoroughly ashamed.

I believe there may be many when the Day of Judgment comes who will be ashamed, because some people who have only heard the gospel once have believed it and others may have heard it Sunday after Sunday and still not have taken a preacher's word for it that Jesus is alive. Faith is taking God at his Word and believing that what he says comes right from his heart and is true of him forever. That is the second principle of true religion. It is based not on visible proof but on the evidence of God's Word. You have heard it and you either take God at his Word or you distrust him, but an evil and adulterous generation would not believe the words. Is it not ludicrous? Jesus had just cast out a demon and restored a withered arm, and they have the absolute impudence to say: Give us a visible proof. It is absolutely clear that they did not want to believe; that no matter how many miracles happened, they still would not believe.

The third principle concerns the danger of emptiness. How do people get like the Pharisees? How do they get so hard that they cannot believe the truth? How can they get so malicious that when they see the Holy Spirit operate they say it is the devil? They get that way through becoming empty, and how do they become empty? Through religion of the wrong sort. There is nothing more dangerous than becoming clean and empty. You are in a far more dangerous condition than you were when evil occupied your life. It is a strange thing this, but we cannot somehow get around it. We cannot get this across to people: that you may be living the most respectable, religious life, and be empty, and you are in a dangerous condition.

Jesus applies the principle to demon possession, though it needs to be applied on a widespread scale. Do you realise that no human being can destroy an evil spirit? If you get them out of one person you have not destroyed them and they will wander around until they find someone else to get into. You have not reduced their number. Evil is a personal force and you cannot reduce that force. Only God can destroy that force, and one day he is going to. He has already prepared the pit of fire and brimstone for the devil and all his angels, but in this world when a demon is cast out it is not destroyed but is simply shifted on. You have moved the problem from one to another, and it is very important to realise this. You have not got rid of evil, you have simply got the evil out of that person, and the evil spirit will look around for someone else who wants to dabble in evil things.

You see, they know that in this world they can have no power, no satisfaction unless they occupy someone and control them. They want power, and they want power over people, and they want power in this world. They can also inhabit animals. I remember a Swiss pastor telling me about a farmer's son who was possessed by a demon and there were Christians seeking to cast the demon out. The demon went out, but they heard the most indescribable noise outside the farmhouse, and when they went into the farmyard, the pigs outside the farmhouse were tearing each other to pieces.

You see, you do not get rid of evil by casting it out, it moves on because it is personal. Evil is not a thing, evil is persons. The devil is a personal being. Do not believe those who deny his existence. You only shift him on, and so Jesus made it clear that when you have cast out a demon you have not finished your job. The tragedy is that if you shift evil, it could easily move back. If you leave a person clean but empty, then that evil being could come right back with seven worse than itself, and the result of your ministry to that person will be to leave them worse off than when you found them. It is vitally important not just to cast out evil, but to see straight away that that person is filled with the Holy Spirit.

You know this is true in nature – in your garden. Shall I tell you the best way to get a really good crop of weeds? It is to clean a bed thoroughly and put nothing in it. Get it beautifully clean, and every weed out, and then the weeds can get all the air and sunlight and they will grow. It is true of human nature.

Many of the sins we fall prey to are sins of idleness because we have got nothing to do and Satan finds mischief for idle hands to do. You see, you find people who are slaves (say to drink or smoking or something else) and they make a superhuman effort for the Lord and pray hard and ask for grace to stop these things, but if their life is not filled up with new activities, new interests, new affections, they are in a more dangerous state than they were when they gave up whatever was getting them down. You know this to be true. The expulsive power of a new affection is a very sound principle and Jesus taught us that someone may have evil cast out of him, he may have cleaned his life right out, be really respectable and really religious, but if he is not filled, other things can come in and you know the things that come in are worse than what was there. What kind of thing comes back into a clean empty life? Pride – "Oh, what a good boy am I!" That is Pharisaism again, and the Pharisees got this way because their religion was negative. "I thank you that I am not as other men are." How negative. A person who thinks they are a Christian just because they do not smoke, and do not drink, and do not gamble, and do not do a hundred and one other things, they are in a most dangerous condition. It is these who give Christianity a bad name because they become narrow-minded, inflexible, intolerant and critical, and they are not filled with the life of God. They are just empty of the wrong things, but they are not full of the right things. It breeds an outlook and a character that is not a delight to know, and I can understand those who say of someone who becomes that kind of religious person: I liked them better when they were a sinner.

The real answer is not just to be emptied of sin but to be filled with what is good. The Pharisees could not do that for people. They could get them to clean their lives up. They could get them to get this, that and the other out of their lives. They could even cast out demons. The one thing they could not do was fill people with the Spirit. That is why it bred such a dreadful religion. It becomes legalism, and you and I know that it is only too easy for Christian fellowships to become legalistic and to become hidebound and narrow, until you can understand a person saying, "Well, if that's Christianity I want nothing to do with it."

There is a negative side. Yes, Jesus wants sin out of our life, but there is a positive side too. He wants good things in their place. He does not just want someone who is free from hate, he wants someone who is full of love. He does not just want a person who is free of pride, he wants someone who is full of humility – which is the positive side. He does not just want people who say, "I've never done anybody any harm." He wants people who are doing positive good. So, our third principle of true religion is: get the positive side. Do not just be emptied of wrong things, but see that you help each other to be filled with the right things.

The fourth principle that we meet here again is seemingly a jump – it is the principle of the basis of relationship. I think of an extraordinary incident. There was one day when I opened my diary in my study and there it said "2.30", and against the time was my wife's name. She had to make an appointment to see me to have a chat, and she thought that was the only way, so she put herself down for 2.30 to see me – that is against me. The family of Jesus came and said, "We would like to see Jesus. Can we have a chat with our own Jesus?" There was a big crowd and they could not get near. They sent a message through the crowd: Your mother, sisters and brother are here – they want to have a chat with you, they want to see you.

Jesus stretched out his hand towards his disciples and said: "Here are my mother, and my brothers." That is a profound statement. Do you realise the full implications of it? The only basis of a lasting relationship is a relationship to God. All other relationships are temporary. Death ends all physical family ties. From time to time I am asked, "What about in heaven? If I am in heaven and my husband [or wife] is in hell, how will I feel?" That question need not be asked. Physical ties end with death. The only ties that survive death are the ones of which Jesus speaks here, and I assure every Christian that all your brothers, all your sisters, all your mothers will be there, because your Father is there, and his whole family will be present. You will no longer regard those who were your physical relatives here as your family. One of the difficulties of being a Christian is that in this world you are torn between two loyalties. Thank God if you are not, and all your family is in loyalty to God. But is it not true, especially for young people, when you became a Christian and you were the only Christian in the house, that it was not long before you felt that your fellow Christians were your real brothers and sisters and were nearer to you, even than your nearest and dearest?

While we are in this world, the Bible makes it quite clear we are to maintain our loyalties to our family relationships. We must go on honouring our father and mother, whether they are Christians or not. We must go on caring for those who are nearest to us. We may be their only link with God. We may be the channel of his grace to them, but let us make no mistake about it, the lasting relationships are not husband-wife, parent-child. The lasting relationships come through getting a new Father. It is significant that Joseph is not mentioned here – he was probably dead, but we learn here that family relationships are entirely dependent on who is the father. Who is my brother? Whoever does the will of my Father. Who is my mother? Whoever does the will of my Father. He had a mother who did the will of his Father. He did not have any brothers or sisters who did at that stage. Later they were so ashamed of what they had said about him. James, the Lord's brother, wrote a beautiful letter, and in it he said: Watch your words.

The brothers and sisters of the Lord, they did come. Out of twelve apostles, seven were relatives of Jesus. Thank God when your physical relatives are your spiritual relatives, but they are not all. The vital thing is that you find your true family that will last forever, and that involves doing the will of the Father in heaven. When you are doing the will of the Father, you have got a whole big new family.

It is a thrill to me to meet so many people from different countries all over the world, and know before I met them they were my brothers and sisters. When you meet them you feel you have known them twenty years. Do you get that feeling? What a family to belong to, and to know that that family is going to go on forever, and that the close relationship I have with my wife in Christ will be as close with everybody in the family, in Christ in heaven. That is something more wonderful than saying, "I hope I'll meet my relatives in heaven." You will meet your true ones, for those are the only relationships that last.

So that is the fourth principle of religion and it matters not whether your parents were Christian, or your grandparents, or your great-grandparents. It matters not whether your brother is a Christian or your sister is a Christian. What makes you part of the family is your relationship to your Father in heaven.

By negative thinking you can make a list of what makes false religion. False religion is to say carefully thought-out things about God and then go home and say things to your own family and your friends that are totally contradictory, and reveal the real you. False religion is to demand visible proof, and really in your heart be extremely reluctant to believe what God has said. False religion is whilst getting rid of what is wrong in your life, remaining empty. False religion is to think that because all your family belong to Christ that you must too.

True religion is to recognise that the words that come out of me in my unguarded moments are the real me, and that an evil tree can never produce good fruit, and I just have to ask the Creator, "Lord, plant a new tree in my heart. Make a new me." Real religion is to say, "Lord, I didn't see the resurrection, I never saw Jonah come out of that whale, I never saw Solomon in all his glory, but I believe. You said it happened, and I believe it. I take your word for it because I believe your words are true to you." True religion, thirdly, is to say, "It's not enough for me to get rid of this bad habit, and that bad affection, I want to be filled to overflowing with the Holy Spirit of God." True religion, fourthly, is to say, "I want to do the will of my Father in heaven." We know what that will is. The Jews once asked Jesus, "What must we do to do the will of God?" He said, "Believe on the One whom he has sent." That is where it starts – that is true religion. Let nothing else ever delude you. Never think that anything less than those four things is true Christianity – it is not the real thing; but it is lovely when you meet the real thing. You know it, don't you? You cannot catch a person in their off moments – they always speak true words.

You know that they have got tremendous faith and that, all appearances to the contrary, nothing could shake that faith. You know that their life is full to overflowing with God, and you know that they have an intimate, personal relationship with God.

16
THE PROBLEM OF EVIL

Read Matthew 13

For centuries philosophers have been grappling with one of the major questions raised by life, namely the problem of evil in our world. There are two questions which philosophers have had to ask. First, how did it originate or how was it introduced? Second, how can it be eradicated? How did evil get in and how can we get it out? Thinkers have argued about these important questions for centuries. They are so related to our daily life that it would be astonishing if they were not dealt with and answered in the teaching of Jesus.

The question "How was evil introduced into our world?" is in the same vein as the question about where the weeds came from ("How then does it have tares?" 13:27). The answer to the question about the eradication of evil is to be found in "Do you want us to go and gather them up?" (13:28) So, we are right into the heart of a profound issue which runs right through our society. There are very few who do not admit the existence of an awful amount of evil in our world. Mary Baker Eddy did try and deny its reality and founded "Christian Science" and tried to teach her followers that if they could only think of evil as a negative charge, as something not quite real, then that might be the way to overcome it. But evil is only too real. You only need to open one newspaper or listen to one news bulletin to know that we live in an evil world. How did that evil get in, and how are we going to get it out?

The answer of Jesus is to be found in a very simple story. We do not have any difficulty understanding this story, for Jesus himself told us its meaning. Where we may have difficulty is accepting what he says and applying it. It is a story that is utterly normal, true-to-life. Anybody listening to him would have understood what he was talking about. He is saying: a man had a field, he sowed wheat in it, and one night an enemy came and sowed tares in it. That sort of thing still happens in some parts of the world. So this was and still is very understandable. In Palestine, they used a thing called a darnel. The plant has some peculiar qualities. The first is that for the first few months of its growth there is no way of telling the difference between that weed and wheat – they look identical. Not until they begin to head out and form the seeds can you tell a difference between a tare and a grain of wheat. It is a mild poison, and even a touch of it gives a very bitter taste to the flour. But if there is a lot of it, it can be quite dangerous and it acts like a narcotic. So, if you were really malicious and angry with someone, you might get some of that seed and gather it from the darnels in the hedgerows, and while the farmer was asleep you might throw it in his field. He would have a big problem. The only thing he could do really would be to try to pull some of it up or, if he went right through to harvest, he would have to hire a lot of people who would sit around the grain and pick out every seed of darnel. It would be grey compared with the golden wheat, but they would have to pick it out by hand – a long, tedious and expensive business. It was a very dirty trick to play, but well known.

Jesus' description of that dirty trick and this situation would have been immediately real to his hearers, and we are shown something about the principles of God's government which apply to the problem of evil in our society. Is it not extraordinary that Jesus could take these ordinary little incidents that everybody was familiar with and put a little twist in them? That approach opens up an understanding of how God works in society, why things are as they are, and there are many people who are asking why God is allowing some things to occur in the world. The answer

Matthew Chapter 13

is to be found in this simple little story.

Let us turn to the two questions: how evil came about and how evil can be eradicated – the solution to the situation. How did evil get in? We are flooded with answers to that question from all kinds of people looking for a natural cause of evil. There are those who tell me it is an evolutionary hangover, and that if only I were a few centuries further away from ancestors in the jungle, then there would be less evil in my heart. Yet if that were so then twenty-first century man ought to be much further away from evil than first-century man, but he is not. We have done as devilish and barbaric things in the modern period as mankind has done at any other time.

Then there are those who say that evil has come from the economic system under which most of us have lived, whereby the means of production have been in the hands of the few to make them rich and to make the many poor. From that unjust and unequal situation comes the evil of people's greed and their pride and all the other sins. One of the reasons why communism appealed so much was precisely because it said that if we can get the right economic system, evil will disappear.

There are those who think it is simply a matter of being overcrowded on a small planet. I once read of an experiment with rats in a box and as soon as the population of the rats became too large for convenient movement within the box there appeared antagonisms and hostilities, and ultimately they fought each other. There are those who say, "That's the answer. Birth control all round. Limit the population, get it down to the right size, and evil will disappear and human greed and wars will go."

Against all that, we can see that Jesus' understanding of the problem is quite different: there is no natural cause for evil. Therefore, that marks him apart from many of the modern philosophers who are wrestling with this problem.

Before we look at the three things that Jesus says about evil and our situation, just notice the remarkable claim in the story.

The claim is this: a certain man had a field and he sowed seed in his field. In giving the interpretation later, in the house after the crowds had left, Jesus said, in effect: The man is myself; or, to put it simply, I own the world. (See 13:37 – "The one who sows the good seed is the Son of Man.")

It is just slipped in as a kind of little phrase that you might not notice. Yet, there was a human being living in the Middle East two thousand years ago revealing that the real solution comes when you first of all realise that the whole world belongs to him. The field belongs to the owner, and the owner is the Son of Man. For a fuller explanation of the Kingdom, refer to my book *Kingdoms in Conflict*.

We are then shown three things about evil which are fundamental to every Christian's understanding of evil. We cannot tackle it properly unless we grasp them. Number one: *evil is alien*. It has no right to be here, it does not belong here, it was not here to begin with. The Lord did not make it and we must never think that God is responsible for evil in the world. He did not put it here – it is not natural; it is an invader. It is alien. It was not meant to be here, and I believe that deep down within every human heart there is an echo to that truth. I believe that fundamentally every human being who has got any sense of decency at all has a feeling that evil is foreign and that it should be pushed out, that it does not belong to the realm of human happiness, and that evil is an enemy invading territory where it does not belong.

Number two, there is something which many people today would not accept: *evil is personal*. It is not a force. It is not something that you can wrap up in a brown paper package. It is not like gravity or electricity. You cannot say of evil: "it". You can only say "he". Evil cannot exist apart from people. You cannot say: Evil is an "it"; how can we get rid of "it"? If you are really going to understand the problem of evil, you have to say: "How can I get rid of him?" In other words, Jesus believed in a personal devil. That may seem old-fashioned, or it did until the mid-twentieth century when at least some kind of belief in the devil began to creep back onto stage and screen and into our literature. But do people really believe in a personal, evil power who is more subtle, cleverer than we are? Jesus did, and we learn that the devil is the one responsible for the evil in the world.

There are many things said about the devil in this story that I want you to take note of. First, the devil usually works secretly. You do not notice when he is working. He often does it when people are asleep. He can be busy in your dreams, but when nobody is looking, he is busy. It also tells you that the devil loves to counterfeit. Planting tares that would look exactly like wheat (for the first few months at any rate) was absolutely typical. If the devil walked into a church dressed in black, with a forked tail and horns, we would have no problem with him.

We once had a worshipper of Satan standing on our church doorstep. He was dressed in black from head to toe. He stood with his arms folded and glared at every worshipper coming to meet Jesus, but at least he gave us the help of dressing up like that. The devil does not usually do that. He prefers to come as an angel of light, if he comes in the light at all. But he loves to plant something that looks good until it grows up and produces fruit. That is why it is often so difficult to spot when he is busy; he counterfeits what the Lord is doing, which tells me something else about the devil. If the Lord sows a field, the devil does not go off and sow tares somewhere else. He wants to get them in there. In fact, one of the marks that the Lord is busy is that you are up against the devil, too. You will find he is busy at the same point. Why? Because he has something more – the devil is motivated by malice. His aim is totally destructive and it is to undo what the Lord is doing. The devil is not trying to build up anything, he is not trying to get a harvest, he is not trying to do anything; he is just so angry, frustrated and malicious he wants to undo anything good. He is, in short, a vandal, an invader, a squatter.

So, evil in the world is alien and personal. Number three, it is *embodied*. The seed the devil sows is people. Satan cannot work unless he can get hold of people through whom he can work. Therefore, the tares represent those who do Satan's work for him or teach other people to do it. You cannot therefore say "Let us try to eradicate evil from the world" without realising that you are saying "We're going to have to eradicate a lot of people." If evil is not a thing but a person, and a person embodied in other persons, then you cannot eradicate it without eradicating human beings. If only we could learn that lesson. Every war that men fight seems to assume that you have eradicated all the people who serve Satan. Within days you discover that you have done nothing of the kind.

These insights into the problem of evil not only tell us that to eradicate evil we would have to eradicate people; they also tell us that no natural force is ever going to remove the supernatural source of evil. We may remove some of the symptoms but we will not be able to touch the actual source. If that is our understanding of our Lord's view of the situation, let us turn to his solution. How can evil be eradicated? How can it be dealt with? Is there a possibility of building a world in which your children and grandchildren will grow up free from evil? Well, look at the stage in the story. It is rather important to realise that this question came up after some months of growing when the wheat and the tares had begun to head out, as we call it, and had begun to form the seeds. By that time, the difference began to be noticed. It was then that they came to the owner of the field and said, "How did these get here?" and he told them the answer.

So, their second question is: how do we get rid of them? Do you want us to go and pull them up? That takes me back to 1948. I could take you back to the very field in North Yorkshire towards a hill called Roseberry Topping, which you can see from Middlesbrough. The first field on the left past the railway is about sixteen acres, and I was sixteen years of age and I was sent into that field "looking". Now, only those who come from those parts will know what is meant by that. I did not know when the farmer said, "I want you to go looking in that field this morning and this afternoon and tomorrow morning and tomorrow afternoon and the next morning."

So I said, "Okay, I will go and look if you'll tell me what looking is." He gave me a thing like a broom handle with a knob at one end and a tiny little blade like a mini spade at the other and he said, "Off you go." What I had to do was to walk up and down that field taking about a yard-and-a-half width at a time and spike at everything that was not wheat – every dandelion, every thistle. Today they would use a chemical spray, but in those days, you went looking and the thing was a looker. Of all the tedious, boring jobs I can recommend that to you. So up and down we went in rain or sun – yard-and-a-half by yard-and-a-half until sixteen acres were done.

That farmer had a reputation through the district for clean corn. So, he could get a good price for his corn from the corn merchant. After I had finished loading up the sacks, got the horse and cart out and gone down to the corn merchant, I knew that the merchant would run it through his fingers and look at it and say, "That's a good clean sample." That was how he did it. It is the instinctive human reaction when something bad appears, to get rid of it as quickly as possible. It is the normal reaction, and these workers came and said to the owner, "Shall we go and pull those up?" It is the instinctive reaction as soon as we have identified evil, to want to uproot it – to want to get rid of it. That is our natural, moral indignation. It is astonishing how much moral indignation we are capable of even before we are Christians, and we often carry a bit over into our Christian life if we are not careful, in that bad form. We have this inbuilt, natural instinct when we get hold of some bad people to say: "Let's get rid of them."

I don't know if you have ever been to Marble Arch in London and looked at that triangle in the road where they hung the triangular gallows. It is only two hundred years or so since at that spot you could be hung for stealing five shillings or a sheep. As soon as evil people were discovered, you got rid of them, you uprooted them, and the awful side of it was that people came with their families and held picnics at Marble Arch and watched them being hanged. It was seen as a day out – a good thing that was happening. Evil was being eradicated and uprooted.

Instinctive as it is as a human reaction, it is a very difficult question for Christians. Are we called to go and eradicate evil – to try to uproot it? It is a question that was tearing apart our brethren in Latin America in the twentieth century. "Liberation Theology" there was asking whether Christians should be involved in revolution. Where there is a corrupt regime, where there is a tyranny, should the church fight with force for the liberation of innocent people? Dietrich Bonhoeffer had this question when he was imprisoned in Germany. He felt that his Christian duty as a pastor was to join in a plot to go and pull up a tare called Adolf Hitler and to remove the evil in that man from the earth. They caught him before the plot was fulfilled, and he was sentenced to death by hanging.

It is a question that has arisen for Christians through the ages. It led to the Crusades and to the Inquisition. Is our calling to go and pull up the tares? Now that we know who is responsible, do we go and deal with them?

This is where the human reaction is so different from the heavenly one. They said to the owner, "Shall we go and pull up the weeds?" and the owner said no. Why? Not because their idea was wrong, but it was the wrong time to do it, and they were the wrong people to do it, that is all. Some day, if there is a God in heaven who has justice in his heart, there must come a separation between good and evil. There must be a final settlement, there must be an eradication of evil. God cannot let it go on forever. The trouble is that we are in a hurry and he is not, and we want to say, "God, let's go and pull them up," and he says, "No, this is not the time to do it, and you are not the people to do it." Why not?

Well, the owner then says something that is the main lesson I want to convey here. Their eyes were fixed too much on the weeds. They ought to have been thinking about the wheat. It is possible for Christians to get their attention so fixed on what to do about the weeds that we overlook the more important question of what is best for the wheat. To spell it out very bluntly, it is easier for Christians in our day to be obsessed with the evils of our society and not to be concerned as they should be with how to establish the good. It is human nature to have moral indignation about other people who are doing wrong. You do not need to be a Christian to have that. It is very easy, when you have found someone else who is committing evil actions or saying evil things, to be highly indignant, to start a protest movement, to blaze away at them. It is not so easy to give one's life to establishing the good, to getting the wheat grown and mature. The concern of the owner of the field is not about the weeds but about the wheat. What is going to be the effect on the wheat? He goes right back to his original desire when he planted the wheat in that field. His desire was to get a harvest. If you go about tackling evil the wrong way, some of the harvest would be lost. If you get so obsessed with uprooting tares, you will either make a mistake and pull up some wheat thinking you have got a tare or, the root systems by now being so intertwined, in the very pulling up of the tare you loosen the root system of the wheat and the wheat will not be as strong as it should be. Therefore, let them both grow together. That is a very hard thing to accept and apply in the right way.

But in our situation, in this nation, I believe this is a word for us. Let them both grow together. Now let us not misapply it. Let none of us ever dare to make this an excuse for letting evil and good grow together within our own hearts.

Towards evil in ourselves, the Bible says to be utterly ruthless: murder it, put to death whatever has come through from your old life that is spoiling the new. Be utterly ruthless, give it no chance to survive – that is within yourself. The owner is not talking about the individual. Jesus is not telling you as a Christian to let evil and good grow together in your life.

Nor is he telling this to the church. In 1 Corinthians 5, Paul makes it utterly clear that though we have no right to judge an outsider (we must leave God to do that), we have the right and responsibility to discipline each other and not just to let good and evil grow together in the church. The field is not the church, it is the world. But it is when we come into the world situation that Christians are on a knife edge. On the one hand, the scripture teaches us absolutely clearly that evil is to be exposed, brought to the light, shown for what it is. But there is not one text in this whole New Testament that I have been able to find that lays on the church the responsibility of seeking to eradicate evil in the world. Expose it, remain unstained by it, but never uproot it. Why not? Because if we did, the Lord of the harvest would have less of a harvest than he otherwise would have had.

When I realised this, I scratched my head about it and thought: Give me an illustration of that from within the New Testament, Lord. Straight away to my mind there came the day when Jesus and his disciples went through Samaria, and people mocked, and they jeered, and they spat at Jesus. James and John (the son of Thunder, that fisherman who had a bit of a bad temper, zealous for his Lord) heard that they were saying such things about Jesus and said, "Shall we call fire from heaven and consume them?" Well, you cannot fault his faith. He shared Elijah's faith. But Jesus rebuked them.

Within a matter of months, there was a revival in that very place and the hundreds came to know the Lord and were healed. There was great joy in that city. If John's fire had come down and consumed them, what would have happened to the harvest for the Lord? Are you beginning to understand? There is something very important here. There will be a day when the owner of that field says: Gather the tares and burn them. But he has not told us to do that. Indeed, it is dangerous to venture into that field if that is our intention. Never avenge yourselves, beloved. Vengeance belongs to him, he will repay. There is a day coming when he will deal with a situation and you do not need to do so. Let both grow together until the harvest.

Psalm 37 seems to give a picture of wicked and good people living side by side in the same land. That is how the Lord has decided it is going to be until the end of history. So if we started praying, "Lord, will you eradicate evil from the British Isles?" I think we would be on rather thin ice. I wonder if you understand his heart. He wants a big harvest and you may be praying for less of a harvest than he would have. He wants to see people saved, he wants corn in that field, and if my mind is preoccupied with all the weeds and the evil and the dirt and all the wrong things and "How can I get rid of those?" and "How can we clean up Britain from that?" – and if I am not concerned with what is going to happen to the wheat and how that can grow strong and be protected and given a good root system, then I have got my priorities the wrong way round. That will affect the harvest because I will begin to see people as enemies instead of those for whom Christ died.

What this parable is teaching is the Lord's amazing patience and our human impatience. As soon as you become a Christian, you get on the right side – you say, "God, why don't you deal with all the evil people? Why don't you deal with all those who refuse your gospel and with all those who doubt you?" forgetting that previously the answer to that prayer is that you would have been gone. Is it not amazing how quickly we become morally indignant and morally impatient with those very people who are living exactly as we lived not long ago? But for the grace of God, we would have been among them.

Praise God for his amazing patience – the wisdom of the delay. Whenever you say, "Why doesn't God do something?" just ask yourself: "If he did, would I be included?" Then you will say, "Thank you, God, for not doing something." Whenever you say, "Why don't you bring this day nearer, Lord? Why don't you hurry it up when you are going to take the tares away?" Ask yourself, "Could I be one of the tares?" You might find yourself saying: "Thank you, Lord, that that day has not come too soon."

There will come a day when the tares and the wheat will be divided, and here I must say another thing which is not popular. I believe in hell. I was asked that by some school sixth formers. I had to say, "Yes, I do," but not because I like the idea. I cannot bear to think about it, really, but I have to believe it because there is one person and one alone in the world who taught it – and that was my Lord Jesus. When he revealed that one day he must take those tares and bind them and throw them into the fire, he was talking about people – human beings. He was talking about a fire that brought conscious agony, suffering, frustration, pain. He talked about weeping and gnashing of teeth. One almost trembles to read the words, but it is Jesus who lets us know that one day his angels will have to take those people and put them in the fire. Do you wonder that he wanted to wait and was putting that off as long as possible? Do you wonder that it would have to be at the end of the story? Praise the Lord that he did not do it then; his patience has meant that we are here.

Look at the wheat for a moment. How does that finish up if the tares finish in the fire? The wheat finishes up like some of those advertisements you see for breakfast cereal – field upon field of golden corn in the sun. There is no more heart-warming sight than that to a farmer – to get it just before it goes brown and when it is really orangey-yellow and there is a gentle breeze. You see the sun trapped in reflection in every little ear of wheat. It is a marvellous sight. Jesus says that the wheat will finish up like that in glory. He does not say "in my Kingdom", he makes a very subtle change: "In the Kingdom of their Father." The irony is that the tares do not belong in the field, but the wheat actually does and yet it is not going to stay there, it is going to be taken into the barn. Jesus' Kingdom becomes the Father's Kingdom,

Matthew Chapter 13

and the glory of the corn shines, and he has his harvest.

Now, what is Jesus trying to do in telling the crowd this story? I took my Bible and turned back a few pages to the very last chapter of the very last prophet of the very last book of the Old Testament. It says that the day is coming, burning like an oven, when all the arrogant and all evildoers will be like stubble. "The day that is coming shall set them ablaze," says the Lord of hosts, "so that it will leave them neither root nor branch. But for you who fear my name, the sun of righteousness shall rise with healing in its wings" (see Malachi 4:1–2).

Four hundred years later and a few pages later in your Bible, John the Baptist says that he has come and he has his winnowing shovel with him to thresh out all the grain, and he will gather his wheat into his barn but he will burn the chaff in a fire that never goes out. In other words, when Jesus came, the Jews, including John, expected Jesus to put the baddies in the fire immediately. They had waited four hundred years for someone to come and do that. They knew that God had promised that one day proud and wicked people would burn. Everybody was waiting for the baddies to be cleared off the Earth and burnt.

Jesus did nothing of the kind. Poor John the Baptist, from prison, sent a message to Jesus: "Are you the coming one or do we look for another?"

Jesus sent a message back: "...blind people regain sight to see, and lame people walk, lepers are cleansed and deaf people hear, dead people are raised and the poor have the gospel preached to them"... Jesus was going to do what Malachi said – to burn the wicked – but not now because he wanted every bit of harvest he could get.

I found myself in Lambeth Palace Chapel one Monday morning service of dedication for the nationwide initiative in evangelism, and there was a voice singing lustily behind me as we sang the first hymn. I recognised that voice – it was the voice of a man who, in Dartmoor Prison, became a Christian. Now he travels the world preaching the good news of Jesus. He had difficulty getting into some countries because, although he wears a dog collar, his passport says he is an ex-convict. They usually keep him for questioning before he gets in. I turned around and there was the lovely face of the man who, if Jesus had thrown the tares into the fire, would be in the fire – but he is part of the harvest. To be absolutely honest, if Jesus threw all the tares into the fire, there would not be one of us left, would there? So, Peter in his second letter says: "It may seem as if God is doing nothing about it. He has fixed the date on his calendar when he will, but praise him for his patience." There is only one reason why he has not stepped in to put it right: he wants as many as possible to be saved.

Every parable breaks down. The Kingdom of heaven is *like* a man who had a field. Therefore, in some respects it will be unlike the man who had the field. Whenever you say, "This is like that" you are making a comparison in which there is a contrast. Caster sugar is like salt, but it is unlike it in taste. Whatever comparison you make, there is an unlike. The Kingdom of heaven is like a field with both tares and wheat growing in it. The unlike is this: tares can be changed into wheat. That is the miracle of the Creator God in Jesus Christ. If Jesus can turn water into wine, he can take a tare and turn it into a stalk of wheat. That is the miracle of the gospel.

So, our task today is not that God calls us to go and eradicate evil and seek to get everyone shut up in prison who is causing others to do wrong. Our task is to see that the Lord gets a harvest of wheat. The real thing that is wrong with Britain is not that there are too many weeds but that there is too little wheat.

If the few Christians there are get hung up on how to uproot the tares, then there is going to be an even poorer harvest.

I am reminded that the Bible Society emblem is of a man sowing seed, not of a man pulling up tares.

17
DEATH AND MORE MIRACLES

Read Matthew Chapter 14–15

Those who think that to become a man of God is to make life easy and comfortable should read the account of John, the greatest man who had ever lived, according to Jesus. This man did not keep his mouth shut, and he lost his head for speaking out. On occasion, I have been told sometimes by people who mean well to just preach the positive side. That is a safer way, but sometimes we are called upon to attack what is wrong as well as proclaim what is right, whatever the cost. John was a preacher like that. He attacked. Repent and believe! He said publicly that there was a man governing that country in which he baptised who was illegally married, who was outraging public decency. He made an enemy the day he said that – not of the man himself, but of Herodias who did not like it one bit. Wherever she went, people now pointed at her and said that she was "living in sin". People looked at her as at a dirty woman. She hated this preacher and resolved that he should die.

She had managed to persuade her husband to put him in the dungeon. Actually, it is still possible to see the dungeons and the iron loops in the wall to which John the Baptist would have been tied. That terrible place is still there. Even though John, down in the dungeon, had been prevented from preaching publicly, every time they had a feast up above, Herodias would have thought of the man below. When you have a guilty conscience it can be hard to forget one's wrongdoings.

There came a day when Herod had all his pals in for entertainment, and he had one of his own relatives do what only a "woman of the streets" would normally do, and she danced in an erotic and obscene way. Herod must have been drunk because he said, "I will give you anything, even my throne as queen." That is what the phrase "half the kingdom" means. If an eastern potentate said to a woman "I will offer you half my kingdom" it meant that he would make her his queen. And Herodias was sitting there! He was saying: I'll get rid of her and you can be the queen in her place. She went and she had a consultation with her mother. Can you imagine the hatred a woman could have to say: I would rather have a man's head than anything else. What an evil woman! It shows her scale of values. And over the rest of the scene one just wants to draw a veil. The head of a man of God is carried in; a preacher who had fearlessly preached the Word of God for years; a man who had lived in the desert; a man who had experienced a hard life. That was how he ended up – killed by a woman's malice.

Herod had this strange mixture: he liked to hear the preacher and yet he did not like it. He was typical of so many men. They enjoy a good sermon and yet they do not like it if it gets near to the bone. This was Herod; he was a man of superstition. Why? Because he was a man of sensuality and the two invariably go together. Once you have given yourself to sensations you lose your sense. Once you have begun to live a life like this you cannot think straight. Here was a man who enjoyed John's preaching yet he did not enjoy it, but he kept him in the dungeon and had him up every now and again to preach, and then put him away again, as a man who listens to a preacher and has his conscience stirred on Sunday but puts it away in the dungeon until the following Sunday. Herod was so like many of us. Herod was the man who misunderstood, and John the Baptist was killed because Herod had to save his face. Do you know what Jesus thought of Herod? We know what Herod thought of Jesus. Herod thought Jesus was this man with his head back on – an incredible idea, but he thought it. Jesus said of Herod: "That fox". This is not "gentle Jesus meek and mild".

Jesus moves out of Herod's territory, crossing the sea. He is hoping to get some peace and quiet, but sometimes a boat has to tack across that sea against a contrary wind, and the crowd saw him going, and they saw the direction of the boat and ran round the lake. It would have been perhaps five or six miles for them but they got there before the boat. So here Jesus, seeking rest and quiet, is faced with a crowd. Any ordinary man would have said, "It's my day off." Any ordinary man would have said, "I have been preaching, I have been working, I have been with you, I must have some rest." But not Jesus. He saw them, and had compassion on them. He taught them and he healed the sick.

Now there comes this great creative miracle, the multiplying of the loaves and fishes. Look at the consideration Jesus showed. He said to his disciples, who wanted to send the people away to find food for themselves, "You give them something to eat." Notice Jesus' carefulness. The first thing he did was to find out how much food they had. I have a little tin of sardines from Galilee. One of these days I will eat them! They had two sardines. From Capernaum in those days salted sardines were a really tasty export. They also had five loaves, although not loaves as we understand them – they were just little rolls, quite thin and flat, about the size of a pancake. That was all they had. Jesus told them to share what they had. He broke the bread and more came. Only God could do that; only God can create something out of nothing, man cannot do it. The disciples gave the food to the people but they were able to gather twelve basketfuls of broken pieces of the food! God's mathematics are not ours; they are not the mathematics my children learned in school. God's mathematics are: what you give away you gain; what you try to keep, you lose. Two fishes, five loaves: God's mathematics says give them away and you will have enough to eat yourself. What have you got that you could share with somebody else?

So, our Lord's consideration as well as his compassion comes through. But the disciples still did not understand one thing about the loaves: that the only hands that could go on doing that must be

God's hands. Although they thought it was something wonderful, they did not understand that this was something supernatural. Their hearts were hard. I suppose they would have been inclined to ask him to repeat it. This is an instinctive human reaction to something marvellous. So they missed the next opportunity that they were given to see the truth.

Jesus now does insist on rest and quiet. He sends the disciples away on their own and he goes up into the hills to pray. Why? Because problems are piling in thick and fast. He is too popular with the crowds; they want to make him king. He has already made some serious religious enemies. He knows now that Herod is disturbed about him, and that probably spells his death, and so he goes up into the hills to pray. Imagine the scene. Here is a little boat that the disciples set off in at about five o'clock in the afternoon, and at three in the morning it was still stuck in the middle of the lake, so severe was the wind, and they were rowing hard. Jesus, up on the hills, saw them. He thought that they would be encouraged if they saw that he was still around and so he walked down the hill and he continued to walk straight out on the water. That should not surprise us. It should not have surprised them. Somebody who can take loaves and fishes and multiply them can surely walk on water. They should not have been surprised in the slightest at such supernatural power. We should not be surprised at anything that God does, but we are, and when we get an answer to prayer we talk to each other in shocked surprise. Why should we be surprised when something supernatural happens?

The boat was already a considerable distance from the land, buffeted by the waves because the wind was against it. When the disciples saw him walking on the lake they were terrified. "It's a ghost," they said, and they cried out in fear.

But Jesus immediately said to them, "Take courage it is I, don't be afraid."

"Lord, if it's you," Peter replied, "Tell me to come to you on the water."

"Come," he said. Then Peter got down out of the boat and walked on the water to Jesus. But when he saw the wind, he was afraid and, beginning to sink, cried out, "Lord save me."

Immediately, Jesus reached out his hand and caught him. "You of little faith," he said, "Why did you doubt?" When they climbed into the boat the wind died down. Then those who were in the boat worshipped him, saying, "Truly, you are the Son of God."

So, Jesus came to the other shore again. Why were there so many sick people? Because Tiberias was a health spa and people came to it from all over to take the waters. Now we find the opposite of what took place in the beginning. In Nazareth, familiarity had produced faithlessness, but here familiarity produces faith. Why? Because they had seen him not mending chairs but mending bodies, and they recognised him, so they rushed to bring the sick to him. Perhaps they brought the sick on the very beds that he had made, as he moved around the villages. But the Jesus who made beds makes bodies. One day he is going to make a whole new universe; without him the stars would not have been made; without him nothing would have been made that was made, and those hands which could multiply loaves and fishes could also heal and make new. I want you to notice that the people still just wanted health. The tragedy is that the demand was for what they could get from him. Nobody came and said, "What can we give to him?" Nobody came and said, "Let's follow him, let's help him with his mission," instead they all came and they said, "You can get health from him." So they misunderstood him. They thought he just came to heal, but he came to forgive, he came to bring people to God. This was what Jesus came up against.

We move to chapter 15 and the tradition of the scribes and Pharisees. We are then shown the problem of this matter of the washing of hands – not to get clean physically, but just in case they had touched the overcoat of a Gentile in the market place. It was a purely ritualistic act, to cover them from defilement.

They would come in and wash their hands, then they would wash between each course, just in case they were unclean according to their religious tradition. It is said to Jesus that his disciples have not washed their hands, and Jesus replied with some pretty severe words. But he was right in what he said. That kind of religion and his teaching would not mix. He taught that they had turned religion into an external instead of an internal matter, so they had become terribly concerned with the outward appearance and outward actions. This is hypocrisy. He points out that Isaiah saw this in them five hundred years before.

To go through the ritual, to perform external religious acts yet to have a heart that is far away from God, is sheer hypocrisy. They had become so concerned about getting their hands clean that they had forgotten that the heart needs cleaning. Let us accept this criticism from our Lord and apply it to ourselves. If we are more concerned about putting on our Sunday best clothes, getting our hair right and getting our face washed before we go to church than about getting our hearts clean and right before we get to worship, then we deserve exactly the same criticism. I apply it like that to my own heart because it is easy to blame those old Pharisees and say they were terrible people, but we all have a dose of this.

Secondly, they had substituted for the divine command a human idea. Jesus told them that they were always doing this, and he mentioned a particularly bad example. The Pharisees gave very generously to God – the trouble was that they began to teach that if you were giving something to God, that released you from other obligations, so you could say to your own aged parents, "I'm sorry I can't keep you because I am giving this money to God", and that was replacing a command of God with an idea of man. I have been asked about this more than once, and my answer is that supporting our family, whether it is our children or our parents, is a divine duty, and we should not be giving to God's work to the extent that those who are directly dependent on us are impoverished. In 1 Timothy 5:8 we are told that if anyone does not provide for his own, and especially for those of his household, he has denied the faith and is worse than an unbeliever. Therefore, this is our first responsibility. And Jesus points out that Moses said in the Law, which is God's Word, that we are to honour our father and mother. They were saying in effect, "I can't. I'm giving all my money to God's work" – and that is putting an idea of man in place of the Word of God.

The third point was even more devastating: they thought of religion as a matter of physical action, when in fact it is a matter of spiritual attitude. In place of this kind of external tradition, the outside of religion, Jesus put the internal truth, and said something that has been described as the most revolutionary statement in the New Testament: "Not what goes into the mouth defiles a man, but what comes out of the mouth, this defiles a man" (15:11). Godliness is concerned with the heart. Being very direct, our Lord is teaching that if something dirty comes in at the mouth, the body has its own way of getting rid of dirt and it goes straight through the stomach and out. It is the things that start inside and come out that are really dirty.

Let us look at some of the things he said were inside. It is a horrid list. Evil thoughts – that means a person who is planning what wrong thing to do next. Fornication – that means extramarital relations before marriage. Theft means petty pilfering. That starts inside and it is dirty. Murder starts with anger. Adultery is the breaking of the marriage bond. False witness and blasphemy are clear evils.

Jesus highlights these as dirty things that you need to get rid of, as the things that make someone filthy. It is not something that a person has taken in, it is something that he has given out. It starts inside and it works out. Fundamentally, Jesus has a completely different view of man from the view the Pharisees held. I have discovered that the Pharisees' view is the one generally held in England today. They believed that a person was basically good and clean, therefore they must be careful of outside influences on them. Jesus taught that a person was basically bad and dirty, and therefore it is the inside that they need to be concerned about. Here are the two different viewpoints and it makes a total difference to your thinking, about yourself and other people in the world in general. Our Lord was saying of these things that he listed that you do not pick them up from other people, they are there inside to begin with. That is a very low view of human nature. Yet when I look into my heart, it is an accurate view. If you are concerned about the traditions of the external things, if you are concerned about the outside of it all, you have missed the real thing that needs dealing with and that is the inside of it all. It is a completely different viewpoint. Jesus was teaching: you are so bothered about washing your hands that you have forgotten about your hearts. They honoured God with their lips but their hearts were far away.

Therefore, what we need is not religion but regeneration; that is why it is no use trying to reform a person and make them behave differently. On the farm we used to have Danish piggeries which are specially designed to keep pigs clean. In a Danish piggery the pig is the cleanest animal on the farm. You can change his behaviour and you can make him quite an attractive animal. But you let him loose out of the piggery and anywhere near the midden, and within five minutes his nature has reasserted itself. This is why sticking religion on the outside will never do the trick. You might manage respectable and decent behaviour, but inside there is the same old heart and the stuff is still there. That is the danger of drinking too much, because alcohol will release what is already inside and it comes out more easily. That is why when we get tired things come out that we are surprised at: irritability, loose speech. These come out when we are under strain. Why? Because they are there already, and that is why we need a new heart, and a clean heart, and the glorious gospel of Jesus Christ is that he does not come to reform you, he does not come to stick a new outside on you, he does not come to get you religious, he comes to clean your heart and to deal with these things at the source and to give you a new nature – that is what is meant by being born again.

It is very interesting that having discussed the matter of "clean" and "unclean" with these Pharisees, who regarded Jews as clean and the Gentiles as unclean, the very next scene shows Jesus in a Gentile country, an "unclean" land – Tyre. It should have been part of the promised land but the tribe of Asher never managed to conquer the people who lived there. It was part of the land that God gave to his people and Jesus was not stepping outside the promised land, but he was going into Gentile territory – unclean territory according to the Pharisees, yet Jesus did not bother one wit. He was escaping from the Pharisees to get a bit of quiet with his disciples, away from this opposition, and he went to a house. A woman heard he was there, even though he told his host not to tell anyone. We now get one of the most extraordinary sayings of Jesus. The woman came in and we read that she begged Jesus to drive the demon out of her daughter. Now come words that, if we did not have them in the Gospel, we would never credit Jesus with uttering. It is a proof of the truth of the Gospel record that nobody would have invented what he said. We read: "... it is not right to take the children's bread and throw it to the little dogs". To us that does not come home with such horror because dogs are our pets, dogs live with us in our homes. But if you go out to the Middle East and call anyone a dog, they think of those mangey beasts that go from dustbin to dustbin scavenging things, animals that you run away from if they get anywhere near – horrible things.

Why did Jesus speak in this way? I think the only way that I can understand it – and I can only give you my understanding and no more – is that he was saying to her that he had come to the Jews with his first duty to God's people. He had left them not because he was coming to start a mission to the Gentiles

– not yet – he had been sent to the lost sheep of the house of Israel. He was saying this to stop this woman starting a mission for him among the Gentiles. He had not come to do this and it was a deliberate discouragement. But he left the door open by including the word "first". He said that the children were to be fed first. He was virtually saying that Jews are the children, you are the dogs – and everything was going to depend on how she took that. The amazing thing is that she took it in just the right attitude. She could have resented it; she could have been proud; she could have been terribly upset. She might never have spoken to him again. But instead, she gave him this witty reply: "Yes Lord, but even the little dogs eat the crumbs which fall from their master's table." But there was more than wit, there was humility. She accepted whatever he said about her, and she was still asking.

Jesus replied, "O woman, great is your faith! Let it be to you as you desire." And her daughter was healed.

The woman had accepted his challenge – she had not resented it, she had not been proud, but in humility and faith she had pressed Jesus for what she needed.

Then, in the remainder of the chapter follow more healings, and the feeding of the four thousand men and their women and children.

18
THE DIVINITY OF JESUS

Read Matthew Chapter 16–17

In the region of Caesarea Philippi Jesus asked his disciples, "Who do men say that I, the Son of Man, am?"

The answer they gave him was that people believed that he was a reincarnation of some great man who lived in the past. Though it was contrary to Jewish ideas to believe in reincarnation they replied, "Some say John the Baptist, some say Elijah and others Jeremiah or one of the prophets."

Then Jesus asked them for their own answer, and Peter was the first to respond: "You are the Christ, the Son of the living God."

Jesus could build on that. Now he could build his church. This was the foundation he had been waiting for: faith in him as the Son of the living God.

When you lose faith in Jesus as the Son of the living God, the church collapses for it has no more rock, no more foundation on which to be built.

This then is the most important question that can ever be asked: Who do you say that I am? Down through the ages for two thousand years there have been a wide variety of opinions as to who Jesus is. Some have so stressed his deity that his humanity has been lost and he is seen as never having become a man. Some have so stressed his humanity that his deity has been lost. He ceases to be seen as divine and becomes the greatest man and no more.

I walked along a street in London and saw a shop window full of booklets – all the same booklet, just published. I stared into that window and wondered why everybody was not stopping and staring into it too. It was the most amazing book title I have ever seen: *The Man Who Was God*. Nobody was looking at it; nobody stopped; I was the only one looking at this incredible title.

I want to tackle it at three levels and approach it from three angles. Number one: the experience of the disciples over three years in which they lived with him. Number two: the doctrine of the apostles as they thought through the implications of the experience they had had. Finally, number three: the creeds of Christians as they have tried to express this amazing truth in human language.

Take first, then, the experience of the disciples over three years. How was it that a handful of ordinary working men who called a carpenter's son "Jesus of Nazareth" and "Teacher" came within the space of three years to go against all they had ever been brought up to believe about God, and to say of this carpenter's son, "My Lord and my God". How did they change over just three years? Well, let me begin by saying they had no doubt whatever that during those three years they lived with a human being, a real man. You cannot live with someone for three years, live in the same room, eat at the same table, walk along the same road and be in any doubt about that. I mentioned in an article in the *Baptist Times* about what Jesus talked about which we have respectable hesitations about discussing, but let me mention that Jesus had all the normal processes of digestion and excretion that you have. The disciples lived in Jesus' presence for three years and they lived with a real man. He was real physically; he got hungry, tired and thirsty. He knew pain, he walked and he talked. He was a real man both physically and spiritually; he was subject to temptation as we are; he went to worship God the Father with God's people; he studied the scripture; he prayed.

The difficulties beg the question: was he was a real man mentally? It is here that statements like these cause hurt. Was he mistaken as we are mistaken? Was he a child of his age as we are children of our age? And did his mind and therefore his words show the influence of his society?

Let me look very carefully at this. It is vital that we be objective and look at the evidence, and not read our own ideas into Christ. There was one occasion and only one recorded occasion when Jesus admitted ignorance. It was about the date of his Second Coming and he said that he did not know the date of his return. But does that mean he was mistaken in the things he did claim to know? Logically, that does not follow.

I want to remind you of two claims that Jesus made for himself which, if accepted, mean that he could not be mistaken in anything he said. One was the claim: "I am the truth". How can a man who says that be mistaken? Either that claim is right or it is wrong. If it is right then we dare not go on to say that he held mistaken views on anything. The other claim he made is this, and it is a very large claim: that he only said to men what God the Father said to him. So, if he was mistaken in what he said then God was mistaken. If his views were the views of a child of his age, then God becomes a child of his age. If his claim that he spoke only as God the Father gave him words to speak was wrong then those words fall to the ground. You see what a morass you are led into when you start saying that Jesus was human to the point of being limited and mistaken in his mental grasp of truth. Rather, the mistake is in the minds of those who say such things for they are judging his humanity by ours.

They have got confused between the average man and the normal man. The average man is a child of his age and is mistaken. I am an average man and you are an average man or woman. The normal man is Jesus, and gets his truth from God the Father. Jesus is the normal, and we are the average. We are not the normal. The real test of humanity is not our humanity but his. So, I believe he was a real human being mentally, but that does not involve my saying that he was mistaken and a child of his age. Indeed, those who say such things go on to say that they believe Jesus co-operated with God the Father. How can you co-operate with him fully and still be mistaken?

I move, then, to the other side of experience. The disciples knew that they had a real human being by their side – that this man they walked with and talked with was a real man. But when you say that Jesus is like us, you have got to specify which of us he is like. When you say that he is a real man you have to say whether it is possible to compare him with any single human being. What category does he fit into? What type of man is he? Very early on in the three years in which they knew him, the disciples began to notice that he is not our kind of man. There were three things that made them say this. First of all, what he did. Secondly, what he said. Thirdly, what he was. These three together made such an impact on these ordinary men that they began to see Jesus as different from us in kind, and not just in degree.

First of all, what he did: no situation is beyond his control. The miracles themselves attest to his unique character. I believe he changed water into wine and is still doing so. I believe he raised men and women from the dead and is still doing so. This is what made them say: "What manner of man is this?" I single out two miracles as examples from many more. Number one: the healing of a man sick with palsy who lay helpless on a stretcher. Jesus in that case knew that his condition was a result of his sin. It is not always so, but in that case it was. For Jesus went straight to the root of the problem and forgave the man's sins.

There were men standing there who came within half an inch of the truth. They said: "Only God can forgive sins." They were right, but they were wrong in the deduction they drew from that.

Jesus proved that he had forgiven the man of his sins by relieving him from the consequences of those sins. When told to get up and walk, he got up. Those men were so blind that though they came close to the truth they went away and said that he had blasphemed. All the sins and evil that people talk about cannot be forgiven by Jesus Christ unless he is divine.

The second miracle, of course, is the stilling of the storm. No scientist will ever be able to control the weather as Jesus did by word alone. I know that we can now fly over a cumulus cloud and drop frozen carbon dioxide or dry ice on the cloud and cause it to rain underneath, but we need an aeroplane and we need some frozen carbon dioxide to do it. No scientist has ever yet been able to say, "Rain" and see it do so. Jesus talked to a storm as you and I talk to a puppy dog. Do you know what Jesus said to the storm? He did not say, "Peace, be still," though I know that makes a good sermon. He said, "Get down! Be muzzled!" He used the phrase you would use with one of your pets. He talked to the wind and the waves as one would to a puppy dog, and they obeyed. The disciples said, "What manner of man is that?" What category do you put that sort of man in? Show me another man who can do that to the wind and the waves. You can then say that Jesus is different from us in degree, but there was something happening there which they did not understand.

The second great area of experience was what he said. Now, there were many claims that he made which caused people to say: "No man has ever spoken like this man." Notice the word "man" there. He claimed to be the exclusive way to God, he claimed to be the arbiter of man's eternal destiny, he claimed to know exactly what God meant in his words spoken in the past. But the two things I want to underline are little phrases which Jesus kept using: "I came" and "I am". No one else uses those expressions. "I came" is an extraordinary way to talk about your life. I do not say, "I came," I say, "I was born in Newcastle upon Tyne in February 1930." But Jesus kept saying "I came." The implication whenever he says it is that he chose to be born. No one else in the human race chose to be born. He came to do a job; he came to seek; he came that you might have life and have it more abundantly. That phrase is a way of speaking that others do not use.

There is also the expression "I am". Even in the Greek language the phrase "I am" is emphasised: *ego eimi;* "I, I am".

Jesus kept using this phrase. Sometimes he put something after it: "I am the good shepherd"; "I am the door"; I am the way, the truth and the life"; "I am the resurrection and the life"; "I am the light of the world"; "I am the bread...." But sometimes he said it without anything after it. When he did, those who heard him were in no doubt as to what he meant. He talked about his friendship with Abraham and they said, "You're not yet fifty, how do you know Abraham?" He said, "Before Abraham was, I AM." They took up stones to stone him because that was the name of God. They had no doubt whatever that Jesus was saying, "I am Yahweh."

They said, "That's blasphemy. A man who says that deserves to die." Jesus escaped because it was not yet his time to die. But that phrase, "I am" standing alone by itself, to his contemporaries meant Jesus was God, or at least was claiming to be God.

Later, when they came to arrest Jesus in the garden of Gethsemane, they were Jewish soldiers who came, temple guards. He said to them, "Who are you looking for?" They said, "Jesus of Nazareth," using a human name. But Jesus said, "I, I am." No wonder they fell on the ground – they expected thunder and lightning to strike from heaven and kill him. They wanted to get away from a man who said that, who was living dangerously, inviting God's wrath. Later still at the trial, when Jesus stood there bound, the High Priest said, "I make you swear, tell us are you the Son, the Christ, the Son of the living God? I adjure you by the living God." So, he had to answer. His answer was, "I, I am." The High Priest ripped his clothes and said, "You heard it! We don't need witnesses. No trial is needed, you heard it!" And they condemned him to death.

The third category was what he was. Being with Jesus gave people the sense that they were in the presence of God. It is difficult to describe this feeling. It is partly the fact that you are looking at a life that is absolutely pure and free from sin. Jesus said, "Which of you convicts me of sin?" They criticised his conversation, they criticised his conduct, but no one ever criticised his character. But it is not just that, it is not that people could not convict him of sin, it was that wherever he went he convicted them of sin. That is the other side of it. He said to a tough fisherman, "Get away from me Satan." There is something supernatural about Jesus – not just a sense of the supernatural, a sense of the holy, the clean and the pure.

There is something about Jesus that makes you feel this: "Woe is me; I am a man of unclean lips; I am undone." There was one extraordinary experience when three men stood on the edge of eternity – it happened at the very top of a mountain. One day, Jesus took Peter, James and John up the mountain and they looked at him and there was light shining through his clothes from the inside. The face of Jesus shone like the sun and his clothes became as white as the light. Peter saw him talking to two old friends who had been dead and gone for centuries – Moses and Elijah. Peter, having said that wonderful thing just a week before, opened his big mouth and put both feet in it. He put Jesus on a level with great men, and he made the mistake of thinking he was only a great man of God. He was willing to put up tabernacles to these three great people. God blotted out the other two with a cloud and said, "This is my beloved Son in whom I am well pleased. Hear him!"

They were not to be put on the same level; they must not be treated equally.

This whole question of who Jesus is reached a climax in the death and resurrection, which Jesus predicted in Matthew 17:22ff. Make no mistake about it, Jesus was not put to death as a political agitator. The political crime put above his head, "This is the King of the Jews," was only an expedient to obtain the death sentence from Pilate. He was put to death because he claimed to be Yahweh. That is what condemned him at his trial, when he used God's name about himself. He died appealing to a higher court and judge. Three days later up from the grave he arose in mighty triumph. He arose a victor from the dark domain, and he lives forever with his saints to reign. What did that do for the thinking of those disciples? They said, "He has been declared to be the Son of God with power by the resurrection from the dead."

It was when Thomas saw the human body again that he said "my God". Looking at that human body back from the grave, Thomas recognised that Jesus is divine. He never did touch those nail prints, and he never did put his hand in the side. Why not? He had seen something bigger than a friend back with them. He had seen God, and he did not want to put out a hand and touch God. "My Lord and my God."

It was the resurrection that clinched it for the disciples. It was this that finally took them to the last stage of the journey from "Jesus of Nazareth" to "my God".

As soon as they realised who Jesus is, their thought was stretched. The disciples became apostles.

The accounts of his birth began to come out. If Jesus chose to be born and chose to come into this world it must have been a different conception from normal. It must have been God's unique act. Jesus was born in a very normal way. He was born as I was born but he was conceived in a marvellous way. The apostles thought further and further back. They wanted to write the life of Jesus. Where to start? Mark started with John the Baptist. Matthew went further back, starting with Abraham. Luke went further back still, starting with Adam. John started at the beginning: "In the beginning was the Word...." The Word was there already. The Word was with God. The Word was God, the Word became flesh. Their thinking was going right back to before Jesus was conceived.

They began to realise that he was consciously alive before he was born. They began to talk about what he was doing, then they realised that he had been telling the prophets what to say. They realised he had been the rock in the wilderness following the Israelites from Egypt. They realised that when God created the world and brought order out of chaos that nothing had been made without Jesus. All things had been made through him. He who had made tables and chairs had once made the very trees from which he later made that furniture. Before there were any hills, before the mountains had been brought forth, or ever God had formed the Earth, there he was. No matter how far back you go, you come to the pre-existence of the divine Jesus.

Here is what they realised: that when the Word became flesh all of his deity came with him. There have been certain theories called "kenotic" or self-emptying theories, that Jesus only managed to bring a bit of godliness into his life, a bit of his "God-ness" into his body, and had to leave some behind. Never! In him the fullness of the Godhead dwelt bodily, and the fullness means he brought the whole lot with him. There was all he left – the position and the glory that accompanies deity – yes, but he brought all his garments with him. He was divine and when he became human all the fullness of the Godhead was embodied. Never let us listen to those who say he left part of his "God-ness" behind. It was an incarnation, and all of his deity came into that little baby's body. I cannot comprehend it, but in him all the fullness of the Godhead came.

Now, the other direction in which the apostles' thought was stretched was forward. They realised that just as when Jesus came to Earth he brought all his "God-ness" into his manhood, so when he went back to where he came from he took all his manhood into his "God-ness". This is the other side of the truth that Jesus was divine before he was human, but this side is that he is still human. Let me say that those who believe firmly in his deity tend, if they are not careful, to overlook his present humanity.

This the apostles saw, and again and again they stressed that when he ascended, he did so as man. This was a man going into space; his body went up with him. He went up in his new glorified body and somewhere in the unseen world that body still exists. One day, when he comes back, we shall see it. This is why they preached that we have a High Priest who can sympathise with us. He has been tempted as we are. We have a human High Priest pleading for us on high. This is why they said there is only one mediator between God and man, the man Christ Jesus. The man – when he comes back, he will come back as the man to judge the world. God the Father has appointed a man to judge the world.

Here then are two fundamental truths which we must not let go of: his deity and his humanity. They are both enshrined in a simple creed of the apostles: "Jesus Christ is come in the flesh." That implies two things: that he came and is now in our humanity. John, the beloved apostle, warned that there are many deceivers gone out in the world who deny that Jesus Christ is come in the flesh. They deny his previous existence as God and deny his present existence as man. He has come in the flesh and he has not left his manhood. He has taken our humanity into godhood – what a mystery. The depth, the unsearchable mystery of it. How can a feeble brain like mine understand that? Therefore, let me beware lest by failing to understand it I deny it, and lest I lose these precious truths – Jesus the man had been God and is still man; he has come in the flesh. John goes on to say that if a man denies those two facts, then you are not even to give him a meal in your home. You are to give him no welcome, for you encourage him in the untruth he is speaking.

Which brings me to my third and last point: the creed of Christians. Our initial knowledge of Christ comes to us through words. Somebody spoke to us about Jesus and our ears heard the truth. That is how the reality of Christ first enters any life – through language, through words. Send up a little prayer in this moment for the man or woman or young person who first spoke to you about Jesus. The gospel cannot be spread in any other way. You may live a Christian life in front of your neighbours, but until you speak about Jesus they cannot know Christ. The words we use are English, they are not Aramaic or Greek such as the apostles spoke and wrote in. English is changing all the time; changing so rapidly that there are teenagers today whose own parents do not understand their own language – maybe vice versa. Maybe they do not want to. So, there is a constant need to translate the reality of Christ into the contemporary language that people around us can understand.

Here we run into two difficulties. One is to find English words that are equivalent to the Greek words the apostles used. The other is a much larger difficulty. A group of linguistic philosophers have said that language cannot be trusted; that all words are relative and like Alice in Wonderland you can make what you say mean anything you wish, and that therefore it is impossible to embody absolute truth in language. All you can do is make a relative approximate statement that is somewhere near the truth, but cannot be argued for or against. So, we live in a day in which people no longer have confidence in words. The result is that people say, "We cannot have a confession of faith. We cannot write down what we believe in a creed. We cannot even be sure that what the scripture says is what God says." Now, that is a difficulty we have to face. To answer this difficulty, I start with God himself. Praise him that he is a God who talks, a God who used words to convey truth to people. If God has confidence in language, so do I. If God can trust words then I can. This is the fundamental belief that I have. I know that Jesus was the Word, but you cannot know the Word unless you know words about him. The scripture claims that God not only gave us the Word but words about him – words through prophets who lived before and apostles who lived after, but words about the Word to make the Word real to me. God inspired both.

19
SAYINGS AND RESPONSES

Read Matthew Chapter 18–19

The disciples of Jesus at this stage were too self-important. They asked him who is the greatest in the Kingdom of heaven. Pride is one of the most difficult things to deal with. He gave them a visual rebuke, with a little child as an example. Failure to be converted and become as little children is a barrier to entering the Kingdom.

If we think we are important, not only must we reverse our ideas but we must also minister to "unimportant" people. A person who thinks he is important will probably spend all his time with important people, name dropping, getting introductions. But Jesus was teaching them that if you give your time to a little unimportant child who cannot give you anything in return, if you do it in his name, you will receive Jesus and the Father. That should be a tremendous encouragement to a Sunday school teacher, to someone who spends a bit of time among young people, to those who are not high in rank or important in society. The disciples are challenged: why are they discussing importance? Everybody is important.

Another thing that was wrong with the twelve was that they could be intolerant of others yet tolerant with themselves. This often happens. You can be terribly strict with other people and slack towards yourself. Jesus' teaching is that it is you yourself that you should be strict with, it is yourself that you should be intolerant toward.

In a host of ways, as we go through life, we can be making others sin. From 18:6, we are given powerful teaching on offences, including causing others ("little ones" who believe in him) to sin. Jesus said that it would be better for you to have a millstone around your neck. Millstones can be seen in Galilee – black basalt rock about a yard across with a hole in the middle, and if you had one of those around your neck you would not even get to the seashore, never mind get into the water. But if others took you to the sea, tied that around your neck and threw you in, you would not stand a chance. Jesus is teaching here that there is a fate worse than death: living with the knowledge that you led others astray, and knowing that one day God will face you with that responsibility.

From 18:7 onwards, Jesus is continuing to teach in a way that challenges the attitudes and behaviour of disciples. It is very clear that the words are not meant to be taken literally, but they are meant to be taken seriously. He talks about parts of the human body through which offences can come. What does he mean? It is picture language and it is clear that Jesus does not mean it literally because if my eye offends me and I pluck it out, I have still got the other eye to look at the same thing. Let me put it into simple English, because we do not think so much in pictures as they did then. Here is what he means: if there is anything you are doing, if there is anything you are watching, if there is anywhere you are going that is hindering you from being a good Christian, cut it right out. It is as simple as that. You will realise that this will vary from person to person, and the tragedy is that we often become so strict with each other that we make rules for one another that Jesus never made. It may be perfectly all right for one Christian to go and watch a good film in a cinema, and it may be thoroughly wrong for another to go near that place. It may be all right for this Christian to have a television in the home but it may be all wrong for another to have one. We must not judge each other in these secondary things. What Jesus is teaching here, he teaches each disciple individually: if this is offending, cut it right out. It may well be necessary for some Christians to be total abstainers, but you cannot establish from the Bible that all should be. It may well be necessary for some Christians to cut out this, and to cut out that, and not other practices. The point is whether this is something that I am doing or watching or going to that hinders me from doing the work of Christ. If so, cut it right out because any of these three things could lead a person to disaster.

In 18:8–9 we come to some very serious teaching about hell. Jesus taught us about hell. He always pictured it as the valley outside Jerusalem. Just imagine the city of Zion, up on the hill with the wall around it. On the south side is a deep, dark valley, the bottom of which never sees the sun but is in permanent shadow. Down in that valley was the rubbish of Jerusalem. If you had any rubbish, you tipped it over the wall and it tumbled down into the valley. There were maggots eating up the food that remained, and bonfires were kept burning to keep the rubbish down – it was just one heap of useless garbage. And Jesus is teaching this: beware; the things a man looks at are enough to ruin him to the point where he is just rubbish and no use for anybody or anything. The things a man does can bring him down to that, and make him utterly useless to man and God. The places he goes to can ruin him. Better to cut these things out and be called narrow and live a narrow life in other people's eyes than ruin yourself and bring yourself to the rubbish heap. Jesus was being so true to life. It was our Lord who described hell in terms of a rubbish heap where the worm dies not and the fire is not quenched, where men and women go who are no use to God and men anymore. It is what the word "perished" means in John 3:16. Rather than perish, rather than become useless, rather than be thrown out as rubbish and ruined, it is better to cut the practice out, right out, for yourself – and enter into life.

We have covered in this chapter some lessons on sin and its effects. The positive side is this: are you one of those who is a little centre of life, neutralising sin, reducing it, dealing with it, and removing it? Every one of us in the church is either a person who is adding to sin by encouraging it, by leading others to do it, or we are reducing it and removing it from the scene. How do you remove it? The answer is by rebuking it and by forgiveness. From 18:14 onwards, we can see this very clearly.

One of the most awful dangers is this: when we see sin, we talk about it to everybody but the one responsible for it. That is an unspiritual and an unchristian attitude. The Bible makes it quite clear that if you see sin there is only one person you should talk to about it and that is the person himself or herself. You should not go to anyone else; you should not gossip about it; you should not criticise them behind their back. You should go to them and – in love – rebuke it. Someone who has the courage and love to go to the individual direct is the person who will remove sin from the scene and not add to it.

Secondly, when they repent, forgive. I have noticed in life this simple fact and I pass it on to you as an observation of Christian fellowship: those who have enough love to forgive are those who have enough love to rebuke. Those who do not have enough love to rebuke do not have enough love to forgive; the two go together. Both are demonstrations of love. In fact, those who do not speak to a person but talk behind their back are those who will be resentful and unforgiving in spirit; the two go together again. This is a lesson Jesus wanted people to learn: he did not want them to be adding to the sins of others' lives, but taking the sins of other people away – reducing the heap of evil in the world, not increasing it; not causing sin, but curing it. It is very difficult to forgive someone else because it involves forgetting it, and putting it right out of your relationship, right out of your mind. Jesus gives us some guidance about how many times we may have to do this. It says something about our lack of spirituality that a person who may have offended us three times is somebody we then can't forgive. In fact, Jewish rabbis of those days used to say: "If you can forgive your brother three times in one day then you are a perfect man." Jesus said seven times in one day. I think that pretty well covers every relationship you have. I would be surprised if you could tell me that somebody has sinned against you more than seven times a day. I have done a little mathematics and that is forty-nine times a week. I once heard a Christian say, "Just wait till he does it the 491st time," because he had been reading "unto seventy times seven" – he had been working that out – that is 490. But what Jesus is teaching is this: don't count; even if the same person sins against you seven times a day, you still go to him seven times, and if he says "I'm sorry", you say, "Right, that is forgiven and forgotten, and it is dealt with."

The reason for doing this is, of course, that it is how you hope the Lord will deal with you. When we say the Lord's Prayer there is only one thing in that prayer that we say about ourselves, have you noticed that? There is only one profession that you make about your own Christian life in that prayer. There is only one ground on which you pray the Lord's Prayer: I have forgiven those who have trespassed against me. It is the only thing you claim when you ask for God's mercy: that you have been merciful. It is a sobering thought, but insofar as you have been merciful to others then God can give you mercy. It is not because it is a bargain, nor because showing mercy merits God's mercy.

In the last verse of Romans 1, having described some pretty horrible features of social life in the Roman Empire which are very common today, Paul writes: "And these people who do such things not only do them themselves, but encourage others to do them also" – as much as to say that is the depth of depravity, not when you have reached rock bottom and wallow in the mud yourself, but when you want to drag everybody down to your level. That is more serious. Far better to be out of this world altogether. To be drowned in the depths of the sea; it really would be better for a person to be at the bottom of the sea, dead, than to be living and doing that kind of thing. But the positive thing that we are to be doing is rebuking sin and forgiving those who sin against us. We are to forgive and forget. Then we are reducing the sin around us – being a follower of Jesus.

In 19:1–12, we read the teaching of Jesus on marriage and divorce. The reader is referred to my extensive discussion of this in my book *Remarriage is Adultery, Unless*....

Then, in 19:13 the section of teaching which began in chapter 18 is completed with a further reminder of the significance of the children as exemplifying the value of all people, not least those of low status.

We then meet the rich young ruler, who I would call the poor rich man. We notice certain things about him. This young man wanted life, and he wanted real life, eternal life. He knew what he was after; he was just existing, and he came running to Jesus and admitted that he had not got life. He recognised that if you are going to get life someone has to give it to you, so he asked what he had to do and he believed the answer lay with Jesus. It is tremendous when somebody realises that if you want real life, the man you need to go to is Jesus.

He said, "Good teacher". Our Lord's comments are very interesting. Jesus says, "Why do you call me good? No one is good but one, that is God." Is Jesus saying that he is not God? No, nothing of the sort. In effect, the young man is being asked whether he thinks Jesus is God. Jesus is asking him why he is calling him "good", since that is only a word that should be used about God – and Jesus is God, and so can give him life. Jesus then went on to ask a question about the Commandments, which would show how good the young man thought he himself was. He answered Jesus, "All these things I have kept from my youth." He was not claiming to be perfect. When he said that he had observed all that from his youth he was saying that he had tried to be good, he had tried to keep the commandments, tried to live decently – and it had not brought him life. Here was a young man who had tried being good and found that it had not led him anywhere. He had tried to find life but he had not found it. He was prepared to do anything to get it, and he asked what he needed to do.

Then Jesus told him of the one thing he needed to do. What was that one thing? Every commentary I have read suggests that the one thing this young man lacked was poverty. But that was not what Jesus said. He said "If you want to be perfect", *not*: there is one thing you have got that is causing the trouble. What was the one thing this young man did not have? Jesus said "come, follow me", but the trouble was that there was something that was going to get in the way. What he needed was Jesus Christ, who brings life.

You cannot have Christ and everything else. I do not care who comes to Christ, there will be one thing in that person's life of which Jesus says: get rid of it, and then you can have me. Go and deal with that and then you can follow me. It may be something you possess; it may be some person with whom you have a relationship.

There are rich people who have found Christ, but it was Jesus that the young man lacked, and at that point the young man turned around and went. Nobody is quite as unhappy as someone who has come as near to Jesus as that and turned away because they were not prepared to pay the price. The young man looked so unhappy. He would have brought that money to Jesus, if Jesus had let him. But Jesus told him to give it to the poor, and "you will have treasure in heaven and come, follow me". Jesus would not reduce the standard; he preferred that the young man went away than follow him under false pretences. Christ lost that young man who did not want eternal life more than anything else, and when the choice came, he let it go.

After the young man had gone away, Jesus explained how hard it is for a rich man to enter the Kingdom of heaven. The disciples were astonished. They thought everything came more easily to the rich. I have met many people today who think that if you have a big bank balance everything is easy. The problem with this is that because things come easily to you on Earth when you have money, you may think that things come easily to you in heaven when you have money. But Jesus was showing the young man that all his money was invested on earth. Give to the poor and get it invested in heaven. So, the disciples asked, "Who then can be saved?" If the rich person could not get into heaven, who could? Is that not a revelation of their outlook? Imagine thinking you can sign a cheque to get salvation! Jesus had taught that little children can walk in. He is now teaching that you might as well try and shove a camel through a needle's eye as try to get a rich person converted. For it is quite impossible, but God can do it. God can get a rich person through the gate of repentance into the Kingdom. And once he is through, what a power that individual can be for good. So, with God it is not impossible.

20

LANDOWNER AND LABOURERS

Read Matthew 20

In the course of the twentieth century in the UK we experienced periods of severe economic disruption, with high inflation and high unemployment. I asked myself: is there any passage in the Bible which we ought to be looking at in this situation? Is there anything that Christians need to be hearing? I found myself reading this remarkable story about work and wages in Matthew chapter 20. I felt that hidden within it there is a very strong word from the Lord to us.

I imagined what each of the political, industrial and union leaders would have commented about it, if asked. I realised that each of them would fasten on part of the story and say that there was biblical justification for their political stance. It proves again that you can prove anything from the Bible if you take parts of it. People tend to pick out parts of the parable. But if you had asked, "What do you think about the whole story?" I think every one of them would say, "It would not work; it is idealistic; it is impracticable, and in fact it would be bad personnel management, a recipe for disaster. If you tried to apply the whole of that story to our economic situation today, we would be over the precipice tomorrow." Indeed, trying to imagine what would have happened, the one person in the story that I feel terribly sorry for is the foreman, wondering what he would do the following day.

These days, the owner of the vineyard would be in an industrial tribunal. But even then, try to imagine what would happen the next day when that owner went out to try to get workers to come into his vineyard. I can imagine that some would say, "We are just not going to work for you." I can imagine others who would work for him but would slacken off straight away and say, "He pays you but it doesn't matter how much work you do or how little." I can imagine still others saying, "I'm not going to get out of bed till five o'clock and then I'm going down the marketplace and he's really a dead winner – you can get in at five o'clock and get a full day's wage." I can imagine a very few who might say, "He was so good to us yesterday we'll go and work the whole day for him for free today." But as a recipe for industrial relationships, it could be a recipe for disaster.

Like so many parables of Jesus, they seem to be going along normal tracks until a certain point and then there is a twist and something happens which is quite untrue to life. It is where the twist comes that the real message of the parable comes. Most of this parable is strictly true to life.

Now, I know that we have to make a culture jump to understand the story. I have never worked in a vineyard, for example. We have to think ourselves into a situation in which men can only get a job day by day and only get twenty-four hours of employment at a time. We have to think of a marketplace as a kind of Job Centre where they wait with their tools to be hired. We have to think of working a twelve-hour day and a return for a twelve-hour day of maybe a few pounds in our money. But the amount mentioned was a normal daily wage then, even for a soldier in the Roman army. Even so, it is easy for us to get into the story. It is a straightforward story, true to life. For those listening to it originally, until Jesus got half way through they would have said, "So what's new, what is he talking about? This is just something that happens every day. It is ordinary – there is nothing special about this story."

Then, by the point we call v. 9 eyebrows would begin to rise. The first funny little twist that is very untrue to life is simply that the owner decided to make those who had worked for twelve hours wait at the back of the queue for their wages. Something is beginning to go a bit wrong at that point. Surely, those who had worked all day in the heat of the day should be able to come to the pay office window first and get their envelope first. But no, they are sent to the back of the queue. A funny owner this – he is already treading on toes. Then comes the shock of the story – they see the first people get a full day's wage so they rub their hands at the bonus that will be in their own packet and are astonished that they get no more. That is the point at which the story becomes shocking.

Many parables are like scorpions – they have a sting in the tail and they really are stinging. In fact, it is a story with a very unhappy ending. Relationships break up; the relationship between the employer and his employees has broken down altogether. What the relationships were between those who came at five o'clock and those who had been working since six in the morning as they went home, I don't know. I would not think they were speaking to each other. The whole thing seems to break up and yet Jesus teaches that this is what the kingdom of heaven is like.

A lot of ink has been spilled trying to say what the real message of Jesus was here. I am going to give you a number of these interpretations and I am going to tell you which ones I think are wrong and why. But I want you to realise that we are not handling an easy passage. Is Jesus commenting on industrial relationships at work and the matter of wages? Is there something in here for our contemporary situation? Or is it something more subtle than that? Let us put the question another way. Is this one of those stories that he told to lift people up, to encourage them, to invite them to something that they would respond to positively? Or is it one of those stories that he is using as a fairly sharp weapon to cut them down, to challenge them, to admonish them, to warn them? Most of the wrong interpretations of the story I think come because people believe that Jesus was telling a story here to encourage us, to fill us with hope – telling a story that had a simple moral in it that would invite us and encourage us in some way. So, they say the essential piece of good news in this story is that everybody finishes up with the same and they fasten on the wages as the key point.

Now, that is all very well but here we get into a real pickle. I am sorry but I am going to confuse you by telling you what kind of a muddle you get into if you believe that is what Jesus is doing. If he is saying in some way that we shall all finish up in heaven with exactly the same, and if that is the message, then you have some very awkward questions to ask. The first question you have to ask is: what exactly is the thing that we finish up with? What does the coin stand for? Some of the Christians throughout the centuries have said the coin is the gift of salvation. That might sound all right until you comment: "Well look, some of them really had to work a long time, and some of them worked a short time for it, and they all worked for some of it. And I thought salvation was something you didn't work for at all. I thought it was free." So, people back off that explanation and they go for a much more common one and say: "This is a story about the rewards waiting in heaven for service rendered on earth and we are all going to receive the same reward in heaven, however much we have done, or however little." That is the most common interpretation of this parable. But it is contrary to so many other scriptures where it says that we must all appear before the judgment seat of Christ and that he will reward us according to our fidelity and our service. Those who take the parable this way have then to ask this funny question: "What do the different times of starting work signify in Christian service?" Here we get very involved. On the one hand, some scholars say that it means that the people who started serving Christ in the first century and the people who started serving Christ in the twentieth century and the people who started serving Christ in the fifteenth century will all get the same reward. That is a funny kind of interpretation.

Matthew Chapter 20

A more common one appeals to a lot more people, namely that it doesn't matter whether you started serving the Lord at ten, twenty, thirty, forty, fifty, sixty, seventy, eighty, or ninety years of age – if you are faithful in service, God will reward your fidelity. There is an element of truth in that interpretation but I do not believe it is what Jesus is saying here. It too runs into difficulties. In fact, the people who interpret the story this way have so scratched their heads that they have had to come up with the extraordinary belief that there is something missing from the story and that our copy of it has a vital fact missed out, as if you have borrowed a detective novel from the library and find the last three pages missing. The vital thing that some say has been missed out is the simple fact that the people who worked for twelve hours worked very slowly and the people who worked for one hour worked so quickly that they did as much as the others and so it was all fair and it was all right. Well, why doesn't it say so?

It is interesting that the Jews had a story very like this. At the same time as Jesus taught this story, a Jewish rabbi taught a very similar story about a king who called men to work in his vineyard, and after they had been working for two hours, he called a man out of the vineyard and for the rest of the day the king and this man spent the time walking through the vineyard talking. At the end of the day, he paid this man the same wage as the others and the others complained and the king said, "Ah, but this man did as much in two hours as you all have done in twelve hours." That is the Jewish version of the story and there is no problem with that, but what a trite story!

We have not got anywhere near what Jesus is really saying here yet. I will tell you why: if you interpret this story as the gift of salvation to us or the rewards of service in the kingdom then you cannot really do justice to the end of the story. It could stop three verses from the end and you would still have the whole story. You see, the story does not finish up in heaven. If heaven is going to involve everybody arguing about what rewards are received, then I do not want to go there. If this is a prophecy of the day when the rewards will be given to us then there is going to be an awful lot of grumbling in heaven – no, it's not going to fit.

Somehow, we have to come to terms with the fact that Jesus finishes this story on a very earthy note, in the kind of grumbling, arguing, grabbing and struggling we saw in the late 1970s. This is not a picture of heaven; it is a picture of something that we are all too familiar with on earth. It is a picture of attitudes which, if we are honest, we have in our very own hearts.

So, we have to come at this story from a very different angle. Instead of seeing it as one of those stories Jesus was giving us to encourage us, let us ask whether he was giving us a warning. Was he admonishing us? Was he rebuking us? Was he exposing something about the fallen human nature that would spoil heaven if it got there? Is he taking the light of heaven to show up the darkness of earth? For, you see, for Jesus the kingdom of heaven was not just something in the future that we are going to enter one day. For Jesus, the kingdom of heaven had broken into the present. It was there and present: repent and believe; the kingdom of God is here; it has come.

The new order is breaking in and therefore it is colliding with the old order. The new attitudes have broken through and are now challenging the old attitudes. The new outlook has broken in and now exposes the old outlook. That is what is happening. Indeed, in this simple story Jesus is showing a confrontation between two totally different outlooks as far apart as heaven is from earth. Yet they are meeting in the very people to whom he is telling the story. This is our situation. The question is whether our attitude is going to be the old earthly attitude or the new heavenly one.

Let us look at the story as a warning. It begins to make sense to me now; it exposes my honest and natural reactions because there is something in this story that we do not like. We love many of Jesus' stories. But if you were to ask people which is their favourite parable, I think that most would not choose this one. There is a feeling that the owner of the vineyard was less than fair. We are born with an inbuilt sense of injustice. Have you noticed that you never need to teach a child to sense injustice? "He got a bigger piece than I did...." My mother used to say what many others said: "If you want to cut an apple exactly in half so that there are two halves, let one child cut it and the other have first pick, and you get it exactly halved." We are born with a nature that never needs to be taught to say: "It's not fair." It is one of the most common expressions on children's lips. As we grow up, we dress it up in sophisticated language but this is the cry of the human heart that readily comes to our lips. This is a natural reaction to this story. It is not fair that a man who has worked for twelve long hours – and especially in the Middle Eastern heat of noon – should get the same wage as a man who has only worked for one hour in the cool of the evening; it is just not fair. There is something in us that rebels against the story.

Have you ever stopped to think what that feeling of "It's not fair" actually does to you? Have you ever tried to analyse what is happening to you when you say it? Let me just spell it out. First, it is making you self-centred because we nearly always say "It's not fair" about our own circumstances. We do not often say it about other people's – have you noticed that? We feel it when we are being treated unjustly much more strongly than when someone else is. So, it is essentially a self-centred feeling. You have to have matured in character to be angrier about someone else suffering injustice than you; it shows a remarkable maturity of character when that is where your anger arises.

There is another thing about saying "It's not fair". Have you noticed what it does to your emotions, and through them what it can do to your health? There are all kinds of unhealthy emotions associated with this phrase. There is anger, bitterness, resentment, envy – and these emotions are bad for us even physically. A person who stays living in those emotions will sooner or later suffer bad health. There is something even worse about this feeling of "It's not fair" – it leads us to make calculated comparisons with other people which destroy our love for them and introduce hatred for them. You see, it is not just that I am being treated unjustly. I may even be treated justly, but if someone else is getting more than they deserve, even if I am getting what I do deserve, then hatred is born within my heart for him, he becomes my enemy. If we are going to go through life saying "It's not fair" we shall finish up a self-centred, envious person with a seed of hatred in our hearts. There is an attitude that is poisonous. It is part of our fallen human nature that we are so ready to have those words on our lips: "It's not fair."

Now, it is that attitude which Jesus is challenging in this story. It is the attitude of saying, "What is in this for me?" The attitude that looks at the neighbour and says, "And what's he getting, too?" That attitude is being challenged here. It is not just asking the question, "Are we getting all that we deserve," but "Are they getting more than they deserve?" The kingdom of heaven is not like that.

So now let us look at the story from a different point of view – that of the owner. We find out that instead of the story being the story of a man who is less than fair it is the story of a man who is more than fair. What a difference that is! The owner is going beyond what he needs to do. His concern is primarily for others, not himself. He is doing favours for people all the way through the story. He is giving them work in the first place. All right, he needs workers in the vineyard but I get the strong impression that he finds people who have not got work and he creates jobs for them; that he wants them to have the opportunity to work and he is giving them work. He wants to help them.

When it comes to giving out the wages, he is a man who looks at the worker and considers: "What does he need and what does his family need?" because that wage was a subsistence wage. You could not save anything out of it; you could only just keep your family going on it, and a day out of work was a disaster. This owner of the vineyard looks at these workers and he thinks of their wives and their children and he knows that if he only pays them one hour's wage those families will go hungry.

Here is a man who is doing more than what is just, he is showing mercy. Mercy is not less than fair; it is more than fair. Now, if you belong to the kingdom of earth and have a worldly attitude you will say of him, "He is less than fair." But if you step into the kingdom of heaven and look at him again you will say, "He is more than fair." As it was, the owner said, "Friend, I am doing you no wrong." That was true. The problem was with the attitude of the complaining labourer.

It is not a story about justice, it is a story about mercy. It is saying that heaven operates on a different principle than the world.

God operates not on what a man deserves to get but on what he delights to give. That is the kingdom of heaven.

Jesus comes with this revolutionary concept: the kingdom of heaven is not built on merit; it is built on mercy. The God who owns the vineyard is a God who treats you not as you deserve but as he delights in treating you. That is the picture of God right through the Bible. The only people who will object to that are the people who still have pride in their heart. For behind the grumblers in the story does not lie greed – they would have been perfectly content with their wage – it was their pride that was hurt.

When did Jesus tell this story? To whom was he speaking? Here comes the awful shock – he was not speaking to crafty businessmen, he was not speaking to angry workers on strike, he said this to his own disciples. Not even to the crowd, but to those who had left everything and followed him and devoted their lives to him, and who had already spent two and a half years with him. Why should he say it to his own followers? It was because although they had left their businesses to follow Jesus, their businesses had not left them. They had not left this calculating comparison behind when they followed Jesus. Do you know what had happened just before this story was told? At 19:27 Peter had said to Jesus, "We were ready to take the step, we left everything for you. What's in it for us?" He actually said that. What shall we get because we left everything?

Jesus was so patient and so tender with his disciples and he did not crush Peter. He taught Peter there was no need to worry about reward. Anybody who has given up anything for Jesus will be repaid a hundredfold. Then he told the story. The kingdom of heaven is like the owner of a vineyard.... So, we should be very grateful to Peter. Situation after situation has arisen when a person has died and the Will is read and the people receiving benefit from it have done nothing to deserve what they get. "If she's got more than I have and if he's got more than he should have..." – then the family breaks up. There have been families that have broken up immediately after a funeral never to get back together again. Even though they did not deserve anything, somebody got more than someone else. We are dealing here with basic human nature.

Jesus had explained that everyone who had left houses, family members and land for his name's sake would receive a hundredfold and inherit eternal life.

What happened immediately after he told the story? James and John went to their mother and asked her to go to Jesus and put in a good word for them and try and get them the chief seats in the kingdom on the right- and the left-hand side of Jesus respectively. The mother came and asked Jesus whether he would do something for her two boys. Jesus did not answer the mother; he knew where it had come from. His reply to James and John meant: could they suffer? He said that it was not for him to give those seats, which would be for those for whom they had been prepared by his Father.

The other disciples were displeased with James and John for trying to get ahead of them. The other ten were angry because they were trying to get an advantage. You can see that still, after two and a half years, all of the twelve disciples were still infected with the concept of merit. They still had not understood that God in heaven is never less than fair, he is always more than fair. That is the meaning of the story. The extent to which you have really grasped the concept of the kingdom of heaven will depend on your reaction to this story; you will either hate it or love it. If you are still thinking in terms of merit, you will say that it is less than fair. If you have got to the realm of mercy, you will say it is more than fair – it is mercy!

That is my understanding of the story. If the three closest disciples of Jesus – Peter, James and John – failed at that point then I need to listen to this warning too. Jesus is teaching us not to let the world around us press us into its own mould.

Mercy seems an alien concept in the jungle in which we live; but that is the message. The story is not a solution to industrial problems on earth, it is a sample of the industrial principles of heaven. Service for the Lord is so different. The clash between the "shop steward" and the owner in this story is nothing else than the contrast between heaven and earth. Recall the time when John the Baptist was preparing the way for the kingdom – wearing those simple clothes out in the wilderness by the River Jordan. He was saying, "Repent and believe, the kingdom is coming!" Have you noticed that when people came to be baptised, he asked them this question: "Are you content with your wages?" That is pretty real and down to earth, but he would not baptise someone who was not content with their wages; he had understood the kingdom.

The very concept of merit can spoil Christian service. The calculating approach that serves the Lord with one eye on the reward that will come will lead to wrong attitudes and broken relationships. It will lead you to begrudge a brother his extra blessing that the Lord in his mercy has given, all the gifts that the Lord in his mercy has given another, which he did not deserve; all the opportunities another is getting that he did not deserve – you will begrudge it all. You will also be led to make that calculating comparison which despises someone else's contribution and says, "Well, they only worked one hour – I worked twelve." All such thoughts would taint Christian service and would result in you forfeiting the reward, so that if you let merit into your thinking about service for the kingdom of heaven you are in for a nasty shock. You will find that the last are first and the first are last. You will spoil what you are doing. That is not to say that it is wrong to think of reward. Jesus spoke about rewards; he left us in no doubt that for certain things there are great rewards in heaven. But here he is teaching us that those rewards are of grace, as much as the work which earned them is given to you by grace; not merit, but mercy – a very different world.

If you are in the world of merit then you talk about the rights of the worker. If you are in the world of mercy you talk about the rights of the owner. That is why the owner of the vineyard says, "Is it not lawful for me to do what I wish with my own things?" God is within his rights to have mercy on whom he will have mercy. He is within his rights to give us more than we deserve. He is within his rights to give gifts to one and opportunities to another. He is within his rights because he lives in a world of mercy and not a world of merit. We have no rights in a world of mercy; if God calls you or me into his service, that is his mercy. I have no right to be a servant of the Lord, and if he rewards me for what I do, that is mercy – I have no right to expect it; but God is more than just and loves to be merciful.

What a lovely message. Could anyone wish to work for a better boss? What then does he expect of us in our relationships with each other? The answer, interestingly enough, was given centuries before this story was told, by the prophet Micah. He said, "What does the Lord require of you but this: to do justly?" That is the absolute minimum: we must be at least fair, seeking to do justly. But that is not all, "To love mercy"– to love to give what people do not deserve, to love to go the second mile, to

Matthew Chapter 20

love to be generous. And that is not enough either, because you could fall into the trap of thinking that loving mercy puts you high up the list instead of walking humbly with your God. Justice is the minimum, and on that we build mercy, but lest that go to our heads and turn into an idea that we have earned merit, we are to walk humbly with our God.

In 20:25ff., Jesus teaches his disciples that they should not be like others who like to lord it over people and tell them what to do. Greatness in the kingdom is about service. The example was Jesus himself who came to serve, and to give his life as a ransom for many.

He was telling them for the first time the meaning of his cross – that it was going to be a ransom. When he died, he was going to be serving people more than he had ever served them before. He was going to be the means of setting them free. That is what a ransom is.

The chapter concludes with the amazing healing of two blind men. There was a big crowd around them and they heard that it was Jesus of Nazareth. The blind men realised this was their only chance. They began to yell at the top of their voices: "Have mercy on us, O Lord, Son of David!" Again, people had the wrong idea about who was important. They thought Jesus would not be interested in blind beggars. Jesus called the men and asked what they wanted him to do for them. They said, "Lord, let our eyes be opened." He had compassion and touched their eyes. Then immediately their eyes received sight, and they followed him.

That the men who had been blind and were healed rose up and followed Jesus was wonderful.

To the rich man Jesus said, "Follow me", but he had too much money and could not follow. Those who had been blind had nothing to lose so they jumped up and followed Jesus. The richer you are when you come to God, the harder it is to follow him; the poorer you are, the easier it is. When you have nothing to lose you can just get up and go. That is why Jesus said in his lifetime that publicans, harlots and sinners got into the kingdom of heaven before respectable religious people. It is still true that when a person is at the bottom and has nothing to lose, they find it easier to follow Jesus than those of us who have so much. That is the first wonderful thing here.

The other wonderful thing is that expression used of Jesus: "Son of David". There was only one man who had called Jesus that before – another blind man. These were blind men who could see, and they saw the truth about Jesus. Just a few days later, a crowd was going to shout, "Hosanna, Son of David" – but it took two blind men to see it first. You cannot physically see Jesus passing through your church, but when he does pass through and you realise that he is present, that is the moment to seize because you may never have that opportunity again. These blind men had not seen Jesus but had heard that he was near, and started calling on him and saying they needed something from him. And they heard Jesus say, "What do you want me to do for you?" Even though you cannot see Jesus, I tell you that you can call on him and say: "Son of David, have mercy on me."

You will hear him say, "What do you want me to do for you?" And you can rise up and follow him, but it is easier to do that if you come as a spiritual beggar. It is one of the hardest things in the world not to come with your hands full of all your good deeds, all your spiritual possessions, saying, "Lord, I have done this, I have done that, I have not done anybody any harm; and I haven't done this and I haven't done that; Lord, will you accept me?" It is much better to come with empty hands and say, "Lord, I am a beggar; have mercy on me."

21
JERUSALEM

Read Matthew Chapter 21

At the Passover festival Jerusalem itself could not cope with the huge number of visitors and they had to camp out on the surrounding hills. This is the setting for what we call the triumphal entry. On that morning Jesus left the home in which he was staying in Bethany, just over the Mount of Olives. That morning he set out and he sent the disciples for that colt. To get on a colt on which no man has ever sat, and then to ride it through a shouting mob numbering thousands, was remarkable. We get a unique impression of our Lord's control of people, of animals, indeed of every situation.

What was really happening in this familiar narrative? To the crowds it was a day of tremendous triumph; to Jesus it was a day of terrible tragedy. The people had waited a thousand years for this day. They were waiting for David's throne to be occupied again. A thousand years before this day they had known a time of peace, prosperity and a king after God's own heart. Back then, it was the golden age of their history, and it had never been the same since.

The people lived for the day when they would have their own land to themselves again. It is quite natural that all these hopes should be expressed in one word, "David". For a thousand years they kept alive the hope that one day there would be another king like David.

Being an enemy-occupied territory, this had bred collaborators, tax collectors, a resistance movement known as the Zealots, and acts of resistance were taking place. If I ask what was the real meaning of the triumphal entry in the eyes of the crowd, one word will answer it: nationalism. It was a nationalist demonstration. It was a crowd of people who were fed up with others ruling their country, fed up with being a colony, fed up with not having their own land to themselves and their own ruler to rule over them. It was a protest movement, a march. That becomes strangely relevant. In their eyes they had found the right leader. They had tried some months earlier, in Galilee, to make him king – and he had refused. Now they thought: he is willing. What a king to have! Imagine finding a king to rule over your land who is a wonderful teacher, a friend of everybody no matter what their class or background, a man who can heal and work miracles, a man who loves the common people, a man who is fond of children, a man who is fair and wise and just and merciful, a man who puts hypocritical religious rulers in their place, a man who can even raise the dead. Would you want a man like this to reign over your country? That was the man they had found, and when he came riding over the brow of the hill, with all the crowds waiting there, they thought this was it: he was going to be king; it seemed he had accepted the offer. No wonder they got excited. So, there was no doubt in the people's minds as to what was happening. The throne of David was not going to be vacant for another twenty-four hours. It was a tide of nationalist feeling, the end of foreign domination, the end of a divided country. You may wonder how we know that it was nationalism. First, look at what they *said* and then at what they *did*.

Every single word they said and every act they did on that day was sheer nationalism. What did they say? They said, "Hosanna!" What does that mean? If you think it means a kind of glorious "hello", some greeting, some act of praise, then think again, for it means nothing of the sort. In modern Christian worship "hosanna" now means "praise him", but it did not then. It is a Hebrew word meaning "save us now". It is an expression of impatience. It is saying get us out of our troubles now; now is the time to fight; now is the time to meet the enemies and tackle them. Shouting "hosanna" was just like singing a freedom song. It was a military expression.

Look at what else they said. Notice how the name David comes in again. You can see that they are thinking of a political coup. Look at the quotation "Blessed is he who comes in the name of the Lord!" It is from a Passover psalm which was about the defeat of the Egyptians. Read Psalm 118, it is all about cutting off their enemies. When they quoted that psalm, they were shouting a political, nationalist, militarist term.

Now look at what they did. We think it is lovely that they took down palms and waved them and strewed the road with them. We think it is wonderful that they took off garments and they put them down in the dust. What did those actions mean? The clue lies in their own history. They had done both these two things on two separate occasions. I wonder whether you have read of the time when they actually took their garments and put them in the road outside Jerusalem. They did it once for a man called Jehu, and he was coming to throw Ahab's house and Jezebel off the throne. He was coming as a resistance leader, and he was coming to liberate the people of Israel from the domination and exploitation of an evil royal family. Jehu was a man who drove furiously. He was coming at a great pace in a chariot up that road and they threw their garments in front of him, and the chariot wheels went over the items of clothing. It was a military action.

What about the palms? This is not in the Old Testament but it is in the Apocrypha. In that period of four hundred years between Malachi and Matthew there was one – and only one – occasion when they got the throne back, and it was under a family of brothers who were very skilled resistance fighters. They were called the Maccabees. Perhaps you have heard of this family of seven brothers who fought the Greeks and who managed for a very few years to put one of their own number on the throne again. When Simon Maccabeus came to Jerusalem, the people waved palm leaves to welcome this resistance leader who was promising to set them free. I hope I have not spoiled Palm Sunday for you, but that is what it was. That was why they shouted "Hosanna"; that was why they took off their coats and put them in the dust. They thought this was a military leader who would set them free, and it was a nationalist uprising. The people were thrilled, bursting with excitement and pride. We might imagine the disciples thinking: this is what we left the fishing for; this is what it is all about – isn't it great; see them looking at us, and we are near him. You can sense what they thought was happening.

But Jesus looks at that crowd who think it is a day of triumph and he sees it as a day of terrible tragedy. Why? What had gone wrong? He loved this place, he loved this people, and his heart ached for them. He could see that this kind of nationalism would lead them to utter disaster. Indeed, in chapter 26, Jesus says that all who draw the sword will die by the sword. In AD 70, only forty years after Palm Sunday, what Jesus foresaw would happen did happen. They rose against the Romans, who crushed that city and killed more than a million inhabitants. It is an appalling story which you can read in the history of Josephus. Jesus knew that if that was the kind of kingdom they wanted, if that was the kind of feeling that was going to stir them, it would lead to utter ruin and disaster.

The thing that they had not noticed, which Jesus had deliberately chosen, was the animal on which he rode. That is the tragedy of Palm Sunday. All their eyes were on him, they had no eyes for the animal on which he rode, and that is the key to it all. If you are coming as a military leader you come on a horse, or even with a chariot as Jehu did, or as Simon Maccabeus did, but Jesus came on an ass and it is the one animal you do not use in battle. He had deliberately chosen this animal. If they had known their scriptures (and he was often telling people that the reason they got wrong ideas was that they didn't know scripture), in Zechariah it says that the king would come to Jerusalem humble, meek; not a fighter, but as a prince of peace riding on an ass. The word "Jerusalem" means the city of peace – the suffix "salem" is the same as the word "shalom", the greeting "peace" used in Israel today. It was always meant to be the city where peace would be, from which peace would flow to the whole world – this was God's intention. Jesus came to bring peace to the whole world from that city, and indeed he has done: he has made peace by the blood of his cross. That was why he came; he was coming for peaceful purposes – to bring the peace of God to a world that needed it, and they misunderstood because they did not see the colt, they only saw him.

Their disappointment with him was great. Imagine the scene. You come down from the Mount of Olives, past the Garden of Gethsemane, over the Kidron brook up the other side towards the magnificent Golden Gate – which, by the way, has been bricked up ever since; it is the only gate of Jerusalem that you cannot go through now, and Ezekiel had said it was for the king, not for anybody else. Back then it was wide open, and when Jesus got through it they would expect him to turn right, because at the corner of the temple area was the Roman garrison.

To their horror, when he came through the gate he turned left and made for the temple. That was shattering. He did not even take one look at the Roman garrison or at the soldiers. He went right into the place of worship and began to look in every cupboard and back room. He wanted to know everything that was going on there. This shook them. They thought he was coming to deal with the Romans, and here he was dealing with them! There were things in those cupboards and those rooms that they did not want him to see, and it was profoundly disturbing. It was getting late and he went out down the valley, up the Mount of Olives, over the hill and away. It is a most disappointing anti-climax. They were so disappointed with him that within days they were shouting "Crucify him", and the mob psychology of it is utterly true to life. If you have once roused a nationalist mob and then do not do what they want you to do, the mob will turn right around, and that is precisely how the cross took place within the week. Only days later, where were the people who had shouted "Hosanna"? They were still in Jerusalem, yet no one would lift a finger to help him. Why not? Because they were disappointed with Jesus. They did not understand the things that belonged to their peace. They had failed to understand how peace comes.

I want to apply this practically, first at a political level and second at a personal level. What does all this have to do with us? Simply this: the crowd was made up of ordinary people like you and me, and in them we can see a mirror to ourselves. Here is the political application. The nationalist spirit is characteristic of our times. The desire to protest, the desire to have big demonstrations, the desire to overthrow those who oppress, the desire to use force, is a desire that is rampant in our world. This world in which we live is an old world. In every continent, this spirit is abroad. And one wants to say to such people again and again: would that you knew the things that belong to your peace. May I say that I do not think it is possible for Britain to be a peacemaker and a world leader in peace because we do not understand the things that belong to our peace. What does belong to our peace? I will tell you. Righteousness exalts a nation, but sin is a reproach to any people, and if Britain is ever going to be a peacemaker in the world we shall need to be prepared to let Jesus come and inspect every cupboard in Britain and look at our lives in all their aspects, and begin with us. Jesus comes to look around *our* lives.

It is easy enough to welcome Jesus as the answer to our troubles. It is easy enough to say, "Jesus, come into my life, I am unhappy and I want to be happy; Jesus come into my life, I'm bored and I want to be interested." But Jesus can weep over that and I believe he would say: I want to come in and put right what is wrong with you. I have not just come to deliver you from your troubles, I have come to deliver you from your sins. That is what belongs to your peace.

Matthew Chapter 21

If we want the peace of Jesus then we must welcome him and say, "Jesus, come in and inspect every part of my life – that is what belongs to my peace." That is why he comes riding on an ass. He is not coming to get us out of our troubles but out of our sins. That is the heart of all true peace.

What Jesus saw at the temple horrified him. In the very place where people should have been thinking about and praying to God he found just the opposite. He found people counting the money and people planning evil; he found crowds, he found noise, he found everything that you would find in the middle of a town, but not in a place of prayer. He was obviously angry about everything that he found in the temple. He has to deal with something that was terribly wrong.

Jesus was angry because the place, God's house, had been made into a "den of thieves". There were two things you needed if you wanted to worship God at the temple: you needed your temple tax to get into the place and you needed a sacrifice once you got in. If you were poor, it would be a pigeon; if you were rich it would be a calf or sheep or something like that. Formerly, you got your sacrifice outside, but they had now started doing this. First of all, the priests had ordered that you had to pay your admission in special temple money which they would make, and you would have to exchange your money for theirs. The charge on the exchange was half a day's wage. Supposing when the collection was taken in your church they said, "We won't accept your money, we have got special money, so you had better get it changed in the porch before you come in." And supposing you were charged, say sixty per cent, before you got in. I guess that not many people would be back soon. It would get around town quickly. But if it was the only church and you had to get to church, it would have a monopoly. They could charge you the Earth in the vestibule.

Let me tell you something else. If I were poor and I needed a couple of pigeons to offer as a sacrifice to God for my sin, I could buy them outside the temple for a certain sum, but inside the temple they would cost more. Why buy them inside when you could buy them outside? For the very simple reason that there were inspectors at the door and they inspected your pigeons. They said there must not be the slightest flaw in a pigeon used in worship, and they would look around for one little blemish and say: Sorry, they are no good, you bought them at the cheap stall down the road; come inside, we have got perfect pigeons here, such and such an amount for the pair. You may think this is ludicrous but it was going on. We have the facts and figures and we can compare the figures with the wages of those days. Jesus saw this in the house of God: exploitation on a wide scale. He turned out those who bought and sold in the temple, overturned the tables of the money changers and the seats of those who sold doves. Why could God not accept ordinary money? Of course he could.

The outer court in which all this was happening was the only part of the temple that you could go into if you were a Gentile, a foreigner. When the temple was built, the innermost court was for the priests, the next part for the men, then for the women, and then came the largest court of all, the court of the Gentiles. If you were a foreigner that was the only place you could go to pray. But it was meant to be a symbol of the fact that anybody could come and pray in that place – and the one place you could not pray for the noise that went on was that court. In other words, they had virtually said by their actions that they did not care about the outsiders as long as they had the temple for themselves; they did not care if anybody else came in, they wanted this to be a club for themselves. That can also happen to a church. We can treat the church as a convenience; we can exploit the church; we can make it an exclusive club that says to people outside that we do not want them inside, we are just in our own church to pray amongst our people.

When Jesus said of the temple "...you have made it a den of robbers" what did he mean? He did not just mean the exploitation that was going on. Once again, the clue is in the Old Testament. Isaiah talked about this being a house of prayer for all nations (see Isaiah 56:7). And Jeremiah in his day said the temple had become a den of robbers (see Jeremiah 7:11) and he tells us what he means.

If you went to the temple from Galilee, you went down the Jordan valley, then you went up from Jericho to Jerusalem four thousand feet higher, and you went up through a very barren wilderness area with caves on either side of the road. And lurking in these caves were people who sprang out at you. That is why the man fell among thieves on the road from Jerusalem to Jericho. And a "den of robbers" refers to the place where they hid, waiting to trap you. Jesus' words mean that the pilgrims have passed all the dens of robbers all the way up and thought they were safe in Jerusalem, but when they came into the temple there was just another hideout of crooks waiting to take their money. It is a most telling phrase. They think they have got past all the bandits, yet all they have done is come into the biggest lot of all. Jeremiah was highlighting use of the temple as a cloak for sin, for crime. They put on this cloak of religious respectability and because it was the temple, they thought that selfishness and greed were all right. The voice of Jesus comes down to us today warning us to never use religion as a cloak to hide sin, never to use the respectability of churchgoing to hide greed. That was what they were doing, so Jesus cleansed the temple.

At this point we have the strangest story, a story that at first sight seems so incongruous, so unlike Jesus, that I have met people who mistakenly believe that it cannot possibly be true. Here is the story in its utter simplicity. Jesus was hungry and he came to a fig tree. It was not the time of year when there should have been figs on it; there were none, so he cursed the tree and it died. That seems the most extraordinary thing for our Lord Jesus to have done. However, when we look at this event, we find a wonderful story. It was not a childish act. He was not in a bad temper and working it out on this tree. We need to remember a number of things if we are to understand this.

Firstly, our Lord was prepared at times to do a destructive thing to nature when there was a purpose in it. Do you remember all the pigs that ran down the hill into the sea to save one man's sanity? Well, he was prepared to do something like that then, and there is no real contradiction between this and the pigs, except that the pigs did feel something and the tree did not.

Secondly, in fact, though it was not the season for figs anybody who grows fig trees (and that does not include me) knows that in the spring when the leaves first come there is a small crop of what are called "first ripe figs", which are not normally good enough to use for any good purpose so they are not harvested, and then later in the summer there comes the main crop. So, our Lord was right in expecting at least something there. The leaves had come, there should have been a little something to eat with them, and that is characteristic of a fig tree.

Thirdly, compare the disappointing fig tree with the temple, which looked tremendous – it was a wonderful building, constructed partly with gold and marble. It was so impressive and it was crowded. Yet when you looked at it closely, it was all show and there was nothing but leaves, no fruit; there was nothing really about God in it all, it was just man the whole way through.

But we can go even further. You will never understand the New Testament until you know the Old Testament well. People who never read the Old Testament miss a great deal in the New. Someone has said: "The Old is in the New revealed, the New is in the Old concealed." When you read the whole Bible as one book you get the clues, and here are some of them. Prophets like Hosea, Jeremiah and Isaiah quite often talk of Israel as first ripe figs; it is a favourite phrase – the first little bit of a harvest that is going to bring in the whole world one day. The prophets also say that if they are not careful, they will not even be able to produce first ripe figs and the fig tree will become barren and withered. In other words, the fig tree was used as a picture of the whole nation, the people of God. The prophets Jeremiah and Hosea both say God will one day come looking for some fruit from you, and if he finds nothing but leaves then your fig tree will wither and become barren and nobody will get any benefit from you. Once you know that that was a familiar picture, and something the prophets had said already, you can begin to see what Jesus was doing – he was acting a parable. Remember when Isaiah took off all his clothes and walked naked through Jerusalem? Why did he do that? He was acting out his message. He said that you will be stripped as naked as I am unless you repent and turn back to God. Or perhaps you remember the story of the day that Jeremiah got hold of an ox yoke and put it round his neck. He staggered around Jerusalem with this yoke round his shoulders. He said: as certainly as I am wearing this yoke, the Babylonians will come and put a yoke on you and lead you away into slavery unless.... The Jews were familiar with this kind of acted out message, and Jesus was doing something the disciples would never forget. He came to the tree hungry. It should have given him something to satisfy him and yet there was nothing. So he said to it, "Let no fruit grow on you ever again." It is precisely what he was doing with the temple. I think he was looking for someone praying there, and all he could find were people changing money, people buying and selling things, the temple crowded with people but nobody praying. He found nothing but show, nothing but leaves.

Jesus comes to churches and he looks for fruit and he looks for some result of all the activity; he looks for something that will bring glory to God; he looks for people praying. The outward signs of prosperity were there: a very expensive building, a lot of busyness, a lot of activity, but nobody loving God. He found nothing but leaves. And when he cursed the fig tree he was damning the temple, and indeed God was going to rip up the veil of the temple in just a few days' time and the temple was going to cease to be the place where people met God. I can see why he did it. He was showing the disciples something in an unforgettable way, and we know they did not forget it because we have it recorded in the Gospels.

Jesus' action impresses a lesson on us, too. God comes to our lives and he comes to our churches, and he looks for fruit, he looks for some result, he looks for something that will bring glory to his name. He may find a nice building and a lot of busy activity, but if he does not find what he is looking for then his Spirit can use some other church and some other people to do his work.

22
CHALLENGES

Read Matthew Chapter 22–23

After the parable of the marriage feast for the son of a king, culminating in the condemnation of those without a wedding garment (see 22:1–14), we begin to see people challenging Jesus, fighting him verbally. Words were the first weapons used by our Lord's enemies.

One gets the impression that the enemies of our Lord – including Pharisees and even the Herodians – team up against him as one. The two things they are aiming at in this verbal battle are, firstly, to discredit him in the eyes of the public and get the crowd on their side; secondly, to try to get a charge with which they can accuse him to the authorities – which meant Pontius Pilate. Everything they say to him has this double objective. They have some pretty acute questions worked out, which seem at first sight to force Jesus either to lose public support or to fall foul of the authorities.

Those who oppose Jesus attack him, but none of their attacks defeats him; Jesus comes on to the attack, and he delivers telling sayings.

Pharisees and Herodians would normally not have spoken to each other. The Herodians were not Jews, they were political puppets in the hands of the Romans; they belonged to the hated line of Esau, they were Edomites, and the Herodians were hated by the Jews because the Romans had set the Herodians over them. The Pharisees were about the most exclusive religious people in the whole land. To see exclusive religious people, who normally see politics as a terribly dirty business and will have nothing to do with it, lining up with Herodians who are just up to their eyes in dirty politics, is to see an amazing coalition. When people hate God, they will make extraordinary alliances.

The question about paying taxes to Caesar was an offensive trap. Israel was an occupied country at this time – the Romans were an enemy occupying power – so this was an appalling trap. Either Jesus could say that they should not pay these taxes to Rome and let this money go out of the country to Rome and Caesar, in which case they could accuse him to Pilate straight away as a traitor, or he could say that they should, in which case he might become so unpopular with the people that that would be the end of his public ministry. It was a cleverly worded question. But my advice to anyone is never try to get the better of Jesus. Many people have tried and nobody has ever done it. Never try to be too clever for him. Jesus saw straight through their question. They were not bothered about taxes at all. Jesus knew their hypocrisy and that means they did not want an answer, they just wanted to trap him. Seeing straight through it, Jesus asked them why they were trying to trap him (v.18) and since, presumably, they did not reply, he went on to give them an answer, and it is a brilliant one.

He asked for a coin. I have heard it said that Jesus was so poor that he had to ask someone to give him a coin. I do not think that is the reason that he asked for one. Judas, the treasurer for the disciples, had some money and Jesus could have asked for one of their coins, but he did not. Why not? Because he wanted something out of their pockets, something that they were already using, something to which they had already committed themselves. So, it was made clear that they were willing to use this money and accept it at its face value. They bought their food and clothing with it. Whose money is it? In other words, you are already committed, you are already involved. It is a very clever answer.

To go a little further, here is something that is not in the Bible but which will help you understand. In AD 6, Jerusalem was under Herod's son Archelaus, who was a thoroughly bad lot. The people got so fed up with him that they petitioned Rome (which had put Archelaus on the throne, and the Herod who had killed the babies at Bethlehem), asking for a Roman governor instead of Archelaus. They thought that even a Roman governor would be better. So they had actually asked the Romans to come. They need not have had a Roman governor at all. And when the Roman governor came, he introduced Roman coins and Roman taxes. Our Lord's hearers were being reminded that they asked for the Romans. They were quite happy to have them come, and quite happy to use their coins. They asked whether they should pay taxes, and Jesus said, "Render therefore to Caesar the things that are Caesar's" and the word used in that reply means "repay". So, they had asked whether they should pay taxes and he told them that they should repay taxes, and that is a different matter altogether. This puts it all in a very different light. Of course, they could not say anything about this because they had benefited from the Roman peace – the "Pax Romana" that for many years had brought security to the whole Mediterranean world, a situation in which you could travel around the Mediterranean without a passport, protected by Rome.

But Jesus goes on to something more in the second part of the sentence: "...and to God what is God's". You also have a duty to God for the benefits you get from him, and he has a right to expect something from you as well as Caesar. Therefore, a Christian is in a double citizenship. He is a citizen of Earth and owes certain things to the earthly country to which he belongs. He is also a citizen of heaven and owes certain things to the Kingdom of heaven to which he belongs. The problem arises for a Christian when Caesar begins to claim something that only God can claim. Then the Christian has to say, "No, I can't give it to you." There would come a day when Caesar claimed to be god and the Christians responded: That is something that isn't yours and we can't give it, and we'd rather go to the lions than give it. But in this case it was a simple issue: Give to Caesar what is Caesar's. You are using his money; why shouldn't you give him his money? The implication is: if you really want to be logical you should not touch his money.

Of course, that was a real dig at those questioners who were fairly wealthy and rather fond of the Roman cash. They were also to give to God what is God's. I use money that I have with the image of an earthly sovereign on it – Queen Elizabeth. I am using her money; she has a claim on it. But what is it which has God's image on it? The answer is: every man and woman on Earth. What I must render to God that he deserves is *me* – he has a right to me. If the money that we use has the image of an earthly ruler who therefore has a right to it, we are made in the image of a heavenly King and he has a right to us. This is what Jesus' teaching here tells us. In this way he turns it very cleverly back on them and, in effect, asks whether God is getting from them what he should have from them – that is the biggest question. Pharisees and Herodians retired. It was a wonderful exchange.

The next encounter is concerned not with the political question but a philosophical one. Now the Sadducees come. They are the wealthy, aristocratic priests of Jerusalem. They run the temple, getting most of the money from it. They are somewhat anti-supernatural in their views – they could be called the liberals of their day. In particular, they said the only part of the scriptures to take notice of is the first five books – the law of Moses, the Pentateuch as it was called: Genesis, Exodus, Leviticus Numbers and Deuteronomy. You had to prove a thing from those five books before they would believe it. One of their strange views was that, unlike the Pharisees, they did not believe in a personal resurrection from the dead after this life. The Sadducees believed that you lived on in other people's memories and in the good that you had done (which is what a lot of British people seem to believe about the future).

They came along to Jesus, and this time they were trying to get him discredited in the eyes of the public by making him look silly. Some people love to do this. I had some sessions at a university and I could pick out the students who just wanted to do that. They had their clever questions; they did not want to know the answer, they wanted to make the speaker look silly in front of others. And if you can make a speaker look utterly silly then of course he is not going to have any effect on them.

So, the Sadducees came with a very funny question. In the book of Deuteronomy, which they did accept, there is a law that if a man died without children his brother has to marry his widow so that she can produce a child for him, and so on down the line. The reason was two-fold. The land was divided up and a parcel of land was given to a family forever. Therefore, the family name needed to be kept alive and there had to be a continuity to the family to keep that land. And it was God's law when the land was so tied to families that this family name be kept alive in this way.

Here was their question. It is not a living issue really; it is one of these logical puzzles. They said that a man died with no children; his brother took his wife and he had none, then his brother took his wife and he had none, seven times down the line. They suggested that there is going to be an awful situation in heaven because all these seven men are going to fight over this woman, each claiming her as his wife. If you think this is a silly question let me put it to you in the form in which it has most often been put to me. I have often had the same basic question in my ministry. People have said to me, "How could I ever be happy in heaven if any of my family were in hell?" It is the same basic question; deep down it is the same basic principle, and the answer Jesus gave would be applicable to both questions. So, before we dismiss the Sadducees too lightly we must realise that it is a problem. The basic problem for people is that they cannot imagine how heaven can be different from earth, and they imagine that everything we know here will be the same there, including our relationships, and we are told quite simply they will not be, that heaven is different in many ways.

Jesus tackled them head on. They had asked the wrong

question, and if they had known their scriptures they would not have asked that question. He points out two very important things of which they were ignorant. He says, "You are mistaken, not knowing the scriptures nor the power of God." So many trick questions show an ignorance of the Bible, and I am more and more impressed with the fact that the more I read it, the more every question is answered. Ignorance of the Bible is one sure way of getting tied up in such knots. Jesus says they do not know "the power of God", meaning the power of God to change things, to make things different (here, to raise the dead).

For all of us to have to live with each other for ever as we are now would not be heaven, but we believe in the power of God to change people. Sometimes at a funeral when we have been burying someone who was known for being a bit awkward, I have said quite openly that one of our hopes for the future is not just a glorified body but a glorified character, and the next time we meet so and so they will be perfect – and that brightens up the relatives no end, and gives them something to look forward to! But the relatives will be perfect too if they die in Christ. In other words, life in heaven will be so different from life on Earth, and we need to remember the power of God to change things and people.

The answer to the Sadducees' question was that in the resurrection they would neither marry nor be given in marriage, but would be like angels of God in heaven. When my wife and I got married we said, "Till death us do part," and we recognised that the particular relationship into which we entered on our marriage day was a relationship for this world only. That is not to say that we do not expect to be in heaven together, but when we get there, it will be a different relationship between us. To put it as I imagine it, it will be a relationship of brother and sister in Christ. We shall all be as closely related to each other; that will be an even more wonderful relationship than we could have known here. Jesus reminded his hearers that this is how the angels live – the angels do not get married, nor do they reproduce and have children. Angels are created, each one. Incidentally, that is the answer to all those who believe that all life must come from evolution. The angels were created distinctly, separately; they do not die, they do not grow old, they do not marry, they do not have children, and that is precisely what life will be like for us in heaven, difficult though it is to imagine. Therefore, the answer to those who have said to me "I won't be happy in heaven if all my relatives are not there" is that relatives will be there, but the people you will count as relatives there will not be the people you count as relatives here. Our relationships will have changed. All your brothers and sisters in Christ will be there, and it is one of the things that God has the power to change. Lest that seem a hard or callous thing to say, let me add straight away that as long as I am in this life my physical relatives are my concern and my burden and my prayer, but in the next life the only relationships will be in Christ, and those are the most important relationships.

So, the Sadducees had gone wrong because they did not know their scriptures well enough and they did not know the power of God to change things. On the positive side, knowing that the Sadducees always wanted to prove a thing from the first five books of the Bible, and wanted to know where in there resurrection is mentioned, Jesus says, "But concerning the resurrection of the dead, have you not read what was spoken to you by God, saying, 'I am the God of Abraham, the God of Isaac, and the God of Jacob'? God is not the God of the dead, but of the living."

Jesus points out that God said, "I am" – not I was. That is a very important difference, and perhaps you could read that story and never notice it. Think of your father or grandfather or great-grandfather, someone who knew the Lord. Do you realise that God, if he spoke to you at this moment, would not say, I *was* the God of your great-grandfather, he would say to you, I *am* the God of your great-grandfather, which implies absolutely certainly that your great-grandfather is still alive. Abraham, Isaac and Jacob are still alive and God is still their God, and you are just joining this wonderful company. This is a tremendous thought.

I remember going to Hebron to look at the cave of Machpelah and the tombs of Abraham, Isaac, Jacob and their three wives. The centuries seemed to roll away as I looked at their graves. Yet I remember saying to myself aloud as I stood there – I could not help it: "They are not dead because God is still their God; whatever has happened to their bodies they are alive, because he is alive."

Now a lawyer comes to Jesus, and asks him (testing him): Which is the great commandment in the law?

Our Lord quotes two texts, one from Deuteronomy, one from Leviticus, and he puts them together and says: "You shall love the Lord your God with all your heart, with all your soul, and with all your mind. This is the first and great commandment. And the second is like it: you shall love your neighbour as yourself. On these two commandments hang all the law and the prophets."

So, he sums it up in those two. Some people have said that Jesus was saying nothing new – there it all is in the Old Testament. But there are at least two things that he was doing that were quite new. The first is that nobody had put those two texts together before; teaching that love is the key to the law of God: loving God, loving your neighbour, the two relationships. The other thing is that he did not qualify the word "neighbour". In Leviticus your neighbour was your fellow Jew, but here it is as wide as the world.

First of all, if you read this summary, you get the idea first that love is not feeling. The trouble is that nowadays if you say the word "love", everybody thinks of emotion. If you listen to the pop songs about love it is always about emotional love. But Christ makes it quite clear that real love is a response of the whole personality. You can love someone with all your heart but you can also love them with all your mind. That is a notion that you will not find in a pop song – that your thoughts can love people. You can love them with all your physical strength, and that is a thought you will not find in a pop song. You can love them with all your soul, and that is a thought you will not find in such lyrics. What Jesus has done is to define the word "love" as something that your whole personality is involved in – all your thinking, all your strength, all your heart and feeling, all your soul – all of you.

Furthermore, he is teaching that before you love your neighbour your first duty is to love God. This is what gives the lie to the idea that you will find many better Christians outside the church than in. When anybody says to me, "So and so is a good Christian and they don't go to church," I say to them, "Now tell me why you think they are a good Christian," and the answer is invariably in terms of the second commandment here, because they love their neighbour. One may then go on to say, "Do you think that person loves God?" – because that comes first. Loving your neighbour is fine, it is good, it is part of the whole law, but it is the second thing, not the first. I remember in one house group a lady said, "Well, how can you love God? The only thing that you can do is to love your neighbour." But Jesus taught that loving God comes first. In fact, I do not think you can really love your neighbour until you love God – not in the fullest sense. Mind you, I think that to love God without loving your neighbour is just as one-sided and just as much a caricature. So, Jesus' teaching meant that love involves more than just our feelings, it involves our whole personality; and love of God comes first.

Jesus now attacks their idea of the one they are expecting. They are expecting a purely human figure from the line of David, a descendant of David. And they keep calling him the Son of David; they called him that when they welcomed him with palms. Jesus challenges them on this idea that they have. They are looking for a purely human descendant of David to come and reign over them, and he challenges them to look at what David himself said about this one who was coming. Jesus is pointing out that David applied the same word to this Christ coming as they apply to God – the word "Lord". In other words, David knew that the Christ who would come would be far more than a human being. He would be divine. So, our Lord attacks their idea of a political messiah, an agitator, a resistance leader, an insurrectionist, and the triumphal entry into Jerusalem showed that so clearly. But Jesus challenges them to think again. They ought to be looking, as David did, for a divine person, someone they could call Lord, someone who is in fact far higher than David. It was always considered in those days that a descendant of someone was lower, that in a sense a grandfather was superior to both father and son. Jesus is teaching that the one who was to come is far above David.

It is "Lord", not just a son of David. That was a technical point, but it was an important one. Jesus was attacking them and their understanding of scripture. Notice our Lord's view of the psalms. David wrote them, but the Holy Spirit inspired them, and therefore they could be appealed to as truth and as proof of truth.

We see from the beginning of chapter 23 that the common people are listening, along with the disciples. He moves now to an ecclesiastical question and he gives a warning. There is a danger of being in religion for what you can get out of it, of covering up greed, pride and hypocrisy with religion. And Jesus now says some very severe words which I find terribly disturbing and challenging. Those of us who have been called to full-time Christian service need to read this again and again and examine our own hearts. But I think all Christians need to do so too.

The teachers were getting prestige out of it, and that is a most subtle thing. They liked wearing long robes. That of course made them distinctive anyway, and different from others. You cannot do any manual work in them and you cannot hurry in them, so it gave the impression of a leisured scholar. They loved special greetings like "father" or "rabbi" [master or teacher]. Jesus taught that you should not let anybody call you father. Incidentally, I found out too late, after three years in the services, that "padre" is of course precisely that. It came from the Italian army originally, and it was simply the word "father" put into Italian for a priest. Papa (Pope) is the same word. "Father" and "master" are terms that imply you are above others, and this is something you are not. The teachers loved titles. They also loved the chief seats, and if there was a feast, they liked the best room in the house where they were staying. They were in it for prestige.

The second thing they were in it for was greed. Widows were easy prey because they had no man to defend and argue for them. I have noticed, again and again, how often cults and sects get hold of women and persuade them to accept their strange teachings, especially if there is no man to argue with the one who has come to the door. There is evidence that many widows lost their money to such people. Jesus pointed out that all this greed, as well as pride and desire for prestige, was covered up with long prayers. I find it very interesting that Jesus did not like long prayers – he mentions this so often. If there is one thing that kills a prayer meeting it is long prayers. Mind you, Jesus could spend all night in prayer without other people around, but he was thinking of public prayer. It is very interesting that in the Book of Common Prayer (a lovely book, and the more I study it the more I feel it is a wonderful book of devotion), the Collect was quite deliberately made to be a prayer of two or three sentences because it was meant to be *common* prayer, prayer that people could follow. If a prayer in a meeting is too long we so easily start thinking of other things. The people Jesus was referring to were professional pray-ers, and because of their privilege, their responsibility, their position, they would receive a greater condemnation. It is quite an attack on some professional religious people, and as I have said, those of us who are called to full-time service need to examine our hearts all the time lest we ever begin to be greedy for prestige or to be thought of too highly by others. But it is a warning that our Lord gives to all the people so it is relevant to all Christians.

23

DESTRUCTION OF THE TEMPLE

Read Matthew 24–25

The temple was a wonderful structure. In those days it was the largest in the whole world. It was far larger than any Greek temple; it was about the size of York Minster. Imagine that stuck in the middle of the Judean hills – a magnificent thing. York Minster is made of stone – imagine it made of white stone and covered with gold. Just think what that would look like in the morning sun. The stones with which it was built were so large that one of them measured forty feet long, four feet wide and four feet high. The temple to which the disciples now referred was not the temple built by Solomon and it was not the temple built when Ezra and Nehemiah came back, it was a brand new one being built by Herod – or at least by his family. He was determined to build for the Jews the biggest and the best temple they had ever had. He was trying to get them on his side and he thought this would be a good way of doing it. He began building it twenty years before Jesus was born. It was not finished until thirty-four years after Jesus died, and it was finished only just in time for the Romans to pull it down stone by stone until there was nothing left. It is the most extraordinary story. But while Jesus and the disciples were walking through the temple at this point it was still being built, the scaffolding was still up. Even so, it was already the most amazing building that had ever been constructed by man and we read just how impressed they were by it. But Jesus said that not one stone would be left there upon another, that would not be thrown down. That came true literally. It would seem impossible for it to have happened.

It took hundreds of people many hours to get one of those huge blocks which weighed many tonnes into place. But Jesus knew that it would only just be finished in time for it to be pulled down.

Some time later, as they sat on top of the Mount of Olives, having crossed the Kidron Valley – a place where you could gaze for hours on end at Jerusalem set out before you – they were chatting, and four of the disciples came to Jesus and said, "Tell us, when will these things be? And what will be the sign of your coming, and of the end of the age?" Our Lord then told them a great deal about the future.

There is something we need to understand about every part of the Bible that deals with the future. Imagine looking through a telescope at two mountain peaks in the distance. The one thing the telescope does not tell you is how far apart those two mountains are. Looking ahead through your telescope you simply see what lies ahead. It will tell you what is there but it will not tell you how far from here to there, how far from there to there. Indeed, the further you look the more difficult it is to see, and you might think that a few mountain peaks in the distance are all in one big jumble, until you get to them and then you might find there is a great valley between. One of the problems in considering what we call prophecy, especially that part of prophecy which is concerned with prediction, is precisely this: all those in the Bible who looked to the future, the true prophets, could see what was going to happen, but in their recorded words they do not usually give any indication of various distances between the events, they just see them all together as they look into the future. By the Holy Spirit they get a kind of spiritual telescope.

Here are some examples from the Old Testament. The true prophets in the Old Testament saw, as they looked through the "telescope" the Holy Spirit gave them, the first coming of Christ and the Second Coming of Christ, and they predict that Jesus will visit the earth twice, but they give no indication whatsoever that there will be a gap of time between the two. Therefore, when you read some of their prophecies you discover that they talk of both comings in the same sentence; they are just describing what they see in the future – two future events. So, they describe them in Old Testament language almost as if they are going to happen together. We now know, of course, that there is a long gap of at least two thousand years between those two events.

Jesus is looking into the future, and he is now looking at not one but two events. The disciples think he is referring to one event, the end of the world, when he talks about this temple collapsing and not one stone being left on another. They cannot imagine that temple being pulled to pieces before then; it will surely last. But, in fact, Jesus can see the end of the temple very much earlier, and throughout the chapter he is describing the end of two things. He is describing the end of the temple and the end of Israel as a state – at least for the time being – and he is describing the end of the world. The disciples had got the idea that the temple would last right until the end of the world, so they asked Jesus to tell them when this would happen, and how they would know when the end was coming. But Jesus has to tell them much more than that. He describes, on the one hand, the end of the temple, which actually took place in AD 70, about forty years after he died. But, looking through the telescope, as it were, he looks through to the end of the temple and to the other end – the end of the world, which cannot be dated. Indeed, he taught us that we are never to try to date it, and that even he did not know the date of that one.

Jesus is so honest with the disciples and he lets them know that they are going to have a tough time. First of all, their minds are going to be very disturbed by false prophets, with whom they are going to have a very difficult time, and false Christs, who do not come with the truth, misleading people. It is very interesting that just before AD 70, when the Romans were pressing very hard on the little land of Israel, man after man stood up and said, "I am the Christ. I will save you," and there was a rash of false messiahs just before the end. One of the best-known ones, who was crucified by the Romans, was Bar Kochba. He said, "I am the Christ. I'll get you out of this trouble" – and some were so desperate and so afraid that they believed him. Jesus warned them so that when it happened the disciples' minds would not be disturbed. I believe that before the end of the world, the same thing will happen: there will be an increase in people making messianic claims. So, Jesus warns that when somebody claims to be the Christ, we are not to believe it. I am afraid we are already seeing something of this, and we have heard in our lifetime of people who have claimed to be the messiah, and we will hear more. It happens before the end, and people's minds can be deceived. Jesus said that, if possible, they will even try to deceive God's chosen people. It happened before the end of Jerusalem, it will happen before the end of the world, and we must not believe such people.

How do we know? If somebody says, "Go to Manchester, the Messiah is there, he has come", how do we know that is not true? The answer is that when Jesus actually comes, every Christian in the world will know it immediately. We will not need anybody to say, "Catch the train to Manchester, he has come"! We shall all know as soon as Jesus has come back, and we are not to believe anyone who tells us that Christ has come. It might be that in our lifetime this kind of rash of false prophets and messiahs could break out. If it does then it could make us very excited because it means the end is near. But if it does our minds must not be deceived, and we must not start running after false people. Jesus even said that they will perform miracles to try to prove that they are the Christ; do not believe them, the devil can do miracles as well.

They will be disturbed by frequent perils, and he lists some. He warns them that they will hear of wars and rumours of wars, and that is precisely what happened before the end of the temple. There was a rash of rumours of war, and petty outbreaks of war, and people thought the Roman Empire was being swallowed up in war. Jesus also warned them that they would hear of widespread famines. Their hearts were not to be disturbed by these. He is not saying that you must not feed the hungry, he is teaching that you must not let your heart be taken away from your faith because of famines. He was predicting that towards the end of history there would be an increasing number of famines – and that is a prediction that is coming true. He added earthquakes.

These were precisely the things that happened before the end of the temple, and will likewise happen before the end of the world. He said, "do not be alarmed" and this is the same word that he was to use one night later. I know of many people who are very troubled by such things, so troubled that they feel they cannot believe in a good God, so troubled that they believe the world is not heading for the fulfilment of God's purpose. But Jesus told you beforehand so that you would not be troubled. It does not mean that you will not be concerned, it means you will not be thrown off balance by them; those things are going to happen.

He taught that your will is going to be under severe pressure because of fierce persecution. The nearer you get to the end, either of Jerusalem or of the end of the world, the more fierce the persecution of Christian believers becomes.

Here, then, are three very severe tests. Peter, James, Andrew and John went through all this before the end of the temple. Christians who are alive when the end of history comes will likewise experience these pressures. See what kinds of persecution Jesus mentions: religious persecution (the elders, the synagogue); political persecution (kings and rulers); domestic persecution (your own family may be against you and betray you), and universal persecution, because you will be hated by all men. In other words, it will come at you from every angle. He was warning them, and I am afraid it all came true in the Acts of the Apostles, which covers the period up to the end of the temple.

But you can be quite sure that in all this pressure the end will not come yet. Or, to put it in very simple English, however bad all this gets you will know absolutely certainly that this is not the end, by one thing: "...the gospel of the Kingdom must first be preached in all the world as a witness to all the nations". That is why I know the end could not come tomorrow. The gospel has not yet been preached to all the nations. One of the things that will tell us that history is drawing nearer to its conclusion is when every nation, every kindred, every tribe, every tongue has heard the gospel of Jesus – then we will know that it could happen.

Then Jesus gives a word of encouragement – it is not a word of judgment: "But he who endures to the end shall be saved." As we persevere, the end is not bitter but glorious.

Now let us return to what we were looking at in the beginning, the two events: the end of the temple in AD 70, and the end of the world. Just as we are coming up to each, this is the kind of thing that we will go through. Forewarned is forearmed, and all Christians need to have these things clear, so that if they should be alive when this pressure comes then they will realise what it is all about and will not be thrown off balance but will endure to the end. It happened most certainly in that period, and it will certainly happen again. There is a parallel between the two events.

We take the first in AD 70 – the end of Israel. We know that God had not finished with them finally, of course. Our Lord knew perfectly well it was going to happen; it was inevitable because God would no longer protect them. They would be at the mercy of their conquerors from now on. There would be dreadful suffering, even for women and children. And he did not tell the Christians to pray that it would not happen because it had to, he told them instead to pray that it would not take place in winter, and it did not, which means that Christians must have prayed hard. That would have reduced the suffering that had to come. He was especially thinking of the children and of the women who were expecting children when he said this.

Many did indeed survive. What would be the sign that this was about to happen? Jesus now said something that was a kind of clue, something that only certain people would understand: "When you see the abomination of desolation spoken of by Daniel the prophet, standing in the holy place..." Jesus says, "then let those who are in Judea flee to the mountains."

When they see that sign, they are to get out of Jerusalem, otherwise they will go down with the temple. We are not talking about fancy ideas now. Did you know that thousands of people were saved from the fall of Jerusalem because they understood what was written in scripture? If they had not remembered our Lord's words and got out when this happened, they would not have survived. If the Jews had believed what the Christians had said, they could have been saved too, but they would not listen, and because Jesus had said it, they would not believe it. It is a most dramatic story. We now look at what it means.

This expression "the abomination of desolation" comes from the book of Daniel, where it occurs three times. Anybody who knows their Old Testament will understand the New, and the clue to this phrase lies in the Old Testament. Daniel was a man who suffered under foreign powers. We read of this "abomination of desolation", or the abominating sacrilege, or desolating sacrilege. Sacrilege is the most apt word because it means something that is absolutely defying God, something that you can see that is set up in the wrong place. Years before, this thing had come true once, when the Greeks came into Jerusalem. When the Greeks came into the temple – in the time of Judas Maccabeus – they put on the very altar of the temple a statue of a Greek god, a graven image standing on the altar of the God who had forbidden graven images. They then killed and sacrificed a pig on the altar, an unclean animal in the Old Testament that God had forbidden them to bring as a sacrifice. Here was something absolutely abominable – sacrilege in the place where it ought not to have been. So, they would have understood this only too well.

In fact, the sign was that the Romans marched on Jerusalem, and they brought with them their gods, their idols, their statues. It was quite clear to everybody that they had every intention of putting them in the temple and of standing them where they ought not to have been. But the interesting thing is that when the Romans came to Jerusalem, they gave them a few weeks' grace to surrender. For that time, they did not interfere with traffic in and out of the city, they surrounded the city with their idols, with their statues, and they waited. As soon as they saw that sign, and the things they were bringing to put in the temple, every Christian in Jerusalem got out. They told the Jews to get out too, but the interesting thing is that the Jews came in from miles around because they thought Jerusalem was safe. The Christians did not even stop to pack. The Christians went over the River Jordan, to a town called Pella. Jesus had told them what to expect; they had seen the sign coming; they had seen the sacrilegious idols on their way – and they left. When Jerusalem fell, not a single Christian died, and not a single Jew need have died if they had believed in Jesus, and had believed that he spoke the truth – but they were determined not to believe a word that Jesus said; they thought of Jerusalem as a safe place and piled into it. What happened then makes for the most terrible reading: 97,000 Jews were taken prisoner as slaves to Rome, 1,100,000 perished as the city fell. They either died by the sword or by starvation. Before they died many of them were reduced to eating dung, sewage, and cooking their own shoes and even their own children.

Jesus had said that the temple would be pulled down in the time of that generation. He could see it coming and he gave them the sign of its coming, so that when they saw the sign, they would know what to do. He gave them the time and the answer was soon, in your lifetime. He also told them what to do: to watch and to flee. Those who did what he said were ready for the end when it came, and the church was saved because they believed that Jesus knew the future and had told them the right thing to do. Within what was left of Jerusalem, false messiah after false messiah claimed to be able to get them out of trouble and the Jews were running around from one false messiah to another during those last terrible days.

Now we look at what Jesus said about the end of the world. The interesting thing is that he says the same type of thing about that. First of all, you will see signs. Certain things will happen which you will notice. You will see things happening in the sky. You will see things happening to the sun, the moon and the stars. We can see when the switch comes. The sun will go out (it did on Good Friday, of course, but it will go out at the end of the world; the moon will go out and the stars will fall). These will be universal signs and everybody will see them. He gave them these signs which have not come yet, of course. On the Day of Pentecost Peter quoted this. He said that the sun will be darkened and the moon turned to blood. That is the first sign.

Secondly, Jesus says, "Then the sign of the Son of Man will appear in heaven, and then all the tribes of the Earth will mourn, and they will see the Son of Man coming on the clouds of heaven with power and great glory" (24:30). I do not know how we shall all see him coming but I believe he can arrange that perfectly well.

The third thing will be the gathering of his elect, or his chosen, by the angels. There is going to be a lot of travelling all at once. We shall not meet him on earth for there is really no place on earth that would be big enough for us all to see him at once, so we are told in scripture that we shall meet him in the air. This, to me, is a most exciting thing to look forward to. Think of all his people coming from all over the world to meet him. What a meeting that is going to be! Frankly, those signs will be enough to tell us that something – the biggest thing of all – is happening.

When will this take place? Jesus had indicated that the fall of Jerusalem would occur soon, before the end of the generation. This time he taught that only the Father knew the day and hour.

Reading church history, I am impressed by the fact that every time someone has tried to date the Second Coming of Christ, they have led people astray. We are to watch and pray. What are we to watch for? Firstly, we are to watch for signs. This does not mean that we walk around the high street looking up into the sky all day. A number of other signs are given to us in scripture, the kinds of things going on around us that we can read in our newspapers or see via other media. We are to watch these things without panicking and without getting silly. Certain things are happening in our world that are so clearly parallel to what happened before Jerusalem fell that I feel that I am much nearer than my grandfather was – beyond that I will not go. The one thing I can predict is this: Jesus Christ is coming back, those who are dead will be the first to meet him, and we shall not be far behind. We can read all about it in 1 Thessalonians 4, and it is very exciting. We are to watch world trends and what is happening around us. One thing that I think is significant that we need to be watching is the spread of violence as a means of settling arguments, the resort to physical force in so many areas of the world.

If you have a garden, I am sure you notice the changes to the trees, especially when the buds come out each year. For "the fig tree" read whatever trees you have in your garden. Jesus tells us that we can look out at our "fig tree" and we can see that something is about to happen soon. Why pray? Because the nearer we get to such events, the more the pressure on Christians grows. The pressure on our minds from false teaching, the pressure on our hearts from world disasters – and it is an awful pressure on your heart – the pressure on your will from persecution and from those who dislike you and even hate you because you belong to Christ.

Why did Jesus take all this time to tell the disciples about the end of the world as well as the end of Jerusalem? For precisely this reason: the more wonderful you think the things are that men build on earth, the more you are tempted to forget that it is all going one day. Look at some buildings people are putting up in major cities, and you think they are building as if they will be here for centuries. We need the constant reminder that this world is passing away, and everything that belongs to it is passing away; you have a different attitude to the world, which does not mean that you ignore it or that you do not contribute to it.

For a fuller account of Matthew 24–25, please refer to my book entitled *Living in Hope*.

We shall now look in more detail at what Jesus prophesied about the signs of the end and his Second Coming.

24

THE SECOND COMING

Read Matthew 24–25 continued

There are three dimensions to the prophetic community's life which will be a message to the world: faith, hope and love. The greatest of these is love but the rarest of these is hope. We are a community of hope and just as we are in a world that is full of agnostics, atheists, animists, polytheists and the rest, we are to be a community of faith. In a world of hatred and suspicion and fragmentation and broken relationships, we are to be a community of love. We are also called in a world that is full of cynicism, pessimism and despair to be a community of hope – and not hope in the traditional sense of the English word hope, which simply means wishful thinking. Saying "I hope it won't rain tomorrow" is pure wishful thinking; in fact, it is worse given the English climate.

But Christian hope is described as an anchor and indeed if the symbol of Christian faith is a cross, then the symbol of Christian hope is an anchor. And we are going to need hope in the days that lie ahead for a mood of pessimism is going to sweep through this nation and God's people will be called to be a people of hope who know where they are going, who know how it is going to end and who remain calm when everybody else is bewildered.

In Matthew 24 we read about how Jesus sought to minister hope to his disciples and told them about the future. But Matthew 24 is followed by Matthew 25 and Matthew 25 tells you how to work it all out in practice and that is very important, but we have got to lay the foundation first. I believe there is a balance needed in Christian teaching between objective truth and the subjective application of truth. I mean by that those truths that are there whether we believe them or not because they are true. That is objective truth – the things that my faith, hope and love will not alter, or the *lack* of my faith, hope and love will not alter. And we need a solid foundation of those objective truths, of what actually is true whether I believe it or not. Only then, on that foundation can we begin to build a practical application of this. And you will find that most of the epistles of the New Testament are based on that pattern. The first half is on objective truth – that it is true whether you believe it or not; the second half is on "work it out because God's worked it in". So, you get a sequence from which we have just read – the first three chapters are objective truth and there is nothing you can do to alter it. It is true. And I think sometimes if we go straight through to the second half, the subjective application of truth, then we get wrapped up in ourselves – in navel contemplation – and we are constantly digging around putting the thermometer in and taking it out to see how we are getting on. And that kind of introspection becomes, I think, a barrier to what God wants to do in the world. So, we need the balance.

With all that in mind, I want you to begin reading at verse 37 of the previous chapter because one thing God never did was to put chapter and verse numbers in the Bible. I wish man had not done that. If he had not done that, we would have really had to know our Bibles. As it is, you can just look up chapter and verse but for a thousand years, Christians did not have that option. And so often, the chapter headings split up what God is saying and spoil the continuity. So, let us read verse 37 of Matthew 23.

I find that people have a kind of dual attitude to the future. They have a fear of it and a fascination for it. They want to know what is going to happen and they do not want to know what is going to happen. Let me just illustrate that. Supposing I had such a strong gift of prophecy that I knew the date of your death and I could say, "You can ask me the date and I'll reveal it to you."

Would you want to know? Even if it was years and years ahead, would you want to know, so that you could celebrate the date every year along with your birth date? There is a kind of fear of and fascination for the future.

I remember reading that something like seven out of every ten women in Basingstoke read their horoscope every day. And the horoscope writers and the fortune tellers would be out of business if they did not give more good news than bad news because people are seeking reassurance. They want to know, is life going to get better or worse.

I was once in the Champs Elysée in Paris and saw a queue of well-dressed people outside a shop in which there was a large IBM computer and they were paying the equivalent of three pounds sterling for 31 pages which poured out of a word processor. And they were feeding into the computer the date, place and time of their birth, and it was then feeding out those 31 pages for the next month to predict their future. And they were well-dressed, educated French men and women paying for one month's horoscope. And *Old Moore's Almanac* is still one of the bestsellers and there are think tanks and professors of futurology. The Massachusetts Institute of Technology constantly works out the end of the world for us and tells us when the oil will run out and when the population will finally really spell famine on a worldwide scale. And there is this kind of dual attitude to the future.

In that atmosphere, when people want to know what is going to happen and do not want to know what is happening, that is where the people of God come right in – "we, who first hoped in Christ". And I am amazed that those who really want to know what the future holds don't get stuck into this Book because its record in predictions is pretty remarkable.

Did you know that 24% of the verses in this Book contain a prediction about the future? Nearly one quarter of the verses of the Bible contain a prediction. And prediction is a vital element in the prophetic and the prophetic people must be concerned with the future. I will give you some more figures. This might stagger you. Altogether in the Bible there are 737 different future events predicted – 737! I do not know of another publication that has dared to make so many predictions. And some of them are predicted up to 300 times within this book, so you can do a little multiplication now. Of those 737, a total of 596 have already happened to the letter, some of them so extraordinary that statistically they should not ever have happened. But 596 – just over 80% of all these predictions have already happened. Does that make the Bible 80% accurate? No! It is a hundred per cent accurate because everything that could have happened by now has happened. Most of the rest are concerned with the end of the world, and when the end of the world happens you will find it was accurate about those too.

There are fewer than 20 things left to happen before the Lord Jesus gets back to planet Earth. Out of 737, there are fewer than 20 to go before that next great world event. By the way, that is one of the events that is predicted 300 times and therefore would seem to be something rather important to our hope.

Now, I am concerned that Christians who ought to be the ones who have a clear view of the future, who know what is going to happen, are in fact very confused, so confused that many have stopped thinking about the future and just say, "Oh well, I'll get on with the present, that's more important." And therefore, they miss out on that vital third dimension of hope. They may be strong on faith and love but weak on hope. And God wants us to be a full 3–dimensional prophetic community.

It is because all kinds of books and films and songs have been thrust on us with all kinds of weird and wonderful ideas. Some of us were brought up on charts. I was not, but some were brought up on charts which were presented to them as the last word. But how vulnerable we are to deception and the Lord's concern was that we should never be deceived and never get it wrong.

He knew that we would be deceived and one of the principles he laid down to prevent you getting wrong ideas is this: Don't trust your ears, trust your eyes, because deception will come through the ears. In relation to the future, keep *watch!* Keep your eyes open. If you listen to everything anybody says about the Second Coming, you will finish up in confusion. Just keep your eyes open – that is his principle. Trust your eyes rather than your ears. Then he told us, quite clearly and specifically, what to watch for. And when you see these things, fine, you will know what time it is on God's clock. He warns us against listening to other people. Watch, therefore!

I give you one illustration of the kind of misleading information that can come through the ears. It is a false prophecy, I believe, which was started off in a place called Port Glasgow in Scotland by a woman called Margaret McDonald. And she gave a prophecy that before the Big Trouble hits this world – and the Bible does say Big Trouble is coming – Christians would somehow disappear and be out of it. The technical term used was *raptured*. And from that place in Port Glasgow that idea, which had never been heard of before and which no one had ever found in the Bible in 1,830 years, was passed to a mansion outside Guildford, a mile and a half from where we used to live – the mansion at Albury. And in the library at that mansion, prophetic conferences were held to which a man called J. N. Darby came and picked up that idea. And from there it went on to a man called Scofield and from there it went on across the Atlantic and now it is coming back over the Atlantic in force from writings like Hal Lindsey and others. And many Christians are reading it, they are hearing it, and they are getting into confusion, I believe.

Now I am going to show you what Jesus said about all this so that you may not be confused, so that you may not be deceived, so that you will know what to look for and trust your eyes and not your ears and see what time it is on God's clock. I mention it also because in recent years, especially among circles where the Holy

Spirit has been renewing people, all sorts of speculation about the Second Coming has been appearing. Back in 1982, some people contacted me after hearing that the planets were going to line up. I had letters asking me what I thought about the planets lining up. I said, "It is very interesting; it has been doing that every 179 years so far and another time will not make much difference, I believe." And in fact, the month of March came and went. Did we *feel* the planets lining up? Did we notice it? Did we notice all the buses going up into the sky and the rest? Well, it came and went without any effect. But you see, many of God's people were disturbed. And there is *nothing* in my Bible about the planets lining up. I mean, they are free to do it but there is no significance.

And there are those who try to tell us, for example, "Look, Jesus could come back tonight and you might wake up in the morning and your family will be gone." I notice the apostles never used such pressure evangelism. It is not scriptural. So, in this maelstrom of confused opinions, Christians are saying, "Oh, well let's forget about the Second Coming; let's just get on with building the church now." I think that is in large part a reaction to all these different views. The proper reaction is to go for the right view, not to withdraw from the debate. And I have found the principle in my own life, and my own study of this is this: I *start* with what Jesus said and I fit everybody else into him. I start with his outline of the future, I start with his teaching, I do not start anywhere else because I believe he is the Truth.

And when I do, I find a clarity and a simplicity that many other Christians do not seem to find in their confusion. Jesus wanted us to know. I just love Jesus for saying to his disciples: "If it were not so, I would have told you." And in this chapter, he says, "See, I've told you ahead of it so you know." Jesus did not want us to be in confusion about the future. He wanted us to be clear so we would know and would not be upset and would not panic and would not rush here and there and get it off balance. And Jesus is that kind of person. He wants to tell you the things you need to know.

Now, we read the last bit of chapter 23 for this reason: It was against the backcloth of his agony over Jerusalem when he wept and said, "Oh Jerusalem, Jerusalem, how often would I have gathered you as a hen gathers her chicks." By the way, the birds of the Trinity are these: Father is eagle, Spirit is dove, but Son is hen. There is a sermon there for you if you are a preacher. But if the Father is like an eagle on high who sees everything down below on earth, and it is the Holy Spirit who is like the dove, which is the nearest bird to human beings, then Jesus said, "O Jerusalem, Jerusalem, the one who kills the prophets and stones those who are sent to her! How often I wanted to gather your children together, as a hen gathers her chicks under her wings, but you were not willing!" And then he said this: "You will not see me again until you say, 'Blessed is he who comes in the name of the Lord.'" Do you know where that is a quote from? It is from Psalm 118, which is sung in Jerusalem during the Feast of Tabernacles. And at the Feast of Tabernacles, Zechariah the prophet said, Jesus will come back again – or rather he just said the Christ will come. The Messiah will come at the Feast of Tabernacles and be King over the whole earth. And in Jerusalem then they celebrate the coming of the King, the coming of the Messiah and they sing Psalm 118, "Blessed is He who comes in the name of the Lord." And Jesus said, "you shall see me no more till you say" that.

I am convinced that Jesus will come right on time. He died right on time at the Feast of Passover, he sent the Spirit right on time at the Feast of Pentecost, but the biggest feast of all, the Feast of Tabernacles has not yet been fulfilled and they are celebrating today in Jerusalem. There will be thousands of Jews – and thousands of Christians – celebrating the coming of the King on that day.

So, the background is his coming, his return to Jerusalem and it is news to some that he is not coming back to Canterbury or to Rome or to Beijing or to New York, but he is coming back to Jerusalem – where else?

Now, I used to be a trainspotter, and I remember as a boy of six on the platform at Newcastle Central station watching the first Silverlink train come in, in the old steam days. But when you were waiting for a train to arrive, there were four signals that you watched for – the distance, the outer home, the inner home and the starter. And when the distance signal fell, you knew the train was in the section, it was in the last few miles. When the outer home fell, you knew the train was much nearer, when the inner home went down, you got ready for it, and when the starter, the last signal of the platform, went down, then you knew if you looked up the line you would see the train in just a minute.

Now, if I can use that illustration, Jesus said that there will be four signals which will go down, and if you are watching for those four, you will know what stage we are at. You will know how near my coming is and if you keep your eyes open, you will not be thrown off balance. And I want to speak about these four signals that are going to go down. They will go down with an increasing speed, so the gap between one and two will be much longer than the gap between three and four. There is an acceleration going on in this chapter.

The first signal I believe has gone down and the first signal is to be seen in the world, the second signal you will see in the church, the third signal you will see in the Middle East and the fourth signal you will see in the sky. So, the four signals are in four different places. And signal number one is a signal in the world at large and the signal is widespread disaster. And the Lord mentions three such disasters you will see on an increasing scale as you watch – war, famine, and earthquake. An earthquake is entirely caused by natural causes; war is entirely caused by human factors; and famine is a mixture of the two. But Jesus is saying that, both from nature and human nature, there will be a great increase in disasters. You can expect to keep opening your newspapers and see another war, another famine, another earthquake. And we have all become aware of these tectonic plates on which we live rubbing up against each other. And we now accept it as a normal part of life; we do not know where the next one will be. And regarding wars, who, in Britain, thought on New Year's Day of 1982 that we would be at war within three months and that our boys would be giving their blood? We had heard of wars in the Middle East, but who would have thought we would be right in one ourselves? Since then, of course, we have been involved in further conflicts.

Jesus asked what your reaction is to be when you read about all these disasters. We know what the world's reaction is; the world says either, "Isn't it terrible?" and "Isn't it awful?" or the world does not want to know and turns quickly to the sports page. But what is the Christian's reaction? The Christian's reaction must not be to say that it is the end of the world.

I have never been in an earthquake. I was hoping to be in New Zealand. I had never had the experience, I am not sure I would like it and yet part of me would like to have been in an earthquake, if you know what I mean, because it would be something interesting to talk about. I would then be able to say, "When I was in the earthquake ..." But I have never had that experience and those who have been in a real earthquake say it is one of the most frightening things and their first thought is that it is the end of the world. If suddenly you found yourself in the middle of a severe war you could well think this is the end of the world. If you were in Sudan right now, or Chad and living in a dry place where there is not a blade of green grass and you had got nothing to eat and nothing for your children, you might well be forgiven for thinking this is the end. And Jesus said that when you see these disasters it is not the end. It is the beginning of the end, but it is not the end. So don't panic, don't rush around and say it's the end of the world. But what you should see is that these agonising things are actually the beginning of birth pains.

Now, I don't know anybody in the world who regards them as that – only Christians. Those who hope in Christ could say, these painful things are the beginning of birth pains, not even the beginning of death pangs, but birth pains. That is a completely different perspective that enables you to read the newspapers and read about the disasters, and say – birth pains. Like a woman suddenly getting her first contraction, earthquakes are the contractions of a creation that is groaning and waiting for your redemption. Now, does that put a different light on your daily newspaper? It does not mean that you gloat because nobody could gloat over disasters that cause such suffering, and Christians will do all they can to relieve the pain caused by those sufferings or they are not worthy of the name Christian. But deep, deep down they do not panic, they are not thrown off balance, they do not say that it is the end of the world. They say, it is the beginning of birth pains, it is the first contraction of a universe that God wants to bring to new birth. Because, you know, some Christians just think that God wants to bring *people* to new birth. He does not; he wants to bring everything to new birth. He wants to restore *all* things. He wants a new earth and new stars and a new heaven. He wants new everything. He wants to make all things new.

He just began this time with us. The first time around, he began with the earth and the heavens and then he finished with us. This time around, the new birth is beginning with us and it finishes with the heavens and the earth. But you see, we hope in Christ and we say, yes, we expect wars and famines and earthquakes and we do not say it is the end of everything. We say it is the beginning of everything – the birth pains.

Now, at each stage of the four signals, there is a danger that comes in and the danger when signal number one drops is the danger of false messiahs. Since the signal is in the world, false messiahs will be in the world and when everything is shaking and when there are earthquakes and famines and wars around, false messiahs can have a heyday. They can exploit the insecurity of people and they do. And that is why we have seen people like

Jones, people like Moon – and you are going to see many, many more false Christs. And the insecurity that this world now offers is going to mean that these false messiahs will get a real hold. I am not surprised at the Moonies. Jesus said it would happen. And it does not upset me. I am sad for those who have been trapped in it by their own insecurity in a world that is desperate for somebody to look after them. But false messiahs are the danger.

Now, I notice that they are not a danger to the church, they are only a danger to the world. That is important because I do not think you would listen for one moment if I claimed to be Christ. You would not listen, but I am afraid that people out in your town might listen because they are very insecure. They are not grounded in their own faith. And so, Jesus said, "Now watch out for false Christs; many will come and claim 'I am the Christ.'" The late Sun Myung Moon claimed to be the Christ and actually used the name of Jesus to do it. And Jesus warned that all this is just a symptom of an insecure world. Well, that is signal number one and I believe signal number one has gone down.

You will see signal number two go down in the church and I believe signal number two is *beginning* to go down. What is it? Well, three things that will happen on a universal scale within the church. First, universal persecution, hated by *all* nations. That has never been true in church history. For 2,000 years, there have been some parts of the world where the church has been under pressure and others where it has not. In this country of ours, we have not been under pressure for a very long time, but I tell you, the number of countries in the world where the church is being persecuted is increasing monthly. I was in Africa, in Zimbabwe, when it was yet another country that was under a communist regime, and I looked at the map of Africa and I thought, how many countries are left where the church is not hated? Very few. And if you look at a map of the world and blot out every country where the church is being persecuted, you will blot out nine tenths of the world in terms of the number of countries. There are very few countries of the world where you are still free to have a celebration in church. Did you know that? And the number is rapidly diminishing.

Jesus said that when we see *all the church* hated, when the whole church is being persecuted, then signal number two is dropping. And then he said, secondly, that the effect that that will have will be a great reduction in the size of the church because there is nothing like pressure to sort people out. I once heard a story out of the former Soviet Union. I don't know if it was true, but I got it from a reliable source. But of course, with stories coming out of Russia at that time, you always had to check them out to be sure and that was not always possible. But I pass it on to you because it has got a real truth in it. It was the story of a prayer meeting in Russia where the doors burst open and two Russian soldiers came in with machine guns and they shouted, "We're going to kill the Christians!" And the Christians thought they were drunk but then realised they were stone sober. And then the soldiers said, "If you're not a Christian, get out!" And a number got up and ran. And then the soldiers said to the rest, "Now can you tell us how to become Christians, please? We had to make sure that we got real Christians so they wouldn't tell on us." My, a bit of pressure soon sorts out the sheep from the goats.

But I believe that we are going to have to get ready for pressure in this country. I believe part of the church's future here is suffering and that we are to get ready for it. And that is the signal, the pressure on, and the purifying of, the church. And Jesus said that we would have to watch out for false prophets at that point. If the danger in the world is false messiahs because the world is insecure, the danger in the church will be false prophets and we shall have to watch out for them. And you know what false prophets do – they tell you, "Peace, peace, when there is no peace." They try to make things easier for you. I would say that is the fundamental thrust of a false prophet, that he cuts down God's standards and accommodates to where the people are and that he seeks to lower moral standards and standards of belief and he tries to keep people happy and give them a security other than God. We will have to watch that when the pressure is on.

But the third feature of this signal is to me the most exciting. Jesus then says, *and* the gospel of the kingdom will be preached to all the nations. He does not say *but* the gospel will be preached. He says the pressure on the church and the purifying of it that will follow will get the job done. And the "gospel of the kingdom will be preached". I find that exciting. Don't you? It may be that God, looking down at a congregation, might say, If I put pressure on that group and got it a bit smaller, I could reach the whole town with them. It is a sobering thought but that is what I hear from this passage. Jesus is saying that the pressure will come on the church worldwide and because of that pressure, many will say, "Oh, let's get out." It is with the rest that he will get the job done. The gospel will be preached to all the nations – because with the rest, he has got an enduring body and "he that endures to the end will be saved," he says here. There is going to be a whole salvation in that. That is signal number two. I do not think it has gone down yet but I think it is going down, don't you? I see the church under increasing pressure everywhere in the world, and a purifying coming that leaves a group of people who can do the job, and who will preach the gospel and evangelise the nations.

Notice the phrase "all the nations" here. Persecuted by all the nations, preaching to all the nations. Invariably, the church has always grown faster when it is under pressure. Read church history. It grew faster in the first 300 years than it grew for many centuries later because the church under pressure grows. Isn't it exciting to find out that the church in China has actually *grown* during the last few decades? We once thought it must have died out because we didn't hear any news. But it was under pressure and it grew.

Now, you will see the third signal in the Middle East. And Jesus here refers to the Prophet Daniel and to a terrible phrase:

"the abomination of desolation", which we mentioned briefly in the previous chapter. I can only tell you what I understand that to mean. Daniel refers to it three times and Paul refers to it a number of times. I understand by this that one day in Jerusalem itself – the place where God set his Name – in the very temple of God, there will be committed the ultimate blasphemy and obscenity: a man claiming to be God. Paul talks about that, the "man of lawlessness" who in the very temple of God will claim to be God. And nothing could cause such an offence to God or be such a cause of suffering to man as a man in Jerusalem claiming to be God and saying, "I acknowledge no laws above me; I make all the laws from now on." It will be the ultimate blasphemy.

It nearly happened 170 years before Jesus when a man called Antiochus Epiphanes, a Greek emperor, came to Jerusalem and he walked into the temple where God's holy Name had been and he put on the altar a statue of Zeus, a Greek god, and sacrificed a *pig* on the altar of God – pork on the altar of the Jews. And then he turned the vestries of the temple into brothels. Nothing so shocking had ever occurred in Jewish history and in the city of Jerusalem as Antiochus Epiphanes. But it is something like *that* that Paul talks about, that Jesus talks about. Something so abominable, so blasphemous, so obscene, so appalling, that God will be offended to high heaven. And from that event will come such desolation, such confusion, such suffering, such distress, which, as Jesus says, the world has never seen before and will never see again. That I take to be the Big Trouble. And Jesus says first that if that were allowed to go on too long, nobody would survive, but fortunately God has already said that will be severely limited in time – that signal number three – or nothing would be left. And so, we can praise God that he is still on the throne and will not let that go on for very long.

But Jesus said the danger during that third signal will be false messiahs *and* false prophets, as if now we have reached signal number 3, Satan is going to throw everything he has got at us, even with signs and wonders. And some people are really fooled by signs and wonders; they do not realise that miracles can come from more than one possible source. And Satan will throw the book at us and you will hear all sorts of rumours – Christ is coming, he's over there. Christ is coming, he's over here. And there will be silly Christians running around all over the place – catching a bus here, getting a train there, flying there – because they have heard a rumour. And Jesus says, *don't run anywhere*. He said, "Wherever there is a carcass, there the vultures will gather." And whenever people are panicking, you will find Satan and his demonic hordes. Just don't listen.

I want you to notice that any idea that Jesus has come back secretly is wrong. Jesus said, don't listen. He said, actually, that when he comes it will be like lightning from one end of the heavens to the other. Everybody will know immediately, so you don't need to move out of your town. Stay right there. You will see, you will know. He has said he will be right there. Don't move. It is only the panicky people who are misled by signs and wonders that the devil produces and by false prophets *and* false messiahs who start running around saying, "It's happened; he's come again, he's come again." And Jesus told us not to listen to them.

There is only one group he told to run and that is the group that lives in the immediate vicinity of Jerusalem, the only group that has to move. And when I was in Jerusalem one October, I had all the Christian leaders together and I pleaded with them to take notice of this. I said, "If you are alive and still around this city when this happens, don't pack, don't do a thing – run! Because you'll be right on the doorstep of this wicked, horrid, filthy man who claims to be God. And any of God's people within reach of his arm will have had it, so you'd better run." And that is the only movement there has to be. Any of God's people who happen to be in Jerusalem – if you are a tourist at that time, you run. And Jesus said, "Pray about that; pray that it will not be in the winter in which it's cold to hide out in the hills. Pray it won't be on the Sabbath because there won't be any transport for you." You see, the El Al Airline stopped all flights on the Sabbath. And in fact, it will be very difficult to get out of that area if it is in winter or on the Sabbath, especially for pregnant women, nursing mothers. How will they cope?

But Jesus said, "I'm telling you beforehand. I want you to know." Now, that signal has not gone down yet, but my, can you see it coming? I certainly can. It seems the most possible thing in the world that that should happen, that a man in the Middle East should claim to be God – "From now on, I make the rules" – and commit that ultimate blasphemy, that abomination, in the very city of God.

Signal number 4. After you have seen signal number 3, start looking in the sky for signal number 4. I get excited by this. Signal number 4 is that immediately after all that trouble, which will be of limited duration, God will turn out every light in the universe. I can remember the first time I was taken to a pantomime and got into this theatre and one by one, the lights went out until we were sitting in darkness. And I was all excited because I knew the next thing would be a blaze of light in front of me and the thing was going to begin. I just want to tell you – that is what it is going to be like. The last signal is that the sun will go out, the moon will go out, the stars will go out; every natural light in the universe will be switched off because the first act is about to begin. And suddenly it will be like lightning from one end of the heaven to the other – and then you will hear a great deal of noise. Some people don't like noise; they think that religion ought to be very quiet and dignified. Well, they are going to have problems on this day. Because 1 Thessalonians 4:16 is the noisiest verse in the Bible – there is an archangel shouting his head off, there is a trumpet blowing loud enough to raise the dead, it really is going to be loud. And you have got this terribly noisy day. But in fact, then you can get ready for your first free trip to the Holy Land. *Then* the angels will come and gather.

Now I want you to notice two things. Up until this point, two things have not happened which some Christians have told me should have happened. Number one, Christ has not come yet, secretly or any way. And number two, Christians have not gone yet. And I think we need to hear it from Jesus' lips. He did not teach, either that he would come secretly, or that Christians would go secretly. He told us the four signals and when the fourth drops, do you know what the big danger is? If the danger of the first was false messiahs, if the danger of the second was false prophets, if the danger of the third is false messiahs *and* prophets, what is the danger of the fourth? Nothing at all! Why not? Because the next thing that will happen will be Jesus is back. So, you will have no time to worry about false messiahs or false prophets because *the* Prophet will have returned, *the* Messiah will have come.

And the fourth one is just so quick. Well, when you see that lightning and when the lights go out, you just get ready – we are off. My grandfather is buried in a graveyard in Newcastle upon Tyne and on his grave are three words. They are not from the Bible; actually, I discovered they are from a Methodist hymn. But they are on his gravestone and people scratch their heads and wonder what sort of an odd man is buried under this stone because on his stone after the details of his age and name, it just says "What a meeting!" And boy, it will be some celebration. There isn't a stadium in the world that can hold it. It will have to be in the air to get everybody in. And it will be loud enough to raise the dead and they will get there first. That is the centre of the Christian's hope. That is the very heart of our hope for the future. There are many other things that we hope for and that does not mean that we wish for it; it means that we look for it in the future. But the heart of it is that the Lord Jesus Christ is coming back to planet Earth – that is the heart of it. Because we know we cannot fully or finally establish the kingdom without the King.

England was a commonwealth for one period of its history under Oliver Cromwell, but there were those who felt it should be a kingdom and to do that, they had to get the king back. And Charles II had to come back. You cannot have a kingdom without a king. And the heart of our hope is that the King is coming back and therefore we do not pray a false prayer when we say, "your kingdom come on earth as it is in heaven." It is a prayer that is going to be answered because the King is coming. And Jesus said that when you see *all these things*, you will know that he is just the other side of the door. Just as when you see the fig tree and its leaves are beginning to blossom and the twigs are getting tender you know that summer is just round the corner. It comes so quickly once the buds come, have you noticed? You are into summer before you know where you are. And Jesus said that when you see *all* these things you will know – that means when you see all those signals drop.

I do not expect Jesus to come back tonight because those four signals have not yet dropped, and I am going to trust my eyes, not my ears. So, I am not going to panic and think I might wake up tomorrow morning and the other Christians I know have all gone. Nor am I going to think that I will have gone and they will all be here. That is often the other side of that kind of thinking. But I look for those signals and it is my dearest hope that it will happen in my lifetime and that they will drop while I am still on earth. That will mean no undertaker will touch this body of mine. That is the hope of every generation. It may not happen in my lifetime and it may be a long way off, but we have got to know what the signals are. Signal and sign – it is the same word.

The disciples asked Jesus, "What will be the sign of your coming, and of the end of the age?" They wondered how they would know when it was near. Jesus told them not to be deceived. Many will come and say this and say that but you just keep your eyes open for these four things. And when you see *all* these things, lift your heads, get excited, it's just the other side of the door. And he said there are two things that will not pass away, and that you can rely on as proof that these are going to happen. One is that this generation will not pass away. He did not mean that particular group of Jews alive at that time. The word is *breed, race,* and he said, the Jews will not disappear before all these things happen. And to me, one of the proofs that what Jesus said about the future is true is that he said the Jews would still be around when it happened. And there they are back in their own nation in their own land, back in Jerusalem, which is no longer trodden down by Gentiles. That is one of the proofs I know that it will happen.

And he told us the second thing that will endure when he said, "my words will by no means pass away". On the last day of history, you will still be able to get hold of a Bible. Other books may pass away. Other men's words will go – but "my words will by no means pass away." And hanging on to the fact that God's people Israel will never pass away and God's Word through Jesus will never pass away, I can face the future and read my daily newspaper without panic and say, Hallelujah! These are birth pains, the contractions of a universe, that are going to be followed by a whole new heaven and a new earth for newborn people with new bodies to live in. I just get so excited.

Read Matthew 24:36–44

Somebody asked me whether I believe in the rapture. Of course, I do; I just believe that it will come when Jesus said it would come. But I believe there will be a separation and a gathering of the elect. That is when Jesus said it would happen – *after the final signal* he will send his angels to gather the elect. Nothing could be clearer. Don't ever get confused; it is crystal clear.

Now we come to the passage that you have just read, which seems to say the opposite, and it is here, I think, that the confusion may have arisen. Having said when you see *all these things, you'll know,* Jesus then says, but you *don't know*, and neither do I and the angels don't know. In fact, nobody knows except Father and he is keeping it a secret. Which to me is exciting in the sense that God my Father already has the date in his diary for the coming of Jesus. It is all settled, it is in the calendar, but nobody else knows. Therefore, you must always be wary of anyone who tries to date the Lord's coming. Martin Luther did and was clearly wrong. John Wesley did and was wrong. You would be amazed how many great Christian leaders have fallen into the trap of saying it will be in such and such a year. The cults have also fallen into that trap. You will find the Jehovah's Witnesses and the Seventh-day Adventists have both fallen into the trap of dating the Lord's return and Jesus said, no one knows.

I am trying to write a book on the honesty of Jesus because I think it is a greatly neglected attribute of his character. The sheer honesty of Jesus! Five times in these chapters that we are looking at he said, "I tell you the truth". One of his favourite words was *amen*. And he used to begin sentences with amen, not end them. And he would begin, "Amen, amen I say to you" – "Verily, verily" – "Truly, truly" I say to you. He was a man who spoke the truth to such a degree that he was able to say, "I am the Truth." And therefore, when he did not know something, he was honest enough to admit it. There is a good example for you. And he did not know the date of his return. He was telling his disciples that he could tell them *what* to look for but he could not tell them *when*. And that is honest, and it behoves every follower of Christ to be equally honest. And no preacher can tell you *when*, but we can say *what*.

But that does not resolve the problem because Jesus seems now to be saying it will be totally unexpected, it will be "like a thief in the night", and that is a favourite phrase of Jesus. And it is used by Peter, it is used by Paul and it is used by John right the way through the rest of the New Testament. They pick this up, that when the Lord comes, he will come like a thief in the night. And that has led many people to say, "Then surely it will be totally unexpected, surely we won't have *any* warning at all."

There are two things about a thief coming. The first is obviously that he tries to come secretly, that he tries to come stealthily. By the way, that is an interesting word – s-t-e-a-l, stealthily. So, a thief tries to come unnoticed. But the second thing about a thief is he is coming to rob you. He is not only trying to come stealthily; he is also coming to steal. Now, do you think Jesus is coming to his church to steal from his church? Never! Therefore, we raise a question as to whether he is coming to *us* as a thief and we shall see that the teaching of the New Testament is crystal clear: To those who are ready, he will *not* come as a thief. He will neither come stealthily nor to steal. But to those who are *not* ready, it will be totally unexpected and it will be certain loss. Do you follow me?

And it is applying the concept of the thief to Christians that is the big mistake that has been made. In other words, let me go a little more deeply into this. The tension between "you *will* know when I'm coming" and "you don't know when I'm coming" is quite wrongly resolved by saying that it must mean two comings, that he must come secretly first and openly second with a gap in between. That is not the way the New Testament resolves the tension.

So, what is the answer to this tension where Jesus at one minute says that when you see these things you will know, and the next minute says, but you don't know? How do you resolve it? There is only one way to resolve it properly and it is the biblical way and it is to resolve it like this: When you *do know*, it will be too late to get ready. That is the only way you can resolve the tension. But it is the right way. In other words, by the time you have seen all the signals and know for sure he is at the door, you will not be able to do a thing about it by then. The time for getting ready will have gone. That is why you need to be ready because you do not know when the final signal will drop. And it is in that way, not by any silly doctrine of two comings, which I cannot find *anywhere* in the New Testament, that if he is coming, he is coming secretly for his saints and openly with them. I cannot find that anywhere. What I do find is this: Those who are not ready will not know *at all*, just as in the days of Noah they had no idea what was going to happen until they were taken away – and lost everything!

And therefore, to those to whom he will come stealthily, he will also come to steal as a thief in the night. To those to whom it is a complete surprise, it will be utter loss. But Paul says in 1 Thessalonians 4–6 so clearly: "But you, brethren, are not in darkness, so that this Day should overtake you as a thief. You are all sons of light and sons of the day. We are not of the night nor of darkness. Therefore, let us not sleep, as others do, but let us watch and be sober." In other words, the whole concept of thieving is a threat only to those who are not ready. But for those who are ready, Jesus says that it is like a man whose house is going to be burgled but he gets a tip-off from the underworld that a thief is on the way and not only that the thief is on the way, but he knows that it is going to be at about one o'clock in the morning. So what does he do? He is ready and he makes sure that his house is not broken into; he is neither surprised nor robbed. Do you follow Jesus' teaching here?

The unexpectedness of it is only for the unready, but those who are ready will be watching and there will be no secrecy, no surprise, and no loss. I tell you this, there are people living in your town now who when Jesus comes again, are going to lose everything that they value. They are going to lose all the love they have enjoyed; they are going to lose all their possessions. They are going to lose *everything* that they value and it will be totally unexpected. It will be like a burglar breaking in. But that should not happen to *you*. And it need not happen to them.

No wonder Jesus says it is like the days of Noah. He was constantly drawing a parallel between what happened in Noah's day and what will happen when he comes back, and therefore if you dismiss the truthfulness of the Noah story, you are not likely to accept the truthfulness of his coming again. But they are both historical events – one is past, the other is future, but they are terribly similar. And do you notice that Noah knew *what* was going to come but he did not know *when*. By the time he knew when it would happen, it would have been too late to build an ark because he knew what was going to happen for a whole year and he got on with getting ready.

The Canberra was the first ship to be designed on the same proportions as Noah's Ark. Did you know that? And most ships since have copied the design. The QEII was based on the Canberra. The Canberra was the first ship to have the same proportions between beam and length as Noah's Ark, and the marine designer did it because he believed God had the best design for ships. Fascinating! It is real. He worked out that Noah and his three sons could have built that thing in the time they had – but they did not know how much time they had. The important thing was that as soon as he knew *what* was going to happen, he got ready straight away. And then, after a year of building that thing God told him to get into it because *in seven days* the Flood would come.

So now at last he knew *when* and it was not a surprise but it would have been a terrible surprise if he had done nothing to get ready until he knew the *when*. But he got ready when he knew *what*. I do hope you are following me in this because I am making a terribly important point. What I am saying is this: From the first part of Matthew 24, it is clear that if we watch for the signals, we will *know when* he is coming. But if we wait until we know *when to get ready*, we will be far too late. We will be like the foolish virgins. Oh, they knew *what was going to happen* but by the time they knew when, it was too late to get ready. And that is the only way I can resolve it. I do not resolve it by having this two-coming theory because I do not believe it is scriptural. But I do resolve it by saying there are two groups to which he will come – those who will know when it is but who have been ready long since, who have got ready *now*, and those who have not even got ready at all. To the latter he will come as a thief, both stealthily and to steal.

Read Matthew 24:45–25:1–46

Now let us turn to the last part of the whole thing. These are four stories which all say exactly the same things. The emphasis in all four stories is on those who were not ready and what happened to them. Each of these stories could finish with the sentence "and they lived *unhappily* ever after". They are not nice stories; they do not finish with all the loose ends being tied up, with all the people in a nice, good place. They finish in just the opposite way. And I want to remind you that when Jesus told the stories he was telling them to 12 men who had been with him for three years. He is not speaking to the crowd; he is not speaking to unbelievers; he is not speaking to the religious leaders of the Jews. He is speaking to those who have followed him for three years – who have eaten with him, slept with him, walked with him, and talked with him. And to them he tells these four terrible stories. And they follow straight through from all that we have looked at thus far.

Instead of going through the four stories separately, I felt the Lord would have me go through them all together and pick out six features of all four stories which are the same so that you get the message. You will be familiar with the stories. You have probably gone through them one by one yourself so let me see them as a whole and look at six things that happen in every one of the four stories.

The first thing that is common to all four stories is that they centre around one person, one man, whether it is the Householder in the first one or the Bridegroom in the second or the Businessman in the third or the King in the fourth. They all centre on one person and there is no doubt at all that Jesus is speaking about himself. And he speaks about himself under a variety of headings, as it were. He is saying, I am the one who is in charge of your household; I am your Bridegroom; I am your Accountant to whom you will account. And I am both King and Shepherd.

I find it fascinating that he combines both shepherd and king in the fourth story because all the great kings of Israel were shepherds first. Have you noticed that? And the Shepherd King is an amazing concept because in the social ladder in the Middle East, the shepherd is at the bottom and the king is at the top – only God could put those two together.

But that is what he used to do. He sent Moses to be a shepherd before he put him in leadership. He got David in the fields before he was king. And the best kings have been shepherds first; they were at the bottom of the ladder before they got to the top – and that is Jesus too. He humbled himself even to his death on the cross and therefore God gave him all authority. Shepherd King – I could spend a whole chapter on that. But that is not the burden the Lord has given me so let us just say this: Have you noticed that Jesus *always* right through this whole discourse refers to himself in the third person singular? He does not say *I*, he always says *he*. He does not use the words "I am the Son of God." He says "neither the Son". Or he talks about himself as the Son of Man or the King. He never says, when *I* come in my glory with the angels. Now, why should he be so reticent to speak the truth about himself in the first person singular? It is one of the marks of a false messiah that he says, "I am the Christ." That is what Jesus says false messiahs will say, and he does not say that. He leaves people to find it out for themselves.

There is a profound lesson here. Beware of someone who says, "I am an apostle"; or "I am a prophet"; or "I am" this or "I am" that. If a man has a genuine gift from God, he never needs to claim it. It will be recognised by faith. It is the false prophets and the false Christs who say, I am this, I am that. And Jesus speaks about himself quite impersonally and says, when the Christ comes or when the Son of Man comes or when the King does this or when the Shepherd does that or when the Householder or when the Bridegroom; he never says *I*. That is very interesting. There are certain things he does claim about himself. In John's Gospel he says: "I am the Bread of Life"; "I am the Door"; and "I am the Resurrection and the Life". But these are not office or status, are they? None of them. They are all functions. So, he is not claiming anything for himself, yet all these stories centre around this one Person who settles the eternal destiny of everyone who comes before him. And the profound thing that we must get hold of here and which all people need to hear is that one day it will be Jesus who settles their eternal destiny. He has been appointed to do that. In every Anglican church this Sunday they will say, "from thence he shall come again to judge the quick and the dead". I wonder if they really believe it.

Jesus will settle the question as to where you spend the rest of your existence. It is he who does it and all these four stories centre on him and it is he who, when he comes, divides people into two groups and only two – those who are ready and those who are not. It is very striking that that is the only division he makes throughout these four stories. He does not go into all their life history; he just asks whether you are ready or not. Because in fact, the test of your faith as to whether it is real is whether you are ready.

Faith and faithfulness are the same thing in scripture. Faith is not one step that you take one night at an evangelistic crusade. Faith is a life you live and a walk that goes on until you die. Faith is not a one-off thing; it is a continuous thing. It lasts from the moment you first believed until the moment you die if it is real faith. It becomes faithfulness. Paul did not say, once upon a time on the Damascus Road I believed in Jesus so I'm going to heaven. No, he would say, "the life which I *now* live in the flesh I live by faith in the Son of God". And at the end of the road, he said, "I have fought the good fight, I have finished the race, I have *kept the faith*." The only faith that saves is the faith you have at the end of the road. That is the lesson of these four stories. It is *faithful* faith. "Well done, good and *faithful*..." You have believed in me enough to be ready. So, we are getting some pretty surprising things out of these four stories.

The second thing that is common to all four stories is something that I have already mentioned. In every story, a crisis is precipitated by the return of the central figure after a *long time*. There are those who have said that Jesus thought he would come back very soon – and there are those who have said that the disciples thought that – but in fact, Jesus' teaching was plain. In every story he puts in the phrase *after a long time*. And he knew that the long time would be the real test as to whether somebody is ready. If you announce to your town that Jesus is coming back next Thursday, you can produce panicked reactions fairly quickly but that will not tell you that they are ready. The people who are really ready can cope with a long wait. Far too often we have used: "He might come next Thursday" to try to get people ready. That is false motivation and it does not produce people who are ready because if he does not come next Thursday, they will be very unready by next week. The people who are really ready are ready if he comes tomorrow or in a thousand years' time. They will still be ready. But it is his coming that produces the crisis and divides people into those two groups.

Let us move on quickly to the third point. In all these four stories, some people were ready. And we ask, how were they ready? And each of the four stories tells us something different here. And we can put them all together. In the first story the man was ready because he had got on with the job he had been left to do. That is the first way he was ready.

There is an old spiritual song which I love and it goes like this:

There's a King and a Captain high and he's coming by and by.
And he'll find me hoeing cotton when he comes.
You can hear his legions charging in the regions of the sky.
And he'll find me hoeing cotton when he comes.
There's a Man they thrust aside who was tortured till he died.
And he'll find me hoeing cotton when he comes.
He was hated and rejected, he was scorned and crucified.
And he'll find me hoeing cotton when he comes.
When he comes, when he comes, he'll be crowned by saints
and angels when he comes.
They'll be shouting out Hosanna! to the Man that men denied.
And I'll kneel among my cotton when he comes.

In other words, I'll get on with the job, whereas there were Christians at Thessalonica who got so caught up with the Second Coming that they left their jobs. And I have had to counsel people over the years who have thrown in their jobs saying the Lord is so near that they just want to get on with this and they are panicking. "And he'll find me hoeing cotton when he comes." If you cannot understand what I am saying you may never see God's purpose in your daily work. But you see, the best thing you can do to get ready for his coming is to get on with the job he told you to do, whether that job is to be a church leader or whether it is to be a butcher or a housewife, or to work at a factory bench. You will find me getting on with the job. "Blessed is that servant whom his Master finds so doing."

In the second story, they were ready because they had built up enough resources for the future to carry on for some time. Now, there are some Christians who are terribly keen on any short-term project. The latest thing in missionary work is to go overseas for a very short time. I once heard a dear old missionary talk about this. He was discussing the change in missionary work and somebody said to him, "What's the biggest change in missionary work since you went out and today?" And he said, "I'll tell you: we went out to stay." And sticking at it means building up resources, not *using* them up – *building* them up. And the five wise virgins had built up their resources so that, even though there was a long delay, they could carry on. And the simple fact is that they knew that they would need their lamps *inside the wedding and after the Bridegroom came*. That is the point of the story. Because they did not have electric light in those days and when you went to a wedding everybody brought a lamp to light up the whole wedding and to help with the celebration. So, they did not just need lamps while they were in the street, they needed those lamps for *after the Bridegroom had come*. And they built up their resources to do something for the Bridegroom after his coming, whereas the others were just looking for the Bridegroom. They were not building up any resources and therefore they could not do anything after he came. They were not ready.

The reward for serving God faithfully is not a large, comfortable sofa in heaven with R.I.P. embroidered on the antimacassar or whatever you like. It is more work. It is serving him and it is those who have built up their resources for what happens after the Bridegroom has come who are ready.

The third story tells us that if God has invested anything in us then he is expecting interest back. He is expecting you to multiply your gift and if you use your gift, it will multiply. If a preacher uses his gift, others will be inspired into preaching. If a singer uses her gift, others will be inspired into singing. And whatever gift you use inspires others to use their gift. And that is multiplying it.

But if you say that you don't have many gifts, isn't it interesting that it was the man with one who said, "Well, it's not worth doing much with my little gift when everybody around me has so many more," and he buried it. He was not ready. Those who are ready are those who increase the investment God has put in them.

The fourth thing is those who are ready are those who are caring for the needs of Christ's brethren – and his brethren are not neighbours. That is too wide an interpretation. Nor are they the Jewish nation. That is too narrow an interpretation. I believe the word "brethren" always meant the same thing when Jesus used it. He said, "Go and tell my brethren", and "whoever does the will of my Father in heaven is my brother". In other words, to do something for a believer is actually to serve Jesus.

A famous preacher went to preach in Yorkshire once and he stayed in a wealthy home and a maid in the kitchen was sent to the butcher to get a joint of meat for the weekend. And she said to the butcher, "Oh, the fuss that's being made about this preacher." She said, "The things they're having to do to get ready for him." She said, "You'd think Jesus Christ himself was coming the way they're carrying on." A week later she went back to the butcher and the butcher remembered what she had said. He asked, "Well, did Jesus come and stay in your house?" She said, "Yes." She had been led to the Lord by the preacher over the weekend and she knew in serving him she was serving Jesus. If you give a cup of cold water to another Christian, you have given Jesus a drink. What an amazing concept that is.

And those who are ready are those who realise that to serve a brother of Jesus is to serve him; to laugh at a brother of Jesus is to laugh at Jesus. To make fun of a brother Christian is to make fun of Jesus. "Whatever you do for the least …"

The fourth thing that these four stories have in common is this. Those who are ready are rewarded but the reward is rather different from what we might expect. In the first story, the reward for being faithful is greater responsibility. Now don't you ever be surprised that if you do a good job in the church you get more jobs. That is the reward of Jesus. We think, "Ah well, just because I did that, now they're onto me about this." But that is the reward – which means that the reward is not something different from what you have done. It is not like a spoonful of jam after you have swallowed a pill. So, if you are not enjoying serving the Lord, you had better watch out because you will hate the reward. Do you follow me? The reward is not rest but more work. Now, of course, the world thinks differently. The world says, "Well, I've worked 40 years in this factory. I deserve a good retirement now." Jesus does not offer retirement as a reward. He offers promotion.

A scientist worked for years in a laboratory – a very rough laboratory, a garden shed really – and he discovered a medical answer to a disease that really had affected the world. And so, the world got together – or at least those who knew of it got together – to reward him and they thought, "Now, what can we reward him with?" And they built him a new laboratory. That was his reward. That is the kind of reward Jesus gives.

In the second story, there is the opportunity to celebrate, to enter into a joyful celebration. That is the reward. In the third story, it is both the first and the second mixed together. It is promotion *and* entering into joy. And in the fourth story, it is actually to reign with Christ on a throne, to enter into a kingship prepared. I love that word *prepared* because Jesus is saying here, if you have prepared for me, I have prepared for you. "I go to prepare a place for you." Are you preparing yourself for heaven as much as Jesus is preparing heaven for you? There are two sides to being prepared.

Now, the fifth thing that these stories have in common is that in each of the four stories, some were *not* ready. The whole point of these four stories is that some were not ready. And the shock that I got when I asked, in what sense were they not ready, was this. They were not ready because they had *not* done certain things. They were not criminals. They were not full of vice. There was not a murderer, an adulterer among them. In fact, none of them is accused of a single vice or a single crime or a single sin. They are only accused of having *not done* something. Now, that is a shock.

Again, in every Church of England church this Sunday, people will recite the General Confession and in the General Confession they will say: "We have left undone the things we ought to have done." Do you know that a man can go to hell, not because of what he has done or anything he has done, but because of what he *did not do?* And therefore, the common defence against accusations – "Well, I've never done anybody any harm" – is not an adequate defence plea because God says, but you never did anybody any good either. Not doing any harm is not adequate. I gave you life, I gave you talents, I gave you opportunities and you did nothing with them.

Now, that is the shock of these four stories. Remember, he is speaking to disciples again and he is saying, you are in danger of doing nothing. In fact, to get to hell, that is all you need to do – nothing. That is the teaching of Jesus.

In the first case, a man had been left to give food to the other servants and he had not given it. In the second case, they were supposed to have enough oil to light the wedding and they had not got it. In the third case, the man with one talent had failed to improve it. He had not spent it on himself; he had not gone out and stolen his master's money and indulged himself. He just hadn't done anything with it. And in the fourth case, the people said, "But how could we ...?" "You never visited me, you never clothed me, you never gave me a drink." And you know, they gave the whole game away when they said, "Oh, Lord, if we'd realised it was *you*..." What social snobbery lies in that implication! In other words, "Oh, we thought it was just some unimportant person. If we'd known it was you, if we'd known it was important we'd have done it." You see, that's awful, isn't it?

The sins of neglect – what are called the sins of omission – are what Jesus is talking about here. Not the bad things we have done but the good things we have not done. Now, that is a serious word. The present year will not be judged by the wrong things we did do, but by the right things we *did not* do. And next year will be judged the same, as to whether we are ready.

The sixth and last thing that there is in these four stories is this. The unready are punished. They are not forgiven, not one of them. They are not given a second chance, not one of them. And the simple fact is that when the Lord comes back again, the chances are over. The door is shut! And there is no appeal, the decision is final. Do you know, I find that I am getting less and less able to enter into Christmas. I am afraid there have been times when I have refused invitations to preach over Christmas. I just could not bring myself to do it. Because if I had done, I would have preached on the Second Coming of the Lord. That is what people need to hear. And it is a wise church that has put Advent just before Christmas and those who observe Advent preach the Second Coming of Christ just before Christmas. That is wise.

The world does not mind a baby in a manger because the baby is not going to judge them. The world does not mind the first coming of the Lord because that was for forgiveness and mercy and salvation. The world *loves* the first coming of Jesus and *hates* the Second Coming. Therefore, the world will celebrate his first coming until the last Christmas but they will not celebrate his Second Coming because he is not coming again to save the world. "From thence he shall come again to judge the quick and the dead." And it is not very nice to be told you are going to be judged for what you have not done. And the world will never celebrate that, but it is as true as his first coming. In fact, it strikes me that you do not need so much faith to believe he is coming the second time when he has been once. It is much easier to believe he will come again, isn't it?

Now look at the punishment that was meted out to those who were not ready – cut to pieces, weeping and gnashing of teeth, shut outside, in the outer darkness, weeping and gnashing of teeth again, cursed, eternal fire, eternal punishment. And you know, I cannot get round those words of Jesus. I am amazed that the only person in the whole Bible that God could trust with the truth about hell was Jesus. He could not trust any apostle with the truth, he could not trust any prophet with the truth. All my teaching on hell comes from Jesus, as if the one person who could warn people about it would be the one who would give his own blood to save people from it. And here we have the profound truth said and we have got to grapple with it: that disciples who are not ready go to hell. We must grapple now with this very serious truth which Jesus is giving us. It is disciples he is talking to. And disciples who are not ready go to hell. There is no trace here of purgatory. There is no trace here of being handicapped in the future life. There is no trace here of forfeiting something. There is only the language which Jesus reserved for hell, which is a place of the most appalling suffering.

Weeping and gnashing of teeth. I used to think that would be remorse. I now realise it is rage and that hell will be full of raving people who are shaking their fists at God for sending them there. And I would not like to be surrounded by a lot of raging people who are angry with God for sending them there. Weeping, gnashing of teeth, outer darkness – it is terrible. I don't think people realise. People outside the church do not realise but people *inside* the church do not always realise who Jesus is talking to or what he is saying.

So, we must finally face very honestly the truth of what Jesus is saying. These are not rank unbelievers. These are not pagan, heathen people on some distant South Sea island. These are twelve men who, for three years, have shared his ministry. These are twelve men who have taught and preached and healed in the Name of Jesus. And in each of the stories, the people who are finally rejected are those who have had a connection with the central figure in the stories.

In the first story, it is a servant of the Householder who is sent to hell. In the second story, it is five of the virgins – the bridesmaids – waiting for the wedding, looking for the Bridegroom coming. In the third story, it is a man who had been given a talent by the

Businessman before he went on the journey. And in the fourth story, the goats have been in the flock of the one Shepherd. This is the challenge of these four stories. You can be as near as that to Jesus and still not be ready. And I am very close now to the burden the Lord gave me for you.

We are not talking about unbelievers and the danger they are in now. We are talking about the danger each Christian is in. So *how* can *we* be ready? Just two things.

They come out clearly in these stories. What was wrong with those who were not ready? What was the root of their failure? Why did they not make it? And the answer is twofold. Number one. Their relationship with the Lord was inadequate. They did not *know* him. They *thought* they knew him but they did not. Think of the man with one talent and he came and he said, "Oh Lord, I knew you were a hard man. You make your money out of other people's labour." A typical man who does not like working for other people. You have heard people talk like this, haven't you? "Why should he make a profit on my labour?" It is almost a shop steward talking here. And he says, "You're a hard man and I was afraid that if I took the risk and lost your money, I'd really get it in the neck so I didn't take any risks because I knew you, you see. I knew what you're like; you're a hard master. You're just after grabbing some money."

Now, he did *not* know the Master. The Master wanted to *share* his joy. The Master wanted to give talents so that he could give people more responsibility. The Master wanted to share everything he had got with the servants. That was the kind of man he was. But this man who buried his talent said, "Oh, I know you." He didn't at all. If you are serving the Lord because you think he is hard and because he pushes you and because he *makes* you do it, you do not *know* him. He is doing it so that he may share more responsibility with you and so that he may say, "Well done, good and faithful servant. Come and share my joy." That is why he is doing it, not because he is hard, because he wants to drive you, but because he wants to share with you.

You see, you do not know the Lord unless you know what he is really like. If you know what he is really like, you will turn your ten talents into ten more, your five into five more, your two into two more, and even your little one you will turn into one more if you know him. They did not know him. In fact, the Bridegroom says to those foolish virgins, "I don't know you!" You may say you are looking for the Second Coming but I don't know you. Wouldn't it be terrible if the Lord said, "I heard you singing that in church but you don't know me and I don't know you. We never got to know each other"?

The second thing that was wrong with those who were not ready was this. Not only was their relationship with Christ – with the Lord – inadequate, but their relationship with his brethren was also inadequate. Not only did *he* not recognise them ("I don't know you!") but *they* had not recognised him either. And they were saying, "But Lord, we never saw you." And he said, "But you saw me many times."

Everyone in church on a Sunday morning has seen the Lord Jesus. You just need to look around and you have seen him. And you could give him a meal today. Do you recognise him at those times? If you do not recognise him in each other, don't you dare take bread at the Holy Communion because if you cannot discern the Body, you should not eat that bread. You could be sick and even die. Looking around, do you discern Jesus? Do you recognise him? Do you know him in your fellow Christians? In other words, those who are ready are those who have a good relationship with the Lord and a good relationship with his brethren. That is all. And out of that will grow all the other things. Out of that will grow a desire to multiply talents. Out of that will grow a desire to build up resources. Out of that will grow a faithful feeding of his household. Out of that will grow the service and the meeting of needs. It will all grow out of those two things.

As I prepared this message my burden was this. How many in your community at church are just hanging on, are just fellow travellers, have just come along to the celebration because it is big and noisy and exciting, and are just tagging along with the community? I tell you, under pressure we would soon find out. But I just felt the Lord say, don't assume because you are singing about my coming again that you are ready. Don't assume that because you have joined yourself to the flock that you are a sheep. Don't assume that because you are among the virgins waiting for the Bridegroom that you are a wise virgin. Don't assume that because you are listening to others use their talents that you are using your talent. Don't assume anything but get to know your Lord and get to know his brethren. Recognise him in each other and get ready.

Now, some readers may want to ask me, "Do you believe 'Once saved, always saved'?" Look, I am teaching on Jesus' Word and we must take Jesus' Word as it stands. And I believe it is possible to be a disciple and to go to hell. And my proof is that out of the twelve men there was one who did not make it; one who was listening to these words, who had gone out preaching and healing in the Name of Jesus, who had left all to follow him, who was part of the inner body of the twelve. And he was listening to these stories and he was the treasurer and he did not know Jesus well enough to know that Jesus knew that he was fiddling the books. And he was faithless in looking after the money of the church. The first church treasurer was crooked. And Jesus, I am quite sure as he told these four stories, kept looking at Judas wondering, will *you* be ready? But Judas was not and Judas went and hanged himself; and it says he went to his own place. Out of those disciples he is the one I do not expect to see in heaven but then, in even saying that, I am being presumptuous about myself.

So, it is a sobering word I have brought you in this chapter. It is a word that will challenge all sorts of traditional ideas. It will challenge all sorts of complacency. We can turn our complacency into doctrine and say, "It's okay, I've got my ticket to glory." We can say, "It's okay, the Christians are all going to be snatched out before the Big Trouble." We can turn all our hopes – human hopes – into doctrine. But I go by the Word of Jesus and I take Jesus' Word at its face value and Jesus wants disciples in your town who will be *ready* – who know *what* is coming but who are getting ready *now* so that when they know *when* he is coming, it will not be too late. You cannot build an ark in seven days.

Hear the final sentence from Saint Augustine: "He who loves the coming of the Lord is not he who affirms it is far off, nor is it he who says it is near; but rather he who, whether it be far or near, awaits it with sincere faith, steadfast hope and fervent love."

25

PASSOVER AND FIRST TRIAL

Read Matthew Chapter 26

Every night, Jesus retired to Bethany, where the temple police could not arrest him. During the day he was with the crowd the whole time and they did not dare to arrest him, fearing that the crowd would riot if they dared to touch such a popular teacher. Every night, when they looked for him and asked where he was staying nobody knew. He slipped out to Bethany. The reason why Judas could betray him was so simple. Jesus said that they were going to stay in the city that night, and Judas saw his opportunity. That was why he was needed. The temple priests and the police needed to know when they could lay their hands on him privately, quietly. I once read about events in another part of the world where the secret police of that country always arrested somebody in the middle of the night because they knew that they would not be able to avoid public riots if they arrested people during the day. This is precisely what happened then.

So, Jesus is in Bethany one evening, the last evening he is going to spend out of the city, and they are having a meal in the house of a man who is a leper. I wonder if it means that Jesus had healed him, because normally he would not have been able to eat with others. They were sitting at the table and a woman brought the perfume. It was a costly thing and may have been an heirloom. If you are interested in the value of it, it was worth about a year's wages. A denarius was one day's wage and it was said to have been 300 denarii's worth of costly perfume. In those days, if you could afford it, you bought some very costly perfume and you put it away for your funeral, for the anointing of your body. That was the only justification for using such an expensive thing. It was the custom to anoint the guest with a few drops of perfume when they came in. We would show someone to the cloakroom or ask them if they would like to wash; they would anoint them with a few drops of perfume – and this was normal hospitality. But to use all of this was scandalous, and she came in and smashed the jar, which meant that it would never be used again. Then, scooping up the perfume, which must have filled the room with a powerful scent, she just poured it onto our Lord. It was a most amazing and moving act. And the commercial attitude of others was immediately revealed. The disciples said, "Why this waste?" This is sometimes how worldly people argue. Here the valuable perfume was used rightly, yet they criticised her. They still had not learned the lesson of the widow's mite, and the lesson is when someone gives something you should not ask about the value of the gift but of what it means to the giver. If they had stopped to ask why she had done this thing they would have understood and approved. I notice that it was men who criticised her. I think the women would have understood.

Jesus said four things about her act. Firstly, he said it was a beautiful act. Secondly, he made it clear that she had done a very opportune thing: she had seized an opportunity that she would not have again. She saw an opportunity to do something that was unique – a once-in-a-lifetime act. All of us have had opportunities to do something and, alas, have missed those opportunities and wished, "If only I had done that" – particularly when the opportunity was in connection with someone who died shortly afterwards. So, Jesus told them not to blame her. Thirdly, she had done a most discerning thing, and here he points out the real meaning of the act. This woman, alone of all those in that room, knew first that he was going to die very soon, and second that no one would have an opportunity to anoint his body, as was the normal custom, after death. How she knew this I do not know. Normally when a criminal was executed on a cross his relatives were not allowed to bury the body. His body was thrown onto the rubbish heap of the valley of Gehenna on the south side of Jerusalem. So, the woman must have foreseen that he was going to die a criminal's death and his body would be discarded and would not receive a proper burial. If she had done it in three days' time nobody would have criticised an expenditure of this kind on a dead body, but she had done it on a live body and that was why she was reproached.

Fourthly, Jesus told them that she had done a memorable act, and he predicted then that wherever the gospel was preached people would hear about this woman – and we are thinking about her. This was a lovely thing to do, it was an opportune thing to do, it was a discerning thing to do and it was a memorable thing to do, so it should not have been criticised.

We step straight from this story into something terrible. I do not quite know the right word to use, so contradictory is it, such a contrast: a lovely woman doing a generous thing, to a dreadful man doing a greedy thing – the contrast is appalling. Here is the incident. Because he realises that Jesus has virtually announced his forthcoming death, one disciple now sees that Jesus is willing to die. Judas is going to cash in on this, getting out of the remaining situation as much money as he can lay his hands on. He had backed Jesus, thinking it was going to be wonderful, that he would be in a wealthy, prospering kingdom, and now he realises that even Jesus is going to let others kill him. So, what can he, Judas, get out of it? This man can only think of going to betray Jesus and making some hard cash out of the betrayal.

It became fashionable in the twentieth century to try to whitewash Judas. In fact, there is a craze to try and turn the Gospel story upside down. Have you noticed this? Newspaper articles, paperback booklets, everybody is on the bandwagon now. Why do people want to whitewash Judas? Why do they want to say that it was not the money, that really he was a good chap and he was just trying to force Jesus' hand and get things moving? Because Judas reminds us too much of ourselves, that is why. Because there is the same kind of covetousness and greed in us that was in him, and we do not like it. Judas is a mirror, so we try to smash the mirror. But the Bible is quite clear that the one reason why Judas did it was because he loved money. We know this from the earliest days. Indeed, up in Galilee Jesus had sadly said to the twelve, "One of you is a devil." Judas was the treasurer, and he was dipping his hand in the money bag for himself quite early on. It was Judas who pointed out that they could have had a year's wages in the fund if that perfume had been sold. I have a feeling that he was already thinking of how much cash he could slip out. Here was Judas, and for hard cash he sold out his Lord.

A thought strikes me at this point. What would those priests think of the followers of Jesus after that? They would say, "You can buy any of them. Grease their palms enough and you can buy them off." We notice that each time Judas's name is mentioned in this chapter, immediately after his name comes the phrase "one of the twelve". Here is a man who has lived with Jesus for three years, yet still he can be so greedy that he can do this. It is an amazing and wonderful story, terrible though it is. How can a man be as close to Jesus as that and not get rid of such covetousness? Well, how can *we?* It is the same problem.

Here is Judas, and he goes to the priests and agrees to sell our Lord for the price of a slave. In those days if you could buy a slave you were definitely "one up". If you wanted to move up the social scale a bit, the status symbol was to say, "I have a slave now, you know," as you might talk about a swimming pool in the garden nowadays. Judas sold our Lord for the price of a status symbol that would move him up the social scale. Of course, he more than regretted it later. Judas, like the woman who anointed Jesus, has been preached about in the whole world; wherever the gospel has gone, Judas's name has been remembered. What would we rather be remembered for: our generosity or our greed;

our sympathy towards the Lord Jesus and understanding of his death or our hardness and callous attitude to it?

Now let us look into the upper room. Again, I am struck by the fact that throughout the whole of this last week our Lord is the master of the situation – he has planned it, he controls it, he decides when, how and where everything happens. At some point he had made arrangements for the use of the upper room and the Last Supper. He had even given a secret sign to find the room. Why these elaborate and secret precautions? Why did he not tell the disciples exactly where they were going? Judas could not know where the upper room was. Our Lord had to have one last evening with them, so he sends two disciples to meet the man with the pitcher of water, who will show them the upper room. Judas still does not know Jesus' plans. Our Lord is controlling and timing the whole thing perfectly, so that when the time comes for him to give himself up he is able to say to Judas: what you have to do, do quickly.

So, we come to the upper room. There are couches and a table, a basin full of water, and a towel for washing their feet, but no servant to do it – we know who did it in the end and who was reluctant to do it. There they are for the meal.

Now comes one of the most terrible things that Jesus ever said. During the middle of the meal he says, "one of you will betray me". The amazing thing is that he had already said five times that he was going to be crucified, and the disciples were puzzled but not upset. But as soon as he states that one of them is going to betray him they get terribly upset. They begin to be sorrowful. Is it not astonishing that they are not sorry for him? There is no word of their sorrow about the cross right until this point, but as soon as he tells them that one of them is going to be involved, that is when they immediately begin to ask, "Surely not I, Lord?" One could put two interpretations on that phrase. If you were going to be kind and generous to the apostles you would say that each of them was prepared to examine his own heart. If you were to be more realistic, I think each of them knew perfectly well that they were capable of doing it. Immediately, they all wanted to be let off the hook quickly. They wanted Jesus to say, "No, it's not you," but he did not say that to any of them – he left them thinking that way. He said that it was someone who had dipped his hand in the dish with him. Judas asked "Is it I, Lord?", to which Jesus replied, "You have said so."

Fancy Judas being able to go through with that. Judas must have had a heart of granite by this time. His feelings must have been so scarred that they were dead. But he took the bread. That one was fully responsible for his act – we must not start blaming predestination or anything – and Jesus said of that one that it would have been better for that man if he had not been born. Jesus, knowing all that, knowing that the disciples would all run away, knowing that there was not one of them he could trust during the next twenty-four hours, took bread and broke it, and he took the cup and made them drink.

The communion service is so full of meaning. This was the new covenant – the old one had been sealed in blood in the broken body of a lamb and in the shed blood of the lamb. Now a new covenant was to be sealed, a new relationship between God and men sealed in the body and blood of Jesus.

Jesus says, "I will not drink of this fruit of the vine from now on until that day when I drink it new with you in my Father's Kingdom." So, the Lord's Supper or communion looks back to the upper room and forward to heaven, back to the Last Supper and forward to the wedding breakfast, and it links the two meals.

They go to the Mount of Olives, and Jesus foretells his death again, and he adds to it the fact that when he is killed they will stumble. Peter, voluble as ever, comes out with a most incredible slur on the other eleven, declaring in front of them (and they would not have liked him for this): "Even if all are made to stumble because of you, I will never be made to stumble." He is told that he would disown Jesus three times. This betrayal would

Matthew Chapter 26

be worse than the others – they were just going to run, but Peter would swear and deny knowing him. Peter has been remembered for what he did that night more than the others.

Jesus says to them: "But after I have been raised, I will go before you to Galilee" Galilee is so lovely compared to the hot, noisy, smelly streets of Jerusalem, which enables us to understand how their hearts would have leapt. To get back to the good old days in Galilee, back to the sunshine, the lake and the open air, without these scheming enemies in back streets and in the shadows. They would have a new start afterwards and, of course, Jesus did what he said, though they did not believe it yet.

The scene switches to the Garden of Gethsemane. They are going to spend the night on the Mount of Olives, and Judas has known this – he has informed the chief priests of their opportunity to arrest Jesus. There is a delay of about two hours while they make preparations for the arrest and the trial, but soon they will be coming. Our Lord's time is now limited to just an hour or two. They go into a garden and Jesus wants to make sure that he has time and quietness to pray, so he asks the first few disciples to stay at the gate. He tells Peter, James and John to come a bit nearer; then he goes a little further still – two lines of defence to secure his prayer time. Luke tells us that Jesus now begins to sweat drops of blood. The words used in the Bible indicate the most terrible anguish of spirit, something that he just could not face. It was not death from which he shrank. What was it? It was worse than death. What could be worse than death?

Twenty times in the Bible the word "cup" is used metaphorically – not a literal, physical cup, but some experience that a person has to go through. It is expressed in terms of a cup that they must drink. Out of those twenty times, on seventeen of the occasions it is a dreadful cup to drink, the cup of God's anger against sin and an experience of being cut off from him. All through the scriptures this is what the cup means when it is used in a metaphorical sense. Do you realise that Jesus had never been separated from his Father? I know that he had left heaven, but he was still with his Father. He could talk to him at any time. He was always in direct communication with his Father. He had never known what it was to be away from God. We who have been estranged from God to a degree cannot understand what it would be like for Jesus to have been in perfect communion with his Father and to face not having that. I do not think we can realise what it would have been like. I do not think that anybody can fully realise what hell will be like because there is no hell on Earth. I have heard so many people say you make your own hell, and hell is what you go through on Earth – but nobody has been in hell yet, because nobody is completely cut off from God yet. But Jesus knew that if he was going to drink this cup what it would mean would be that for the first time in all eternity Father and Son would be separated. "O my Father, if it is possible, let this cup pass from me; nevertheless, not as I will, but as you will."

Within hours he was going to cry out, "My God, my God, why have you forsaken me?" He was drinking the cup when he cried that. That is what hell is like – to be forsaken by God – and it is dark, thirst-inducing and a place of loneliness. You will understand the sufferings of Christ when you realise that on the cross for those few hours the Son of God was in the hell of experiencing separation from the Father. That is why he shrank. Three times he fought this battle, and each time he came back to the disciples and they were asleep. If you have ever taken part in an all-night prayer meeting you will know the truth of the words: the spirit is willing but the flesh is weak. You would love to see it through, but by about two in the morning you are beginning to feel heavy, and then you can get your second wind.

Now comes the contrast. There were two gardens – the Garden of Eden and the Garden of Gethsemane: the first a garden of disobedience from which a disobedient man went out to die for his sins; and, here, the Garden of Gethsemane, a garden of

Matthew Chapter 26

obedience from which one man went out to die for everybody else's sins. Can you see the connection?

Then comes Judas. I do not know how Judas could do it except I know that I could, and I suppose you could too. He used a token of the utmost affection, a kiss. Our Lord must have been horrified at this. How could Judas betray him in that way? Could he not just have pointed? How could he use a symbol of affection and friendship to do such a dastardly act? So low can a man sink that tokens become the opposite of that which they were meant to express.

The disciples forsook Jesus and fled. When it came to the decisive moment when they could either stay or run and save their lives, they all ran, and so would we. Not one of them was man enough to stay, and nor would we have been. This is human nature; the spirit is willing but the flesh is terribly weak, and self-preservation took over in that moment.

Our Lord had two trials, a Jewish and a Roman one, and both of them were rigged. Both of them were rank injustice. Fifteen things about the Jewish trial before the priests were illegal:

1. Jesus was arrested without a charge being made. Even in those days if anyone was arrested they had to be told at the time why they were being arrested, but no charge was laid against Jesus.

2. The arrest was organised by his judges, who thus became accomplices to the arrest.

3. The trial was held at an illegal time. Such trials had to be held during daylight hours and this one was held at night.

4. It was held in someone's home, which was an illegal place to hold it. It should have been held in the public law courts.

5. The trial began without a charge.

6. The witnesses for the prosecution had no consistent story, so there was no case.

7. The witnesses who disagreed with each other were not punished for perjury, and the prisoner was not released as he should have been when the witnesses did not agree.

8. The judge became a witness for the prosecution and therefore partial.
9. The judge asked a leading question of the prisoner.
10. The judge condemned him on his own confession.
11. He called no witnesses for the defence and made no examination of our Lord's claim.
12. He condemned the prisoner for speaking the truth by calling him a liar.
13. No vote was taken from the members.
14. A full quorum of the council was not present.
15. The execution was organised for the same day, not allowing the normal time for a legal appeal to be made against the sentence.

This was judicial murder. The one thing that I would draw from this is that the priests were desperate men. Desperate men do dreadful things, and they were doing dreadful things to our Lord and Saviour Jesus Christ.

Let me underline our Lord's words on which they incriminated him. The high priest asked a direct question: "Tell us if you are the Christ, the Son of God". The reply was an astonishing one: *"It is as you said...."*

The high priest never stopped to ask whether it was true. For a man to have said this was seen as being blasphemous, the worst crime in the Jewish book. They rushed through toward the execution. Jesus added, "Nevertheless I say to you, hereafter you will see the Son of Man sitting at the right hand of the power, and coming on the clouds of heaven." He was claiming to be the fulfilment of one of the predictions in Daniel.

The next incident takes place out in the courtyard: Peter's denial. It is so human. You and I have done exactly the same thing in school, in the office. There has been an opportunity when we could have said openly that we belong to Jesus and we flunked it, so let us not throw stones at poor old Peter. But let us notice certain things.

Firstly, at least he got as far as the courtyard, which the others did not. I am not trying to whitewash him; I am just trying to put it in balance and remind you that at least he followed and at least he was there. But when it came to the push, he could not go through with it.

Secondly, he did deny Jesus. Both his face and his speech gave him away, and our face and our speech should give away that we belong to Jesus.

Thirdly, he did weep. It broke this man's heart. Judas could not have wept, except for himself, but Peter wept. It is all in that word. There is something very cleansing about tears, especially when a man weeps over something he has done.

Fourthly, Peter himself must have told this story or we would not have it recorded. So, the man who did this was the man who wanted us to know about it, which tells us of his humility. He wanted to encourage us by telling us that he failed and that he let the Lord down, and that the Lord picked him up again, as we learn elsewhere.

26
ROMAN TRIAL AND EXECUTION

Read Matthew 27

We turn to the Roman trial. It is now six o'clock in the morning. Peter had denied Christ at three in the morning. At three o'clock every morning a Roman bugler blew his trumpet. It was the changing of the guard, the end of the first watch of the day (from midnight until three). And it is interesting that the bugle blown at three o'clock was called the "cock crow". It may be that this was what our Lord was referring to.

Pilate has had to be dragged from his bed early, and the trial is now shifting from a religious to a political one, and the charges have been changed. The Jews condemned Jesus for blasphemy, but now when they come to Pilate, they indicate that it is a political crime, not a religious one. Claiming to be the king would have been seen as a challenge to Roman authority. See how they twist the truth again and again, changing the charge on which Jesus is tried. Pilate would not have been interested in blasphemy, so they presented a political charge.

Pilate tried a number of things to get out of this dilemma and evade what they were trying to get him to do. At least he tried.

First, he demanded that the case be re-opened and re-tried, and he demanded to know the charge. He was not going to take their word for it.

Secondly, he could have taken the easy way out and simply rubber-stamped their decision, but instead he examined the prisoner himself, by a direct question – again it was a leading question. Pilate asked, "Are you the king of the Jews?" and Jesus simply replied, "It is as you say." In other words, they should not be asking him, they should be examining the evidence. You do not say to a defendant, "Did you do this? Right, you are condemned." Even if he pleads guilty you must examine the evidence.

Thirdly, Pilate did give Jesus a chance to defend himself, which the others had not done. But our Lord would not defend himself.

Fourthly, Pilate had a brainwave. At every Feast when there were so many hundreds of thousands of Jews in Jerusalem, it was a very tense situation. To keep the crowd happy, he always used to give them a sop or favour at this time, and agreed to set loose from the prison any prisoner they named, and it kept them reasonably happy. So here was a ready-made prisoner to hand back to them. They were not having any of that because they wanted another man, Barabbas, who was a political resistance leader, an insurrectionist. The crowd had welcomed Jesus on Palm Sunday, thinking he was going to fight for them and set them free. They are so disappointed with Jesus now because instead of going to tackle the Roman garrison he simply cleansed the temple. Pilate could not escape that way.

Fifthly, he tried to stand there on the steps of his house and ask them why. What crime had Jesus committed? But they shouted all the louder, "Let him be crucified!"

Sixthly, he decided to have Jesus flogged to within an inch of his life. That was a very naughty thing for Pilate to do. He had no right to condemn an innocent man to a flogging like that. Again, he was trying to give them a sop to buy them off. But they were not going to let him off. Whipping Jesus was not enough for them, and they demanded that he be crucified.

In handing over Jesus to be crucified Pilate ensured that for two thousand years at least his name would be linked with the death of Jesus. For wherever Christians have recited the Creed they have included one man apart from Jesus, and it is Pilate: "He suffered under Pontius Pilate".

Matthew Chapter 27

Many people ask, "How could Pilate have come to do such a terrible thing?" The real problem, however, is precisely the opposite: how was it that Pilate ever tried to get out of it? Why do I say that? Because of Pilate's history. He started life as a slave. He was the first slave ever to be a Roman governor and he was the last, and he was no good at the job. This was a man with a petty mind, a bully. When he came to the Holy Land in AD 26, he did certain things that were the blunders of a bully. For example, he set up a Roman eagle in the temple and caused such a riot that he ended up ordering soldiers to go in dressed in civilian clothes with their swords under their cloaks and kill the rioters. We are told that the blood of Galileans mingled with sacrifices in the temple. That was one major blunder.

Another time, he was building a water supply into Jerusalem, an aqueduct from the pools of Hebron. You can still see it today – a wonderful construction. It cost a lot of money, and Pilate was very short of money, so he thought about how they were getting good collections at the temple at that time, and he decided to borrow a bit from the treasury, only he forgot to tell them that he had borrowed it, and it started another riot. Again, he sent Roman soldiers in among the rioters with swords inside cloaks and killed the rioters – again, the act of a bully.

Word of these two blunders had got back to Rome and Caesar sent a warning letter to Pilate. One more blunder like that and he would be finished. Pilate knew that if he were to cause another riot among the Jews, that would be the end of Pontius Pilate the Governor. So, the mystery is not why he let them crucify Christ – you would have expected that, knowing his background – the mystery is why he tried to stop it. The reason was that his wife had a dream, and Romans were superstitious, setting great store by dreams. We learn that his wife sent him a warning: "Have nothing to do with that just man, for I have suffered many things today in a dream because of him" (27:19). We can see Pilate's dilemma – caught between Caesar and his wife; caught between the Romans and the Jews; caught in this dilemma: if I let Jesus go it will cause a riot; if I don't, I will have betrayed justice, and that dream will certainly bring disaster to me. Disaster faced him both ways, and Pilate, caught in that dilemma, did what every one of us would have done in such a dilemma and tried desperately to save his own skin. Pilate was a man caught between his past and his future. We have been caught like that, and we have behaved like this – certainly without such far-reaching consequences, but have we not done this? It is instinctive in us to behave this way.

It was not Jesus who was on trial that morning. The people who were really on trial were Annas and Caiaphas, and Herod, and the soldiers who spat on Jesus, and Pontius Pilate and his wife, and Caesar and everybody else. It seems to me, as I look at this trial, that Jesus stands there as Judge and that all the others were on trial that day. The other thing that strikes me is if anyone ever suffered for the sins of others it was Jesus. You can see the sin even of Peter as well as the sin of Pilate and the high priest, and all that sin seems to come onto him so that the one who suffers for their envy, their cowardice, their cruelty is Jesus, and so he is led away to be crucified.

Two things strike me about this part of the account. One is the restraint of the writer. You could paint a terrible picture of crucifixion, you could play on the emotions, you could really touch the feelings, and yet it is stated in simple fact. There is no attempt to move our feelings, and only the facts are presented to us. So, I do not want to lead you to pity Jesus, nor to dwell on all the gory details. I am going to give you some of those to try to help it to be fresh to you, but not in any way to play on your feelings.

The other thing that strikes me is the restraint of Jesus. I say it reverently, but he could have blasted them off the face of the Earth. They spat at him, but with one word he could have just blasted them to eternity, and he was so restrained, he did not lift a finger against them. Let us just go through the five things they did to him.

Matthew Chapter 27

They scourged him. This was totally unnecessary. A man who was crucified was never made to suffer beforehand – this was totally wrong, but Pilate did it and allowed it. The scourge was a terrible thing. It was a long leather thong with pieces of bone and metal fastened to it at intervals. A man who was flogged with that not only had his back torn to ribbons but he could be blinded very easily, he could be paralysed, or even killed, by a flogging. It explains why Jesus could not carry his cross more than a few hundred yards; he must have been half dead before he ever set out on that journey.

I remember a preacher once saying something which I found to be a remarkable insight. He pointed out that in all the sacrifices of the Old Testament, in all the hundreds and thousands of lambs that had been killed up to that point, not one had been made to suffer – a quick, clean cut with a knife and it was all over; not one lamb offered to God as a sacrifice for sins had ever been tortured first. But when the Lamb of God came, men added to the sufferings that God had ordained for him. God did not ordain this scourging – man added that – and we see that something of the suffering of Jesus was added by the cruelty and malice of human nature.

They also mocked him. It was a bit of barrack room buffoonery and they dressed him up. They took his clothes off him, they plaited that crown of thorns, they put a purple robe on him, and they said, "Hail, king of the Jews!" Still to this day in the place where they did it, you can see scratched on the floor the games of the soldiers, and one of the games they played was "Mock King". They would cast lots and one of their number would be chosen as "king", and they would dress him up and make him "king" for the day and bow down to him and take orders from him. They decided, this day, to laugh at Jesus. I remember going to see a lady who had been offended because of something that happened in church. Somebody had said or done something to her and off she went, she was never going to that church again, and so on. She told me the whole story in detail even though it had happened many years ago. I asked, "Did they spit at you?" And she replied, "I should think not." I said, "Well, they did spit at Jesus and he said, 'Forgive them, for they know not what they do.'" They spat on the Lord of Glory, they mocked him, the Son of God who made the universe.

They marched Jesus through the streets and made an exhibition of him. Picture the scene. The crime was written on a board, and a soldier walked in front carrying the board so that everybody might learn the lesson of Roman justice. Pilate had wondered what to write on this board because he knew that Jesus was going to be led through the streets and the people would want to know why he was being crucified. So, he wrote down in language that everybody could understand – the last burst of courage he ever showed – THIS IS JESUS THE KING OF THE JEWS. So, in spite of Jewish protests Pilate's board was carried. Then behind the board came a ring of soldiers, and in the middle of the ring was the prisoner, carrying the heavy wooden beam that was to be the crosspiece of the cross. Jesus could not even carry it.

They did not go straight from Pilate's house to the place of crucifixion. They used to go round and round the town, making the procession as long as possible so that everybody might learn their lesson and never do anything against Roman law. A short way round this tortuous route Jesus fell, and the Roman centurion (Regimental Sergeant Major would be the equivalent rank) was in a dilemma. No Roman would carry a cross because it was beneath his dignity. He dared not ask a Jew to carry the cross because that would render him unclean for the Passover the next day and would start a riot. What was he to do? He picked on a man because of the colour of his skin, to carry the load. He got hold of Simon and made him carry the beam. It was an African who carried the cross of Jesus up to Golgotha. Reading between the lines in the rest of the New Testament, I can tell you what happened to that man. As he carried that heavy cross,

Matthew Chapter 27

he saw Jesus, his flesh torn to ribbons, staggering along in front, and he must have wondered who it was. Becoming increasingly interested in him he began to ask questions, and he became a leading Christian in the first Gentile church at Antioch. The first African became a Christian because on this day he had to think about the cross of Christ.

Then they crucified Jesus. They came to the hill called Golgotha, which does not mean the face of the skull but rather the cranium, the dome. As it happens there is a hill outside the city wall where you can see the sunken hollows of the eyes, the nose and the mouth of a skull carved out by the wind and the erosion of centuries in the cliff. But on that day, they came to the top of it which they called the dome, the "brow" of the hill, so we use the same word. There they crucified him.

They gave him sour wine to get him drunk and to deaden his sensitivity a bit. He would not take it. Why not? Partly because he was going to go through with it all, and partly because of what he had said the previous night. He is keeping to his word. It had myrrh in it, which would have helped to deaden the pain, but he did not take it. If he had taken it, we should never have had the wonderful words from the cross that came; he would have been too drunk to give them. It was normal to make a criminal drunk to help him through the dreadful pain.

They took his clothes off him. By the way, in spite of every picture you have ever seen, a person crucified was naked; it was part of the public shame. Then they gambled for his clothes. It was part of the execution party's right that they could have anything that the prisoner had on him at the time of execution. They did not want to split his clothes so they cast lots for them. If ever gambling was condemned it is there. Six feet below the cross they gambled, and they missed the most important thing that was happening in the universe. They drove the nails through him at nine o'clock in the morning. They pinned the board above his head, the board they had carried through the streets, bearing the words "THE KING OF THE JEWS". They put criminals on either side – the last jest. Hundreds of years before this, the Prophet Isaiah had said, "He poured out his life unto death, and was numbered with the transgressors. For he bore the sin of many, and made intercession for the transgressors." That night as the Regimental Sergeant Major filled up the day book he would write down: 9 a.m. – three criminals executed. And somewhere in a Roman record that may be lost now, Jesus was "numbered" with transgressors.

Then came the reviling. You would think they had done enough to him, wouldn't you? You would think that they had done all they could do. But no, they had to add to all the pain and the suffering their mockery. The passers-by reviled him.

At midday, when the sun should have been so bright that there were no shadows on the ground, when the sun should have been overhead, it was as dark as midnight. It was not just a human conflict for the powers of darkness were there. But the reason the sky went dark was that God is light and God had gone. "My God, my God, why have you forsaken me?" God is light, and where God is there is light. There had been a star in the sky at Jesus' birth, and when he comes back again there will be lightning in the sky from east to west, but now the sky went absolutely black.

This was the first time in all eternity that Jesus and his Father had been away from each other. If that is a sorrowful experience for a little child, think what it must have been to the eternal Son of God – to be separated from his Father. Then there was Jesus' final cry. It was finished.

When Jesus' time on the cross was finished it was only just the beginning. He had done all that he came to do, and the effects of it would now begin. He expired at three o'clock, and in fact he would not have been expected to die then, even though he was in a very weak physical condition. A man usually took two to seven days to die on a cross. If they wanted to hurry the death, they broke the legs with a spear so that the one crucified then suffocated because they could not support their own weight to breathe. When they came to do this to Jesus, he was dead. Jesus chose to die; Jesus decided to die; he had done it – it was finished, there was nothing more to do, and it was Jesus who laid down his life. He had said that no one would take his life from him, he would lay it down of himself. If he had not laid it down, he would have survived perhaps two or three days longer, except that they would probably have hastened his death before the Passover. He died at three o'clock, at the very moment when thousands of lambs were being killed for the Passover.

The next thing that happened was that the screen divided. In the heart of the temple was a huge, beautiful curtain maybe forty feet high, embroidered all over, keeping people out of the holy place where God lived. The moment Jesus died it was ripped in two from the top to the bottom. It was so high that no man could have done that. Man would have ripped it from the bottom to the top – this was God saying that it was finished. The temple, priests, vestments, altars, incense, sacrifices – all that is finished. No Christian needs priests, temples, sacrifices. God has ripped them out. When they looked in, there was nothing there. God was no longer to be found in a temple made with hands – he had gone.

The tough centurion, when he saw how Jesus died, how he breathed his last, felt blood on his hands. He said, "Truly, this was the Son of God!" You can see him turning to the other soldiers in the execution party with the realisation that they had just killed the Son of God. A pagan Roman was the first to realise who was hanging on the cross that day. The women were last at the cross. Finally, they went too.

A man who was a secret believer who really believed that Jesus was right but had not dared to say so, now that he was dead took courage and went to Pilate. He could not bear to think of Jesus' body being left on the cross for the vultures or thrown out with rubbish, and he came right out and boldly approached Pilate to ask for the body so that he could give Jesus a proper burial.

Here was Joseph of Arimathea, a man who until this moment had been afraid to stand for Jesus, afraid to acknowledge that he really thought he was right, a man who had a lot to lose by giving him this burial, a man who was part of the council, a man who had not consented to the death of Jesus, who even if he had not consented did nothing to protest – this man at last came out. He was trying to make up for the fact that he did not openly accept Christ when he believed in him. It seemed too late, but Joseph was to find out it was not. The tragedy is that there are many who will one day say, "He was right." In fact, everybody will one day acknowledge that Jesus is the Lord; one day it will be popular to say that Jesus is Lord. It is wonderful when people can get over their inhibitions and say: "I belong to him now; I believe in him now, whatever it costs."

So, they buried Jesus, laying the body in the tomb. But if that was the end of the story, we would have to close our churches now. If this were all we had to celebrate, wouldn't it be terrible? It would have finished in utter gloom and tragedy, ending in a grave – the death of all our hopes and all our dreams, and with the disciples creeping away, shattered men. If that were the end of the story there would be nothing left. It would mean that all our hopes for the future would be dashed by death. It would mean that however wonderful Jesus' teaching may be, it would be impracticable and idealistic and it would not work in this world. It would mean that Jesus was deluded. But that is not the end of the story. Even while we were yet sinners Christ died for us and he went through all this for each one of us as if we were the only person in the world.

27
RESURRECTION

Note: First read Matthew 7:62 because it describes what happened the previous day (the day after Jesus died) then read Matthew 28.

In the 1920s, two Oxford men, Lord Littleton and Gilbert West, decided to spend an entire summer holiday studying the records of the resurrection with a view to proving that Jesus never rose from the dead. Separately they went into the matter in depth. When they met, they embarrassed each other by having to admit that the evidence had convinced them that Jesus rose from the dead. They published a book, a typical long-winded title of that period: *Observations on the History and Evidences of the Resurrection of Jesus Christ*. About ten years later, a young man called Frank Morrison, who was studying law, decided to do exactly the same thing, realising that if you could once prove that Jesus was in a grave somewhere, Christianity as a religion would collapse. So, he examined the evidence, started writing his book to prove that Jesus was dead, and finished up by having to write a totally different book: *Who Moved the Stone?* Morrison, too, was convinced that Jesus is alive.

I heard Professor of Modern History in Cambridge Herbert Butterfield say that the resurrection narratives convinced him also of the historical accuracy of those who have given us the story of the resurrection.

Dr Arnold of Rugby was also convinced by a study of the stories of the resurrection that Jesus Christ is alive.

If a person does not believe that Jesus is alive, there is only one reason for that: they want to believe that he is dead. They cannot have studied the evidence; they cannot have studied the narratives of those who were there at the time. One of the most striking features of the stories of the resurrection in our Bible is that there are discrepancies between the accounts of Matthew, Mark, Luke and John. It is those very discrepancies which convince us of the truth. If men are making up a story, if they are concocting an alibi, one thing that marks out such an invention is the way in which their stories agree in every detail. Any detective, any magistrate, any judge, any jury will tell you this. But when you study the four Gospels, the very kind of discrepancy that occurs when you have different people witnessing the same sequence of events occurs.

J.B. Phillips, who made a translation of the New Testament into English, produced a book entitled *Ring of Truth* and in it he says that, as he translated these stories, every one of them had the ring of truth in it. Real people, real reactions, real events – he too was convinced.

These discrepancies are not contradictions. When looked at closely, they fit together into a sequence of events which you can reconstruct. The kind of discrepancy is this. Luke says that Peter ran to the tomb. The Gospel of John says that Peter and John ran to the tomb. There is a discrepancy there but not a contradiction. It is clear that both statements are true but the ring of truth comes in that one person noticed Peter and someone else knew that there were two. That is the kind of "discrepancy" that if this story had been invented would not have been included.

Another one is that Mark and Matthew say that when the women came to the tomb a shining angel spoke to them. When Luke recorded these events, he says two shining angels came. Discrepancy yes, but naturally one of those two would be the spokesman. Luke mentions both, and Matthew and Mark mention the one who spoke. There is not a contradiction there but there is the kind of discrepancy that true witnesses would record. So, as we read these accounts the thing that hits us again and again is that this is straight history. These things actually happened, and the way the people behaved is the way that we would have behaved in the circumstances.

Have you ever seen what you think is a ghost? Have you ever confronted a visitor from the supernatural world? If you have, then I bet you were as afraid as these people were. You would have behaved just like those women.

If some women came to you in an excited condition and said they had just been to the cemetery and they had seen an open grave and had seen somebody who had walked out of the grave, would you say, "I believe you, thanks for telling me"? No, you would be excited, maybe overwrought; that is how the men behaved here.

We are reading about real facts. Our faith is squarely based on history. I am so glad that it is because unlike every other sacred book in the world, the Bible is simply a string of historical facts – things that actually happened. We do not follow flights of philosophy; we do not let our fancy take us into the clouds of mysticism. We base our faith on what has happened in this world of ours; things that once done can never be undone. They put Jesus in the tomb and put a stone over it and sealed the stone and guarded the seal, but once Jesus was out of that tomb, they could never put him back into it. History cannot be unwritten.

Now we are going to look at two groups of people. First, we are going to look at the women and how they reacted. Then we are going to look at the men and how they reacted. The ladies had the honour of being the first to know that Jesus had risen. In a sense, that offsets and balances two other firsts for women. First, it was through a woman that sin entered the human race. It was through Eve, a woman, that the darkness of Satan first entered into human thinking and relationships. It is as if God wanted to do something appropriate to respond to that: it was through a woman that salvation first entered the human race. It was two women, Mary and Elizabeth, who first knew that the

Son of God was coming to earth, and subsequently that he had come. A woman brought salvation into the human race in the person of the Son of God; and it was to women first that the news of the resurrection was given – to the women who were there because they had plucked up enough courage to come and do something that needed to be done but which was distasteful and unpleasant to do.

I must mention the funeral customs in those days. I want you to understand how the women felt. When a person died, if they were to be given a funeral of honour, their body would be semi-embalmed. Special spices with aromatic and antiseptic qualities would be strapped to the body to counteract the natural process of decay and corruption that sets in so quickly, particularly in that climate. That process of decay really set in on the fourth day in a cool tomb there. Therefore, there was a limited time in which you could counteract that process and try to stop it or try to delay it or try to fill the grave with a sweet smell. So as soon as a person was dead, they would take forty yards of long linen bandage and anything up to a hundredweight of these sweet spices. They would wrap the body round and round, tipping in the spices as they went. It was a loving act, the final thing that you could do for someone.

When Jesus died, they had hastily wrapped the body but they only had three hours between Jesus' death and the beginning of the Passover. Jesus died at three o'clock in the afternoon and the Passover began at six, at sunset. In that time Joseph of Arimathea had to go to Pilate, persuade Pilate to release the body, take the body from the cross, carry it to the garden, wrap it up in spices, put it in the tomb, put the stone there and seal it. They had three hours in which to arrange the entire funeral and the job was not properly done.

I believe Jesus died on Wednesday afternoon at three o'clock. That is the only time that really fits everything said in the Bible, but I would not be too dogmatic. It might have been Thursday;

Matthew Chapter 7:62 and 28

I am almost sure it was not Friday. He was three days and three nights in the tomb according to the Jewish calendar. Yet by the Roman calendar he rose on the third day, which means that he rose sometime between six o'clock on the Saturday and midnight. It is difficult for us to get into the thinking of Jews whereby the day begins at six o'clock in the evening. So, any time after six o'clock on Saturday evening, Jesus could have been raised. We know he had risen long before dawn on Sunday. The grave had been empty long before the women got there, and they arrived before the sun was up, just at the first light of day, so some time between 6 p.m. and midnight.

The Sabbath that followed Jesus' death was a high Sabbath, a special holiday for Passover. That would have been followed by the weekly Sabbath, the Saturday. So, the women were kept from doing the job properly until first light on Sunday morning. It was the very earliest opportunity they had to do this. During the Passover you could not touch a dead body or you would be defiled. During the Sabbath you must do no work. So as soon as they could, they got out of bed early that morning and went to complete the embalming. They would only have just been in time.

Do you realise that by this time rigor mortis would have set in, and the task of wrapping those bandages around the body would have been very difficult? Do you realise that, having had to wait that long, the process of decay would have begun? Those dear women loved the Lord so much that they were prepared to come even while it was just the beginning of the day and still dark, and to come to an eerie place, without men, and to come with spices and be prepared to tackle that job. What courage and what love! That is what they did, and because of that they became the first to know that Jesus was not there.

You can understand that their nerves would have been in a state of tension. They would already have been pulling themselves together to do the job. They would have been wondering what they would find in there. No wonder then that they were perplexed and puzzled to find things totally different – to find the stone which must have weighed many hundredweight pushed aside by the angel of the Lord. The stone probably weighed a tonne and a quarter – that is the average weight of these stones that you can still find in the Middle East. Seeing that rolled away and going in and finding the body gone, on top of the tension in them that had been building up to do this thing – to find all that! They were now thrown off balance. They were bewildered, their minds had come to a full stop, and they did not know where to go next.

Do you know that is usually what God does just before he is going to show you something wonderful? He brings your plans to a full stop, he throws you into a turmoil; he brings you into a place where you don't know where to go next, and that is a lovely place to be. It is a place where God is going to step in and say something new. To a lesser degree, we have all had experiences like this with the Lord. We have made plans to do something, we thought we were doing it for him, and we thought it was right to do it. We went ahead and somehow it all fizzled out, it all came to nothing. It seemed as if we had come to a dead end and we did not know where to go next.

There are people who do not even believe angels exist. There are people who don't realise that we are surrounded by myriads of intelligent beings other than human beings, and that they are watching what goes on here on earth. It is not childish to think about the angels guarding you while you sleep. The hosts of the Lord encamp around those who fear him. The angels are there. We should not think this universe is an empty place – that away from Earth there is no life. There is life throughout the universe. The skies are full. With angels and archangels, we praise God.

At point after point in crises in Jesus' life, the angels are there, helping and speaking, ministering in some way, doing something positive. They were there at Jesus' birth putting it right with Joseph, explaining to him what was happening, preparing Mary for this event, warning Joseph and Mary to take the little child down to Egypt. They were there with our Lord in the wilderness when he was tempted by Satan and desperately in need of succour. The wild beasts were around him and the devil was tempting him but the angels came and ministered to him. They were there when Jesus desperately needed company in Gethsemane. Jesus said to his disciples, "Will you stay here and watch and pray?" When he came back, they were all asleep and an angel appeared to him and strengthened him. When there is no one else to help you, remember the angels.

An angel was tidying up the grave. It was an angel who came and rolled that stone away. They were God's messengers releasing that tomb. The stone was rolled away, I believe, not to let Jesus out – for in his resurrection body he could pass through closed doors and through the very grave clothes – it was to let the world in. So, the angel rolled the stone away and sat on it. What a lovely picture of strength. Jesus had ten thousand angels as his personal bodyguards. It only took one of them to roll that stone away, and a couple of them came to meet the women; it was a frightening experience.

Those women were there at the grave because they were letting common sense dictate their action. Common sense says that when a person is dead, they are dead. Natural reason assumes that what happens naturally is normal. Therefore, the normal thing to do is to go to a cemetery if you want to find Jesus. But death is not the normal end, decay is not normal. Sickness is not normal. These things are invaders, intruders, abnormalities in God's world. He never intended people to be sick and to die. These things have come in with sin and spoiled our world, so in this world common sense can be mistaken. Common sense says it is not *natural* for dead people to rise. But I tell you, it is normal. There was one person who came to our world who lived a normal life, and his name was and is Jesus. He lived a normal life because he lived a good life, a pure life; he was God's Holy one. That is the life you were meant to live. When you are living a holy life, you are living normally, properly, you are living as God intended you to live. God has said in his Word that a person who lived a normal life would not see corruption (in Psalm 16). Let us never accept the state of the world as it is. Let us never accept sickness and death as inevitable natural events. Even the scientist has no biological explanation for death. Whilst the scientist can point to the immediate cause of a death, he cannot point to the ultimate cause: that it is not normal. You were not made to die, you were made to live. You were not made for sin; you were made for goodness.

The second reason why they came to the graveyard that morning was that they had forgotten the words of the Lord. The angel said to them, "He is not here; for he is risen, as he said."

Jesus had indeed told his disciples that he would be handed over to wicked men, and that he would be killed, and that he would rise on the third day. The Bible contains many predictions, and if you remember the words of the Lord you can be assured that its remaining predictions will happen. By engaging common sense alone, it is not possible for a person to believe in the resurrection. Common sense might say there will be a tomorrow and a tomorrow after that and a tomorrow after that. The Bible says it is going to come to an end, and the heaven and earth that we know will pass away. Are you going to believe the Word of the Lord? Common sense says that human nature will always be sinful, we will always be imperfect, no one is perfect and you cannot make bad people good. But the Word of the Lord says that if any man is in Christ, he is a new creation. These women were being reminded of what Jesus had predicted.

Then the appearances of the risen Lord began to happen, recorded from 28:9 onwards. Do you know that it is literally true that the evidence for the resurrection of Jesus is far stronger than the evidence for the existence of Julius Caesar? There are many more documents and far earlier documents about the resurrection than about the existence of Julius Caesar. Yet I never met anybody who did not believe that there was a man called Julius Caesar who once invaded this country.

You should know that Jesus is alive. I want to plead with anyone who does not know. The evidence is there – study the evidence. Read the record, listen to the testimony of those who have had supernatural experience of the Lord. But then you need to get away by yourself and think it through; let Jesus come into your life. I know it sounds crazy but you can meet today a man who died two thousand years ago. I know that common sense is all against it. But I want you to believe the Word of the Lord because that is how people meet Jesus – when, in this particular case, they leave what appears to be the common-sense approach behind and say, "If God says it, it is true. If Jesus is willing to come into my life, then I am going to ask him, and when I ask him, I will thank him for coming because he keeps his word. I am going to believe in his Word." When you believe in his Word, you find that he is real. You can say, "I serve a risen Saviour. He walks with me and talks with me." You will have a real relationship with him.

How gently these people were introduced to the risen Jesus. I suppose that Jesus could have stood outside that tomb and waited for them to come. I suppose that he could have come to them first thing on that morning but to most of them he did not come until the evening. Do you see that God gently leads people? He showed them the stone rolled away first, then the grave clothes, then that the body had gone. Then he sent them an angel, then they shared testimony, then the Lord Jesus appeared to Mary by herself, then to Peter by himself, then to two walking down the road to Emmaus, then to eleven, and then to five hundred at once. Do you see how gently it grew? The evidence, the testimony, the direct relationship with one, then two, then eleven, then five hundred, and that is how it happens today. Quietly, unnoticed, Jesus makes someone take the Bible and read the record and study the evidence. Then he introduces them to other Christians who testify of their relationship and what God has said to them. Bit by bit he prepares them and draws them until the great day comes when they meet Jesus. I think of a young man who got hold of a Bible and started reading it and then came and talked with me. I gave him my testimony and told him what I knew and had experienced. Then he went off, and two or three days later he said, "I was just walking down the High Street and I met Jesus." That is when it really means something.

I could spend a lot of time going through the evidence – it is very convincing. (Note: For more on this subject see the Addenda below.) You might agree intellectually that it is a sound case, but that would not make you a Christian. I and countless others could give you our testimony and that would not convince you either and it would not make you a Christian, even though you would say, "Well, I envy them their experience, it seems real to them." But one day you will meet Jesus. Then you will have no doubt about the resurrection. You will just say what a friend of mine said. He was a converted bookmaker in County Durham. Somebody said, "How do you know that Jesus is alive?" He said, "Well, I was talking to him only this morning!"

Thousands upon thousands of people every day come to know Jesus and move from the spiritual blindness where they could not see him to the stage of longing to go and tell people who do not know him.

In the period between the resurrection and the Ascension, the risen Jesus showed the disciples his body; he taught the meaning of scripture, and he promised his backing to those disciples. The message of Jesus' death and resurrection was to go out to the whole world. That is God's will and intention – that every nation on earth should have Christians in it; that every tribe on earth should hear the gospel, that every tongue should praise the Lord.

In 28:18, we are told of the universal authority of Jesus. He said: "All authority in heaven and on Earth has been given to me."

In 28:19–20, he gives the Great Commission:

"Go therefore and make disciples of all nations, baptising them in the name of the Father and of the Son and of the Holy Spirit..." and there is the instruction to teach what he has commanded and an assurance of his continuing presence: "...teaching them to observe all that I have commanded you; and lo, I am with you always, to the end of the age."

It can seem a frightening thing to go out as a witness to make disciples. We know what we have got to do as witnesses. A witness must not embellish; a witness must not say what is not true. A witness must stick to the facts. Witnesses must simply tell what they have seen and heard, and must pass on what they know to be fact. But who has believed our report? Who will listen to us? Who is convinced, unless God promises his backing? Unless the Lord works with us confirming the Word, nothing will happen. In order to spread the Word, you have to be clothed with power from on high.

Addenda

1. BETHLEHEM (2)

Read Matthew Chapter 2

Bethlehem is, I suppose, the most famous little town in the world. You would never have heard about it unless one day the baby Jesus had been born right there. We are now going to think about Bethlehem as though we were on a pilgrimage. As the shepherds said, "Let us go even to Bethlehem and see this thing which has come to pass which the Lord has made known to us." I want to take you to Bethlehem, but not as it is today – I want to take you way back beyond that.

Seventeen hundred years ago, Bethlehem was destroyed, razed to the ground by a Roman emperor called Hadrian, who at the same time was building the Roman wall in the north of England. About a hundred years (or a little more) after Hadrian, the emperor Constantine became a Christian. He had an ambition to go and visit the far corner of his empire, to see where Jesus lived and had been born. He took his aged mother, the empress Helena, on that pilgrimage to Bethlehem. When they got there, the place was absolutely ruined; there was nothing to be seen. The houses had been pulled down. So, they began to search the ruins, and all they could find was a little group of caves down in the ground, caves that had obviously been used by people to store things. Helena and Constantine decided that they would regard one of those caves as the stable where Jesus had been born. So they said, "This shall be the cave." Today you can go to the Church of the Nativity. You go into the large, old building with its terribly low doorway that makes you stoop almost double to get in – a low doorway to keep out marauding horsemen originally. But it makes you bow, and that is rather a nice thought, and then you go down into the crypt and down a flight of steps into the cave. There is a silver star set in the floor. It is surrounded by gaudy trappings, which I don't really think help worship at all. There is no ground for believing that this was where Jesus was born; it was just a cave. It was all that the Emperor Constantine and his mother Helena could find.

It is almost certain that Jesus was born in the open air. The Bible does not mention a stable and it does not mention a cave. These are the two things that legend has added. It only mentions a manger, and a manger was in the middle of the courtyard of an inn, open to the sky. The animals were tethered around it. So, it seems quite clear that Jesus was born not below ground in a cave but above ground, where the stars shone down, and in the middle of the courtyard. But there is that cave today, and thousands file through. They look at the silver star and they remember the birth of Jesus.

It is today a place of pilgrimage, and it is still a wonderful place to go. Even though you know the cave is not the actual site of the events, you know the place is. The town is built along a hillside, looking down into a valley, which is clearly a valley of vineyards, olives and sheep. You can see the shepherds with a little flock of sheep going through the valley. A way over further, you can see the wilderness of Judea and, fifteen miles away, you can see the great cleft in the Earth's crust, which is the Jordan Valley – far below the sea level of the Mediterranean, and down at the bottom you can see the Dead Sea, that amazing dead lake of salt water.

I have a table lamp carved by a carpenter in Bethlehem from two solid pieces of olive wood. It is a most beautiful carving, and it was a lovely present I received from a party of people that I took for a fortnight to the Holy Land. It depicts a date palm, and lying underneath is a shepherd lying down with his crook and two of his sheep. He is shown watching over his sheep by night. That tells you a number of things about Bethlehem. The interest in sheep is one, the interest in fruit trees is another.

Now this little town has a population of over 25,000 people, about five miles southwest of Jerusalem, on the top of the ridge of hills that runs north and south up Judea. This little town, 2,550 feet above sea level, is the place that God chose for his Son's coming. Why did he choose Bethlehem? What is the history of this little town? What led up to this?

Let us go back seventeen centuries before Christ, when the story of Bethlehem begins. It begins with a tragedy and with sadness. It begins with a couple, coming down the road towards Bethlehem, and the woman is soon to give birth. That is the very first mention in the Bible of Bethlehem. Is that not amazing? She did not make it. Within sight of Bethlehem, her labour pains started. By the side of the road, they managed to get a midwife, but it was there that she gave birth to a little boy – yet it was obvious that she was going to die, and she knew it. It was a painful and terrible birth. Her name was Rachel and her husband was Jacob. As she died, knowing that she was dying, she said, "Call my little boy Benoni," which means, "son of my sorrow". But Jacob could not bear that and after his wife died, he changed the boy's name to Benjamin. It was like the original name, but it means "son of the south; the journey to the south". Then, sorrowfully, he buried his wife, and put up a tomb.

I shall never forget seeing that tomb. The last time I saw it was just after the Six-Day War. The Israelis had been allowed through. They had got through to Rachel's tomb, and they had come to see it. As mentioned in the previous chapter, the stone was drenched with tears. That is the beginning of the story of Bethlehem. It is a story of tragedy.

From there right through to the day that another heavily pregnant mother came down the same road and reached Bethlehem and had her baby, there is a kaleidoscope of human experiences: sorrow, joy, meeting together, parting, tragedy and triumph, and I want to unfold that story for you. From a place of tragedy, it became a place of scandal. The name of this town was not Bethlehem at first. It was called Ephrathah, which means "the place of fruit". They grew dates, they grew vines, they grew olive trees, and it was a centre for fruit.

So, when Jacob made his journey to the little town, it was to Ephrathah, which the Bible says was later called Bethlehem, that he went. In the days of Joshua when Joshua led the people of Israel into the Promised Land, and they got this land for themselves, they renamed the towns. When they took over a town, they took away its pagan name, giving it a new name. So now they called it "The house of bread" and it became known as Bethlehem. They began to keep sheep there, and they began to develop the flocks for which Bethlehem later became famous.

Now, the interesting thing is that there were two villages they called Bethlehem: one in the south and one in Galilee in the north. There is one Bethlehem of which you have never heard, and the other which the whole world knows about. Both villages were about the same size, noted for the same thing, and there was Bethlehem of Galilee and Bethlehem of Judea. You had to add the second bit so that people knew which one you were talking about.

Let me draw the first lesson that I want to draw, which will come up again and again: the only things that will last for ever are those things that Jesus is associated with. Other towns and villages may be built and they will crumble; other achievements of human beings may be mighty in their day, but unless Jesus is there, they are forgotten; they fade. One day they are forgotten even by those with the longest memories, but not where Jesus is.

It became a place of scandal. During the days of the judges, they had no kings. They were ruled over by judges, and the ninth judge was Ibzan. He was a native of Bethlehem, and this little town gave the nation of Israel one of its first judges. But now come two very shameful stories. If you have a morbid curiosity, you can read all about them in Judges 19 and 20, but there are two very sad and sordid tales telling us that Bethlehem was no better and no worse than any other place. It had its rogues and here were two of them.

In Judges 18, we read first of all of a Levite priest who lived in Bethlehem. One day he went on a bit of a journey to have a look around Israel and a man said, "I'm looking for a private chaplain, and I'll offer you a lot of money if you'll become my private chaplain." This Levite, instead of saying, "God, where should I be minister?" was tempted by the money, and he became a private chaplain in a wealthy home elsewhere. A short time after that, some wandering people from the tribe of Dan were heading up north to break fresh territory (where in the twentieth century new kibbutzim were established, on the Syrian border).

These people of Dan came by this wealthy man's house, and they met the priest. They said, "Wouldn't you like a better job than you've got as a private chaplain? You could be chaplain to our whole tribe if you'd come with us. Bring this man's gods and come with us." So, he picked up all his paraphernalia, which didn't belong to him – his altar furniture – and he took it from his employer and ran away. His employer ran after the tribe of Dan and said, "Here, you've taken my altar. You've taken my priest." They said, "So what? We're more than you are, so you try and get him back if you can."

The Levite went off with them to the far north, to Dan, what is now Panias – or Caesarea Philippi – and they settled there. The priest, because he had been tempted by money, by status, by authority – who had allowed where he ministered to be decided by such matters – became the corrupting influence in the tribe of Dan. They built a magnificent temple, and the priest approved of building a golden calf. The tribe of Dan disappeared later because of that one priest for whom money and status were the decisive factors. He came from Bethlehem.

The next chapter tells us about another rather horrible story of a man who picked up a mistress from Bethlehem, a young woman. They called them concubines in those days, and he took her away. He went on his journey with this concubine from Bethlehem, and they came to Jerusalem which was not then a Jewish city, it was pagan. The man said, "We can't stay here the night, and the sun is going down. We mustn't stay in a pagan city, it is dangerous." They left the pagan city and went on to Gibeah. They went in and the men of Gibeah came, and they came in a threatening mood. They were going to harm this man. Now these were Jews and the man said, "All right, for my safety I'll give you my mistress," and he pushed her out of the door. They abused her all night. In the morning she lay dead on the doorstep. You probably know this story.

When the man discovered his concubine dead on the doorstep, he took her body, then with a knife cut it into twelve pieces, and he sent a piece to each of the twelve tribes, and he said, "This is what happened when I turned away from a pagan city because it might not be safe, and I came to the people of God." The Bible simply says: "Such a thing has never happened or been seen from the day that the people of Israel came up out of the land of Egypt until this day. Consider it. Take counsel and speak." It was a poor young woman from Bethlehem who was at the heart of that story.

You see, Bethlehem is not a story of a village in which everything was nice and happy. It is the story of the human race. That sort of thing would have made a great story for the Sunday newspapers. Indeed, it was a scandal throughout the land for a long time. This is Bethlehem, and it got a name for being a source of scandal, and the name got associated with human sin.

Step number three: it became a place of romance. One of the loveliest love stories in the whole Bible is linked forever with this little village of Bethlehem. It is the story of a woman's love for her mother-in-law. That is such a pleasant change from all the

Matthew Chapter 2

music hall jokes and all the things that are said about mothers-in-law. Incidentally, I had one of the sweetest in the world, so none of the jokes apply in my case.

This was about a girl called Ruth and this is how it all happened. There was a famine in Judea, and a woman and her husband in Bethlehem said, "Where can we go to get food for the children?" They had two boys. There was no food, and they heard that down through the wilderness, across the ford of the Jordan near Jericho, and up in the Moab hills there was food. So, they left Bethlehem, went down to the Dead Sea and up the Moab hills and beyond into what is now the land of Jordan. They found food, and their two boys grew up. Both boys married, and they married Moabite (Gentile) girls. One of them was Ruth. The mother-in-law was Naomi, the mother of the two boys. Then tragedy struck the family: Naomi's husband died; Ruth's husband died; Ruth's brother-in-law also died. One after the other, they had three funerals of their men. They were left, three women on their own. By this time, Naomi had heard that back in Bethlehem there was food, and she said to her two daughters-in-law, "I'm going back to my people, going back to my town. You stay here, marry other husbands, have families; you stay here among your people." One of her daughters-in-law said yes, she would, but the other said no. Here were her words: "Where you go, I will go. Where you lodge, I will lodge. Your people shall be my people. Your God shall be my God."

Ruth and Naomi, together, with that deep love between two bereaved women, came down to the Dead Sea and up the hills to Bethlehem again, and they got food. Ruth went out to glean the fields. You know the story, and she saw a relative of her husband – a man called Boaz. She gleaned in his field. He fell in love with her, and she fell in love with him. You can read this lovely story in the tiny little book of Ruth, one of the most difficult books of the Bible to find if you don't know where it is. It is right between Judges and Samuel. Four chapters, four pages, it is the story of how Boaz and Ruth fell in love with each other. Bethlehem became a place of great romance. It is a delightful story told with an eastern flavour. Ruth's approach to Boaz and Boaz's approach to Ruth – so delicate and so beautiful.

They became man and wife, and they had a son, and they had a grandson, and they had a great-grandson. The grandson's name was Jesse and the great-grandson's name was David. In every genealogy of our Lord, in all the family tables in Matthew 1 and Luke 3, you will see right there the name of a Gentile woman, Ruth, who so loved someone of the people of God that she said, "I want your God to be my God, and where you go I will go." Bethlehem became the place of this Moabite woman, and Jesus had Gentile blood in his veins as a result. Jesus was not a pure Jew; he had mixed blood and it is there in his family tree. But he was going to have royal blood too, because that great-grandson of Ruth and Boaz was a man called David.

Now we come to the fourth chapter in the Old Testament story of Bethlehem. It became a place of fame. It happened like this. Israel was being governed by a judge called Samuel, a wise old man, but his two sons were not – they were bad lads. They could obviously not take over.

Israel said, "We want a king. Everybody else has a king; why don't we? Please, can we have a king?"

Samuel said, "Well now, a king is a mixed blessing. God is your king; isn't he enough?"

"No, because we can't see him; we want a king we can see. We want a leader."

Samuel said, "All right. I'll get you one, but he won't be any good to you." They chose a man who looked the part: tall, strong, handsome – a big man. His name was Saul. They chose him from the little tribe of Benjamin, the tribe of the little boy who was born by the roadside on the road to Bethlehem, but he was no good.

God said, "Samuel, you will have to choose someone else."

"Where shall I find him?"

"Go to a little village called Bethlehem. Go to a farmer who has seven sons."

Samuel went, and there were six of the sons lined up – the eldest down to the second youngest. They were handsome, they were fair, they were strong, they were big, but God said, "No. You mustn't judge them by appearance."

Samuel asked Jesse, "Have you got any more boys here?"

"Yes, I've got one, but he's only a little lad, and he's out in the fields. He looks after the sheep." That was the lowest job of all, to go out and stay in the fields and watch sheep.

"Bring him," said Samuel, and when he saw him God said, "That's the king."

David became the greatest king, a man after God's own heart and a man after the people's own heart. They loved him. He was a man of the people, he was a fighter, he was a musician, but above all he was a human being. They understood him and he understood them. He had been through tough times as they had been through tough times, and he was a great king. Bethlehem forever afterwards became David's city, the royal town to which you looked for the great king.

That is why Bethlehem became a place of hope. There was a time later on when Bethlehem sank back into insignificance, because David took Jerusalem as his capital, taking it from the pagan Jebusites. Ever since, Jerusalem has been the royal city of Zion. Bethlehem faded into the background. But one day a prophet, Micah, said, "You, Bethlehem of Judea, you may be little. You may be the least among the rulers of Judah. You may be a tiny little community, but don't worry, there's a great big future for you, and that future is that out of you shall come a Ruler for the people Israel." It is a wonderful promise, quoted in Matthew 2.

I want to take the second lesson now from this study, namely: God chooses the small and the weak. He chooses places that nobody else would look at. God chooses people of whom other people might say, "Oh, he is only the shepherd boy." God did not choose that his Son should be born in a palace in Jerusalem but in a manger in little Bethlehem. That is the way God works.

Now the last thing in the Old Testament is that Bethlehem became a place of parting. A great big inn was built outside Bethlehem and we have the name of the innkeeper: Chimham. He saw that Bethlehem was a key town for travellers so he built a lodge there which became known as "The Inn", so large was it. It was the starting place for journeys to Egypt. We are told that when the Babylonians came to Jerusalem, the refugees fled to Egypt, and they stopped for their last night in their home country in the Inn of Chimham. You can read about it in the book of Jeremiah.

So, it became the place of parting, the place of separation. Jeremiah saw in the partings that took place there refugees going to a strange country. He saw there a little foretaste of a weeping that would come to that area and he spoke of "the voice of weeping and wailing in Ramah". It is a place of tears again. The whole cycle has come round from the place of sorrow; it has come back to the place of weeping and wailing in Ramah. There is an awful lot of sadness connected with Bethlehem.

We have seen the cycle of the Old Testament from sorrow to joy and fame and back to sorrow. It has gone the whole way round. Let us look now at the New Testament cycle. It begins in Matthew's Gospel, and Matthew 1 mentions Jacob, Rachel, Ruth, Jesse, David and Boaz. The people we have been thinking about are in Matthew 1. But now we start the cycle again. Once again, a man and his wife are coming down the road to Bethlehem and the wife is heavily pregnant. It is as if it is all happening all over again – a wonderful pattern of God in the Old and the New Testaments. They seem to correspond to each other again and again. This time, she makes it. Though she did not make it to a room or a house, she made it to the courtyard and camped with the others who could not get rooms in the inn. They camped inside the courtyard around the manger where the animals were tethered, under the clear sky. It was not December. We know, of course, that Jesus was not born in December. No shepherds watched their flocks by night in those cold months. It was around April, as far as we know – the spring; the time of new life, the time of birth. Jesus was born in Bethlehem of Judea. We love those words – they take us back.

He only just got there, but it was as the result of a decision made in an office, hundreds of miles to the west, when the Emperor Caesar Augustus said, "We must tax the people more efficiently." There is something strangely modern about this. There in that office, with his civil servants gathered around him, a decision made by the emperor got Joseph and Mary to Bethlehem just in time for the birth. Can you see that God can overrule even the civil service? God can overrule even the emperor. God can overrule all the machinery of man. God can overrule decisions and he could cause an emperor to make a decision in Rome that would accomplish his purpose in a little village near the borders of the empire. So, they came. God already had Joseph and Mary on his register but how wonderful it is to human beings that God, through the emperor, was going to see that human records, too, had it down in the books that Joseph and Mary came from the royal line of David. All overruled, God was 'stage-managing' the nativity events.

Think of the wonder of that year, which as we now know was 4 BC. There has been a mistake made with the Gregorian calendar, but that does not matter. The important thing is Bethlehem became a place that divided BC from AD. Bethlehem became the little village that broke history in two. Bethlehem became the pivot of world events because everything is going to hang on what happened at Bethlehem that day.

It is a place of worship and wonder. The angels look at a little village. The wise men from the east come to the village to look at a baby. It is the most amazing account, but it became a place of horror, a place of sorrow. The cycle went round again. King Herod was so angry; we need not go into the reasons why except that it was sheer jealousy, fear of losing his status, his position. He did something that I have never seen yet on a Christmas card, but it is part of the narrative. He foully murdered hundreds of little babies. It shows what the sin of man can do when God steps in. Even thirty-three years before the cross, here is the hatred of men trying to kill a little baby whom God has sent.

I have seen it depicted in some of the great paintings of the medieval and Renaissance artists. It was a theme that seemed to haunt them: the slaughter of the innocents, they invariably called their pictures. You can see them in the National Gallery in London, but the trouble is that at Christmas we want to be nice and emotional and sentimental. That is why many prefer carols without sermons and Christmas cards that are all holly and ivy and all the rest of it, but not the slaughter of the innocents. Yet Christians are not sentimental. We face the whole truth, and the whole truth is that Bethlehem became again a place of a voice weeping in Ramah, Rachel crying for her children. It became again a place of mothers mourning. It became a place where wailing was heard in every young household; it became a place of tragedy. Jesus got out just in time. His parents fled as refugees to Egypt as the result of a dream. So, I say that Jesus only just got into and out of Bethlehem. He was only there for a very short period, just long enough to belong to Bethlehem, and then he was gone. Bethlehem owes its fame to that very short period.

Now I come to the most amazing part of the story of Bethlehem. There are two amazing facts in the Gospels. One is that Jesus never visited Bethlehem. Have you ever noticed that? He went everywhere else. He went to Samaria; he went to Galilee; he went to Judea, Jericho, Jerusalem and Emmaus. He went round and round Jerusalem and Bethlehem was within sight all the time. He must have seen it many times. Was he not

Matthew Chapter 2

interested in going to see where he had been born? Wouldn't you be? If you had been born in a manger, wouldn't you want to go back and see it some time? But he never went back; never darkened the doors of Bethlehem, never healed anybody in Bethlehem, never preached in Bethlehem, and it was only just a few steps down the road from Jerusalem.

Even more remarkable is this: he never mentioned it. When I read a passage in John's Gospel, I was absolutely staggered. He was in Jerusalem and when he had finished preaching, it says: "When the Jews heard these words, some of the people said, 'This is really the Prophet,' and others said, 'This is the Christ,' but some said, 'But is the Christ to come from Galilee? Has not the scripture said that the Christ is descended from David and comes from Bethlehem, the village where David was?'" So, there was a division among the people over him. Yet he never said a word. All he would have needed to do was to say, "But I was born there. I am of the royal line." But he never did. The disciples, as far as we know, were never told that he was born in Bethlehem. So, everybody called him "Jesus of Nazareth" – where he had been brought up. Yet he wasn't. He was Jesus of Bethlehem.

Even when he was put to death as "Jesus of Nazareth, King of the Jews", still he did not say, "Look up your records; I am Jesus of Bethlehem, King of the Jews." Now why? Can you not see why? Jesus was not going to persuade anybody to believe in him unless they saw in him the Messiah. He was not going to argue them into belief. If they chose to call him "Jesus of Nazareth" he was not going to correct them. He wanted them to come to faith in him because of what he was, not because of where he was born. So, when they said, "He can't be the Messiah; he's from Nazareth," Jesus kept quiet. I am sure he never told his disciples so they didn't say, "You're quite wrong; he was born in Bethlehem." So, Bethlehem is not mentioned again. It fades out again into nothing.

That is the account of Bethlehem. Even on the cross they got his birthplace wrong because when a criminal was put to death, his birthplace had to be linked to his name. His address had to be put there from the Roman records to make sure they had got the right one. There are two more things I want to mention about Bethlehem. Here is a place of scandal, sorrow, romance, tragedy; an ordinary human place of human experiences and emotions, but it has become the place it is because Jesus was in that place. I do not know whether for you Christmas is a time of joy or sorrow, shame or romance. Allow Jesus to be at the centre of it. Let Jesus come in. Whether it is sorrow or joy; whether you have a wonderful time or not such a good time, let Jesus come.

The other thing is this: the sheep of Bethlehem were rather special, not because they were a different breed but for the purpose for which they were bred. The sheep of Bethlehem were not bred for wool and they were not bred for mutton. The sheep of Bethlehem were bred for sacrifice. We now know that there was an arrangement between the temple at Jerusalem, five miles away, and the shepherds at Bethlehem, that the sheep they prepared would shed their blood on the altar in the temple. Those who came to see Jesus were looking at the Lamb of God, the Lamb prepared in Bethlehem for slaughter in Jerusalem as a sacrifice for sin.

For, you see, it is no use going to Bethlehem today if you want to find Jesus. People do go looking for an experience and maybe God graciously gives them that, but Jesus is not there. I came across a lovely little poem about Bethlehem:

We went to Bethlehem but found the babe was gone,
The manger empty and alone.
And "Whither has He fled?"
"To Calvary," they said. "To suffer in our stead."
We went to Calvary but found the Sufferer gone,
the place all dark and lone.

"Whither?" we asked,
"Into the heavens," they said.
"Up to the throne for us to intercede."

So then to heaven we'll go, the babe is not below.

Addenda

2. THE PROBLEM OF EVIL (2)

Read Matthew Chapter 13

There was a woman in Vancouver who invited her neighbours to a Tupperware party and about eight or ten of them came and she put out all the containers. There were a couple of neighbours who came who were not interested at all. They had just come to gossip with their friends so they just picked up the Tupperware stuff and put it down and ignored it. There were a couple of others who were quite interested and they looked at it and they said, "We'd love to have it," but then they remembered that their husbands had ordered them not to spend any more money on that kind of thing. So, they said, "If we get these there'll be trouble so we'd better leave it this time." There were another couple of housewives there, neighbours, who looked at the containers and said, "Those would be jolly useful but really our cupboards are pretty full already and we don't have much room for them," but they liked them. But they soon started talking about other things they wanted to buy – dresses, hats, other things for the kitchen – and they didn't buy anything ultimately. But there were three of this lady's neighbours who actually were interested enough to buy. One spent $10, another $15, another $25. And if you're not hard of hearing, just you listen.

Do you realise that if you had been in Galilee in Jesus' day, that is about all you would have got from him? Do you seriously realise that is how he talked? When he was teaching the crowd, that was his teaching. He did not mention God, he did not quote from the Bible; he told little stories from everyday life and he didn't even add a moral at the end. As a little child said about her minister, "I like our minister when he talks to us; he has no morals." But Jesus did not mention God and he did not quote the scriptures and he had no morals to tell; he just told a little everyday event and said, "If you're not hard of hearing, then listen." And that was all they got.

And it was his disciples who later said, "Tell us what that was all that about. We don't understand. Explain it to us." But he spoke nothing but parables to the crowds – nothing but those little stories. That was all he did. Now, I am writing on a chapter I have never written on before, but it is a group of parables about the kingdom and I believe somewhere in it God has a very direct message for churches. But since it is parables, you might miss it and there is a sense in which everything depends on the hearer when you are telling parables. And some will go away with *more* than they came with and some will actually go away with *less*. Parables do that to you. They either add to your understanding or they take away from it. They are very two-edged – and Jesus said that about his parables.

So, having given you a little bit of a shock, we turn to the chapter. I wanted to start there because you need to realise how Jesus taught. I have seen people trying to teach the crowd out in a street and all they do is throw the Book at them and make a string of statements about God and point out the moral very, very strongly and think they have got the *art* of speaking to the public. They should go back and study Jesus again. He never did people's thinking for them. That is an important point. He did not spoon-feed them. He told them something and left them to find out what it was all about, and many of them could not even be bothered to ask what it meant. He might be preaching to hundreds and then only twelve men would come and ask him to please explain it to them – which he then did because he was waiting for that eagerness to have more.

It is Matthew chapter 13 now and the first parable he told is

Matthew Chapter 13

almost identical to the Tupperware party. It is as ordinary as that and there is no mention of God, there is no mention of the Bible, there is no mention of heaven, there is no moral. He just describes something that could have happened on any day, at anytime, anywhere.

Having now read it, do you see what I mean? There is not a word about God, not a mention of scripture, no moral. Actually, it was probably something they saw happening at that very moment because right behind the place where he was in the boat is a field where I have seen sowers doing just that. There is nothing extraordinary there. I am quite sure the response of most people was, "So what's new? I thought he was a great preacher, I've heard a lot about him, but what's new?"

I hope that by the end of this chapter you will be able to understand all these things. Then you will be among those who can bring treasures new and old together.

About half a mile south of Capernaum there is a horseshoe-shaped bay with sloping banks down to it and I *know* that is the place where Jesus sat in a boat. The acoustics are perfect for thousands of people. And in a boat, out in that horseshoe-shaped bay, everybody on the bank can hear every word. You know, that sound carries well over water. Furthermore, right behind that bay is that sloping field which, to this day, is still a field in which men sow seed in exactly the same way as they did 2,000 years ago; I have seen it. And out behind that bay you can see the fishermen out there with their nets. The whole scene is set. There is hardly anything that Jesus said on this day which they could not see as well as hear. And all through the Bible, eye and ear go together. Your town is not waiting to hear the gospel but they are waiting to see it. And on the Day of Pentecost, Peter says, "For we cannot but speak the things which we have seen and heard." And you will find that again and again these are partners through the New Testament – seeing and hearing.

"I didn't just come to you with words," says Paul, "but with a *demonstration* of power." You could see something. Seeing and hearing go together and so Jesus mentions that the two main gates into the human spirit are the eye and the ear. The eye and the ear are the two main senses through which we receive communication. But how deeply they both go in is the question. And Jesus explained that he used parables so that "Seeing they may see and not perceive, and hearing they may hear and not understand; lest they should turn, and their sins be forgiven them." And that last 18 inches is probably the longest journey.

So, Jesus quite deliberately used parables as his teaching method to the public. They were stories from everyday life which were perfectly credible, perfectly ordinary, sometimes so ordinary that when people heard one of them, they must have wondered why on earth he had mentioned it. And he did not point out the moral and he did not mention God and he did not quote scripture. He just told the story, and he was waiting for a response on which he could build. That is excellent teaching and I commend it to you, especially with people outside the church. Yet these very ordinary, earthly stories were about the kingdom of heaven. I find that astonishing. He could explain heaven in ordinary, everyday terms. And he did it because he believed that his Father had created both heaven and earth and that there is a correspondence between earth and heaven. There is a correspondence between natural and spiritual laws, for example. The more you understand nature the more you will understand God's nature.

I am glad that I had to do three years of science before I studied theology. I learned, I think, more about God doing science because it was higher critical theology at Cambridge that I had to wade through after that. But I think I did. So, for Jesus, the earthly and the heavenly were very much closer than they are to most of us and he could take the ordinary earthly and use it to illustrate the realm beyond. Again, that is good teaching, taking what people know and understand and filling it with a meaning, linking on to what is part of their own experience and knowledge, and building on that an understanding of things that are way beyond their reach.

But there are two things that I want to get very clear. Parables had a positive and a negative aspect. The positive was to help people to understand, the negative was to hinder them from understanding. The positive was to reveal, the negative was to conceal. The positive was to add more understanding to those who already had some and the negative was to take away from people what they already had. And Jesus' teaching was a sharp, two-edged sword and the Romans had two kinds of sword – a long, thin one and a broad, fat one with a ridge down the middle. It looked exactly like a large tongue and Jesus' tongue was as sharp as any two-edged sword. You used the long, thin one when you fought with one man, but the broad, fat one you used when you were dealing with a crowd. You flashed it from side to side and it was a heavy, sharp thing and everybody got out of your way. And when Jesus spoke in parables, he was using the broadsword, the sharp, two-edged sword of his tongue to slash through the crowd. Some of his parables are really terrible weapons – they cut people if they understand them.

So, we must realise that there is this double edge to the parables; they are not just sermon illustrations or children's addresses and they are not just to bring light in, they are also to bring darkness in to some. They divide whoever listens to them into two groups – those who go away with no interest, even the interest they came with, and those who are so fascinated that they want to know more. It is a bit like doing a crossword. I am not a crossword fan, except very easy ones. I don't know if you are but I have *sometimes* got interested in a crossword. I start doing it and I get about three clues and fill them in and then I get stuck and I read these clues and I think, "Well, what on earth is that about?" I don't have that kind of a mind and I give up. So, what happens? I lose even the interest I brought to it. It has gone dead on me. Have you had that experience? I literally *lose* interest. But if I get on to a few more clues, I *gain* interest and I get a bit more and a bit more and I begin to see where it fits and I see that word will go there and so on.

Now that is what happens when you listen to Jesus' teaching, when you listen to anything about the kingdom, but particularly parables of the kingdom. I think it could happen to readers of this book; some may lose what interest they had. That might be my fault, it might not be. But others will *gain* interest in the kingdom. Which brings me to these particular parables which all hang together; and the key word is *understand*. The bad soil, the hard soil is the man who hears the Word and does not understand. The good soil is the man who receives the Word and understands. And all the way through you will find *understand* is the key word. It is whether the Word not only gets through the eye and the ear – not just whether you see and hear while reading this – but whether you understand in the heart. And if it gets through there, then you will have more understanding of the kingdom.

But they all hang together. They are all about the same theme. And I would say they are all about *expectancy*. What you can *expect* to happen from the kingdom – that is the thread that ties them all together. And here I want to say that I meet many Christians who are wavering between a naïve pessimism about the kingdom and a naïve optimism about the kingdom, both of which are of the flesh. The Spirit leads you into realism. Now, it is very important what expectancy you have of the kingdom. If you have too low an expectancy, you are going to be surprised. If you have too high an expectancy, you are going to be disappointed. If you are realistic, your hopes will come true. "Hope deferred makes the heart sick." And if your hopes are not realistic hopes, then you are in for trouble.

Let me spell this out. I meet some Christians who are very pessimistic about the future of the church. They say, "In the last days there's going to be a great falling away. There'll only be a few of us left – it might be just you and me at the end. And I'm not sure if you're sound." Have you met pessimists like this? I caricature, but you know who I am talking about; perhaps you have been there and you thought the church was going to shrink and shrink, with only a handful of people remaining at the end to greet the Lord. As long as he brings the angels with him, we can hold a meeting but there won't be enough of us.

Then, at the opposite extreme, I meet a naïve optimism which is often grown out of a reaction to the naïve pessimism I have just mentioned. I meet many today who are naïvely optimistic and think we are about to sweep Satan off planet Earth, that the church is going to grow and grow and take over the nations and rule them and then present them to the Lord. That is naïve optimism. It is not realistic and it will also be disappointed. There is a realism in what we expect of the kingdom in the future before the Lord returns that gives us a good hope. And all these parables put together a picture of what we can expect of the kingdom in this age and they spell it out very realistically.

I begin, then, with the first parable, which is the Parable of the Sower and you know it backwards – you could recite it. You may have preached on it. You have been taught it in Sunday School. You have heard it again and again.

I want to give it the title The Incarnation of the Kingdom. That is the first insight we are going to get, the incarnation of the kingdom. The question is how can the kingdom of heaven be re-established on earth? The answer is always by incarnation. It can only be done by being embodied in human beings who rule the earth. Therefore, the Sovereign of the kingdom of heaven must be incarnate in a human being on earth to re-establish the kingdom – and the Son of God was. But a kingdom is made up of subjects as well as a sovereign. You cannot have a kingdom without subjects as well as a sovereign. The Sovereign has been incarnated; the kingdom of heaven is now being incarnated in subjects. That is what is meant by sowing the seed. The seed is the message of the kingdom and it is to be embodied in men. The soil is human. And we are taking the message of the kingdom and embodying it, incarnating it in human beings. That is how the kingdom will be re-established on earth. The Sovereign was incarnated and the subjects are now being incarnated here on earth. Something of heaven is being put into human beings here and now.

That is the basic message of this. God nearly always does what he wants to do by words. He created the whole universe with words. He recreates through words. It is through his Word that a man becomes a new creation. It is by words that God does most things he does. That is why most of the gifts of the Spirit are word gifts – word of knowledge, word of wisdom, word of prophecy, word of interpretation. He does most of what he wants to do by words. Most of the ministries of the church are word ministries. Apostles use words, prophets use words, evangelists use words, pastors and teachers use words. And the kingdom is incarnated in human beings through words. That is the seed and it is to be implanted in human nature.

Now I want to look at two things – the statistics of sowing and the rewards of reaping in this parable. Both are very interesting. The first thing I want to say that I think may begin to touch the burden the Lord gave me concerning this is that the method of sowing is *broadcasting*. It is *scattering* the seed.

Now, you would have to watch a farmer in the Middle East to understand this. That field behind that bay where Jesus sat in the boat and talked is a field you could not plough. It is covered with hard basalt rocks and stones, which would wreck a plough – it is almost the hardest stone around. It is black, it is hard and there are thorns – some of them six to eight feet high – with spikes on them longer than my thumb. Two and a half inch spikes, the thorns in the Middle East. You can't get near them. And you have no idea whether the soil is shallow or deep, you just see a little patch of soil here and a little patch there. But those people have to use that land. It is the only land they have got.

And I have watched a sower going down through that field. And he does what I actually did in my earliest days on the farm. You carry around a container of seed and you develop a rhythm. And you take a handful out and just do that down the row. That is how they sow. It is the only way you *could* sow in that territory – you have to *broadcast* it; you cannot place it. You have to scatter it and hope for the best.

Now I am beginning to say something which you need to hear. Right at the end, I shall come to the great contrast there is between fishing and shepherding, between evangelising and pastoring. There is a total difference and we have real difficulty adjusting to the two because the seed has to be broadcast, thrown all over the place. You cannot place it as you can plant your house plants. You scatter it, you broadcast the message of the kingdom. Sometimes it feels like trying to fill a lot of jam jars from a hose pipe. That is broadcasting. Hoping that some will drop into some jam jar. But that is the method Jesus used. It is a wasteful method but there is no other way to sow. And the statistics of sowing – let us assume that the four times Jesus said, some fell, some fell, some fell, some fell means a quarter fell, a quarter fell, a quarter fell, a quarter fell. It may not have been exactly that but for the purposes of understanding the parable, just assume that he is talking about four quarters of the seed. And what he is saying is three quarters was wasted. And you have got to live with that and face it. Otherwise, you won't sow.

Now, you know perfectly well what caused the wastage. I am not going to draw that out. You may have preached on it yourself. Jesus knew what was in man. He had no illusions. He knew there were some so hard, maybe gospel-hardened or they had heard preachers so often or they had had tough experiences in life that had hardened them. So many people had trampled over them that they just were not receptive to any good news.

Have you met people like this? He knew some were hard and he knew that they had no sooner heard than what had been said would be forgotten within minutes and that Satan would see they forgot it and keep them hard. He knew there were people like that, no penetration of the Word. It just went.

I saw a secretary in London who had two new earrings. One said, "In" and the other said "Out". And that is exactly what he was talking about. Now, he also knew there was a second group of human beings who are too shallow. They will get very emotional, they will receive the news with joy, have a good old sing and dance about it but it does not lead to anything – especially when the way gets a bit tough and trouble begins. And I am afraid that some people make Christian professions and nobody told them that that is the beginning of trouble. I could not tell you that when I came to Christ my troubles were over. They began when I came to Jesus. And they got much worse when I got filled with the Spirit. I was asked by a minister, "What's the infallible sign of being filled with the Spirit, how do you know?" I said, "I can tell you: trouble." If you have not got into further trouble, I question whether you have been filled with the Spirit.

I have a sound scriptural basis for that because the most frequently mentioned sign of being filled with the Spirit in Acts is not tongues but boldness. And the boldness always got them into trouble. So, there are those who, as soon as they realise that getting to know Christ gets you into trouble, and being filled with the Spirit gets you into more trouble, are off. They like the choruses and the singing, they "hear the Word with joy", but it is very shallow. It gets no deeper than their feelings.

And then there is this third group whose lives are already too full of other things, who think of the kingdom as a nice optional extra: "I've got the job I want; I've got a nice house and I've paid the mortgage off; I've got a nice car, it would be lovely to have a nice church to go to on Sunday as well." Do you know what I mean? As if Jesus is just the icing on the cake, as if a bit of good religion would just complete it all. But their lives are already too full and it is interesting that Jesus said that they are too full of wealth and worry. Those two go together. The more you have the more you are worried about how to keep it. And you start reading the stock exchange more than your Bible. Jesus knew there were people like that. And he said that it is all wasted on those three groups; three quarters of the seed is wasted – it has gone.

Actually, many evangelists would not say that. They would say that only a quarter was wasted because, in fact, three quarters made a decision. Three quarters made a response. Three quarters received the Word. And those are the evangelists' statistics we usually give, right? But Jesus said that he counts those who get through to producing fruit. The others are all wasted because the whole point of sowing was to get some more grain. So, in fact, three quarters was wasted. That is how you should count. Not who starts the Christian life but who finishes it, because it is not the faith you start with that saves you, it is the faith you finish with, according to my reading of the New Testament. It is not those who make a great response in an evangelistic crusade, it is those who, twelve months later, are producing fruit, of whom you can say it was worth it.

But the point is that the sower went on sowing though he knew that three quarters of what he was throwing out was wasted and would produce nothing. Now that is important to notice because that is evangelism. And the farmer was a realist. He was neither a pessimist nor an optimist. A pessimist would have said, three quarters was wasted. An optimist would have said, three quarters grew. A realist says, a quarter will produce fruit.

But now look at the rewards of reaping. Just do a little mathematics. I have tried to do a bit; I think I have got it right. Twenty-five per cent of what he sowed produced an average increase of just over sixty. And if that is so, a hundred seeds got into good ground and produced 1,500 results. In other words, each seed that got into good ground produced fifteen seeds. Do you follow me in that? Twenty-five per cent produced on average a sixty per cent increase. So, in fact, he was getting back fifteen times what he put in, even though three quarters was wasted.

Now, I am saying something about evangelism here. I have heard mass evangelism criticised because many do not last. True. But the Word is to be broadcast and from those to whom the Word does get in, you will get the return that the farmer was looking for. Now, this is profound in its implications because shepherds find it difficult to cope with wastage. Evangelists do not. It is the difference of gifting. It is very hard for them to understand each other. How can you preach and get all those decisions and then see three quarters of them go to nothing? The shepherd cannot bear that but the evangelist can because he is a sower. In Australia I found some very good fishing churches who were bad at shepherding and some very good shepherded churches who were bad at fishing.

As one evangelist said to me, "I'd rather lose eighty per cent of a thousand people than eighty per cent of a hundred people." That sounded a bit odd to me but what he was saying positively was that he would rather catch twenty per cent of a thousand than twenty per cent of a hundred. Do you follow me in that? I thought that was pretty logical. He had understood the parable of the sower. I'll go after as many as I can reach even if I only keep a few because the few from a large crowd will be more than the few from a small crowd. Broadcasting – the method of incarnating the kingdom is to broadcast the seed of the Word of the kingdom, to get it out as far and wide as possible, forgetting the wastage and doing it for the sake of the one that produces thirty, sixty and a hundred.

A missionary in Ethiopia, before the Italians invaded it in the 1930s and turned it into Abyssinia, laboured far and wide, scattered the Word wherever she could but the only convert that missionary had was a blind beggar – one. Then the Italians came and pushed out all the missionaries and they had to flee and there were atrocities of gassing and so on that went on. A terrible time. For years, the missionaries were kept out. When that missionary went back, that blind beggar had a church of 3,000 converts. And the missionary realised that broadcasting # the Word, as she had done, only got it into one, but look what the one produced which made the whole operation worthwhile. I hope you are feeling a word of encouragement coming through here. The pessimist says, so much waste; the optimist says, look how many responded immediately. The realist says, let's wait and see, but it was worth doing for what we will see, the fruit we will get.

Jesus, in the early days of his ministry, scattered the Word wide and got up to 5,000 listening and he got twelve. I mean, Jesus preached one sermon and lost 5,000 people. One sermon did it. They said, "No, this is too much for us," and off they went. In fact, he only got eleven out of that crowd who said, "Explain the parables to us; we want to go further." When he asked, "Are you going to leave me too, like the 5,000 have done?" Peter replied, "No; you're talking about what we want to know."

I am dealing at length with the first two parables and then we are going to deal briefly with the rest because the first two are the vital ones. The second of these is the parable of the wheat and the tares, and it tackles the questions of basic philosophy which the greatest minds of the world have been tackling ever since ancient Greece – and before. And the question of evil is still the biggest philosophical question. How did evil get here and how can we get rid of it? What is the cause of evil and what is the cure for evil? How was it introduced? How can it be eradicated? These are the questions which every major philosopher has tried to think through and Jesus gave the total answer in a very ordinary little story about six sentences long. And they won't accept his answer.

As a man once said to me, "The world's in a hell of a mess." I said, "If you're using that word like I'd use it, you're not far off the truth because hell means godless." But he recognised that the world was in a mess. Now, the two questions are how did it get this way and how can we put it right? How did evil get in here and how will we get it out?

So, in this parable Jesus tells a very ordinary story about one field, two sowings – one by the Owner and one by an enemy. And in that little story, he has told it all. This is not a made-up story; this actually happens in the Middle East. I have known it happen in India, and it used to happen in Ireland. And it is this. If you really want to play a dirty trick on a poor farmer, what you do is, after he has sown his wheat, you go and sow darnel – that is a semi-poisonous, narcotic weed that looks exactly like wheat for about half its life. And it is only when the ears begin to form that you can tell the difference between darnel and wheat. It is a really dirty trick when a man's livelihood depends on what little grain he is going to get because he cannot use that as food. It is dangerous to use. It has wrecked his little crop.

So, Jesus was not making it up. He was just telling them what happened in the sense of "once upon a time", and they all said, "Um, yes, that's happened; so what's new?" And the disciples said, "Tell us the meaning." And the meaning that Jesus was explaining to them was the introduction of evil and the eradication of evil. The two basic things everybody wants to know about.

You notice that Jesus says evil is not an evolutionary hangover, nor is it due to the economic system we live under, nor is it because we live on an overcrowded planet. These are quite irrelevant factors. They are not messing up the world and therefore, to get us under another economic system or to get us a bit further down the evolutionary road of progress will not get us anywhere. Why don't we listen to Jesus? He is the only one who has told us the truth about it.

He says three things about evil. Number one: Evil is alien to this world; it does not belong here. That is a profound philosophical statement. Evil was introduced to this world; it did not belong here. It is not part of creation. The Owner sowed wheat in his field, that is all. Therefore, let no one say that God is responsible for introducing evil to this world. It is a libel on the Creator. Evil is alien, it is unnatural, it was not here to begin with. The only thing you can "blame" God for is that he made a world that was vulnerable to it. But I do not think you can say that is blame, just as if you have your garden and you plant things in the garden and someone else comes and wrecks it and you call the police and the police come and say, "Well, it was your fault for having a garden. It was your fault for making it nice. If you had left it as it was before you built the house, nobody would have bothered with it; it's your fault." You see how crazy this argument is? But men use it of God.

The second thing about evil is that it is personal; it is not a thing, not an *it* but a *he*. And until you understand that you cannot talk of evil as a *thing*, you won't understand the problem. Evil does not exist apart from personal will. It is not a thing you can package up and introduce somewhere, you have got to *incarnate it*. Evil is personal – the Lord's Prayer we always say wrong. I think we should say it more. It is a prayer that keeps you right in your own praying, but the end of it has always been translated wrongly in English Bibles. Jesus said, "Lead us not into temptation but deliver us from *the evil one*," not deliver us from *evil* – it – but from the evil *one – him*. And you need to pray every day that you may be delivered from *him* and that God will not leave you exposed to him – which is the meaning of "Lead us not into temptation". If God wants to teach you a lesson, he just exposes you to temptation. He says, "Okay, you're on your own; see how it works out." And in the Lord's Prayer, you are saying, "Lord, please don't ... May I not need that lesson. Don't put me in that place where I'm vulnerable to him, but deliver me from him today."

So, evil is personal – it was *an enemy* that sowed the tares. There is a personal enemy of the Owner of the universe who is responsible for the mess we are in. Oh, it says so much – you could almost preach a whole sermon on the devil from this one parable. For Jesus, the devil is a fundamental belief. You could hardly be a follower of Jesus and not believe in a personal devil.

The devil is an invader who can actually treat this world as if it is his. He can go sowing as if he owned the place. We know we are of God and the whole world lies in the grip of the evil one. He treats it as if he owns it. The devil is motivated by malice and hatred toward the Owner of the field; that is why he did it. The reason the devil destroys us is because he wants to get at God, not at us. He is using us to get at him. That is his motive.

The devil's method is counterfeit and what he does can deceive people for a time – until the fruit appears. The darnel looks like wheat until it begins to fructify at the top. His aim is always destructive, it is never constructive. He is never trying to build something up; he is always trying to break something down and destroy it. He *always* works where the Owner is working; now that is a very important understanding of Satan. Wherever the Owner sows wheat, that is where the devil sows darnel, so if God is working in your church, you had better be ready for the devil to work too – because that is where he will sow *his* seed.

But another clue – he always works in the dark, whereas the Owner sows in the light. He always does it secretly; he does not want any publicity for it, whereas what the Lord does is open and seen. You can see the Lord sowing but you cannot see the devil. I could go on, but this is not a book on the devil. So let us push on.

The third thing about evil is something I have already mentioned – that evil is not only alien to this world, and personal, it is incarnate and the devil's method of planting his kingdom is exactly the same as heaven's. Hell has to get hold of people and embody. The seeds that are sown are the *sons* of the devil – they are people. The wheat is personal, the tares are personal – and that is his method, incarnation again. He has got to get hold of human beings. And he looks around for something in your life or in mine that he can get hold of. It is usually something we keep in the dark and if you think of something you could not share with someone, that is usually where he will incarnate himself and grab you. Well, let us leave the devil now. I do not like giving him a lot of publicity.

Jesus does not answer all the questions but he tells us enough about the introduction of evil to tell us how to tackle it. And the basic insight is: something that was supernaturally introduced can only be supernaturally eradicated. If human beings had introduced evil to this world, human beings might eradicate it. But we won't. It will take angels to eradicate the devil. We won't do it. It is a false hope that we will. We *are* promised that if we resist him, he will run away from us, but we are never promised that we will eradicate him or his kingdom.

We are coming now to the eradication of evil. As the wheat and the tares matured, the differences became obvious and the sons of the kingdom of heaven – the servants of the farmer – became greatly concerned. They had a righteous indignation that this should have been done. And moral indignation can often lead to mental impatience and you say, "Let's deal with it straight away. Let's root it out straight away." And I am afraid that moral indignation slips into mental impatience very quickly if we are not careful. So, they came to the Owner of the field and they said, "Look what's happened; look at these weeds in your field. You didn't sow them, did you?" And the Owner said, "No, I had nothing to do with it. An enemy did it. Well then, let us clear the field up straight away.

I want to tell you that one of the most subtle temptations on Christians today is to become tare-pullers. I say that carefully because I do not want to be misunderstood. I believe in church discipline. I believe in social action by Christians but I do not believe in tare pulling. It is very important that you understand this. There are Christians who are getting all steamed up about a tare pulling crusade and you can work up a good head of steam on that. When you are filled with anger about some evil things and perhaps you say, "Come on, let's clear it out, let's root it out, let's eradicate it." And I am just putting a cautionary word against this, lest we try and do what we cannot. That is the human reaction: let's have a purge. It is the reaction of the flesh all around the world. Let's purge our nation of evil people. That is the human reaction to the tares, isn't it? Everywhere you go. If we could only get rid of *that lot* the field would be fine. And every election we have I hear it. Let's kick that lot out and then we'll have it – then we'll have the kingdom of heaven on earth. Let's get rid of the Tories, let's get rid of Labour. They are saying, Let's purge, get rid of the people who are causing the problem. That is *not* heaven's method – and it won't work. It is the right idea but the wrong time and the wrong people. The right idea is that someday every tare has to be removed from this world, that someday everyone who sins and everything that causes sin must be eradicated. If this is God's world, that has got to happen someday. It is the right idea, but listen, we are not the people who will do it and this is not the time for it to be done. That is what Jesus is saying.

The right time will be at the end of the age and the right people to do it will be the angels; they will not be the sons of the kingdom. The Farmer will bring in another team to deal with that. He is not going to entrust us with that job of eradicating evil. He must have his own reasons for that. I could think of some of them but they would be speculation. We need to go back again to the Owner's original intention, which was to have a full barn, not a pure field. Do you hear me on that? I am going to return to this theme; it is heavy on me now. The Owner's original intention was a full barn, not a pure field. But we keep wanting to give him a pure field when he wants a full barn. And if you start tare pulling now, there are two things that could happen. First of all, a case of mistaken identity could happen and you could pull up wheat. Boy, if somebody had managed to pull up all the tares in this world, I would not be here now. Would you? And the other mistake that you can make is that because the roots are so interwoven you will disturb the wheat itself from growing properly and you will do more harm than good.

Now, these are profound things. The orders of the Owner are: Let both grow together until ... Which means, quite simply, that where the pessimist says the tares are going to take over the world, and the optimist says the wheat is going to take over the world, the realist says, both will grow together until ... Do you see how Jesus' teaching keeps you balanced? The wheat is not going to take over from the tares in this age, nor are the tares going to take over from the wheat. Both are going to increase, which means increasing confrontation to the climax of the final struggle between Antichrist and Christ. But the outcome is certain, the harvest will begin it and the barn will be full. But we must not engage in a crusade to eradicate evil. We must not try and live in the barn yet. Many Christians would like to live in a nice, sheltered Christian community up in "them there hills" and milk cows while singing choruses. Listen, the wheat and the tares have got to grow – both of them – together. Did you hear that? Together.

It is tough being in the world but that is where the church has got to be. And the tendency constantly is to build a barn where we can all be sheltered. You cannot live in the barn now. You can only live in the field now together with the other kingdom. We are too interwoven to start separating now, and indeed Jesus prayed, on his last night: "Father, don't take them out of this field. *Keep* them *in it* and *from him*." That was his prayer. We can protect ourselves and our children too much. Sooner or later our children have to live *in the world*, with their roots interwoven with the kingdom of Satan. I would not let our children go away to boarding school partly because I had unhappy memories of boarding school. But one of the reasons was we both wanted them in the world but in close touch with us so that they could discuss what they were encountering. And I am happy to say they still share everything with us. And that was what we wanted – so they came home and *told* us what they had seen of the tares. And we could talk it over. "In the world but not of it." Let both grow together.

Sooner or later, we have got to be in there; salt is no use in the salt cellar. Both will grow bigger and stronger; but here is a word of encouragement. The growth of the weeds will not hinder the growth of the wheat, otherwise we would be told to pull up the weeds. The wheat will grow strong. The Integrity of the Kingdom would be my title for this parable.

Heaven's way is patience and the Owner will do it in his time with his way with his agents. But you notice a little phrase in there when Jesus says, "The field is the world, the good seeds are the sons *of the kingdom*". Did you notice that? The kingdom of Christ is not the church, it is the world. There are things in his kingdom that should not be there but the world is his kingdom. When I preached in Canada, I said that Canada is his kingdom. Even if it became a republic, it could not really be one because Canada has a King and always will have. And all authority in heaven and on earth is given to Jesus. He said that the field is the world and the field is his kingdom. And one day, everything that is wrong in it will be eradicated from his kingdom. Really, we need to see the kingdom as far bigger than the church. The kingdom is the world and it is already the kingdom of Christ, though many people do not realise it. But one day they will, when he calls his angels – not us – and tells them to take out of his kingdom everyone who does not belong there. And to bring everyone who does belong there into the barn, and the barn is the kingdom of his Father. There is a lovely switch there. The field is the world, which is the kingdom of the Son of Man. The barn is the kingdom of Dad. Mind you, one final thought: Isn't it beautiful that a Creator can change tares into wheat? I think that is why he does not want to pull them up yet. We might have pulled up some lovely saints.

Matthew Chapter 13

We talked about the incarnation of the kingdom and the integrity of the kingdom. I think that is the right word. It can stand on its own. You do not need to purify the field. It stands in its own integrity. You do not need to clear the world up before the kingdom is strong and growing.

The third area that Jesus talked about was what I would call the Increase of the Kingdom. And he rounds off his public discourse with these two very short parables. And usually when Jesus gave two short parables to the public, he always gave one to the men and the other to the women. I find that interesting – like the lost sheep and the lost coin. There is one from agricultural life and one from domestic life usually, and true to form, here he talks about the garden and the mustard seed and then he goes into the home and talks about the yeast and a woman. He wanted to include all his hearers, get something that everyone could identify with. Again, a study of his teaching is a marvellous study.

Every parable so far has included this theme of growth but the question arises: How much growth can we expect? A little? Or a lot? What *expectancy* can we have? Can we expect the kingdom to grow until everybody in the world is in it? No. But can we expect it to grow just a little? No. The two parables he tells tell us that we can expect a lot. I am glad about that. There are differences between the two. The mustard seed tends to emphasise the *quantity* of growth whereas the yeast or leaven tends to emphasise the *quality*.

The first is growth in size, the second is growth in influence – and these are two aspects of growth. I am afraid some people are only interested in growth in numbers but God actually wants a threefold growth in his kingdom – growth in size, maturity and influence. That is true growth. But the mustard seed, the story for the men out of doors, simply says the kingdom which was tiny will be huge, like the smallest seed you sow in your garden. You can only just see a mustard seed with the naked eye but it actually becomes the largest plant in your garden and is a tree big enough for birds of the air to come and nest in. Incidentally, that phrase *birds of the air nesting* comes in the Old Testament and is used of Gentiles coming to the King of Israel and nesting in Zion, which is an interesting little reference. But I am just thrilled to report that the church is growing faster today than it has grown for 2,000 years.

Jesus said, "I will build my church". I am so glad he did not tell us to. He is doing a very good job and it is growing faster today – it is *huge!* I have got some figures for you just to strike you. Let's take 1900 to 2000. And let's take Africa and Asia. In Africa and Asia between 1900 and today, the population has doubled, but by 2000 it will have trebled – that is the speedup. So, 1900 to today doubled; today to 2000 trebled. You can see how the speeding up is coming. Now, what has happened to the church in Africa and Asia over the same period? Has it kept up with that growth? Between 1900 and today, the church in Africa and Asia has multiplied by 13 times when the population has only doubled. And by the year 2000, the church in Africa and Asia on present trends will multiply 34 times when the population has only trebled. Does that encourage you? That is what is happening in our world.

A businessman said to me at a party a few years back, "What's your job?" I said, "I'm a minister of a church." He said, "What's it like to belong to a dying organisation?" I said, "I wouldn't know." He said, "Come off it; churches are closing everywhere, it's on the way out." I said, "Well, the church I belong to isn't." He said, "What's that one?" I said, "The church of Jesus." And he looked at me a bit sideways, but I said, "Listen, every minute I talk to you – every *minute* – the church has 15 more members, even allowing for deaths. A net gain of 15 members a minute around the world – that's a thousand an hour, 25,000 a day." I said, "If your business had 25,000 new customers a day would you talk about a dying organisation?" Well, that impressed him. And I am one of those who having impressed someone, then tries to improve on it – and I lose them. Do you do that? I thought, well

I've really impressed the man so I'll say something even better. I said, "And I'll tell you another thing: we never lose a single customer by death." And he looked at me as though I had gone way beyond and he dismissed me as a crank and walked away.

That was a few years ago. The figure today is 45 per minute. There is a net gain of Christians in this world of 64,000 a day. That is the church you belong to, the church you should get excited about. The mustard seed is becoming a *huge* plant, and the birds of the air are nesting in it – the Gentiles all over the world are getting in on the act. It is an encouraging parable. It tells us to expect from tiny beginnings – 11 men – a huge church, a multitude that no man can number. It will not cover the world. It will not be everybody, but it is growth, real significant growth, and it is faster, much faster, than the population is growing in this world. And all you hear is the population explosion. Somebody should give a bit of publicity to the church explosion because it is fantastic.

I met a Korean minister – not Yonggi Cho – a Presbyterian minister from down the road from Yonggi Cho, and his church is growing almost as fast, but he gets no publicity. Many churches are growing like mad in South Korea. They have Christian rallies of just under 3,000,000 people, you know. And this minister was telling me about them so I tried to look as though I was in the same league! Look, I thought these people had *colossal* faith but in Yonggi Cho's church the target he sets per month is 10,000 new members – for his church – and he is seeing it. But actually, that target is well within reach because his target is actually that each house group should win two people for Christ every six months. But when you have got thousands of house groups it adds up. I can relate to that target now. Every house group has to win two people in six months. Would your faith stretch to that? The growth in South Korea is exactly that rate so I want to encourage you into growth.

And the second parable about the yeast is more on the quality than the quantity, on the influence. If the first is very visible growth, the second is invisible. But what Jesus is saying is that the kingdom will permeate every part of society and every part of this world. It will just spread like yeast in dough until every part is feeling the effect. I am not talking about converting everybody but every part will be affected. There will be a day when there will not be any part of this world that is not being affected by the kingdom of God. Something will be happening in an area that is the result of the kingdom being here. That is encouraging, isn't it? And he is promising that that will happen – the kingdom is like yeast that goes on operating until every part of the dough is touched.

So, the first parable says the small will be big, and the second says the part will affect the whole. It is an encouragement. But you notice that it only happens when the seed is planted in the soil or when the yeast is mixed with the dough. I am back to something we touched on earlier. Separation of the church does not lead to anything. The church has got to be mixed right in there. The yeast has got to be in the dough. The seed has got to be in the garden, otherwise neither the seed nor the yeast would produce a thing.

The next thing I want to talk about is the Incentive of the Kingdom. At this point Jesus stops talking to the crowd and he talks for the rest of the time to the disciples only, and therefore to men only. All his parables are to men. It is just little things I notice like this that make Jesus such a superb teacher. He switches his style from outdoors to indoors, from the public to the disciples; suits his material to the people. These men have *received* the message, they are sons of the kingdom and it has cost them a lot. It has cost them their jobs; it has cost them their homes. So, he is going to encourage them a bit now with *expectancy*. And he tells these two beautiful little stories – and again there are differences between the two as well as similarities. The stories are the treasure in the field and the pearl of great price and there are certain differences between them. In the treasure case, the man is *not* looking for treasure and therefore not wanting it, but is suddenly surprised by it. In the other case, the man *is* looking for a pearl; he is a trader, and he is wanting it. And some people find the kingdom through a long search. They are wanting something better and so they go looking and they find the kingdom. Other people just trip up one day and there it is before them in the street. It does not matter how you find the kingdom. There are many different ways, and there must have been differences among the disciples as to how they first either stumbled on it or came seeking for it. Nathaniel was looking for something. I do not think some of the others were. Matthew was not looking for anything, and suddenly he stumbled on something that was even more profitable than tax collecting.

So, again, in the first case, no one directed him to it. In the second case, someone was trying to sell it to him. In the first case, the man had a sudden change of outlook, his future changed like that when he saw that treasure. In the other case, it was a slow build-up of resources, a search. There are many ways to find the kingdom. In one case, the owners did not know what the field was worth, in the other case, the owner must have known what the pearl was worth. But I notice that there is one little word that is different. The man who stumbled on it suddenly, who was not looking for it, had joy. The other man did not have such an emotional experience. His long search found fulfilment but it does not say any joy, and I have noticed that again with people who have come suddenly into the kingdom, when almost out of the blue, they find how wonderful it is – there is such a surge of joy. And I could *almost* wish I had been a cannibal or a criminal when I was converted. Have you ever felt like that?

Listen, the important thing is not *how* you found it. The important thing is just twofold. Number one, this is the biggest thing in your life. It is the biggest thing you ever found. It is number one now. It is *the* central goal, ambition, desire of your life once you have really found the kingdom. You cannot tack it on as an extra. You cannot say, "Well, I'll give an hour a Sunday morning to church and I'm in the kingdom." This is it! It has got to be everything! If you have really discovered the kingdom, nothing else matters from that moment. If you have really understood what it is all about, it is *now* your life. That is the first thing – it is number one.

And the second thing is that it is worth making any sacrifice whatever to get that one thing. Everything else pales now. You would give up anything else for this. Both of these men sold *everything* they had and did not feel the loss. The kingdom has a way of taking you over. It really just so grips and almost obsesses you, if you like, that you just say, "Right, that's the lot. I'm prepared to let anything go for this." You don't lose by it. Jesus said, "No man has left family, houses, lands for my sake and the kingdom's but he'll receive a hundredfold – with persecutions." I love the honesty of Jesus. He put that in the "small print" but it is there – with persecutions. Do not listen to anybody who teaches prosperity unless they preach it with persecutions because that is honesty. Jesus did promise to prosper those who had left all – with persecutions. Oh, I am not sure I want to be prosperous – it is honesty.

Well, let us move to the last one. I did not know what to call this, but being a slave to alliteration, I wrote two words down – you can take either of them or reject them both, but you will get the idea. The first was The Indiscrimination of the Kingdom but that is a pretty complex word and people don't use it. So, I wrote down a second – The Inclusiveness of the Kingdom. This last parable is the hardest of them all to take and I have never heard it preached on. Have you ever heard the parable of the dragnet preached on? Have you ever heard a sermon on the parable of the sower? I am sure you have. How we pick and choose in the Word of God! Now, this is a problematic one. It is a difficult one, but it has got a message and I think the heart of my burden for you is going to come out with this one.

Go back to Galilee. They never fish with a rod and line. I have been out in the middle of the night with fishermen right in the middle of the Sea of Galilee fishing with them. I never saw a rod and line, never saw a hook. They use nets and the problem with the net is that it is indiscriminate in what it catches. It is inclusive. It just catches everything that is there whether you want it or not. Now, with a rod and line you can say, "Right, I won't bother with those little ones; there's a big salmon just over there under the shade; I'll go for that." And you go for it. You are picking. Or you choose a fly or a particular bait and you go for that one. But fishing in the New Testament and in the Middle East is not that kind of fishing so we must forget that picture and get it out of our minds. Fishermen use nets and therefore they get a real mixture in the net. Their aim is quantity first. Now, that is going back to the first parable again. Their aim is to get as many as possible into that net. Their aim is not to catch good fish but to get the net full and when the net is full, they take it to the shore and they say, not that one, this one; not that one, this one. A good fish is one that is either edible or saleable, something they can do something with. A bad fish is one they can do nothing with so they throw it back. But they do it after the net is full.

There is an important point coming here. If you will forgive the pun, here is the catch. Oh, groan! Forgive that! Firstly, the *angels* will do the sorting, not us. Here we go again; we would *love* to do it but it is not our job. It is our job to get the net full, not to throw the bad fish out. The angels will do the sorting of them.

Secondly, they will do it at the *end* of the age – not now. Thirdly, some fish that have been in the kingdom net will go to hell. It is quite clear. Matthew repeatedly warns us of those who have related to Christ who can yet go to hell. Matthew 25 gives five warnings like that of those who are *waiting for the Bridegroom's coming* who will be in outer darkness. Now, we have got to take these warnings pretty seriously. The kingdom net will catch people who are not going to be in heaven and we must face the full implications of that. It is a big net and it catches all kinds of fish and we must not do the sorting out. The angels will.

My conclusion is that as of this point in time, the net is not yet full. Do you follow me in that conclusion? Because the angels are not kicking the bad fish out yet. The net is not yet full. Our concern is to get *any fish* into that net and get the net full. Now again, it is difficult for us to accept that concept if we have got a heart for quality rather than quantity – and yet here is Jesus saying that the kingdom is like this, and it gets sorted out in the end. But it gets a net full.

While spending two weeks in Australia some years ago with the ministers of the Sunshine Coast, I found that there was great tension between some of the leaders out there. Some of them had not even spoken to each other in years and had not shared the same platform in years. But praise God! God put them together on a platform side by side in full view of the whole church of the Sunshine Coast. He did a miracle. But one of the basic things that was coming between them was that some of those men were fishermen and some were shepherds and they did not understand each other. The fishermen were going for the big numbers and had a lot of wastage, whereas the shepherds said, "No, we believe in real care of each one and we go for quality not quantity." And they could not understand each other. And the risen, ascended Christ gave to his church pastors and evangelists – and they have never understood each other. And Jesus says that his church needs both – and he wants the Word to be broadcast wide and he wants the net to be cast wide and you are just going to have to cope with the bad fish you catch. You are going to have to cope with the wastage and the disappointment because it will be worth it for the harvest at the end of the age. And we need both.

You see, I meet lovely shepherding churches that tend to stay the same size or grow slightly. I meet marvellous fishing churches – they get huge numbers but cannot keep them. And I think the risen Lord Jesus is just saying, Couldn't you get it together? Couldn't my church have fishermen and shepherds together? Couldn't they be casting the net wide *and* caring for those they get and get it together and have quantity and quality *together!* And neither saying they're the best because they have the biggest quantity or the best quality, but saying, "Hey, we need what you've got; you need what we've got." That is my burden. I believe the Lord is sharing that burden of his heart to have a fishing, shepherding church.

I have brought forth from my treasures, things new and old. Jesus said, "If you're instructed in the Law and the kingdom, that's what you'll do, bring familiar things and fresh things together." What a beautiful balance in Jesus' teaching. In just one chapter he has spoken of the kingdom as present and future. Get the balance right, it is both. He has spoken of the kingdom of heaven, and yet on earth. He has spoken of divine sovereignty and human responsibility. He has got almost every major doctrine in balance in just one chapter.

But just before I began preparing this message I said, "Lord, how do we finish this?" And he told me to tell you about Peter whose first call was to be a fisher of men but who, three years later was told, "Feed my lambs." And he had to learn both. And on the Day of Pentecost, he was a great fisherman; he caught 3,000. But when he wrote his letter later, he wrote as a shepherd to other shepherds about the chief Shepherd. Peter was one of the very few who managed to get it together in his own leadership. Very few manage to do that. Very few pastors are evangelists; very few evangelists are pastors, so in most cases you have got to get a team together. But what he told me to tell you is this – just to quote one verse – "After the resurrection, Peter said to the other disciples, 'I'm going fishing' and the other disciples said, 'We're coming with you.'" I thought that was beautiful.

Addenda

3. WORK:
LANDOWNER AND LABOURERS (2)

Read Matthew Chapter 20

My subject is how to make Monday the most exciting day of the week. Do you realise that we spend a third of our life asleep and a third at work and a third doing other things? One of the great tragedies is that that part of our life, which is the major part, is often wasted. I just want to tell you how you can extend your time to serve the Lord by at least forty-five hours a week.

No wonder if we feel that our work is really a waste of time, we press for more and more money and less and less work and early retirement. This worldly attitude to work has infected the Christian church too, so that Christians themselves are thinking this way – that life is to be found in leisure rather than in work. I want to tell you how to serve the living God through your daily job because if you limit it to your leisure time you are very limited as to what you can do for the living God. But, if you see your daily work as an offering of praise, it means that at least eight hours a day can be spent in worship, serving the living God – but if your job is a dead work, then it really is a deadly thing.

I am going to begin by going back two thousand years and looking at three different views of work: the Greek view, the Hebrew view, and the Christian view. The tragedy is that we are more influenced in English society by the Greek philosophy than by the Hebrew. We owe much more to Plato than we do to Jeremiah and the result is seen in all kinds of wrong attitudes. For example, the division between the physical and the spiritual

– that is a Greek division not the Hebrew way of looking at it. The division between the natural and the supernatural, which finds the concept of a miracle difficult, is a Greek view; it is not the Hebrew view. But in relation to work, let me tell you now that the Greek view is that you cannot live through work.

The Greeks said that leisure is the secret of life and the more leisure you have and the more money you have to enjoy it and the more you can get others to do work for you, the more you can live. It is that view that is gripping this plastic world in which people feel their life must be filled with entertainment for them to be living. Let me quote three Greeks. Plato said, "No artisan can ever be a citizen of the state." Aristotle said, "Until you've dropped your trade for ten years, you are not fit to be a citizen." And Cicero said, "No gentleman will ever work for a wage." It is that view that crept through to England because our education is so based on the Greek philosophy that somehow in England, we look on a gentleman as a man of leisure. A gentleman is certainly not someone who works with his hands and probably not someone who works very hard. We got this view straight from the Greeks. It is that view that leisure provides the secret of life that we owe to the ancient Greek world. That is why in the Roman Empire when the New Testament was written, two out of every three people were slaves doing the work for that other one who was the gentleman and who was the man of leisure and he was the one who really lived.

Every man's ambition was to be a free man with slaves to do the work for him so he was free to enjoy life in his leisure. It sounds strangely modern, doesn't it? Now, against that there came into the world these writings – nearly all of them by Hebrews with a totally different philosophy. This book is the most revolutionary book that ever hit the human scene. It had a totally different concept of work and it contrasts with the Greek religion with its gods of leisure. If you study the God of this book, you will find a God who is a worker. From that springs life. Your religion will colour your whole outlook on life. The gods you worship will determine the kind of person you are. Study the Greek gods and you will find them eating, drinking, and dancing because they are gods of leisure, as are the modern gods. These gods were supposed to enjoy themselves through leisure. Even the labours of Hercules were exploits rather than employment. There is not a single Greek god who is regularly employed and you can study all the myths and prove me wrong.

When I turn to the Bible, I find it begins with a concept of a God who is hard at work and a God who is on a six-day week. A God who says, "Let there be . . ." and there was and then he gets busy working on something else and says, "Let there be . . ." and there was. We are presented straight away with the message that in the beginning God was busy creating. He was working and that is where the Bible starts – not with a God who is enjoying his leisure but a God who is a worker. Now, he is not a God who lives entirely for his work; he is a God who takes a rest. He is a God who works a six-day week and rests for one day, in that proportion. It is from that there springs the notion that God, deriving great satisfaction from his work, made man in his own image as a being to find his true vocation in his work and find his deepest satisfaction in his work. So that when God finished that six-day period he said, "Let us make man in our image," and "God saw everything that he had made, and indeed it was very good". So, he made man in his own image.

A man derives tremendous satisfaction and fulfilment from a job that is well done and because God is a worker and we are made in his image, we are made to be workers. Not entirely though because there are times when we must step aside for the proportion to be six to one if we are really going to enjoy God's life; then we shall have to understand that we enjoy God's work and we become workers too. I read in a Christian book that work is the result of the Fall and is part of the curse. The author cited God's words to Adam, "Because you took of the tree, in the sweat of the brow you shall get your bread and till the soil," as meaning that work is the result of the curse. It is nothing of the kind.

If you study Genesis 2, before man sinned, God put Adam in the garden to sit in a deck chair and enjoy the flowers – no, it doesn't say that! There is no mention of a deck chair. It says, "He put him in the garden to till the ground and to cultivate the garden," to work. What happened after the Fall was that work became drudgery, work became a negative thing. There were thorns and thistles now to be pulled out and you have not seen thorns or thistles until you have been to Israel. The thorns are up high and so are the thistles – a real thicket of spikes. Suddenly, work turned sour and instead of being the most fulfilling thing, it became a battle. You are fighting against factors instead of working with the Lord and cultivating that garden.

So, the Fall brought the curse upon work as it spoiled marriage, it spoiled work; as it spoiled family life, as it spoiled every aspect of man's freedom in the Garden of Eden. Therefore, work itself is not the result of the curse. When you turn to the book of Exodus you find God saying these are the rules of life to enable you to live to the full: "Six days shalt thou labour and on the seventh rest." I am still waiting for a tract from the Lord's Day Observance Society pleading for a six-day working week. Yet it is part of the commandment and it is as much a part as the second part. Which Christian today is pressing for a six-day week? Yet God is saying if you want to live life to the full, share my pattern of activity, "Six days shalt thou labour and on the seventh rest."

Turn later in the book of Exodus and you will find that when they built the tabernacle God gave special skills of craftsmanship to Bezalel and Oholiab, making them skilful in stones and wood and metals so that they could use these skills to build something beautiful for God. It is written right in the Psalms, "The work of our hands", but we spiritualise it. "The work of our hands established it." When you have done the washing-up say, "The work of my hands established it." Make it worthwhile; make it something lasting for God. So, the Psalms talk about man going to his toil and to his labour until the evening. They are full of work – that is the Hebrew view. When the Greeks conquered Israel, the Greek view of leisure came in as something alien to this view. Stadiums were built, theatres were built in Jerusalem, and suddenly everybody was living for leisure and for entertainment and some of the Jews realised that this was distorting life. It was spoiling their life and they rebelled against it.

They tried to get rid of that Greek influence. They never entirely succeeded but I will tell you this: you name any profession, any trade, any branch of human activity and I will give you the name of a Jew somewhere near the top of it. It is because from a Hebrew doctrine of work there comes an inner motivation to be stretched to the limit and to go to the top and to be used for the glory of God in work rather than in leisure. It is written into their nature. In the dispersion over these two thousand years, many Jews lost this and found that money could do their work for them, but when God took them back to their own land within our lifetime, he took people who had worked with their heads and who had worked way up in a rarified intellectual atmosphere and he put them to work digging ditches to drain swamps. One of the secrets of modern Israel is that people were ready to go back to work with their hands on the land and saw in menial and manual labour something dignified and not degrading. It upsets the world's notions to rethink our attitude to work and to realise that a man who works with his hands is higher in God's scale of values than a man who works with his head, which is why his own Son was a manual labourer – it is upside down to the world's way of thinking.

I wonder if you know what Israel's biggest export is today. Perhaps you guessed fruit. Well, that is still a major export, but number one is diamonds – the cutting of diamonds, that is the South African connection and the Amsterdam connection. They import the rough diamonds from South Africa; they cut them, send them to Amsterdam and then to Hatton Garden in London. You see, they get most of their money from what they do with their hands, either through the skill or toil of their hands – that is how modern Israel was established, that is how it survives – through the work of their hands, establish thou it, Lord. What is the Christian attitude to work in the light of all that? The answer is that Christians have been torn between the Hebrew and the Greek view. Whenever Christians have really got back to the Bible, the Hebrew view has prevailed and a new attitude to work has come back. Whenever they have been more influenced by the world around them, the Greek view has got back in and the leisure view has prevailed.

Let us go to the New Testament written by Hebrews. Jesus was a Jew and Jesus came and he said, "My Father has been working until now, and I have been working." Out of thirty-three years, Jesus spent twelve years being brought up, eighteen years working with his hands as a carpenter in Nazareth and three being the Saviour of the world. If he had not done the eighteen years as a carpenter, well, God the Father would not have given him the job as Saviour. It is a fact of Jesus' life that we often overlook. Our advice to young people is often to do three years in a job first and then eighteen serving the Lord, but the Father said to his own Son, "Do eighteen years working with your hands, Son, then you will be ready for a three-year ministry for me." It is a scale of values that is alien to our thinking. So, you can turn page after page of the New Testament and you find in 1 Corinthians and Ephesians and Colossians and Thessalonians that again and again there is mention of daily work.

Indeed, Paul says, "If a man won't work, don't let him eat." We do not want beggars among the Christians. If a man can work and he won't, it is your duty not to give him anything to eat. I once had to put that into practice with a young man who was a professional student. Do you know what I mean by that?

He had been on eight courses and each time he had managed to switch courses just towards the end of the course and got a new grant and he had gone on and had every intention of continuing his life that way. Then he came and asked for lunch at our house and I said, "I'm sorry, the Bible forbids me to give it to you," and he was shaken. He said, "Where?" And I showed him in Thessalonians. Do you know what happened? He went away and he came back and said, "I got a job," and he came and had lunch with us. You read Paul writing to slaves and he says that they should do their work not to please men or as if men were watching them but with God's eye upon them. We are to work for him. We work as if he were our employer and as if he were going to pay our wages. That is the New Testament teaching – it is utterly clear and utterly practical.

Now, what has happened to Christian thinking over two thousand years? I tell you, Catholic thinking has been too heavily influenced by Greek philosophy and Protestant thinking recovered the Hebrew. I am speaking historically now. I am not speaking about today. One of the great joys of life today is that many Catholics are getting back to the Bible and recovering a Hebrew view of life. Hallelujah for that. I am looking back over two thousand years and the Catholic view of life was the Greek view that if you want to live you must withdraw from the world; you must withdraw from daily work. That has noticeably marked hundreds of years. When the Protestants came with their Reformation and got people back to the Bible it began to be obvious that work was changing.

Do you know that in Scotland the Bible got such a deep hold of people through John Knox's ministry that to this day the Scots have a far better record for men in business and in education and in many other fields than the English? The Bible in the Reformation never really got a hold of England as it did Scotland and the result was that in England the image of the life of leisure of the gentlemen prevailed and it went on; it did not in Scotland. You can argue with me if you feel that is offensive. The outstanding exception to this was when John Wesley in the eighteenth century rode through England with a horse between his knees and a Bible in his hands and preached the Bible.

The early Methodist view of work affected the Coniston Miners and the Daw Mill Coal Miners, and a new work ethic developed out of that eighteenth-century revival, but it was an exception. Right until today the idea has persisted that a gentleman does not work with his hands or work too hard if he can help it – that is English class society, it is not God's way of looking at things. Here, then, are the three ways: the Hebrew, the Greek and the Christian, which has wavered between the two. What I want to say in this chapter is that there is a desperate need for a revolution in our society. I want to apply now the Hebrew teaching in the Bible, the Christian teaching in the Bible, to our contemporary society, first by applying it to ourselves as individuals and second by applying it to our society.

First to ourselves as individuals. There is going to be a lot of re-education needed, a lot to unlearn as well as to learn. Unconsciously, we are always adopting the attitudes to work of those around us if we are not careful and then we become so coloured by the world around us that we cannot tell the difference. Some people think that leisure is life; no, it is not – to work-allergic people I want to say life is work; to the workaholic I want to say life is more than work. I think more of us are work-allergic than workaholic. So let me deal with the first group. Our daily job is not a necessary evil to pay the bills; it is a necessary good in order to live. For the Hebrew, life is work. There is this saying that for a rabbi not to teach his son a trade is to teach him to steal. That is why every rabbi has to have a trade with his hands – why Paul was a tentmaker. In order that those who preach would first work. And though the Lord let me off fairly lightly with a fairly short period, I do praise God that he put me out cleaning cow bile before he put me in the pulpit.

Life is work. I can remember people in the church when they saw me in dirty, smelly dungarees, somehow found something terribly fascinating on the other side of the street. Now, those who work with one eye on the clock and the other on the pay packet and a third on the boss, if possible, have not understood that life is work. This is where life is to be found. Ruskin said, "Life without industry is sin." Now, in terms of the scale of values that I used to encounter in Christian circles, it was often considered that the very highest thing you could do in life was to be a missionary, with a minister a good second, but to serve God full-time, that really was great. If you could not do that then the next two best careers were medicine or education – for that was serving your neighbour in their need. So, you came down the line, and a dirty, manual, menial job was bottom of the list. Where did we get that idea from? Not from the Lord of glory who washed feet.

People say that the church has lost the working class in England. We never had them and the reason is because we had a wrong scale of values towards work. Somehow when a Christian parent says, "My son's really got on," or "My daughter's really made it," and you ask, "Oh, what's she doing?" they don't say, "Well, she's cleaning out toilets in a local hospital." I think of a lady in Beijing, in Communist China. She was China's top lady surgeon, a brilliant surgeon with hands full of skill and when they found out she was a Christian, they set her to cleaning out the toilets in that hospital in Beijing. She cleaned them out with a smile on her face and she said, "My toilets are the cleanest in Communist China." She had understood the biblical attitude toward work. My spiritual grandfather was Samuel Chadwick. I mean by that that my father owed more to him than anyone for his faith and I have inherited something from Samuel Chadwick. Have you heard his name? He was Principal of Cliff College.

When he was a teenage boy, he went to a church one night and the preacher really preached the gospel and he made a decision for Christ that night. The next morning his father gave him his boots to clean and they were as filthy as usual, covered with caked mud, and Samuel Chadwick with a rather disgruntled spirit began to scrape the mud off and give them a bit of a brush and he put them down. As he put them down a horrible thought struck him: "Would I have cleaned them that way if Jesus was going to wear them today?" He picked them up again and he brushed and he polished until he could see his face in the toe caps. Samuel Chadwick says, "That was my real conversion that morning, not my decision the night before; I was really converted to Jesus cleaning my dad's boots the following morning." Monday was the best day of his life.

There was a road sweeper in Leeds who every morning took his brush and shovel into an empty but open Church of England church and he went up to the communion rail and put his brush and shovel against the rail and he would pray. Do you wonder that they were the cleanest streets in Leeds? There was also a tennis player who attended the church of which I was pastor, and he told me that he gave the Lord his tennis because, as he put it, so much of his working life was spent in tennis that if the Lord didn't get that, then most of his life was going to be kept from the Lord. He began playing for the Lord and I could just imagine him doing a really good drop shot and saying, "Did you see that, Lord? Wasn't that great?" This is a totally new way of approaching work. We have so many choices of job today.

In the past, if your dad was a cobbler, you would be a cobbler. If your dad went down the pit, you would go down the pit. Now young people are confronted with such a choice that there are whole books written: careers for boys, careers for girls, so that we have got a distorted view of Christian vocation. Let me get back to the biblical view. Your vocation is not what you do, it is how you do it. That is the Christian calling to which you were called. If you are a Christian slave, Paul says that you should remain in the calling in which you are called. Be a slave for the glory of God. I find so often that young people become Christians and they drop their jobs because they feel it is not a Christian job and they are sitting, waiting for the Lord to tell them what their calling is. Their calling was to do that job for his glory. You will find the man who gets the next job is the man who is so busy doing this one well that people notice him.

Work so that God is able to give you a reference for the next job and pull you out of the one you are doing well; not looking for another job because you are dissatisfied and frustrated and giving up on your present one but because you are working so well at it that he has to pull you out for the next. If you are a butcher when you are converted, your vocation is quite clear: to be a good butcher for the Lord. It is not to stop and say, "Does he want me to be a missionary?" It is to be a good butcher. Here is the calling of God in Christ Jesus. It means that instead of just a few of us being able to rush off and be a missionary somewhere else, all of us are able to be in full-time service for the Lord – all of us. We do not put on a pedestal those whom God moves away to work as missionaries, neither do we degrade them. We just say, "We're all in full-time service for the Lord." God has put you in Africa and he has put me in Billingsgate but it is the same Lord we serve full-time.

I came across the following little poem that was written by a Scots engineer who loved building steam engines. So much were his faith and his work interlocked that he wrote this: "From coupler flange to spindle guide / I see thy hand o Lord / Predestination in the stride / Of yon connectin' rod". Isn't that lovely? You can almost see that man with a rag in one hand and oil can in the other and he sees God in the connecting rod. He sees God's predestined laws operating in a steam engine.

Another wonderful poem that I came across was written by George Eliot and it is about Stradivarius. I will give you the gist of the poem, since it may be a little difficult to follow. It is a conversation between Naldo, an artist, and Stradivarius the violin player. Naldo is saying to Stradivarius, "Instead of saving people for God, you're just making violins. You'll go to purgatory." Stradivarius's reply to that really grasps the Hebrew view of work. The gist of the poem is that God himself might conceivably make better fiddles than Stradivarius but by no means certainly since, as a matter of fact, God orders his best fiddles from Stradivarius. She really understood Stradivarius making violins and saying, "God might be able to make a better violin than I can but he orders the best ones from me." I love that. That is why there is a place for ambition in the Christian life, and that is why a Christian who has understood the Hebrew doctrine of work will labour to be the very best that he can be, will want to find every gift he has inside himself, will want to realise to the very full every potential that God has given him. There is a place for holy ambition in the Christian life. Another little poem says: "When I work for myself and live for myself, I exhaust myself, but when I work for others wisely and well, I work for God also and for my work I get that bread which comes down from heaven." A very short poem, but the poet is someone else who discovered it.

Now to the workaholics. A workaholic is someone who lives entirely for his work and it makes more widows and orphans than any war – it robs people of their family life; it robs people of their holidays. A workaholic is a person who for the first three days of their holidays is unwinding and then for the next three days is enjoying it and for the next three days is planning their work that they are going back to. A workaholic is a person for whom work becomes a god and for whom their business is their sole business. To the workaholic the Bible says, "Remember the Sabbath day." Come apart and rest awhile; switch off and remember God. Now, that is the application of the Hebrew doctrine of work to ourselves.

Now let me turn to the Hebrew doctrine of work applied to our society. I want to begin by saying something that may outrage you but I want you to think it through. Karl Marx's book Das Kapital is nearer to the Bible in its attitude to work than Bunyan's The Pilgrim's Progress. The Pilgrim's Progress is concerned with the other world and how to get there. Das Kapital is concerned with this world and how to work. Marx was a Jew, and that is significant. A Jew who came to Manchester, and when he saw the conditions of work in Manchester, his whole conscience revolted against the exploitation of human labour. I want you to realise that communists sometimes have a greater conscience about working conditions than Christians do. I want to spell out seven things in connection with daily work that a Christian needs to be very conscience-stricken about if they apply to his society.

Religion is the opiate, or the heroin as we would say today, of the people. It was not Karl Marx who said that but Charles Kingsley, the author of Tom and the Water Babies, and he said it because he was writing that book about the chimney sweeps, boys of nine and ten who were pushed up the big chimneys and a fire was lit underneath them to force them to go out and brush the chimney. He was so furious about the fact that people were doing that to chimney sweeps and could come and sing hymns in church on Sunday that he said, "Religion is the opiate of the people," and communism took up that phrase. Now, if religion blinds us to working conditions in our society, then it is indeed a drug that is giving us a false sense of security. Here are seven things connected with work that a Christian is concerned about in his conscience.

Number one: that there should be full employment. Do you realise that if what I have said from the Bible is true, a man rots in idleness? A man loses his chance of living his life when he has got nothing to do with it. In the 1890s there was no dole, no unemployment, no social security, and there were thousands of men with unlived lives. Now, one of our major concerns at a general election should be: which party will employ more people? Which policy will increase employment?

The second concern: healthy conditions. Lord Shaftesbury, in the nineteenth century, was concerned that children were working sixteen hours in factories, that women were going bare down mines and tugging trucks of coal with chains around their waist – he was concerned. When you read of some of the working conditions then, especially among the match makers, you will see why. They made the matches by dipping little pieces of wood into yellow phosphorus. It was the cheapest way to make them and they would get it on their hands and three grains of yellow phosphorus was lethal and they would just wipe it on their face and they would get what was called "fussy jaw" and their jaws rotted and they became first green and then black and then covered with puss. If you turned the lights out in a match factory you could see the workers with phosphorescent jaws, rotting their lives away. Christians were concerned. I am glad they were concerned about asbestosis and silicosis and other industrial diseases. A Christian should be in the forefront of that concern that a man's body is being damaged or that his moral health as well as his physical health is being damaged by that employment. We should be right at the front of the protest.

A third concern should be adequate incentives. Again, to go back to the match makers, I read of a mother and two children under nine who worked together for sixteen hours a day to produce a thousand match boxes a week and they got the equivalent of seven and a half pence for that – praise God that is gone. A Christian will be concerned that there are adequate incentives and that a man should work, and work knowing that he will get a living wage and that he will get what he needs at the end of it. Society will not work without incentive. I believe nationalisation was a psychological disaster even if it was an economic necessity. The thought was that if people owned the factory, they would have work and they would work even better for themselves. It just did not work out; people need incentives.

A fourth concern of Christians is equitable compensation,

which means that wealth should go to those who helped produce it and not just to the shareholders who make their money work for them.

A fifth concern is that we should have meaningful occupations for people. The vast majority of people have to take the jobs that are open to them. I went around the Vulcan bomber factory at Weybridge years ago when I was minister in Chertsey, way back in 1954. They were then building the Vulcan bomber and I saw a man all day and every day pull a leaver down and the hydraulic press changed a flat piece of aluminium into a shaped piece of aluminium and I said, "What are you doing? What part of that is for a Vulcan bomber? What is the point of that piece? What does it do?" He said, "I don't know. I don't know," and he pulled the lever again. I thought, "God doesn't want menial occupations," and our technological society is making us machine-minders and button-pushers in which the machine is cleverer than we are and can do more and is more skilled and we are just a button presser. A Christian should be concerned about that.

Sixth: that there should be personal recognition in a man's work. A Christian man should work for personal recognition so that he may take pride in his achievement and know that he is a person and not a hand and not a button-pusher and not a machine-minder.

Finally, the seventh concern I believe a Christian should have is that industry should not be a jungle of them and us but should be a place of cooperative endeavour. England is the most class-ridden society in the world. It pervades our military life, it pervades our social life, our industrial life, even at last sometimes our ecclesiastical life. There is a "them and us", which Christians will seek to break down. I think America is ahead of us here, and will continue to be until employers and employees are part of one endeavour and partners, not competitors or rivals.

Am I pointing you to some political conclusions? I don't mind that because I think God is interested in politics. It is the memories of days when these things were not the concern of people and the fear that these will never be the concern of people who want to make money that has produced a phobia that in turn produces the closed shop, the restrictive practice, the go-slow strike. We may find these thoroughly inconvenient; I just want to tell you that behind these practices is a fear that has been handed down from generation to generation that these concerns will not be felt by those who want to make money and Christians should be in the forefront of this social concern.

Men should be able to work, take a pride in their work, and be able to offer it and find in their work their life. Back in the early 1980s, a psychologist found that in British Leyland, the primary reason why the strike-ridden concern had so many walkouts was not the conditions, the pay, or the issue under dispute – the primary reason was boredom with work and a strike broke the monotony. Brethren, this should never be and yet it happened in our land. I want you to understand why it happened.

I now come to man's two greatest fears – and I deliberately say man's and not woman's because women have other fears. Man's greatest fear is death – ceasing to exist. His second greatest fear is unemployment – ceasing to be useful. These are the two greatest threats to a man's self-respect and a man's integrity. We need to recognise them. I am old enough to remember the Depression of the thirties and I recognised in some of the excessive behaviour of trade unions, in living memory, the fear of those days coming back. When the unions were in a position to defend themselves and workers had the power to defend themselves, their fears led them to act as they did. Let Christians recognise those fears and work for a society in which those fears are groundless.

Now, let me close this study of work by saying two things. I want to look first at our contemporary society and then say to you and plead with you in the name of Jesus to go to your workplace tomorrow morning to present the alternative society. First, I look at our contemporary society – our society is sick of work. Sectional selfishness, a welfare state that has taught us to think of rights rather than responsibilities, and nationalisation have helped to make us a nation of beggars. We are a nation of beggars with a Prime Minister going cap in hand to the International Monetary Fund to bail us out yet again, in order that we may go on living on money that we have not earned. There is no difference between the Prime Minister doing that and a young man perfectly capable of doing a good job sitting in an underground tube and playing his guitar hoping to get a few pennies from commuters.

We have become a nation of beggars. I am old enough to remember this: I was told when I went out to spend my Saturday money, or if I saved it up to buy a toy, that if I saw the words "Made in Japan", I mustn't touch it. It was shoddy rubbish. If I saw the words "Made in Britain" that would be good value for money and quality. Do you remember? Now we go cap in hand to Japan, "Please don't send any more cars to our country, they're such better cars and they run so much more reliably and British Leyland is going to fold up if you go on selling cars to us." "Made in Japan" now spells quality and "Made in Britain" will have to go back to the makers five times before you get it good – that is not a caricature.

I am afraid we are now getting a reputation for being lazy and shoddy. We find a bit of oil and we cheer it as a beggar would cheer winning the pools. There is not one ounce of work that we did to deserve that oil in the North Sea. God put it there, "The earth is the Lord's and the fullness thereof." There it is and we say, "We're out of our troubles, we've got oil." Until Britain realises that and until we live within our means and do a fair day's work for a fair day's pay we will never get out of our economic problems. Until we realise that, we are just heading for further and further economic disaster. It is a fact that productivity in 1978 and in this month of June is exactly the same as it was during the three-day week – that is where we are. Now that is our contemporary society.

I read a poem by Rudyard Kipling written long ago which seemed just to sum it up:

> *"From forge and farm and mine and bench,*
> *Deck, altar, outpost lone–*
> *Mill, school, battalion, counter, trench,*
> *Rail, senate, sheepfold, throne–*
> *Creation's cry goes up on high*
> *From age to cheated age:*
> *"Send us the men who do the work*
> *"For which they draw the wage!"*

That is contemporary society. Now let me talk to you about the alternative society. It is to be found in the Bible in the book of Nehemiah and I have looked at the very stones that are involved, where they rebuilt the walls of Jerusalem and each man built his section and it says they completed it on time and even before time. Why? There is this little phrase: "Because the people had a mind to work."

That is the alternative society. It is the fulfilment of the prayer "Your kingdom come on earth as it is in heaven." It is applying kingdom principles to Monday morning. It is bringing the government of God to your office and to your factory and to your kitchen. It is to establish his government on Monday morning. I want to send you to your work tomorrow morning feeling like this: "I'm on my way to serve the living God. I'm on my way to establish his government. I'm part of the revolution. Jobs for Jesus." I am going to let people see the alternative society. I want them to see who tackles the nasty jobs. I want them to see who stays back to finish a job. I want them to see who gets on best with their colleagues. A man came to a vicar and said, "I want to be a Christian." The vicar asked him, "What made you want to be a Christian? Have you been listening to a preacher or reading the Bible?" "No, nothing like that." "What made you want to be a Christian?" "Well," he said, "you see it's like this, it's the foreman at work. It's the way he treats us, it's the way he does his job and I've just found out he's a Christian and I want to be one too." That is the alternative society. That is the revolution. That is the Hebrew view of work.

Did you realise that that is bringing heaven to earth? Some people think that in heaven it will be a place of bean bags and armchairs with RIP embroidered on them. There was the char woman who was dying and this is what she wrote as a little poem when she was dying: "Don't pity me now, / Don't pity me never; /I'm going to do nothing / For ever and ever." Frankly, that would be utterly boring. Do you want a heaven like that? I don't. In my Bible heaven is a busy place. Heaven is a place where you are on a twenty-four-hour shift, you serve him day and night and there is no night there. Aren't you dying to know what job God has for you in glory? The work of your hands, something to do for him, something to make for him, something to express creativity for him. Again, I am going to go back to Rudyard Kipling and a lovely poem he wrote:

When Earth's Last Picture Is Painted
When Earth's last picture is painted
And the tubes are twisted and dried,
When the oldest colours have faded,
And the youngest critic has died,
We shall rest, and, faith, we shall need it –
Lie down for an aeon or two
Till the Master of all good workmen
Shall put us to work anew.
And those that were good shall be happy;
They shall sit in a golden chair;
They shall splash at a ten-league canvas
With brushes of comet's hair.

They shall find real saints to draw from –
Magdalene, Peter, and Paul;
They shall work for an age at a sitting
And never be tired at all!
And only the Master shall praise us,
And only the Master shall blame;
And no one shall work for money,
And no one shall work for fame,
But each for the joy of the working,
And each, in his separate star,
Shall draw the thing as he sees it
For the God of things as they are!

Do you like that poem? That is heaven. Jesus was a carpenter and somebody has conjectured that above his shop, at the carpenter's place in Nazareth, was a hoarding, a poster, advertising his words and it said on the poster in this legend: "My yolk is easy." Do you know what a yoke is for? It is not for resting; it is for pulling, it is for working. Jesus spent eighteen years carving yokes for oxen, carving them so carefully that they didn't rub, they didn't chafe, but an ox could go on pulling hard, hour after hour after hour. The yolk was easy and Jesus said, "Take my yoke upon you and learn from me, for I am gentle and lowly in heart, and you will find rest for your souls. For my yoke is easy and my burden is light." "The trivial round, the common task, / Will furnish all we ought to ask; / Room to deny ourselves, a road / To bring us daily nearer God."

"Hallelujah, it's Monday morning!" Are you going to say that? I am going to say that. Monday is my day off but I want you to be on that train going to your office, saying, "Hallelujah, it's Monday morning. I'm part of the revolution. My work is my worship. Lord, I'm starting another week for you. Take my work and just lift it into the glory of your presence." Let people see what society can be like in Jesus.

Addenda

4. DESTRUCTION OF THE TEMPLE (2)

Read Matthew Chapter 24

As they left the temple after that scene, if you like, when Jesus wept openly and publicly, the disciples were not so much awed by what he said as by their surroundings. They were looking at these stones which King Herod was already using to build the temple. In fact, I remember listening to a programme on the radio about King Herod's buildings when they were being excavated in Caesarea. And King Herod, who was not a Jew, wanted to please the Jews and to please them he thought he would spring clean their temple – in fact rebuild it. And he was rebuilding it while Jesus was alive on a scale that is almost unimaginable. The foundation of the temple was big enough to hold 13 English cathedrals. And some of the stones are 40 feet long by four feet wide by four feet high and weigh 110 tons and he had no cranes. He had nothing but human muscles to get those stones in place. And they were piled up; the foundation of the temple was already 120 feet high; the columns of the temple carved out of one block of stone were 37 feet 6 high and three men holding hands could just get round them. This was Herod's sop to the Jews. And as they walked through the temple, the disciples were not discussing Jesus' agony or his words, they were saying, "Look at all this, Jesus. Isn't it magnificent! Isn't it amazing?" And Jesus said, "Not one stone will be left on another."

I got a thrill the last time I was out there. I went to the south-west corner of the temple area where they have excavated the stones of the temple that were thrown down. And you can actually see them – it gives me a shudder up my spine to look at something Jesus said would happen and they have found it at last. They did not know where the stones had gone, they just knew that all that was left was the platform with the Wailing Wall, the edge of the platform – but nothing on top, not a thing on those 13 acres is left, and they did not know where they had gone. Now they have uncovered them and you can actually look at the stones that the Romans somehow pushed over the edge of the platform and they were just lying there in one gigantic heap.

The disciples could not imagine such a thing happening except at the end of the world and so they poured out their questions: "Jesus, when will this happen? What will be the sign of your coming? And what about the end of the age? Surely, you're describing a disaster that can only happen when the world comes to an end." They had missed something that Jesus tried to tell them – that, in fact, that would happen before the thing was completed. And less than 40 years later, it happened and those stones were thrown down. So, Jesus said, "Sit down; I don't want you speculating about the future; I don't want you to see – I'm going to *tell* you what will happen when I come and you will know."

Addenda

5. EVIDENCE FOR THE RESURRECTION

Read Matthew Chapter 28

This is Matthew's account of part of the resurrection story. If we could have seen the disciples on that Saturday before Easter Sunday, we would have found them in utter, abject misery. Their hopes and their dreams had been sealed within the tomb by that stone. They had nothing left to live for and one of the worst things that can happen to any man is to lose his self-respect and these men had lost their self-respect. They had made utter fools of themselves. They had dropped their jobs, they had left their homes, they had followed a stranger who suddenly appeared and they had said, "This man is the greatest and we are going to give our whole lives to serving him" – and now it was all over and they were left looking silly. Stunned, bewildered, hopeless, very tired after losing some nights' sleep and all the excitement of the last few weeks, dazed, heartbroken, numb. That was Saturday and there is not a word in the Bible about the disciples on that Saturday. The Word of God draws a veil over their utter dejection. And if that were the end of the story, we certainly would not be attending church this Sunday. Their leader was dead, one of their own number had committed suicide and the other eleven were wishing they were dead too. That is the Saturday picture, but it is not the end of the story.

It is against that backcloth that Easter Sunday shines in all its glory. It is only when you realise that when Christ died, Christianity died, that Easter Sunday means so much. There is one play entitled "The Trial of Jesus" by John Masefield in which Pilate's wife meets Peter the day after the crucifixion and Pilate's wife (in the imagination of the playwright) says to Peter something like, "You must go everywhere into the world now and spread this good man's teaching for he was a good man and this is the right way to live." And Peter replies something like this and says, "But we can't do that without him. We can't go without him." You see, if you take Christ out of the centre of Christianity, there really is nothing left; there is only religion left and religion never helped anybody – not eternally. It might comfort their emotions for a time but religion cannot save.

Now, these disciples were in the position where they could not even go back and pick up the threads of their former life. They didn't even feel like that. They did not feel like going back to their homes and their jobs. They just got into an upper room to sulk and they locked the doors. Perhaps the man in the worst state was Peter, who had been their leader under Jesus. He had been the main disciple and was to be the first pastor of the Christian church but he was broken, and all he could do was weep as he remembered that he had sworn he did not know his best friend and watched him be taken away and crucified. Jesus spoils you for everything else. If you ever come to Jesus and know him and the life he can give and then lose your touch with him, you can never be happy again. You have been spoiled for everything else. No other relationship could ever satisfy you as much. No other life could ever give you the joy and the peace and the sense of purpose. And I have met people who, having known Jesus Christ, have drifted away from him, and you know, they are miserable, they are lost, they are worse off than they were before they ever met him. A man who puts his hand to the plough and looks back is just not fit for the kingdom.

These were the disciples, their hopes and dreams shattered. But Easter Sunday dawns and all that misery is going to be swallowed up in a joyous excitement which is almost too much even to read from the Bible. I want to look at the resurrection from two points of view. First, I am going to look at the miracle itself, the event itself, the amazing events of Easter Sunday morning. And then I am going to look at the meaning of the miracle, the significance of it. What is it all about? What was happening? Why did Jesus come back? What was he hoping to do? What is the meaning of it all?

We first of all look at the miracle, a supernatural event, because this does not happen. It has not happened to anyone else. No one else has been put in a grave and come out of it three days later. There was one person in the lifetime of Jesus, Lazarus, whom Jesus had raised from the dead in a similar way and yet not in a similar way. As we shall see in a moment, there is a profound difference between the resurrection of Jesus and every known case of someone coming back to life. But first of all, let us look at the miracle from two angles.

I want to look at it from the point of view of the evidence that convinced the disciples that something supernatural had happened and then I want to look at it from the point of view of the experience, which was so much more to them than the evidence. There are two approaches you can make to the resurrection. You can sit down and use your brain and your reason to study the evidence and if you do so with an open mind, you will be convinced that Jesus got out of that tomb. No one who has studied the evidence impartially has ever come to the conclusion that the story is false. That is a challenge I dare to throw out because it has happened too often that men who set out to disprove the resurrection as an historical event have been convinced by the evidence that it actually happened. But the evidence points to the *absence* of Jesus from the tomb. It is the experience which points to his *presence* with us. It is one thing to prove his absence; it is another thing to know his presence.

I remember a man who had a great influence on me. He had been a bookmaker before I first knew him but by the time I knew him, Christ had got hold of that man and changed his life. He was one of those who when people talked to him about Jesus turning water into wine, would say, "Well, he turned beer into furniture in my house." This dear man, Jack Harrison, is now in glory. I remember him once being asked by one of his fellow coal miners – for he became a coal miner after he left the bookmaking – "How do you know that Jesus is alive?" And his reply came like a flash: "Because I was talking to him only this morning."

It is the evidence *and the experience* which together make up full Christian conviction. Either without the other is inadequate. You may have all the evidence in your mind and be able to reason it out rationally, logically, persuasively, but if you do not know Jesus, there is something missing and you will not be able to convince people. You may know Jesus and you may know that he is alive, you may have talked to him this morning – I hope you have – *but* we are told to be ready to give every man a *reason* concerning the hope that is in us – that he may be persuaded that this is not irrational folly but that we know what we are talking about, that we have thought it through. It is intellectually sound as well as emotionally satisfying. And it is this combination of heart and mind – of the evidence and the experience – which makes us want to shout about the resurrection from every hilltop.

The evidence for his absence consists of four things and these four things together convinced the disciples that Jesus had escaped from the tomb. Even before they met him, even before they knew his presence, the absence of Jesus from the tomb was clear and convincing. The evidence is fourfold: first, the deserted garden. Soldiers do not desert. Soldiers put on sentry duty stay there until they are relieved. If they desert, they will be court-martialled. They do this at peril of their career and even in those days, in peril of their life. A soldier who is ordered to guard a place but deserts is wide open to disaster. Yet the simple fact is that the soldiers ran. Something happened that gave them a fear greater than the fear of their commanding officer, greater than the fear of death. What was it? The Bible explains that they met supernatural beings and that there was an earthquake and when a man faces the supernatural, he does not give a second thought to his commanding officer. He is off. And the deserted garden – the fact that soldiers deserted their duty on that day – was the first piece of evidence that convinced them something supernatural had occurred.

The second thing that was evidence for his absence was the rolled stone. A stone rolled in front of a tomb weighed about a ton and a quarter. But not only was that stone pushed into place by a team of men, it was sealed; it was immovable. No man could move it without chipping away at the seals all round. And yet, that stone was not only rolled aside in its groove, it had been pushed over and was lying flat. Hitherto, an angel had sat on it as if to say, "That's what I think of it." And it just takes one angel to push one and a quarter tons over, and to sit on it in contempt of it. Of course, the stone was not rolled away to let Jesus out, but to let the disciples in. It was rolled away for men. Jesus, who could pass through closed doors would find no difficulty with a stone. But it was opened to let the world in, to see that it was empty and that the body had gone.

The third piece of evidence for his absence was the empty tomb and *no one ever challenged the fact that the tomb was empty*. It is true they spread the word around that the body had been stolen. They had to because no one could produce it. They knew that they had put a body in there, they knew they had sealed it, they knew they had set a guard, but when they went in, they found that it was empty. The disciples, the women, the Jews – everybody found it empty. The one thing that would have finished Christianity forever would have been to produce the body. Nobody did – because nobody could. Jew and Christian alike were agreed that that tomb was empty, stark empty – and that was the third piece of evidence. Just fifty days later, they were preaching openly within 200 yards of this tomb that Jesus had been raised, and anybody could just have gone to the tomb and proved it otherwise if the tomb was not unoccupied.

The fourth piece of evidence consisted of the folded grave clothes. Jesus' body was wrapped the same way after he died as he was wrapped after his birth. Swaddling clothes consist of a long bandage wound round and round a little baby's body almost like a mummy. And when a person was buried in those days, a thirty-yard strip of cloth was wrapped round and round from the shoulders right down to the feet and a shorter bandage was wrapped round the head from the eyebrows upwards like a turban. The body was wrapped with just the face and the shoulders exposed, then the body was laid in the tomb. Normally within the folds of the bandage were put spices and ointments and other sweet-smelling things. That was the way they dealt with their dead.

Jesus never got the ointment, at least not after his death; he got it about a week before when a woman anointed him with perfume beforehand for his burial. But he did have the bandages and when Peter and John ran to the tomb after the women's startling message that it was empty, they found it was not quite empty. There were bandages still wrapped round but collapsed, lying flat – except for the head cloth which had kept its shape, and the translation of the literal Greek language for the account in John is that it was still rolled up and lying by itself, separated from the bandages. You cannot get a body out of bandages without unravelling them. They would have been spread for yards, not only over the tomb floor but out of the tomb into the garden, and yet there they were rolled up. And when John went in and saw those, he knew that no man had been in that tomb, no man could have done it, no man could have got Jesus' body through those bandages and through that stone.

This was the evidence and it convinced them. It convinced them that something supernatural had happened. It convinced them of his absence from the tomb, but some of the saddest words in the Bible are in Luke 24 where it says, they went to the tomb and found it even as the women had said, but him they saw not. It is one thing to be convinced in your head that Jesus is alive, that Christianity is true, that the historical evidence on which our faith is based is accurate, and it is another thing to meet Jesus.

I suppose there are many people who accept basically the historical truth of the Christian faith, many people in England who have been brought up on this. And a Gallup poll by independent television revealed how much Christian truth is generally accepted in the population. But how many of these people who believe these things basically with their heads know Jesus personally? They may have found it even as the preacher had said – "but him they saw not". The evidence must become the experience.

Now let us see the experience of his presence. Again, four cases are known on Easter Sunday. And Jesus made himself real in different ways to different people; so typically of him he adapted himself to every personality. And the first people he appeared to were women – the men were all behind that locked door. But the women got on with what needed to be done while the men, frightened, huddled together in an upper room. It was to Mary and the other women that he first appeared – humble, obscure women. One of them had been demented. Take Mary, still wanting the body and still calling the body "him". The last thing she had to hold on to was a corpse, but like any woman, she wanted that corpse. She wanted to touch it, she wanted to stroke that cold forehead and now she could not even do that. Where have you put him? Those who think that feminine intuition is infallible get a rude shock here. Feminine intuition is not *always* right and she saw a figure standing there, but assumed it was the gardener.

I do not know how Jesus spoke: "Mary, Mary." But she knew that voice and she started to hold on to him and she put her hands round those ankles and she held on. I am never letting you go again. He told her to let him go. That was the first time. And then she went to the men. And the one proof that the resurrection was not hallucination is that the disciples would not believe it. They were sceptical; they were not credulous; they were not ready to believe anything. They were not ready to be lulled into a false idea; they were not gullible men. They were suspicious men; they were cynical men at this stage. "No, you've got up too early; it's a spooky time of day to go into a cemetery. It can't be true." Now, it was men like that who were convinced – not soft, silly men but men! And it was they who accepted the experience later.

The second appearance on Easter Sunday was one which is nowhere mentioned in the gospels. It is the greatest untold story in the Bible. I would love to hear it but it is not here. He appeared to Simon; we do not know where, we do not know when, we do not know what was said, we just know that Simon was feeling the lowest of all the disciples and Jesus met him first. He came to the one who was right at the bottom. That is where Jesus becomes real – when you are right at the bottom, when you are low enough to meet him, to look up into his face. And it was to Simon that he came. Do you notice that his name has gone back to Simon? It is no longer Peter. When Jesus first met him he had been called Simon and Jesus called him Peter but now he has appeared to Simon. Why the change? I will tell you why. Simon means "a reed", something easily blown about and shaken. Peter means a rock. And when Jesus met Simon, he said, "Simon, you're a reed, easily shaken, but I'll make you a rock." But on the night before Jesus died, Peter had discovered he was still Simon, a reed – easily moved, easily disturbed, easily shaken. And the Lord appeared to Simon and said, "Go and tell Peter." You see that? The Lord has a way of coming to weak, easily vacillating people who are tossed around, and he says, "Look, with me it's still rock. I'll still make you firm and stable."

And the third appearance, the third experience, was one that I am going to focus on now – to a man and his wife. We do not even know both their names. And they were on a sad, weary journey of eight miles just before the sun set. They were just an ordinary couple. They had been there at the cross – or the wife had – and now they are to experience the presence. And late on Easter Sunday after dark in that upper room with nobody even needing to open the door, a well-remembered voice said, "Peace be to you." There were only ten by this time. One had committed suicide; one could not stand being spoken to and he was out in the streets wandering alone. His name was Thomas. And he just did not want to be with people. He was crawling away like a wounded animal into the jungle. And there were just 10. But to 10 Jesus came and he was back.

Now for the rest of this chapter, I want to ask this question: Had they really got Jesus back with them? What is the meaning? Is it true to say that Jesus had come back to life? Yes, it is true that it was the same Jesus. He said, "Handle me and see. It is I myself." It was the same voice, the same gestures, the same love, the same memories, the same conversation, the same patience, the same wisdom, the same love, the same gentleness and yet, he was different. How different? Well, for one thing, most of those who met him failed to recognise him at first. Mary did not recognise him; Cleopas and his wife did not recognise him. There must have been something different.

The second difference that I notice is that he did not want them to touch him after they had first discovered that he was real. And to Mary he said, "Don't hold on to me. Don't cling to me." To Thomas it is true he said, "Handle me and see; put your finger through the hole in my hands and your hand into that gash in my side. Come on, do it." He never did actually. But for those who seized his body he said, "Let it go, let it go." Why?

A third thing that surprises us is this. He only appeared to believers. Pontius Pilate never saw him. Annas never saw him. Caiaphas never saw him. Herod never saw him. Why? Before he had allowed them to see him. Now he does not show himself. Something had changed.

And the fourth thing I notice is that now he keeps disappearing. He never once did that before his death but now they are talking to him and suddenly he has gone. Now they are walking with him and he has gone. He keeps disappearing, he is elusive. Not only slipping *into* a room through closed doors, but slipping out of it again unnoticed. What has changed? There is a change in the disciples that reflects the change in Jesus, there is an atmosphere of reverence, of awe. No longer is this the Jesus they walk arm in arm with up Galilee and lean on his breast at meal times. They are almost pulling away from him now. It says again and again, they worshipped him – and you know, they never did that before his death. Search the Gospels and not once does it say anybody worshipped him but now, when they saw him, they worshipped. They drew back a bit. There is something different about this Jesus. What is it?

I will tell you. Four things are new in the resurrection. Four things are going to happen now that changed the whole picture. First of all, Jesus has a new body. It is not the old one. It has all the appearance – and even the wounds – of the old one, but it is a new one. Now, when the disciples realised this, I don't know. Just let me put one question to you in case you are wondering where I am off to now and where I get this from. Let me ask you this simple question: Where did Jesus get his clothes from for the resurrection? He died naked, he was wrapped in bandages for the tomb, but when he rose, he had clothes. Where did he get clothes from? Did he go to a tailor? Did he go to a shop? Did he go and borrow some? I will tell you where he got them from. He got them from the same wardrobe that you and I will get them from when we go to heaven. We are going to wear fine linen. And God can make clothes. He did for Adam and he did for the second Adam. And the clothes were new and the body was new too.

We are told in the Bible that resurrection bodies are like this: Take a potato or a grain of wheat and look at it as a body, as

Matthew Chapter 28

a material thing. Bury it in the ground and one day, from that body, will come new bodies – new potatoes, new grains of wheat just like the old ones to look at, but new. It is not the old body resuscitated; it is a new body resurrected. It is a creative act. If Jesus had come back with his old body that body would have come back at the age of 33 and a year later 34 and a year later, 35 and 20 years later, 53 and 40 years later, 73, and 60 years later, 93. Then it would have died. But Jesus still has that 33–year-old body now in its prime. It was a new body. It was no longer subject to the natural limitations of our earthly bodies. It was a glorious body and we are promised that in heaven we shall be fashioned anew according to his glorious body – not the body he had before he died but the body he had after he rose.

This is the difference from every other resuscitation of a corpse. You can, I gather, even up to an hour and a half resuscitate a corpse on the operating table of a hospital. But you only bring them back in their old body. It is the old one still operating and it will still be tired and it will probably need another operation in a few years' time and it will still die again. Jesus got a new body.

Secondly, Jesus when he rose from the dead, had a new life. It was another and a higher sphere of existence. It had nothing more to do with evil and temptation. Christ could not be tempted after his resurrection. Satan could not and did not speak to him. Before his death, Satan had troubled him right up to the cross. But there is no record whatever of Satan saying or doing anything to him after his resurrection. He is now living above that. He has died to sin – that is what the phrase means. He has finished with the old devil. It is a new life altogether now. And as we share his resurrection life, we are finished with Satan and we can enjoy that even now according to the New Testament.

And the third thing. Not only did he have a new body and live a new life, a life at a new, high plain that had nothing to do with evil, now he is also part of a new creation. When God made the old world in which we live, he made the mountains and the oceans and the plants and the fish and the birds and the beasts. Then he made man and he built up to this climax and he said, "Now it's done – that's good." But sin came in and spoiled it all so God has promised to make the whole thing all over again, to make a new creation, to make a new heaven and a new earth; new mountains, new valleys and new men and new bodies to go with the new earth and the new heaven. And the resurrection is the first part of that new creation.

This is the thing that I am most excited about. God has already begun rebuilding and when Jesus got his new body, he became "the first of the new creation" – the first fruits, the beginning of all that God is going to unfold. Isn't that exciting? It has already started. This old world is on the way out already. Someone has said, "On Easter Day, tomorrow has become today." That is a wonderful saying. Tomorrow has become today and all that God has promised to do in the future has begun to happen already. Indeed, tomorrow is now yesterday and God is going on with his new creation. The difference is this. In the old creation, he made the mountains and the valleys and the beasts and the birds first and then he made new men last. But in the new creation, he is making new people first and then he is going to make a new world to put them in. The reason is very simple. Before he started the old creation, he had no people to start with but now he has – and God loves the people he has and God wants to save them and God wants to make them new people and get them ready for the new world. And everybody who believes in his heart that God raised Jesus from the dead and confesses it with his mouth will become a new creature. They will be given new life and one day they will have a new body to go with it. And then they will be given a new heaven and a new earth to walk around and enjoy. That is what Easter means to me.

And therefore, I have already mentioned the fourth thing. First, the resurrection means to me a new body, not the old one spring-cleaned and renovated – a new one. It is a new life lived above Satan, lived above evil and suffering and death. For Christ coming back to life lives to die no more. A new creation of people, and Jesus is the first to get the new body and others will follow. And finally, a new world. For his body which could be handled and touched and seen was the first part of the new heaven and the new earth, which will be as real as his body.

Jesus did not come back to life. Lazarus came back to life; the widow of Nain's son came back to life; Jairus's daughter came back to life. And sometimes we would wish that we could bring people back to life that we have loved and lost. But I will tell you something that is even more wonderful for them: that they should go on to new life, that they should go to be with Jesus and await with us the resurrection when the new bodies will be given to us "in a moment, in the twinkling of an eye" and we shall be changed. Oh, don't let us want to drag people back into this world. Let us rejoice that they have taken a further step on to the next and to the new heaven and the new earth for which we wait.

Look at these disciples now. Look at them two months later, radiant, confident, challenging, aflame, absolutely fearless, overwhelmingly happy with a message for the whole world, a message that people have to listen to. And they go out to plan the conquest of the earth in the Name of Jesus. That is the difference that Easter has made and so we continue to meet together to praise Christ – alive, risen, ascended, returning, reigning.

www.ingramcontent.com/pod-product-compliance
Lightning Source LLC
Chambersburg PA
CBHW070105120526
44588CB00032B/886